THE EUROPEAN UNION

CW00447156

This is a strong collection of incisive and detailed analyses of the state of relations between the European Union and Japan. The book takes a close look at what the relationship is today, what it has failed to be, and what it could and should be in the future. Its central message deserves broad attention: European and Japanese contributions to global governance are essential, and will become even more important in the future.

Hanns W. Maull, University of Trier and Adjunct Professor of Strategic Studies, Johns Hopkins University Bologna Center

The world desperately needs actors such as the European Union and Japan who tackle, head-on and with professional expertise, mundane daily life issues such as trade and regulations, environmental and energy security, and political, food and health security issues. This volume is a must-read for those who wish to know what these two civilian powers aspire to achieve.

Takashi Inoguchi, University of Tokyo and University of Niigata Prefecture, Japan

This excellent book could not come at a better moment. Japan and the EU are negotiating a bilateral economic partnership agreement which has received less attention than counterpart negotiations between the US and Japan and between the US and the EU. This book offers a precious analysis of the relatively little-known relationship between Japan and the EU. It also suggests that the chances of cooperating, learning from each other, and possibly providing a model for global governance may actually be higher in the Japan-EU endeavor than between these two societies and the US—a fascinating perspective.

Patrick Messerlin, Sciences Po, France

The European Union and Japan *takes a long overdue and fresh look at this inter-regional relationship, which is of considerable potential importance to international stability and governance. The book gathers together some of the leading scholars, both established and emerging, working in this area today in Japan, Europe and North America. This book demonstrates the continuing problems in maximizing the potential of EU-Japan relations, but also demonstrates key areas of cooperation across economics, security, and a broad range of new and pressing global governance issues. It is essential reading for students, scholars and practitioners alike.*

Christopher W. Hughes, Warwick University, UK

Globalisation, Europe, Multilateralism

Institutionally supported by the Institute for European Studies at the
Université libre de Bruxelles

Mario TELÒ, Series Editor

As a leading research institution and a Jean Monnet Centre of Excellence in European Studies, the Institut d'Études Européennes of the Université Libre de Bruxelles (IEE-ULB) supported the launch of this global series with a view to bringing together multidisciplinary research in global governance and EU studies. The series can draw on a wide and global network of partner universities across five continents. Among its numerous resources special mention is to be made of the Erasmus Mundus GEM PhD School on 'Globalisation, Europe, Multilateralism' and the GR:EEN European research project on 'Global Reordering: Evolving European Networks'.

Volumes included in the series share innovative research objectives centred on: globalisation, the EU's changing position therein, resulting forms of multilateral cooperation, and the role of transnational networks as well as multipolarity in the contemporary international order. A wide array of possible approaches to these shared themes are welcomed, including among others: comparative regionalism, public and foreign policy analysis, EU governance and Europeanisation studies, discourse analysis, area studies, and various institutional perspectives.

With a shared aim to contribute to innovations in the study of both European Integration and International Relations, the series includes: collaborative volumes, research based monographs and textbooks. Each publication undergoes an international refereeing process, and enjoys the advice and feedback of an international editorial board.

The European Union and Japan
A New Chapter in Civilian Power Cooperation?

Edited by

PAUL BACON
Waseda University, Japan

HARTMUT MAYER
University of Oxford, UK

HIDETOSHI NAKAMURA
Waseda University, Japan

ASHGATE

Published by
Ashgate Publishing Limited
Wey Court East
Union Road
Farnham
Surrey, GU9 7PT
England

Ashgate Publishing Company
110 Cherry Street
Suite 3-1
Burlington, VT 05401-3818
USA

www.ashgate.com

British Library Cataloguing in Publication Data
A catalogue record for this book is available from the British Library

The Library of Congress has cataloged the printed edition as follows:
The European Union and Japan : a new chapter in civilian power cooperation? / edited by Paul Bacon, Hartmut Mayer and Hidetoshi Nakamura.
    pages cm. -- (Globalisation, Europe, multilateralism series)
    Includes bibliographical references and index.
    ISBN 978-1-4724-5746-2 (hardback) -- ISBN 978-1-4724-5749-3 (paperback)
ISBN 978-1-4724-5747-9 (ebook) -- ISBN 978-1-4724-5748-6 (epub) 1. European Union countries--Foreign relations--Japan. 2. Japan--Foreign relations--European Union countries. 3. European Union countries--Foreign economic relations--Japan. 4. Japan--Foreign economic relations--European Union countries. I. Bacon, Paul, editor of compilation. II. Mayer, Hartmut, editor of compilation. III. Nakamura, Hidetoshi.

    D1065.J3E95 2015
    341.242'20952--dc23

2014039549

ISBN 9781472457462 (hbk)
ISBN 9781472457493 (pbk)
ISBN 9781472457479 (ebk – PDF)
ISBN 9781472457486 (ebk – ePUB)

Printed in the United Kingdom by Henry Ling Limited,
at the Dorset Press, Dorchester, DT1 1HD

Contents

List of Figures, Illustrations and Tables

Figures

Illustration

Tables

Notes on Contributors

Paul Bacon is Deputy Director of the European Union Institute in Japan at Waseda University, and an Associate Professor of International Relations at Waseda's School of International Liberal Studies. Professor Bacon received his PhD from the University of Kent (UK) and his research interests include European Union foreign policy, EU–Japan relations, human security and human rights protection. In 2014 he co-edited two monographs, *Human Security and Natural Disasters* and *Human Security and Japan's Triple Disaster*, and has published a number of book chapters and articles in leading international relations journals.

Dimitar Bechev is Senior Visiting Fellow at the European Institute, London School of Economics, and also lectures in International Politics at Sofia University, Bulgaria. His former positions include Director of the European Council on Foreign Relations office in Sofia, Lecturer at Worcester College, Oxford, and Visiting Professor at Tokyo's Hitotsubashi University. Dr Bechev received his DPhil in International Relations from the University of Oxford in 2005, and specializes in the study of EU foreign and enlargement policy, and politics in Turkey, the Balkans and Eastern Europe. In 2011 he authored *Constructing South East Europe: The Politics of Balkan Regional Cooperation*, and has also published in leading academic periodicals such as the *Journal of Common Market Studies*, *European Politics* and *East European Politics and Societies*. He is a frequent commentator on current affairs in international media, and has been quoted by the *Financial Times*, *The Economist*, and the *Wall Street Journal* amongst others.

Gijs Berends is an official at the European Commission. He was posted to the Delegation of the European Union to Japan from 2007 to 2012, where he was responsible for energy, climate change, agriculture and food safety. He edited (together with Dominic Al-Badri) the volume *After the Great East Japan Earthquake: Political and Policy Change in Post-Fukushima Japan*, which was published in 2013. Previous publications have appeared in the *European Law Review*, the *Journal of World Trade* and the *Food and Drug Law Journal*. He holds degrees from the universities of Rotterdam and Cambridge (Queens' College).

Koji Fukuda is Professor of International Public Administration at the School of Political Science and Economics, Waseda University. He is Director of the Waseda Institute for European Union Studies, and received his PhD in Political Science from Doshisha University. He has published widely in both Japanese and English on the European Union. He co-edited (with H. Akiba) *European Governance after*

Nice (2003), and his most recent publication in English can be found in *Economic Crises and Policy Regimes* (2014, edited by H. Magara).

Yasue Fukuda is a Lecturer at Waseda University and Visiting Lecturer at Osaka University. She received her PhD in Medical Science from Osaka University. Recent relevant publications include *Cross-border Health Care in the European Union: Recent Trends in the Movement of Health Service Professionals and Patients and Their Implications* (2009) and 'The Fukushima Nuclear Power Plant Accident: Issues with Radiation Monitoring and Their Relation to Public Health' in the *Journal of Epidemiological Community Health* (co-authored, 2012).

Bart Gaens is a Senior Research Fellow at the Finnish Institute of International Affairs in Helsinki. He is also Adjunct Professor at the University of Helsinki. In the recent past he has worked as Acting Professor of Japanese Studies at the Department of World Cultures, University of Helsinki, and has led a research project on the EU's relations with Asia at the University of Helsinki Network for European Studies. He has published in the field of Japanese Studies as well as on Europe–Asia inter-regional relations, with a special focus on the Asia-Europe Meeting (ASEM) process. He obtained his PhD in Japanese Studies from the Graduate University of Advanced Studies (Japan).

Martin Holland holds a Jean Monnet Chair (*ad personam*) and is Director of both the National Centre for Research on Europe at the University of Canterbury and the European Union Centres Network in New Zealand. Professor Holland is a visiting lecturer at Chulalongkorn University in Thailand, Renmin University in China, and the University of Malaya. He is internationally recognized for his work on EU Development Policy, Common Foreign and Security Policy and Perceptions of the EU. He has held a number of notable awards, including: a Jean Monnet Fellowship, European University Institute, 1987; an Alexander von Humboldt Fellowship, Freiburg, 1992–1994; and a Rockefeller Bellagio Fellowship, 2000.

Hartmut Mayer has been Official Fellow and Tutor in Politics (International Relations) at St Peter's College, University of Oxford, and a member of Oxford University's Department of Politics and International Relations since 1998. He is also Adjunct Professor of European and Eurasian Studies at Johns Hopkins University's Paul H. Nitze School of Advanced International Studies (SAIS) in Bologna, Italy. Dr Mayer holds a BA from the Free University of Berlin, an MALD from the Fletcher School of Law and Diplomacy at Tufts University, an MPhil from the University of Cambridge (Gonville and Caius College) and a DPhil from the University of Oxford (St Antony's College). He has held visiting professorships at Hitotsubashi University in Tokyo (for six months), the University of Hamburg and the GIGA German Institute of Global and Area Studies (for three years). Most recently, he has visited at the Université Libre de Bruxelles (ULB) and at SciencesPo in Paris. He has also been a visiting researcher at the European

University Institute (EUI) in Florence, the Finnish Institute for International Relations (UPI) in Helsinki, at the Stiftung Wissenschaft und Politik (SWP) in Berlin, and for 10 months as a JSPS Fellow at Waseda University in Tokyo.

Hidetoshi Nakamura is currently Associate Professor of International Relations, Faculty of Political Science and Economics, Waseda University, and also Deputy Director, European Union Institute in Japan at Waseda University. He studied Political Science and International Relations at Waseda and the University of Oxford. His recent publications in English include 'The Efficiency of European External Action and the Institutional Evolution of EU–Japan Political Relations' in Mario Telò and Frederik Ponjaert (eds), *The EU's Foreign Policy: What Kind of Power and Diplomatic Action?* (2013), and 'Regional Security Communities' in Mario Telò (ed.), *Globalisation, Multilateralism, Europe: Towards a Better Global Governance?* (2013).

Hiroshi Ohta is Professor at Waseda University's School of International Liberal Studies, and is project research leader on global governance and international fisheries governance at Waseda. He received a PhD in International Relations from the Department of Political Science, the Graduate School of Arts and Sciences, Columbia University. Some of his recent works include 'Climate Change and Human Security: The Convergence on Policy Requirements' in *Human Rights, Human Security, and State Security: The Intersection* (forthcoming), 'The Arctic and Japan: Energy Security and Climate Change' in H. Peimani (ed.) *Energy Security and Geopolitics in the Arctic: Challenges and Opportunities in the 21st Century* (2012). He has also published a number of book chapters and articles, in both English and Japanese, on the international politics of the environment.

Frederik Ponjaert is Researcher and Lecturer at the IEE-ULB and the KULeuven, and Associate Lecturer in Comparative Regionalism at SciencesPo, Paris. His research is centred on comparative regionalism, with a focus on European and Asian realities, the foreign policies of Germany and Japan, and regional policy processes. Recent publications include: 'Public Research Projects in Europe and East Asia: Cooperation or Competition? A Comparative Analysis of the ITER and Galileo Experiences', *East Asia* (2010), 'The EU and Its Far-Abroad: Interregional Relations with Other Continents' in *The European Union and Global Governance* (2009) and 'Japan in East Asia: The Dynamics of Regional Cooperation from a European Perspective', *Studia Diplomatica* (2007).

Miranda A. Schreurs received her PhD from the University of Michigan, and researches in the field of comparative environmental politics and policy in Europe, the United States and East Asia. In 2007 she was recruited to the Freie Universität Berlin as Professor of Comparative Politics and Director of the university's Environmental Policy Research Centre. In 2008 she became a member of the German Advisory Council on the Environment. She is Chair of the European

Environment and Sustainable Development Advisory Councils, a network of advisory councils across Europe, and member of the Berlin Climate Change Advisory Commission and the Enquete Commission for a New Energy System for Berlin.

Min Shu is Associate Professor at the School of International Liberal Studies, Waseda University. He received his PhD from the University of Bristol. Before moving to his current position, Professor Shu was Lecturer at Fudan University and Visiting Associate Professor at the Waseda Institute of Advanced Studies. His research focuses on international political economy, comparative regionalism and EU–Asia relations. Dr Shu's works have appeared in *European Law Journal*, *European Journal of Political Research*, *Current Politics and Economics of Asia* and several edited volumes. He is currently completing a research monograph entitled *The Rise of State-Led Economic Regionalism in East Asia*.

Mario Telò is Emeritus President of the Institute for European Studies, Université Libre de Bruxelles, and Professor of European Institutions and International Relations at the ULB and LUISS University, Rome. He holds a Jean Monnet Chair *ad honorem*, and in 2006 was elected as a Member of the Royal Academy of Sciences, Belgium. Professor Telò has served as an advisor to all of the EU institutions for many years. Among his 30 books, the most recent are: *The European Union and New Regionalism* (3rd edition) (2014), *Globalization, Europe, Multilateralism* (2014) and *The EU's Foreign Policy* (2013). His monograph *International Relations: A European Perspective* (2009), complete with a Foreword by R.O. Keohane, has appeared in French in 2007, 2010 and 2013, and in Mandarin in 2009. For the last 40 years he has taken part, on a regular basis, in the media debate about the future of the European Union.

Yves Tiberghien received his PhD from Stanford University in 2002, and is an Associate Professor of Political Science and Director of the Institute of Asian Research at the University of British Columbia. Yves was an Academy Scholar at Harvard University in 2004–2006. He has also been a Japan Foundation Scholar at the Japanese Ministry of Finance and at Keio University. He specializes in East Asian comparative political economy, international political economy and global governance, with an empirical focus on China, Japan and Korea. He is the author of *Entrepreneurial States: Reforming Corporate Governance in France, Japan, and Korea* (2007), *L'Asie et le futur du monde* (2012) and *Leadership in Global Institution-Building: Minerva's Rule* (edited volume, 2013).

Henri Vogt is Professor of International Politics at the University of Turku, Finland. He holds a DPhil in politics from St Antony's College, Oxford, and an MSocSc. in political science from the University of Helsinki. His research has focused on democratic transitions, globalization and European foreign policies. His books include: *Between Utopia and Disillusionment: A Narrative of the*

Political Transformation in Eastern Europe (2004), *A Responsible Europe? Ethical Foundations of EU External Affairs* (co-edited with Hartmut Mayer, 2006) and *Europa zwischen Fiktion und Realpolitik* (co-edited with Roland Marti, 2010). Over the past 10 years, approximately 80 master's students have finished their theses under his supervision.

Foreword

Herman Van Rompuy, President of the European Council

This is an important book at an important moment. As the world seems to be entering a new phase of geopolitical instability, it is essential that Europe and Japan, the world's two foremost civilian powers, act together to strengthen the international order. This starts with understanding each other better. In my time in this European office, I have always underlined the crucial importance of our relations with Japan.

It so happened that Japan was the first country with which the European Union held a summit outside Europe during my Presidency. It took place in Tokyo, in April 2010. Alongside the summit meeting with Prime Minister Hatoyama itself, my trip included a memorable encounter with the Emperor and Empress. Both sides felt it was a new starting point in the political relationship.

The visit rekindled my deep interest in Japan and its culture. From a previous visit, in the late 1990s, I remember having been impressed by its dizzying architecture, the speed of city life, the advanced transport technology. It struck me how this busy modern day Tokyo contrasted with the stylized, traditional expressions of Japanese culture that I also admire: Japanese rock gardens, landscape painting and haiku poetry. In recent years, I have felt privileged whenever, as amateur haiku poet, I could build another modest bridge between our cultures – not through official diplomacy, but via 'haiku diplomacy'!

The world has changed since that new beginning of April 2010, and the authors of *The European Union and Japan: A New Chapter in Civilian Power Cooperation* do not eschew analysis of these new realities. Public opinion in both Europe and Japan has become more concerned with geopolitical developments closer to our respective neighbourhoods – tensions with Russia around Ukraine and turmoil in the Middle East in Europe's case, tensions in Eastern Asia in that of Japan. Both our societies struggle with weak economic growth, another potential source of a more inward-looking attitude.

So could we risk losing sight of each other? No, not at all. Since that innocent spring of 2010, we have also experienced how deeply interlinked all major global actors are. The European Union's sovereign debt crisis, which erupted around the same time in Greece, was for two years a global economic concern – until we overcame it. The triple disaster of March 2011, comprising the earthquake, tsunami and Fukushima nuclear accident, a nightmare for so many Japanese and the society as a whole, made itself felt far away in Europe; it had a lasting impact on our energy policies, not least in Germany (as one of the chapters in this book sets out in more detail). 'Fukushima' also resulted in a moment of international solidarity. These experiences of modern interdependence, usually for the better and sometimes for the worse, will have a lasting impact.

These past years, we have also worked hard and actively to strengthen the partnership. The progress on a Free Trade Agreement is the most obvious case. From the timid start back in 2010, when a preliminary feasibility study was the maximum possible, we are now in a much more committed mode and the real talks are already proceeding toward their conclusion. The global climate debate will be another good occasion for European-Japanese cooperation. During the last EU summit I chaired, European Union leaders reached an ambitious deal on climate and energy that we hope will set the tone both in the run-up to and beyond the United Nations' Paris 2015 Conference on climate change. Our global leadership as civilian powers also requires engagement in the field of security. Here EU-Japan cooperation, from Somalia to Afghanistan, is good, although it could still be developed further.

The results, the opportunities and the challenges of the thriving relationship between the European Union and Japan in all these and many other sectors are solidly addressed in the contributions to this volume. Seemingly technical issues – from energy security to food safety standards – in many cases involve deeply political stakes, as the authors convincingly explain. It is also inspiring to discover that we can often learn more from each other than we think.

It is always important to remember that the 'civilian' nature of our two societies has a common origin: the Second World War. From that terrible period of suffering and destruction we must draw all the appropriate lessons, and keep in mind that reconciliation, through rebuilding trust and establishing cooperation between former regional rivals, is the best way forward.

It is my strong conviction, the way the world goes, that Europe and Japan can both be stronger if we work more together, as civilian powers. We can help shape a global order that is more just. This book correctly recognizes that such an enterprise starts, not with lofty speeches or declarations, but with everyday progress, with men and women working together to achieve concrete results. I am confident that the new European Union leadership will bring that same approach to the table.

Herman Van Rompuy
President of the European Council (2009–2014),
21 November 2014

Acknowledgements

This edited volume is the direct product of a host of academic activities organized through the European Union Institute in Japan at Waseda University (EUIJ Waseda). Accordingly, we must first and foremost acknowledge the continued support, both financial and principled, that EUIJ Waseda has enjoyed from the European Commission, through its various programmes, and the European External Action Service, by way of the EU Delegation in Tokyo.

The genesis of this project harks back eight years, when in December 2006, Hartmut Mayer and Hidetoshi Nakamura started a comprehensive research project 'Assessing the European Union and Japan's Joint Responsibility for Global Security'. This project enjoyed financial support from the Japanese Society for the Promotion of Science (JSPS). We are grateful for this financial support from the JSPS, which made Mayer's year-long stay at Waseda possible. In August 2007, an international workshop was convened with the support of the Waseda University 21st Century Center of Excellence (COE) programme on 'Constructing Open Political-Economic Systems' (GLOPE). In March 2008, Mayer and Nakamura also co-chaired a similarly themed panel at the 49th Annual International Studies Association (ISA) Convention in San Francisco.

This favourable context allowed Waseda University to seize a unique opportunity and become the host of an EU Institute (centres are referred to as institutes in the Japanese context). In the summer of 2008, following Hidetoshi Nakamura's advice, Professor Koji Fukuda presided over the successful application to see an EU Institute created at Waseda University. Paul Bacon joined this foundational effort, supporting the application process. Waseda officially launched the EU Institute, named EUIJ Waseda, in April 2009.

Since its creation, EUIJ Waseda has conceived and financially supported several international symposia and workshops, many of which are directly relevant to this edited volume. EUIJ Waseda has also pursued a wide range of outreach activities in partnership with the EU Delegation, the embassies of EU member countries, Diet Members, MOFA and various civil society organizations. These activities have often provided us with invaluable insights into EU-Japan relations.

In 2010–2013, some of our academic activities were also funded by a JSPS KAKENHI award (Grants-in-Aid for Scientific Research Grant Number 22530167). This grant supported visits to Oxford University by Nakamura and Bacon, thus allowing for further editorial meetings with Mayer.

Since February 2010, Professor Mario Telò and Frederik Ponjaert, both at the Université Libre de Bruxelles (ULB), have conducted close working relations with the three editors through the Erasmus Mundus GEM PhD School, and the

GR:EEN project (FP7 Number 266809). Our initial Waseda-Oxford joint research has therefore effectively evolved into a Waseda-Oxford-ULB joint project. With this final evolution, the project had reached full maturity and was ready for the necessary practical and substantial push towards the definitive publication of this edited volume.

This publication also profited from invaluable support from several collaborators such as David Attewell, Mayer's research assistant who provided valuable support during the compilation and editorial stages of the book's production, and Johan Robberecht, who supported the series editors in the management of the GEM series.

We are extremely grateful for all the kind support and contributions this project has enjoyed over the years, which have culminated in this edited volume.

Paul Bacon, Hartmut Mayer and Hidetoshi Nakamura

List of Abbreviations

ACEA	Association des Constructeurs Européens d'Automobiles
ACP	Africa-Caribbean-Pacific States
ACTA	Anti-Counterfeiting Trade Agreement
AOSIS	Alliance of Small Island States
ARF	ASEAN Regional Forum
ASEAN	Association of Southeast Asian Nations
ASEM	Asia-Europe Meeting
AU	African Union
BFL	Basic Food Law (EU)
BICHAT	Program of Cooperation on Preparedness and Response to Biological and Chemical Agent Attacks
BoJ	Bank of Japan
BRIC	Brazil, Russia, India and China
BRICS	Brazil, Russia, India, China and South Africa
BSE	Bovine spongiform encephalopathy
BWC	Biological Weapons Convention
CAA	Consumer Affairs Agency (Japan)
CAP	Common Agricultural Policy
CARIFORUM	Caribbean Community + Dominican Republic
CCP	Common Commercial Policy
CDM	Clean Development Mechanism
CEE	Central and Eastern Europe
CEFP	Council on Economic and Fiscal Policy (Japan)
CETA	(EU-Canada) Comprehensive Economic and Trade Agreement
CFSP	Common Foreign and Security Policy
CJD	Creutzfeldt–Jakob disease
CSDP	Common Security and Defence Policy
CTBT	Comprehensive Test Ban Treaty
DAC	(OECD) Development Assistance Committee
DG	Directorate General (EU)
DG AGRI	Directorate General for Agriculture and Rural Development (EU)
DG DEVCO	Directorate General Development and Cooperation-EuropeAid (EU)
DG ECHO	Directorate General International Cooperation, Humanitarian Aid, and Crisis Response (EU)
DG ELARG	Directorate General for Enlargement (EU)
DG RELEX	Directorate General External Relations (EU)

DG Trade	Directorate General Trade (EU)
DPJ	Democratic Party of Japan
EC	European Commission
ECB	European Central Bank
ECDC	European Centre for Disease Prevention and Control
EDF	European Development Fund
EEAS	European External Action Service
EEC	European Economic Community
EFSA	European Food Safety Authority
EFSF	European Financial Stability Facility
EIDHR	European Instrument for Democracy and Human Rights
ENP	European Neighbourhood Policy
EP	European Parliament
EPA	Economic Partnership Agreement
EPC	European Political Co-operation
ESDP	European Security and Defence Policy
ESM	European Financial Stability Mechanism
ETS	Exchange Trading System
ETUC	European Trade Union Confederation
EU	European Union
FAO	Food and Agriculture Organization
FDI	Foreign Direct Investment
FSA	Food Safety Authority (UK)
FSC	Food Safety Commission (Japan)
FTA	Free Trade Agreement
GDP	Gross Domestic Product
GFL	General Food Law
GHGE	Green-house Gas Emissions
GMO	Genetically-modified Organism
GNI	Gross National Income
GoJ	Government of Japan
HR	High Representative (for Foreign Affairs and Security Policy)
IBRD	International Bank for Reconstruction and Development
IEA	International Energy Agency
IMF	International Monetary Fund
IO	International Organization
IPE	International Political Economy
IPPC	International Plant Protection Convention
JBIC	Japan Bank for International Cooperation
JETRO	Japan External Trade Organization
JEUFTA	The Japan-EU Free Trade Agreement
JICA	Japan International Cooperation Agency
JSPS	Japan Society for the Promotion of Science
JSS	Joint standard-setting

LDCs	Least Developed Countries
LDP	Liberal Democratic Party (Japan)
LICs	Lower-Income Countries
MAFF	Ministry of Agriculture, Forestry and Fisheries (Japan)
MDGs	Millennium Development Goals
METI	Ministry of Economy, Trade and Industry (Japan)
MEXT	Ministry of Education, Culture, Sports, Science and Technology (Japan)
MHLW	Ministry of Health, Labour, and Welfare (Japan)
MICs	Middle-Income Countries
MITI	(Former) Ministry of International Trade and Industry (Japan)
MLA	(EU-Japan) Mutual Legal Assistance Agreement
MOD	Ministry of Defense (Japan)
MOE	Ministry of the Environment (Japan)
MOFA	Ministry of Foreign Affairs (Japan)
MOJ	Ministry of Justice (Japan)
MRA	(EU-Japan) Mutual Recognition Agreement
MS	Member State (of the EU)
NATO	North Atlantic Treaty Organization
NCGM	National Center for Global Health and Medicine (Japan)
NESID	National Epidemiological Surveillance of Infectious Diseases (Japan)
NGO	Non-governmental organization
NIBIO	National Institute of Biomedical Innovation (Japan)
NIID	National Institute of Infectious Diseases (Japan)
NSC	National Security Council (Japan)
NSS	(Japan's) National Security Strategy
NTB	Non-tariff Barrier
ODA	Official Development Assistance
OECD	Organisation for Economic Co-operation and Development
OIE	World Organisation for Animal Health
OMT	Office of the Ministry of Trade (Korea)
OPEC	Organization of the Petroleum Exporting Countries
PCA	Partnership and Cooperation Agreement
PMO	Prime Minister's Office (Japan)
PP	Public Procurement
PRC	People's Republic of China
PTA	Preferential Trade Agreement
QMV	Qualified Majority Voting
RASFF	Rapid Alert System for Food and Feed (EU)
RCEP	Regional Comprehensive Economic Partnership
RH	Regulatory Harmonization
ROK	Republic of Korea
ROKEUFTA	Korea-European Union Free Trade Agreement

R2P	Responsibility to Protect
S&T	Science and Technology
SAA	Stabilisation and Accession Agreement
SAP	Stabilisation and Association Process
SCJ	Science Council of Japan
SCO	Shanghai Cooperation Organization
SDF	(Japan) Self-Defense Forces
SME	Small and Medium-sized Enterprise
SPA	Strategic Partnership Agreement
SPS	Sanitary and Phytosanitary Measures
TAM	(EU-Japan) Trade Assessment Mechanism
TEPCO	Tokyo Electric Power Company
TEU	Treaty on European Union
TFEU	Treaty on the Functioning of the European Union
TFEU/TEU	Lisbon Treaty
TICAD	Tokyo International Conference on African Development
TPP	Trans-Pacific Partnership
TRIPS	Trade-Related Aspects of Intellectual Property Rights
TTIP	Transatlantic Trade and Investment Partnership
UK	United Kingdom
UMR	Unconditional Mutual Recognition
UN	United Nations
UNCAT	United Nations Committee Against Torture
UNCED	United Nations Conference on Environment and Development
UNDP	United Nations Development Programme
UNFCCC	United Nations Framework Convention on Climate Change
UNHRC	United Nations Human Rights Committee
UNICCPR	United Nations International Covenant on Civil and Political Rights
UNSC	United Nations Security Council
US	United States of America
UTCs	Unfinished Tariff Cuts
WHO	World Health Organization
WISH	Wide-area Information-exchange System for Health, Labour and Welfare Administration (Japan)
WMD	Weapons of Mass Destruction
WTO	World Trade Organization

Introduction:
EU–Japan Relations in a Fluid Global Order

Hartmut Mayer

In the beginning there was enthusiasm. When in April 2010, the new President of the European Council, Herman van Rompuy, the President of the Commission Manuel Barroso and the fairly new Japanese Prime Minister Yukio Hatoyama (from the Democratic Party of Japan, hereafter DPJ) met for the 19th EU–Japan summit in Tokyo, there seemed to be the possibility of a new dawn in European-Japanese relations. Since the 1991 Hague Declaration on EU–Japan Political Relations (Declaration of 18 July 1991) nearly 20 years of half-hearted summitry had formalized the gradual institutional evolution of EU–Japan political relations (Nakamura 2013) but it had failed to deliver on greater promises. 2010 was therefore optimistically dubbed the 'year of renewal' (MOFA 2010, Japan-EU Joint Press Statement). It was hoped that relations between Europe and Japan could finally be elevated to a higher level, in order to achieve the significant potential that closer cooperation between two large economic entities with shared values certainly promised. Back then, negotiations on a Free Trade Agreement and on a Comprehensive Political Agreement between the EU and Japan were already set in motion. The newly upgraded EU foreign policy instruments, namely the foundation of the EEAS and the strengthened role of the High Representative for Foreign Affairs, Baroness Catherine Ashton, provided further impetus for optimism. All looked set for a fundamental upgrade of one of the EU's oldest and most valued strategic partnerships.

As it happened at the time, the Tokyo summit was also Catherine Ashton's first formal engagement outside Europe. As part of the delegation, she held various closed meetings with officials, think tanks and academics. The roots of this book go back to these meetings and the spirit of optimism at the time. The three editors and several other contributors to the volume participated in a series of closed reflections around the summit. To some extent, those reflections between policymakers and academics on EU–Japan relations became midwife to this book. This project therefore developed through seminars and open international conferences held before and subsequent to Ashton's visit, at Waseda University's EU Institute in Japan (EUIJ Waseda), one of the primary hubs for EU studies and research in Asia. These workshops and conferences all aimed at providing a new stimulus for enhanced political cooperation between Europe and Japan, both with regard to research on the subject and its potential political implementation. From its very inception, this book was therefore located at the juncture between academic research and actual policy debate.

At the time of publication in 2015, the original optimism has faded slightly but the ambition is still very strong indeed. Japan and the European Union are still in careful negotiations on a new bilateral trade treaty as well as a comprehensive political agreement that was always the envisaged twin sister of the trade deal. Many of the original strategic aims surrounding these talks have now been influenced by parallel inter-regional trade negotiations on the TPP (Trans-Pacific Partnership) and the TTIP (Transatlantic Trade and Investment Partnership). Furthermore, the emergence of new geo-strategic tensions and hot-spots in Gaza, Syria, Iraq, the South China Sea and Ukraine have altered the external environment surrounding EU–Japan relations. Domestically, sluggish economic growth in both the Eurozone and Japan, as well as rapid changes in the domestic political outlook, with right-wing tendencies on the rise in both Europe and Japan, have provided new challenges for mutually beneficial co-operation between these two advanced and demographically aging industrial societies. It nevertheless remains timely to take a fresh look at the past shortcomings and the future potentials of the relationship between Europe and Japan, in our view still one of the central axes of world order.

Against popular notions that EU–Japan relations will face an inevitable decline as both Europe and Japan become less significant in the world as a whole, and more pre-occupied with domestic economic challenges and regional security, it remains our view that the EU and Japan can still provide a vital axis for future global governance and become an essential pillar in the emerging fluid global order. The book's general point of departure is one of modest optimism. As others have noted, the EU–Japan relationship transformed over 40 years from 'confrontation to global partnership' (Keck, Vanoverbeke and Waldenberger 2013) but it is time to consolidate this partnership with concrete results. On the whole, this edited volume intends to counterbalance gloomy notions of joint decline by analysing the positive effects of European and Japanese contributions to global governance. The book asks how the changing EU and Japan jointly respond to global challenges and how they can cooperate on such diversified issues as trade, finance, development, human rights, food security, post-conflict nation-building, renewable energy, climate change, nuclear safety and infectious diseases. Implicitly, the book also attempts to make theoretical contributions to debates on co-operation in global governance and global norm-setting.

Our research focuses on both the political and strategic co-operation between the European Union and Japan that were supposed to have intensified ever since the 2001 Action Plan for EU-Japan Co-operation. The evolution of the EU–Japan political relationship during that period has also been examined in a number of other places (Hook et al. 2012: 257–309; Söderberg 2012; Frattolillo 2013). Ueta and Remacle have also edited four volumes addressing the current state of EU–Japan political relations throughout the 2000s (Ueta and Remacle 2001; Ueta and Remacle 2005; Ueta, Remacle and Ponjaert 2007; Ueta and Remacle 2008). Although these volumes mentioned the concept of 'civilian power' (particularly Ueta and Remacle 2005), it was not used as an organizing device in any of them. As explained below, our book does deploy the concept, and is also forward-looking, rather than historical in focus, and makes a significant contribution to the *ongoing* debates on the necessary upgrade of EU–Japan relations that underpins the current negotiations on trade and a Strategic Partnership Agreement. A renewed reflection about the often overlooked and undervalued partnership between the EU and Japan remains essential for many reasons. Despite an intensification of formal contacts between the two entities since 2001, both Japan and Europe remain in real danger of losing sight of each other. The last five years have not altered this picture significantly.

The internal dynamics of EU–Japan relations remain dependent on larger geo-strategic concerns. Europe's overall Asia strategy seems to be pre-occupied by an obsession with China and India. Energy concerns and the re-emergence of an aggressive Russia in the European neighbourhood have led to a regional concentration on Russia and Central Asia. Terrorism and traditional security fears resulting from various conflicts in the Middle East have reaffirmed Europe's concentration on the near abroad. Japan is far away and, wrongly in our view, is currently out of focus for most European citizens and policy-makers alike. Meanwhile, Japan enhances its economic role in Asia, focuses on its increasingly difficult relationship with China and is reconsidering some aspects of its regional security strategy, with an upgrade of the classical self-defence forces. Research has shown that Europe looks increasingly peripheral to many people in Japan, and that Japan also looks peripheral to Europe. In this climate, we argue that, more than ever, a new emphasis on joint tasks and responsibilities for enhanced EU–Japan co-operation is needed.

In addition to an appreciation of shared and common values, one should also ask how Europeans and Japanese could jointly address and manage global problems concretely. This will never mean full harmony between the two players under investigation here. However, even where views on policy issues do not completely converge, a better understanding of each other's point of view is crucial. Despite the shifts in global outlook, great potential for enhanced co-operation with measurable results can be identified in many areas: general foreign policy co-ordination and transparency beyond the respective regions; multi-lateral trade co-operation in the WTO and through bilateral and regional agreements; the deepening of regional integration efforts, in particular in Asia, as well as sustainable development, climate change and the environment, health, science and technology.

In all these areas, the economic resources available and the civil society attitudes present in Europe and Japan are much closer to each other than in many other parts of the developed and developing world. If one aims to enhance results in these areas globally, joint efforts and activities between the EU and Japan remain a powerful, and in our view, essential tool. It is with a normative agenda in mind that the various chapters of this volume have been chosen. The emphasis on the concrete co-operation potential is the common glue that holds the empirical chapters of this book together.

Academic Debates as Background for this Book

In addition to normative desires and concrete policy recommendations, the book offers modest reflections on how one can conceptualize EU–Japan cooperation. The book is not intended to enhance theory building in International Relations or to commit our broad range of authors to one particular theoretical or conceptual straitjacket. Open pluralism as an intellectual point of departure characterizes the volume. However, that does not mean that research on EU–Japan relations should, as it has often done in the past, sit firmly in its specialist and purely empirical niche. It must be linked to leading mainstream debates in International Relations, where the larger significance of EU–Japan co-operation should be highlighted. While the design and scope of the book does not allow for theoretical innovation, various generalist approaches have informed the above mentioned conferences and workshops and thereby shaped the chapters of this volume.

Foreign Policy Analysis

The first cluster of approaches that informed the writings stems from classical foreign policy analysis. These look for domestic, bureaucratic, institutional, psychological and ideational factors that explain the shifts of European and Japanese foreign policy over time. The EU and Japan are both interested in enhancing their international standing in order to overcome their traditional respective images as 'economic giants and political dwarfs' and to reposition themselves as significant actors in a changing global order. While there is the pre-disposition that the two traditional 'civilian powers' are somewhat natural partners with many shared responsibilities in global governance, there has also been a long-standing benign and mutual neglect of each other over the years (Reiterer 2013: 296). The changing roles and significances of the two polities in global governance can therefore be explained to some extent by the application of Foreign Policy Analysis. A classical rationalist power-calculation would provide a first cut. With the European fixation on China and a world view that sees the US, Europe, Russia, India, China and possibly Brazil as future poles of global order, Japan has been somewhat marginalized in European thinking. Meanwhile, Japan's foreign policy elite, refocusing its security policy and global engagement, seems to lose confidence in the EU's ability to play any significant role in global politics apart from trade and aid. The variety of classical studies on foreign policy-making, including institutional and ideational approaches, could lead to a better explanation of a somewhat surprising indifference that Japan and the EU have in the past displayed towards each other. Nakamura identifies and explains some of the domestic Japanese political constraints which have contributed to this state of affairs in his contribution to this volume. Furthermore, every new Japanese leader that recently came into office has had a different set of ideas on the general direction of Japanese foreign policy. Ignoring these dimensions in a general narrative about the structural potential of EU–Japan co-operation would do injustice to the topic.

Larger Visions of World Order

The second approach places EU–Japan co-operation within a wider macro-perspective and analyses its function in the context of larger debates on world order. While acknowledging the rapid shifts in global order, many Europeans and Japanese still seem to be trapped in traditional perspectives. As Nakamura (2013) notes, the origins of EU–Japan relations are rooted in a world and time that saw economic power directly translated into global political influence. EU–Japan relations were a second-order sub-set which were important due to economic resources, but were anchored around undisputed US leadership in a generally liberal world order (Ikenberry 2008). The emerging new power configuration, uncertain as it is, obviously raises questions about global leadership, in particular for those states and regions that have held positions of responsibility in the past. A legitimate but nearly extinct sub-text of EU–Japan relations is the question as to whether a new trilateralism between the US, Japan and Europe would be needed for sustaining global stability. While this might be in the minds of some of the advocates of closer relations between the EU and Japan, a mere restoration of old patterns is a highly unlikely avenue for future relations between Europe and Japan. Whether the West's general political domination is coming to an end remains to be seen, but there can be no doubt that the relative weight of the US, Europe and Japan is declining. Considering the persisting economic and political power and the enormous potential for innovation in the old triad, the challenge is to foster and integrate co-operation between the US, Europe and Japan in a rapidly changing world. The classical triangular relations need to be redefined and rejuvenated for larger global purposes. The future of EU–Japan relations will likely continue to be a somewhat second-order question, but this question no longer depends on the US alone, but on a variety of players and circumstances.

Debates on the EU and Japan and their future relationship are clearly influenced by larger waves of change in global politics. World order is indeed constantly reshaping and affecting the bilateral ties under consideration here (Maull 2005). Without summarizing the debates on global order in detail (see for example, Hurrell 2007a; Krause 2007; Zürn 2007; Walt 2005; Haass 2008), larger visions of world order have come in different forms and fashions over the last 25 years. They include roughly 10 versions, which I have analysed in detail elsewhere (Mayer 2010). Some of these alternative visions of order have quite different implications for the significance of the EU–Japan relationship.

The first vision, US hegemony in a uni-polar world (Krauthammer 1990/91, 2003) would be closest to the established pattern of EU–Japan relations. Tokyo, Brussels and the European capitals would look for clear US leadership and would have limited room for independent positions and action. As in the past, different policy initiatives could come out of European–Japanese co-operation, but their fate would ultimately be decided in Washington.

The second vision, neo-realist instability on a global scale, where no power or group of powers would dominate, and where no hegemonic leadership would manage to stabilize any regional or global order, provides a huge challenge for European–Japanese relations. In this image, the likelihood of wars and crises spreading around the world would make European nations and Japan rely first and foremost on themselves. Some voices in the Pentagon have recently referred to a 'vuca-world' (Sommer 2014) as a general guideline, with vuca standing for volatile, uncertain, complex and ambivalent. In such a world view, EU–Japan relations would likely be reduced to ad hoc co-operation on a case-by-case basis, rather than a shared sense of common values pointing the way to joint action.

The third vision of world order, multi-polarity with several distinct poles or concentrations of new powers such as Russia, China, India and Brazil more or less challenging established powers in the West, is a real factor in debates on EU–Japan relations. Multi-polarity could become cooperative assuming that the few major powers would cooperate on defining the rules and would discipline those who violate them. There would be a central role for the EU and Japan as joint guards protecting the existing norms of global society. In the 1990s, a well-received variant of this vision was the concept of tri-polar regionalism (US, EU, Japan) with competing trading blocs all roughly committed to similar values. Alternative visions of multi-polarity foresee world order as fiercely competitive with the possibility of dialogue between major powers breaking down. In that scenario, the EU and Japan could move further apart as rivals rather than be partners in a multi-polar world.

A similar ambiguity for EU–Japan relations derives from the fourth image of world order. This concerns hierarchical notions of power with regard to different policy fields. In such an image there would be a stark contrast between great powers, middle powers, small powers or, alternatively, super-powers, great powers and regional powers that would create a 'layer-cake model' of world order, with unipolar, multipolar, multi-regional and transnational layers and logics defining different policy areas. The EU and Japan would be different players in different fields, with potential for sector-specific co-operation and rivalry. An EU–Japan axis as such would have limited general meaning.

The opposite is true for the fifth image, a return to bi-polarity in a G2 world, with the US (West) and China heading for a new clash in the twenty-first century. The EU–Japan relationship would be firmly anchored on the US side of this global rivalry. However, the image of a G2 world is a general burden and distraction for the current EU–Japan dialogue, as the Europeans have no interest in importing Japanese–Chinese or US–Chinese rivalries into their general Asia strategy. The delay in the EU–Japan trade talks can be partly explained by Japanese desires to use such agreements as safeguards against China, while the Europeans do not wish to direct the EU–Japan relationship against Beijing.

A similar ambivalence for EU–Japan relations results from the sixth image, a world of economically and culturally integrated and distinct regions with inter-regional dialogues and agreements at the heart of world order. Rhetorically at least, this has been the preferred vision of the European Union for a long time, but it no longer seems to resonate strongly in Japan. Deepened regional integration in

Asia would in Tokyo's view translate into enhanced Chinese dominance. Hence, EU–Japan relations are therefore not seen as a building block for mature inter-regional co-operation between Europe and Asia as a whole.

The seventh scenario of world order offers optimistic hopes for a structured and well-governed New World Order, centred in strong institutions of global governance, the general power of the rule of law and well-functioning international regimes. Such an order would provide a strong platform for EU–Japan relations. In such a world order, inter-regional agreements based on the same values would provide an opportunity to reaffirm and strengthen the global order through complementary regional arrangements and interregional dialogue. It would give room for regional and cross-regional initiatives to travel into the central institutions of global governance. A forum such as a strengthened G-20 not ruled by the US would certainly benefit from a layer of functioning inter-regional arrangements. In such a world, the EU–Japan alliance could punch much above its current weight.

The three remaining world visions would, however, downgrade the specific ties between Europe and Japan. The eighth vision, that is, a world of cultural friction, clash of civilizations, asymmetric warfare and globally networked terrorism as the defining feature of an unstable world, would pull Europe and Japan further apart. The ninth image, the powerful notion of a more transpolar order where economic actors, rather than state-based political power is decisive, and where states are in rapid decline, would place limits on both the EU and Japan. They would be overtaken by business, markets and other non-state actors as the relevant players defining world order.

The last image, more recent debates on a non-polar world (Haass 2008; Roberts 2008), paints a picture of numerous centres of meaningful power. Haass defines such order to include six major powers (like the multi-polar image): China, the EU, India, Japan, Russia and the US. Unlike a simple multi-polar image, there is a second significant layer of regional powers including Brazil, Argentina, Chile, Mexico, Venezuela, Nigeria, South Africa, Egypt, Iran, Israel, Saudi Arabia, Australia, Indonesia and South Korea. Most importantly 'meaningful power centres' include the major international organizations (UN, IMF, World Bank, ASEAN, AU, OPEC, Shanghai Cooperation Organization among others) and even 'states within states' (California) and global cities (New York, London, Sao Paolo, Tokyo, Shanghai). They also include the largest world energy, manufacturing and financial firms. Each of these power centres will then be constantly challenged from above (by international organizations), from below (by militias such as Hamas, Taliban, Hezbollah) and from the side (by NGOs and corporations). Churches, networks of political parties, global media, drug cartels and global charities all play an independent additional and powerful part (Haass 2008). Most significant for this book, Haass's comprehensive vision of a 'non-polar world' does not consider a fixed place for Japan or European nations as such, or for a stable axis in world order. There is no danger of overburdening expectations for EU–Japan co-operation, as this would be just another fluid element in a 'a world of many worlds' (Hurrell 2007a).

Normative Commitments

In addition to internal insights derived from foreign policy analysis and external constraints that result from notions of world order, there is a third element that binds the chapters of this volume together. There are two implicit normative commitments that have shaped this book. The first is the well-known concept of civilian power (Duchêne 1972; Bull 1982; Orbie 2006; Telò 2007). The term was developed in the Cold War context and applied mainly to the EU, Japan and Germany (Maull 1990). The editors of this volume are supportive of the concept, but believe that it needs to be re-examined and provided with a new substance. The substance as provided in the various chapters in the volume will be vital, as empty labels are already abundant. For the EU, for example, we can already find terms such as 'normative power' (Manners 2002), 'soft power' (Nye 2005), 'soft empire' (Hettne and Söderbaum 2005) 'transformative power' (Grabbe 2006), 'ambiguous power' (Gasteyger 1996), 'green normative power' (Falkner 2007) or even, most bizarrely, 'metrosexual superpower' (Khanna 2004).

While discussing the terminology is important, it strikes us as crucial that the EU and Japan will continue to take leadership positions and engage in joint advocacy in areas where other powers are less well equipped or willing to engage. These areas concern the following:

- sustainable development and energy
- leadership in development aid policies
- egalitarian principles and non-monetary concepts of well-being
- human security
- regulation and standard-setting

The various chapters of this volume elaborate in detail but they are committed to supporting this unique civilian power role that Europe and Japan might be able to play.

The second normative commitment that the book subscribes to is the notion of 'global responsibility' that I have developed in previous works elsewhere (Mayer and Vogt 2006). As a general guideline, we suggest that a shift away from regional interests to global responsibilities could provide a common narrative for successful co-operation between Japan and Europe. While the EU and Japan themselves, and the supporting global order have changed significantly over the last 25 years, the EU's and Japan's traditional rhetoric have not altered accordingly. A new narrative for both the EU and Japan in world affairs is needed. Due to the decline of America's intellectual leadership and its loss of general prestige as a result of the mistaken ideology and policies under President George W. Bush – a period that saw its policy peak between 2001 and 2005 but whose outside echoes are likely to last for decades – the EU and Japan might be well placed to feed into a new global discourse that emphasizes ethics, sustainable economic development, global justice and responsibility. The other rising and regional powers are certainly less equipped to fill the vacuum, if one agrees that there is such a demand. The contribution, however, has to be concrete and well-founded.

As far as Japan is concerned, since the end of the Cold War there have been significant shifts, with periods of confidence and lack of confidence in foreign policy. The quick turn-over of governments and leaders that characterizes politics in Japan has not helped in producing a consistent direction in Japanese foreign policy, as Nakamura indicates in his chapter in this volume. The outlook has been, on the whole, still too much confined within the parameters of the nation state and the perceived national interests of Japan, be it with reference to global trade, as a regional leader or as one of the most powerful states in the world. We argue that both the EU and Japan would benefit from a conscious shift in their perspectives, towards that of true global responsibility. In doing so, the real danger, for both the EU and Japan, would be an ever-increasing, self-congratulatory and self-centred debate along the old lines that 'Europe is doing good for the whole world' or that 'Japan must be the natural leader in Asia'. In a world in which Europe (and possibly Japan as well) is likely to become increasingly peripheral in terms of population, economic growth and innovation, this decline in relative power might lead to a decline in normative and ethical power. This is not to say that Europe and Japan should not continue to advocate civilian and ethical norms, but that both have to explain the substance, the intellectual origins and the meaning of norms much better to sceptical audiences worldwide. They also have to show to the developing world that the EU, and most likely Japan as well, follow such norms themselves. In any case, hypocritical 'ethical or civilian powers' would be self-defeating, less ethical and less powerful probably than hard-nosed interest driven actors (Mayer and Vogt 2006) .

Naturally, the proof for Japan and Europe as responsible global actors is in the pudding. This is why the book takes a sector-by-sector approach and analyses concrete policy areas in detail. In order to be ethical actors, a notion of 'global responsibility' should become the reference point for the EU, for Japan and indeed for any major actor in international affairs. One would have to define global responsibility first and then ask what the EU and Japan, with their specific sets of instruments, values and capacities, ought to do to qualify as responsible actors in world affairs.

Chapter Outline

Inspired by the different strands of conceptual reflection referred to above, the various chapters of this book help to test the theoretical guidelines and provide new conceptual underpinnings for a desired boost to EU–Japan relations. In any case, the empirical studies on the achievements and limits of EU–Japan cooperation in selected policy fields are already a worthwhile major contribution to the debate in themselves. The guiding hypotheses for all authors were that European and Japanese contributions to global governance are essential, and that they will become of ever greater importance. The book is committed to identifying such a concrete agenda, and to capacity enhancement. In our view, it reaffirms the vital importance of EU–Japan relations in a drastically shifting global order, as outlined above.

Part I of the book therefore tries to contextualize in more detail the role of the EU and Japan in a fluid global order. It provides the conceptual background for the various case studies that form the main empirical and concrete contributions to the volume. Hidetoshi Nakamura's chapter (Chapter 1) explains the place of EU–Japan relations within Japanese politics. He analyses domestic constraints on the development of Japanese foreign policy, and also identifies other Japanese international priorities which compete for attention with EU–Japan relations. Nakamura also traces the emergence of Japan as a 'normal' state, and argues that normal statehood is not, in fact, inconsistent with the notion that Japan can be thought of as a 'proactive' civilian power.

Mario Telò (Chapter 2), a leading expert on EU external relations, asks whether the EU will remain a civilian power in global affairs, or whether its new ambitions after the Lisbon Treaty and the development of the European External Action Service (EEAS) will transform the EU's general global outlook. He offers a special focus on Germany as the EU's emergent hegemon, and suggests that the EU's global aspirations will be more decisively shaped in Berlin than has been true in the past.

Paul Bacon and Martin Holland (Chapter 3) then respond to Europe's new global ambitions by looking at them through the eyes of Japan. Their chapter analyses Japanese perceptions of the EU, an essential ingredient for an understanding of the future potential of EU–Japan relations. The research is based on an extensive and systematic analysis of the Japanese media, demonstrating the high visibility of the EU in the Japanese media, but also offering a clear suggestion that the relationship suffers as a result of significant 'untapped potential' (Barroso 2006). The chapter sets the scene for the main body of the edited collection, which brings together a distinctive list of genuine experts in their respective fields.

Parts II, III and IV of the book provide empirical case studies on selected policy areas. In each of the fields we are tentatively asking the following broader questions:

1. Are the EU and Japan actively co-operating together, either with a declared or implicit, institutionalized or non-institutionalized intent to lead, in the development of norms and policies?
2. Are the EU and Japan learning from each other with regard to the development of particular policies? To what extent, and how can we tell?
3. Is EU policy, or Japanese policy, providing a model/having an impact on how states or international organizations develop their own norms and policies?

The general aim of the chapters is to examine actual areas of co-operation, and individual or joint contributions by the EU and Japan to good global governance. At the same time, we identify areas of contestation and disagreement, as for example in the field of human rights. In each of the chapters, we have also used the concept of civilian power as an organizing device, leaving it to individual authors to engage with it as deeply as might seem appropriate. The policy areas under consideration are naturally wide-ranging, and we have clustered them under distinct headings.

The first and most important issue in the context of EU–Japan relations has always been trade. Part II of the book is therefore allocated to this subject. Min Shu (Chapter 4) opens the section by arguing that the importance of the EU–Japan negotiations needs to be highlighted, but also contextualized within the EU's wider Asia strategy. Shu examines important changes in trade relations between Europe and East Asia, charts the recent development of EU–Asian trade relations, analyses institutional reforms to the Common Commercial Policy, and assesses the challenges facing the EU's external trade strategy towards East Asia. He shows that growing trade with the Far East has not only created a large trade deficit on the EU side, but has seriously divided domestic interests within the EU. He discusses the 'Global Europe' strategy, the Lisbon institutional framework, and the new policy guideline of 'Trade, Growth and World Affairs'. Shu then discusses how these policy and institutional reforms have reshaped the EU's trade policy towards East Asia, detailing recent trade disputes and negotiations between the two regions. He identifies three balancing acts that the EU is facing in dealing with East Asia, mediating between 'Bilateralism and Regionalism', 'Trade Protection and Market Access' and 'Economic Interests and Foreign Policy Goals'.

Frederik Ponjaert (Chapter 5) moves us from the global/regional level to the bilateral level, and offers a detailed and valuable history and assessment of EU–Japan relations. He notes that there has been a significant trend towards PTAs, and explains the reasons for increased recent momentum behind the negotiations for an FTA/SPA between the EU and Japan. Ponjaert looks in some detail at vested interests and domestic institutional, political and economic constraints operating on both sides, which influence the likelihood of successful negotiations. He notes that the EU–Japan relationship suffers from an 'expectations deficit', but argues that this can be a good thing, in that it reduces the possibility of more substantial critical scrutiny from within both polities. Ponjaert offers a cautiously optimistic assessment of the prospects for the negotiations, arguing that political conditionality has a role to play in moving them forwards, as long as this is accompanied by an appropriate degree of 'constructive ambiguity' regarding how rigorously conditionality would in fact be applied.

Within all global and bilateral trade negotiations, some specialist issue-areas are always particularly significant. This volume provides chapters on some of these specialist and often contentious topics. Gijs Berends (Chapter 6) analyses European and Japanese food standards. Although the overall volume of EU–Japan trade in food is relatively small, he highlights an area where both sides worked together successfully, in a post-Fukushima context, to overcome a specific standardization problem with regard to food security. This detailed case study potentially shows a way forward for practitioners looking for middle ground on other standardization issues under negotiation in the trade talks. Furthermore, this is clearly an important policy area, where EU–Japan co-operation seems to have real promise for enhancing standards of global governance. The way in which this issue is addressed in these negotiations could therefore also be relevant for other trade talks, such as TPP and TTIP.

Part III of the volume moves away from trade, and looks at co-operation with regard to energy security, economic development, and international environmental politics. As with Part II, general overview chapters are followed by more specific ones. Miranda A. Schreurs (Chapter 7) opens the section by examining one of the most high-profile and contentious issues over the last few years, namely energy policy. Since the triple disaster in Fukushima, mutual learning and adaptation between Europe and Japan has been remarkably fast and has had influential consequences. The impact of the Japanese tragedy on energy policies in Europe, and in particular Germany, has been decisive. However, even though Fukushima occupies a prominent place in the chapter, its scope is far more wide-ranging. Held together by the concept of cross-societal learning, Schreurs' coverage ranges from traditional areas such as sanitation and pollution control to more recent policy areas such as the promotion of renewable energy. She argues that mutual learning between Europe and Japan takes place between environmental civil societies, established state institutions, and within the context of international negotiations on global treaties, such as those on biodiversity and climate change.

A second area where the EU and Japan have impacted significantly on global affairs has been in their respective contributions to development and worldwide poverty alleviation. Bart Gaens and Henri Vogt (Chapter 8) compare the development policies of the European Union and Japan, both portrayed as 'aid superpowers' in the global development regime. Civilian powers would be expected to take a lead in this area and set global examples and norms. The chapter shows that, despite sharing the common label of 'civilian power', the principles, goals and instruments of Japanese and EU aid policies in fact differ significantly. However, in recent years there have been increasing signs of convergence, suggesting some form of inter-regional or global norm diffusion. What has certainly united European and Japanese aid polices is the external perception that both actors use aid policy to enhance their respective interests, rather than fully subscribing to the ideal of global responsibility.

Hiroshi Ohta and Yves Tiberghien (Chapter 9) then look at concrete co-operation in environmental politics. They analyse joint attempts by Europe and Japan to save the Kyoto Protocol on Climate Change. Global warming has been one of the flagship topics for co-operation between the EU and Japan, as the views they share seem to differ from those expressed by the United States and the emerging BRICS. The EU was certainly a key player in defining the general conditions lying behind the Kyoto regime, while Japan seems to have been more reluctant in the beginning, but quite influential at key moments in the process of establishing institutions. According to the authors, however, the record of EU–Japan co-operation has been mixed. Periods of joint leadership have alternated with periods of limited impact, suggesting that Europe and Japan might in the future need to reach out to China, to seek trilateral initiatives with regard to climate change.

Part IV, the final section of the book, investigates issues of political, food and health security. It was noted briefly above that civilian powers should promote and seek to implement the concept of human security. Political, food and health security are three of the seven dimensions of human security identified in the landmark UNDP report introducing the concept (UNDP 1994; Bacon and Hobson 2014). The practices of human rights promotion and post-conflict nation-building are discussed in chapters by Paul Bacon (Chapter 10) and Dimitar Bechev (Chapter 11), respectively. Both of these practices are subsumed within and, if successfully prosecuted, contribute towards the overall condition of political security, for both individuals and communities. Dual-use governance regimes, which are addressed in Yasue Fukuda's chapter (Chapter 12), seek to mitigate the risk of biological, chemical and nuclear terrorism, all of which obviously present threats to health security. Successful food governance regimes mitigate the risk to food security presented by such issues as BSE crises, which occurred within both the EU and Japan. These crises are discussed in Koji Fukuda's chapter (Chapter 13).

Bacon and Bechev look at two different aspects of political security, but also at two areas where the EU and Japan have not been natural partners in the past. In the field of human rights, Bacon identifies areas of disagreement and contention behind the surface of common declarations. He focuses on EU human rights strategy with regard to Japan, and argues that there has been too much symbolic and one-dimensional focus on the death penalty. Bacon argues that there are other human rights issues in Japan which are actually more important than the death penalty, relating to the criminal justice process. Reform is more likely with regard to these criminal justice issues, rather than on the politically-charged subject of the death penalty, and the EU therefore needs to adopt a more nuanced and tailored approach to the specifics of the Japanese context. Drawing on the work of Amitav Acharya, Bacon calls for a more 'localized' EU human rights strategy, with regard both to Japan, and to Asia more generally.

Dimitar Bechev also looks beyond declarations, and researches actual joint efforts to provide stability in the Balkans over the years. He analyses the various stages of the EU and Japan's efforts to address the violence, war and uncertainty in the Balkans since the break-up of Yugoslavia. Bechev points to the usefulness of the civilian power concept, both as an analytical tool, and as a normative guideline for actual policies. One further fruit of his chapter is a systematic analysis of the Japanese contribution to global efforts to stabilize the Balkans, a contribution which has often been overlooked in standard accounts of this prominent and ongoing regional crisis.

A further widely neglected area of EU–Japan relations, namely the global governance of dual use in biomedical research, is investigated by Yasue Fukuda.

This innovative chapter also directs us to the untapped potential of and the further mutual benefit for the EU and Japan through enhanced co-operation. Dual use means the potential to use new research in the biomedical and life science for good purposes and, unfortunately, for ill. Research outcomes in these areas require strong international supervision and monitoring, in order to prevent and minimize misconduct and misuse, which constitutes a clear threat to health security. The chapter provides a systematic comparison of the EU and Japan's respective codes of conduct for scientists, and makes a strong normative plea for enhanced co-operation between the two actors as a building block for a global regime.

Koji Fukuda concludes by looking at the accountability and the governance aspects of food safety policy. This is an example of both political risk management between Europe and Japan, but also of EU–Japan influences on the universal dimensions of food safety governance. Here again, EU–Japan co-operation is a useful tool in itself, but also a vehicle for the globalization of food safety standards, and thereby for the mitigation of threats to food security. Fukuda concludes by noting that there has been policy convergence and mutual learning between the two polities with regard to the development of a food safety regime.

All in all, the volume should be of interest first and foremost to academic audiences. However, it has been the result of a very fruitful collaboration between academics and practitioners from Japan and Europe. It will naturally appeal to a wide readership beyond academia. By doing so, it hopefully provides inspiration to policy-makers and publics in Japan and Europe who, in the end, are responsible for sustaining and enhancing close relations between the two main actors under consideration in this book. The editors and authors of this volume still believe in the necessity of a fundamental upgrade for EU–Japan relations. As the following chapters will show, cross-societal learning is an important task for experts, leaders and citizens in both Europe and Japan. If not enthusiasm, there is still substantial ambition, and also a genuine need to tap the fantastic potential of EU–Japan civilian power co-operation in an uncertain and fluid global order.

PART I
Japan, the EU and Civilian Power Relations

Chapter 1

Japan as a 'Proactive Civilian Power'? Domestic Constraints and Competing Priorities

Hidetoshi Nakamura

Introduction: The Hague Declarations of July 1991 and March 2014

How much has the EU–Japan political relationship evolved since 1991, and what have been some of the main factors impacting on this evolution? *The Joint Declaration on Relations between the European Community and its Member States and Japan* was adopted in The Hague on 18 July 1991. Japanese Prime Minister Toshiki Kaifu, European Commission President Jacques Delors and European Council President Ruud Lubbers met there for the first summit meeting. The EU and Japan were keen to stress that they share a number of political values, such as a common attachment to freedom, democracy, the rule of law and human rights. This notion of shared values has regularly been referred to in subsequent summit Joint Press Statements and other such pronouncements. Among 10 or so of the EU's strategic partners, Japan has been identified as a like-minded partner, along with the US and Canada.

The EU–Japan relationship has been further institutionalized since 1991. This chapter offers a brief indicative sketch of these developments, but for a fuller account of this institutional history, please refer to Nakamura (2013), which is drawn on in places within the current chapter. At the ninth EU–Japan summit in 2000, the EU and Japan jointly declared a 'Decade of Japan-Europe Co-operation', to commence from 2001. Both parties affirmed their intention to translate the EU–Japan partnership into coordinated policies and concrete actions. An 'Action Plan for EU-Japan Cooperation: Shaping Our Common Future' was adopted at the tenth EU–Japan summit in 2001. The Action Plan had four main objectives: promoting peace and security, strengthening the economic and trade partnership, coping with global and societal challenges, and bringing together people and cultures. This Action Plan was intended to operate for 10 years.

To mark the tenth anniversary of the Action Plan, an attempt was made in 2011 to inject fresh momentum into EU–Japan relations. In the Joint Press Statement issued after the May 2011 summit, leaders agreed to start the process for parallel negotiations for:

- a deep and comprehensive Free Trade Agreement (FTA)/Economic Partnership Agreement (EPA), addressing all issues of shared interest to both sides including tariffs, non-tariff measures, services, investment, Intellectual Property Rights, competition and public procurement; and
- a binding agreement, covering political, global and other sectoral cooperation in a comprehensive manner, underpinned by their shared commitment to fundamental values and principles.

Summit leaders decided, to this end, that the two sides would start discussions with a view to defining the scope and level of ambition of both negotiations, with such scoping to be carried out as soon as possible. On 31 May 2012 the European Commission announced that it had finally ended its 'scoping exercise' for a deep and comprehensive free trade agreement with Japan, but the 27 trade ministers, who met the same day in Brussels, did not immediately give the Commission a mandate to open formal negotiations. The decision to begin negotiations was instead approved at a meeting of trade ministers in November 2012. On 25 March 2013 these negotiations towards an EPA/FTA were formally launched through EU–Japan summit talks via telephone, instead of the scheduled meeting in Tokyo, which European leaders were forced to cancel because of the Cyprus crisis. However, the negotiations commenced on condition that the process could be suspended after a year if Japan refused to eliminate a range of nontariff trade barriers. EU Trade Commissioner Karel De Gucht said at the time that he believed it would take three to four years to conclude the envisioned EPA. In the end, there were five rounds of increasingly productive talks from April 2013 to April 2014, before the EU's mandated review. Neither the European Parliament nor the Council took the opportunity provided by this unprecedented additional review to politicize or influence the negotiations. They simply endorsed DG Trade's expert opinion, noting the progress made throughout rounds 1–5, and it was therefore possible to hold the sixth round in July 2014. The 'one-year test' was passed, and negotiations now proceed in a routine and constructive manner. Frederik Ponjaert charts these developments in some detail in Chapter 5 of this volume.

Although this bilateral framework has been firmly institutionalized, as the brief discussion above demonstrates, EU–Japan relations have largely been played out within the G7 (Group of Seven) framework. The annual EU–Japan summit itself, the regular meeting between the Japanese Prime Minister and the two EU Presidents, of the European Council and the Commission respectively, was firmly institutionalized as long ago as 1991. Table 1.1 shows the names of Japanese and European leaders who attended these summits. The locations for the summits indicate the following established practices: since 1992, the hosting of the summit has rotated every time between Japan and Europe. However, the timing of the EU–Japan summit shows that Japanese and European leaders often effectively meet on the fringe of the G7/G8 summit: nine out of 22 EU–Japan summits were held within just a few days before or after a G7/G8 summit.

The EU and Japan have been able to cooperate not only reactively, but also proactively, with regard to the US within the G7 framework. And it is not only the economic field, but also the security field where the two international actors cooperate proactively with regard to the US. Although European countries and Japan had little substantial political cooperation during the Gulf conflict and they were both responsive to the US, there have been some cases of proactive cooperation since they adopted The Hague Declaration. In December 1991, for example, the EU and Japan drafted the joint proposal for a universal register of conventional arms transfers under UN auspices.

After Russia joined the G8 Summit, the EU and Japan successfully persuaded Russia to ratify the Kyoto Protocol on climate change, and they were able to help the Kyoto Protocol to come into force without US ratification. This is an important example of earlier civilian power cooperation. However, the G8 has not entirely replaced the G7, and the Ukraine crisis may well be understood as offering unfortunate evidence that Russia has never quite been a fully like-minded partner of the G7. Indeed, the G7 leaders condemned Russia's 'clear violation of the sovereignty and territorial integrity of Ukraine' in their statement issued on 3 March 2014 (European Council 2014a). The G7 leaders also met in The Hague and issued a Declaration on 24 March 2014. They stated: 'International law prohibits the acquisition of part or all of another state's territory through coercion or force' (European Council 2014b). The Japanese Prime Minister also said that 'changing the status quo by force is completely unacceptable', thereby sending an implicit message to China (MOFA 2014).

Among the five permanent members of the UN Security Council, we still frequently observe conflict between the US, the UK and France on the one hand, and Russia and China on the other. Cooperation among the P5 has yet to become business as usual, and it is natural that any attempt to expand the G7 into the G8 (plus China) has not been successful, particularly in the political and security fields. Although the attempt to expand the G8 into the G20 in the economic field has been successful so far, the originally planned G8 summit was not held in Sochi on 4–5 June 2014. Instead, a G7 summit was held in Brussels on the same day. This summit was hosted by the EU instead of Russia. The 41st summit will be held in Germany, but it remains unclear whether this will be a meeting of the G7 or the G8.

Whether in the G7, the G20 or elsewhere, some EU–Japan political cooperation can be observed. But such cooperation remains limited in the politico-military field. Japan was almost indifferent, for example, to Libya. And on North Korea, for example, the EU has little to say. The roles which the EU and Japan have played in these respective multilateral frameworks are still limited: the EU and Japan are still described as two civilian powers. Although the EU and Japan make some military contributions to international peace and security, both actors are not necessarily described as normal military powers, but still viewed as civilian powers with some military capabilities.

Table 1.1 The annual EU–Japan summit (names of leaders) and the G7/G8 summit

EU–Japan Summit		Place	Japanese Prime Minister	President of the European Commission	President of the European Council	The G7/G8 Summit		Place
1st	19 Jul 1991	The Hague	Toshiki Kaifu	Jacques Delors	Ruud Lubbers (Dutch PM)	17th	15–17 Jul 1991	London (G7)
2nd	4 Jul 1992	London	Kiichi Miyazawa		John Major (British PM)	18th	6–8 Jul 1992	Munich
3rd	6 Jul 1993	Tokyo		Henning Christophersen (Vice President)	Jean-Luc Dehaene (Belgian PM)	19th	7–9 Jul 1993	Tokyo
						20th	8–10 Jul 1994	Naples
4th	19 Jun 1995	Paris	Tomiichi Murayama		Jacques Chirac (French Pres.)	21st	15–17 Jun 1995	Halifax
5th	30 Sep 1996	Tokyo	Ryutaro Hashimoto	Jacques Santer	John Burton (Irish PM)	22nd	27–29 Jun 1996	Lyon
6th	25 Jun 1997	The Hague			Wim Kok (Dutch PM)	23rd	20–22 Jun 1997	Denver
7th	12 Jan 1998	Tokyo			Tony Blair (British PM)	24th	15–17 May 1998	Birmingham (G8)
8th	20 Jun 1999	Bonn	Keizo Obuchi		Gerhard Schröder (German Ch.)	25th	18–20 Jun 1999	Köln

9th	19 Jul 2000	Tokyo	Yoshiro Mori		Jacques Chirac (French Pres.)	26th	21–23 Jul 2000	Okinawa
10th	8 Dec 2001	Brussels			Guy Verhofstadt (Belgian PM)	27th	20–22 Jul 2001	Genoa
11th	8 Jul 2002	Tokyo		Romano Prodi	Anders Fogh Rasmussen (Danish PM)	28th	26–27 Jun 2002	Kananaskis
12th	2 May 2003	Athens	Junichiro Koizumi		Constantinos Simitis (Greek PM)	29th	1–3 Jun 2003	Evian
13th	22 Jun 2004	Tokyo			Bertie Ahern (Irish PM)	30th	8–10 Jun 2004	Sea Island
14th	2 May 2005	Luxemburg			Jean-Claude Juncker (Luxemburg PM)	31st	6–8 Jul 2005	Gleneagles
15th	24 Apr 2006	Tokyo			Wolfgang Schüssel (Austrian Ch.)	32nd	15–17 Jul 2006	St Petersburg
16th	5 Jun 2007	Berlin	Shinzo Abe	José Manuel Barroso	Angela Merkel (German Ch.)	33rd	6–8 Jun 2007	Heiligendamm
17th	23 Apr 2008	Tokyo	Yasuo Fukuda		Janez Janša (Slovenian PM)	34th	7–9 Jul 2008	Hokkaido Toyako
18th	4 May 2009	Prague	Taro Aso		Václav Klaus (Czech Pres.)	35th	8–10 Jul 2009	L'Aquila
19th	28 Apr 2010	Tokyo	Yukio Hatoyama		Herman Van Rompuy	36th	25–26 Jun 2010	Muskoka
20th	28 May 2011	Brussels	Naoto Kan			37th	26–27 May 2011	Deauville
						38th	18–19 May 2012	Camp David
21st	19 Nov 2013	Tokyo	Shinzo Abe			39th	17–18 Jun 2013	Lough Erne
22nd	7 May 2014	Brussels				40th	4–5 Jun 2014	~~Sochi (G8)~~ Brussels (G7)

Note: This table is updated from Nakamura (2013).

Source: http://www.mofa.go.jp/mofaj/area/eu/shuno.html; http://www.deljpn.ec.europa.eu/modules/relation/chronology/ (both last accessed 14 October 2014).

This book examines the prospects for greater EU–Japan cooperation, and one of the recurring themes is that the relationship has unfulfilled potential (Barroso 2006). This obviously suggests that Japan's approach to its relationship with the EU could be improved, and vice versa. However, although the EU has not always been a priority for Japan, it is not only Japan's relations with the EU that could be criticized. Japan's relations with the US, China and Korea, to name but three, could be significantly improved. Internally, Japan faces a persistent debate about what 'normal statehood' is, and whether Japan is a normal power, or needs to become one. A disproportionate amount of Japanese political energy is also consumed on intra- and inter-party conflict. This chapter therefore attempts to explain why EU–Japan relations are not as well developed as they could be, not by focusing on the institutional history of the relationship itself, but rather on identifying and explaining some of the other factors which have distracted Japanese attention and energy, giving insights into what Japan's main international priorities are, and what domestic constraints are placed on the development of Japanese foreign policy, and how these factors impact on EU–Japan relations.

While the first part of the chapter attempts to identify and explain shortcomings, the second half of the chapter assumes a more positive tone. It looks at debates about what kind of international actor Japan is, and notes an emerging consensus that Japan is moving in the direction of assuming 'normal statehood'. The chapter also analyses the Abe administration's promulgation of the concept of a proactive contribution to peace, and asks how original the concept actually is. It is suggested that although there is room for considerable improvement, Japan has in fact already been a proactive civilian power, in post-war Iraq and the Horn of Africa for quite some time. In short, the chapter argues that it is possible to maintain a credible distinction between the concepts of 'civilian power' and 'military power', to question the primacy and legitimacy of the latter type of power, to reclaim the notion of proactivity and to be a proactive civilian power.

Japan's Foreign Policy and Domestic Politics: Continuity and Change

The first issue of the *Diplomatic Bluebook*, published in September 1957, listed the following three major principles of Japan's diplomatic action: (1) UN-centred diplomacy, (2) cooperation with other free nations (democracies) and (3) firm positioning as a member of Asia (MOFA 1957). Since Japan was admitted to the UN in 1956, the three pillars of Japan's foreign policy have been: (1) US–Japan relations, (2) the UN and (3) Asia. Historically, Europe had played a more significant role in Japan's foreign policy. After the Second World War, although most West European countries were democracies as well as the US, Europe–Japan relations have been less salient than those provided for in these three pillars.

It is frequently mentioned that Japan's foreign policy, including that towards Europe, has long been made by a 'tripartite elite': the central bureaucracy, big business and the LDP or the governing party of the time (Hook et al. 2012: 38–64).

EU–Japan relations have also been formulated through this established policy-making mechanism. Japan's foreign policy towards the EU and European countries is primarily drafted by the Ministry of Foreign Affairs (MOFA), but also the Ministry of Finance (MOF), the Ministry of Economy, Trade and Industry (METI), the Ministry of Defence (MOD) and the Prime Minister's Office. Secondly, big business, particularly through the Japan Federation of Economic Organizations (*Keidanren*), has often played a significant role in EU–Japan economic relations. Third, Diet members have also played some role in EU–Japan political relations, but to quite a limited degree. For example, the Interparliamentary Conference was institutionalized in the late 1970s. However, these exchanges of opinion with their European counterparts have not directly influenced the making of Japan's foreign policy.

Domestic politics often matter, and it has been the ruling political party which has had a direct influence upon the making of foreign policy as a part of the 'tripartite elite'. From 1955 to 1993, during most of the second half of the twentieth century, the ruling political party was always and only the Liberal Democratic Party (LDP). However, in June 1993 an intra-party LDP political conflict led to the successful passage of a no-confidence motion in the Miyazawa government, and to the dissolution of the lower house (House of Representatives). General elections were held, and the LDP lost their majority in the lower house for the first time since their foundation in 1955 (although it should be noted that the LDP won 223 out of 511 seats, a far larger share than that secured by any other party). In August 1993 an eight-party coalition government, excluding the LDP, was formed and Hosokawa of the Japan New Party became the new Prime Minister. In April 1994 Hosokawa suddenly resigned and Hata of the Japan Renewal Party became the Prime Minister, by forming a new coalition government. Among the eight original coalition partners, the Japan Socialist Party (JSP) did not join and the New Party Harbinger (NPH) refused to cooperate with the Hata government. Following this, in June 1994 the three party leaders of the LDP (Kono), the JSP (Murayama) and the NPH (Takemura) struck a deal and formed a new coalition government. The LDP was therefore quickly able to return to power, at the cost of ceding the post of Prime Minister to the JSP, which had been an arch-enemy in the so-called 1955 political system. The JSP ceased to oppose the US-Japan Mutual Security Treaty under its own Prime Minister (Stockwin 2008: 80–87).

In January 1996 Murayama stepped down from the premiership and Hashimoto of the LDP replaced him. The same month, the JSP changed its name to the Social Democratic Party (SDP), but was losing parliamentary seats. In September political forces of the moderate left formed the Democratic Party of Japan (DPJ), absorbing the SDP's right-of-centre factions, the NPH, the New Frontier Party (NFP) and others. The following governments were formed under LDP Prime Ministers. In October 1999 Prime Minister Obuchi decided to form a coalition government with Komeito (Clean Government Party), and Komeito has since become a major coalition partner for the LDP.

The arrival of Koizumi as Prime Minister in April 2001 marked a significant political change, with his neo-liberal economic policy of deregulation, including privatization of the postal services. In this policy area, Koizumi was confronted by the central bureaucracy and many powerful members of his own party. However, his stance with regard to foreign policy was basically in line with that of the central bureaucracy, as exemplified by the dismissal of Foreign Minister Makiko Tanaka in January 2002. Foreign Minister Tanaka was alleged to have asked her German and Italian counterparts about a potentially negative aspect of the US-led missile defence system while she was attending the ASEM (Asia-Europe Meeting) of Foreign Ministers on 25 May 2001. The media somehow revealed the contents of their meeting, and this revelation surprised, and to some degree, shamed Tanaka. In the following months Koizumi's decision to visit the Yasukuni Shrine in April and Pyongyang in September did rather break the traditional mould. However, he placed great emphasis on the US–Japan alliance by morally supporting the US invasion of Iraq and by initiating the subsequent dispatches of Self-Defence Forces (SDF) for reconstruction activities there in 2003.

In 2003 the DPJ, led by Kan, and the Liberal Party, led by Ozawa, reached an agreement for the latter to be merged into the DPJ. The DPJ and the LDP issued party 'manifestos', and fought against each other in the November general election. A two-party system was expected to emerge. The LDP kept a similar number of seats, but the DPJ won 50 more seats than it had in the previous election. In September 2005, however, Koizumi surprisingly dissolved the lower house and called a general election, mainly focusing on the single issue of postal service privatization. The election gave a huge majority to the LDP, with 296 out of 480 seats, while the number of DPJ seats was reduced to 113. One year later, Abe succeeded Koizumi as the new Prime Minister. But in September 2007 a combination of the loss of upper house elections two months previously and his own health problems forced him to resign, and Fukuda replaced him. A year later, Fukuda was replaced by Aso. Throughout this period, the LDP lost popular support, and two-party alternation was expected to become the norm in the future.

In the August 2009 general election the DPJ won a huge majority, with 308 out of 480 seats, while the number of LDP seats was reduced to 119, and Komeito seats to 21. In order to secure two-thirds of all seats, the DPJ formed a coalition government with the SDP and the People's New Party (PNP). This political change was undoubtedly historical in many aspects, and there was also potential for a real change in many policy areas. The DPJ particularly pledged to break the long-established dominance of the central bureaucracy during the election campaign, and Prime Minister Hatoyama and his government attempted to change the traditional domination of the 'tripartite elite' in foreign policy as well. European commentators naturally expected the new DPJ-led government to announce a moratorium on the death penalty. Justice Minister Chiba and several other new ministers had previously been vocal abolitionists. Kamei, the PNP leader, was a particularly well-known abolitionist, and headed the Parliamentary League for abolition of the death penalty. Over time, however, it became clear that his real priority was rather to fight back against Koizumi's reform agenda for postal services privatization and other deregulation policies (Bacon 2010).

Meanwhile, the new Hatoyama government attempted to change many of the foreign policies which previous LDP-led governments had established. One of the major attempts at reform was to change the policy of relocating the US Marine Corps Air Station in Futenma to Henoko. Hatoyama explicitly pledged to move the Futenma base outside Okinawa during the election campaign in August 2009. The possible relocation of the US base in Okinawa naturally caused huge tension with the Obama administration as well as the established Japanese 'tripartite elite'. As early as May 2010 Prime Minister Hatoyama realized that the Futenma base relocation policy was difficult to change. This led to disagreement with one of his coalition partners, the SDP, which subsequently withdrew from the coalition. In early June, as a result of respective personal scandals being revealed, Hatoyama resigned as Prime Minister and Ozawa resigned as DPJ Secretary-General. The confused relationship between the US and Japan was one of the reasons why Hatoyama was replaced by Kan as the new Prime Minister. The entire episode shows that it can be risky to challenge the primacy of the role of the US in Japanese foreign policy considerations. This episode also demonstrates the limits on the extent to which Japan can reach out to other partners besides the US, or promote alternative multilateral visions of international relations.

In July the DPJ lost the upper house elections, leading to a hung parliament, but Kan stayed in power. In September Kan won a DPJ leadership contest with Ozawa. In February 2011 the DPJ suspended Ozawa's party membership due to a scandal revolving around Rikuzankai, his political fund management organization. In early September Noda replaced Kan, after defeating Kaieda, who Ozawa and his followers supported, in another party leadership contest. Dissatisfied with the DPJ leadership, Ozawa and his followers eventually formed a new party in July 2012. This was a structural repeat of what happed to the LDP in 1993, but Ozawa was no longer powerful enough to form an opposition party which could effectively form and lead a coalition government. Ozawa has belonged to eight political parties so far. These bitter intra-party political struggles within the DPJ consumed massive amounts of energy, time and attention. They also prevented the party from making good on their promise to establish a new style of policy making, and new innovative foreign policies. The innovative ideas were there, but it became politically impossible to translate them into an effective policy agenda. This is one of the most important reasons on the Japanese side for a lack of momentum in EU–Japan relations during this period.

Furthermore, the EU–Japan political relationship can often be influenced by turmoil in domestic politics. As mentioned above, since July 1991 the EU–Japan summit has been institutionalized as an annual event, but there have in fact been two years when the summits were not held: in 1994 and 2012. It is a somewhat uncomfortable fact for those of a social democratic disposition that on each of these occasions the LDP were not in power. It was three non-LDP Prime Ministers who missed the summit: Hosokawa, Hata and Noda. In October 2010, when the

ASEM summit meeting was held in Brussels, Kan had not planned to attend, but decided eventually to go, in large part because he needed to meet with his Chinese counterpart in order to ameliorate China–Japan relations, after clashes near the Senkaku/Diaoyu islands. This is further evidence that the EU–Japan relationship is still less salient than those provided for in the three established pillars of Japan's foreign policy listed above. As these three examples show, the US dominates Japan's international agenda, domestic politics absorbs much political energy and European summits are used as proxy opportunities to address other, more pressing issues such as China–Japan relations.

With regard to the impact of ideas on Japan's foreign policy, Ozawa himself famously proposed a new Japanese state identity: that Japan should become a 'normal state' (Ozawa 1994). Ozawa was at that time the LDP General-Secretary, and was forced to deal with the Gulf conflict, and also with persistent requests from the US administration for Japan to make more of a military contribution. He has since attempted to re-balance the three pillars of Japan's foreign policy, by placing less emphasis on US–Japan relations and greater emphasis on Japan's relations with the UN and Asia. Although other ideas, such as 'Peace-Creating Nation' and 'Country of Co-Creation', were floated under the Kan and Noda governments, the debate around what normal statehood entails, and whether Japan has or should have these attributes, has become a central and defining feature of debate about Japanese foreign policy. The idea of 'normal statehood' heavily influences any 'disposition in Japanese state identities' (Hook and Son 2013).

In the November 2012 general election there was a significant political swing from the DPJ back to the LDP: the LDP won a huge majority, with 294 seats, and the DPJ only won 57 seats. The LDP formed a coalition government with Komeito, which gained 31 seats, and Abe became Prime Minister again. The DPJ had blown its chances due to infighting. It is an interesting counterfactual question whether the DPJ would have really changed the established policy-making mechanism. Nevertheless, that is now an academic question. The facts are that the LDP has quickly returned to power, and the 'tripartite elite' in foreign policy is alive and well. What is the impact of all of this for Japan's state identity in international security?

Is Japan Still a Civilian Power?

Japan is easier than Europe to classify in terms of international relations theory: it is a traditional type of actor in that it is a nation-state. Nevertheless, similar difficulties of definition are encountered when one attempts to define Japan as a single (independent, assertive or autonomous) actor in contemporary international affairs. Europe was a group of states with a range of inhibitions preventing it from pursuing assertive foreign policies independent of the US, and Japan is a nation-state with similar inhibitions. In the mid-1970s, as Hedley Bull argued, next to the US, the USSR and China, Japan was 'only a potential great power' (Bull

1977/2002: 197). After the Cold War, Deudney and Ikenberry (1999) regarded both Japan and Germany, rather positively, as 'semi-sovereign and partial great powers' in the Western liberal order. Japan became one of the G7, which is a kind of great powers' club, at least economically. But what kind of 'great power' has Japan been?

The existing literature on Japan's foreign, security and defence policy has struggled to describe or prescribe what type of international actor Japan has been or should be: is Japan a new kind of superpower (Garby and Bullock 1994), an economic superpower (Drifte 1996), a hesitant superpower (Bridges 1993) or a global civilian power (Funabashi 1994).[1] Inoguchi and Bacon (2006) have argued that Japan's foreign policy has evolved through the following five phases since the end of the Second World War: an unstable phase of contestation between pro-alliance and anti-alliance sentiment (1945–1960); a stable phase of Yoshida doctrine (1960–1975); a third phase as a systemic supporter of the US (1975–1990); a fourth as a global civilian power (1990–2005); and the current phase as a 'global ordinary power', on the UK model (from 2005 towards 2020). Depending on how to define each concept, there may be a disagreement over how to describe Japan's actorness in the current phase, whether as 'a civilian power' or 'an ordinary power'.

Developing and supporting Inoguchi and Bacon's argument, Welch and others observe that the 'general tendency is clearly towards a pragmatic embrace of normalcy' and that this is part of Japanese 'national strategy' (Soeya, Tadokoro and Welch 2011: 13). Hook and Son examine cases of overseas SDF dispatches in the post-Cold War period, and focus on the transposition of Japanese state identities. They conclude that 'Japan has shifted from a passive state with a peace state identity to a proactive state with a humanitarian state identity' (Hook and Son 2013: 51). Interestingly, they distinguish between 'a civilian power' identity since 1991 and 'a humanitarian power' identity since 2001.

The Japanese Constitution has not been amended since 1946. Any Japanese foreign, security and defence policy should be made under constitutional constraints. If the Constitution alone is said to determine state identity, it logically follows that Japanese identity should not change, unless the Constitution is amended. But, depending on how one interprets the Constitution, there is manoeuvring room for any government to change policy. With the return of Prime Minister Abe in late 2012, his government has gradually revealed a relatively clear position on the form that Japanese state identity should take. Abe rather quickly abandoned his political desire to amend the Japanese Constitution itself, but he has attempted to re-interpret the Constitution, and to change Japan's foreign, security and defence policy.

In 2007–2008 the first Abe Cabinet had tried but failed to carry out such a change. The Advisory Panel on Reconstruction of the Legal Basis for Security, consisting

---

1   Hughes (2004) and Serra (2005) describe the more recent development of Japan as an international security actor within the historic context.

of a group of like-minded experts, issued its report in June 2008, recommending the Abe government to change the interpretation of the Constitution, in order for Japan to exercise the right of collective self-defence. However, the Abe Cabinet failed to approve that interpretation before his resignation. Abe has been keen to push through his foreign policy agenda in his second term in office, while 'Abenomics' remains perceived as successful, and before he loses popularity. The new 'Report of the Advisory Panel on Reconstruction of the Legal Basis for Security' was published on 15 May 2014 and paved the way for a possible 'exercise' of the right of collective self-defence. The LDP and Komeito agreed to support the basic idea of this report, and the Abe Cabinet has approved the modified interpretation of the Constitution. Public opinion surveys show that most Japanese are still reluctant to support a more militarily active posture, but if Abe stays in power, the Diet would eventually pass a bill enabling the SDF to be dispatched for new types of case, such as the exercise of the right of collective self-defence. This would change the substance of the US–Japan alliance.

During the Cold War the Peace Constitution and the US–Japan military alliance co-existed, and Japan's passive/responsive attitudes were allowed by the US and others. But the end of the Cold War and the Gulf conflict required Japan to be more positive/proactive with regard to international security and peace. The proactive nature of the contribution relates not only to the US–Japan pillar of foreign policy, but also to the UN pillar, if not yet to the Asia pillar. For example, the growing number of UN Security Council resolutions offers a significant and legitimate basis for Japan to dispatch its SDF forces overseas. The recent case of EU–Japan security cooperation over anti-piracy operations off the coast of Somalia is one positive example of this phenomenon. Japan is now able to make more military contributions within the UN context of collective security, not necessarily by exercising the right of collective self-defence.

The current Abe government also seems to 'embrace normalcy' by adopting the first ever 'National Security Strategy (NSS)'. In December 2013, the Abe Cabinet successfully established the National Security Council (NSC) of Japan, which is headed by Shotaro Yachi, who was the Administrative Vice-Minister for Foreign Affairs from 2005 to 2008. The first Abe Cabinet had submitted a bill to establish an NSC in April 2007, but this was eventually discarded in early 2008. This time, Prime Minister Abe was successful. The NSS 'elaborates on Japan's peaceful orientation to date and the policy of a "Proactive Contribution to Peace", based on the principle of international cooperation' (Cabinet Secretariat 2013: 1). The concept of 'proactive contribution to peace' used in the official document is translated into English. Interestingly and importantly, however, the original concept in Japanese (*Sekkyoku-teki Heiwa-shugi*) may directly be translated as 'positive pacifism', which has similarities with the pacifist concept of 'positive peace' of Johan Galtung. However, it is clear that this is *not* the way in which the Abe government understands this key strategic concept. The Abe administration places emphasis on 'proaction', rather than 'peace' in the 'pacifist' sense of that term.

The Gulf conflict was an almost traumatic experience for many bureaucrats in Kasumigaseki. The then Vice-Minister for Foreign Affairs, Kuriyama, regarded the Gulf conflict as a test case for Japan's proactive foreign policy (Kuriyama 1997: 25), but MOFA received serious criticism, as Japanese foreign policy was dismissed as mere 'cheque book diplomacy'. As a result of this stinging criticism, MOFA, the Prime Minister's Office, and the central bureaucracy have ever since embarked on the 'quest for a proactive policy' (Togo 2010). The collective quest for a 'proactive foreign policy' has now developed into the intense articulation of a strategic concept under the current Abe administration. As Fukushima has noted, 'Japan has already been proactive in its contribution to peace' (Fukushima 2014), and the NSS's key strategic concept has in fact developed through several episodes of trial and error by previous governments. This concept is obviously consistent with the three pillars of Japan's foreign policy, but it is important to note that it is also relevant to EU–Japan political relations, and to their possible re-invigoration.

EU–Japan Political Relations

Indeed, it could be said that although major dispatches of SDF forces have taken place within the context of support for US visions of world order, in practical terms the SDF has worked closely on the ground with European partners. There has therefore also been a significant European-Japanese dimension to the activities of the SDF. Even the Iraq War of 2003 was a case in point. Of course, there were differences of opinion between Japan and some European states over whether to support the invasion. Leading EU Member States were divided: the UK, Italy and Spain supported the US, but France and Germany did not. Compared with the 1990 Gulf conflict, Germany changed its attitude from that of a responsive follower to that of a proactive opponent. Japan, on the other hand, responded more quickly and militarily to the US request than it did with regard to the 1990 Gulf conflict, under the leadership of Prime Minister Koizumi. The Japanese action might have been intended to be 'proactive'.

In December 2003 Japan decided to dispatch SDF contingents to Samawah, southern Iraq, so as to provide humanitarian assistance and help in the reconstruction of Iraq, even though some major European countries did not send forces to Iraq, and others withdrew at an early stage. The Japanese ground forces were deployed to Samawah from January 2004 to July 2006, engaging themselves in 'reconstruction' missions. Japan's policy was not made solely within the US–Japan context. The security of Samawah was rather maintained by Dutch forces until March 2005, and later by British and Australian forces. It should be noted that Japan was not regarded as a military power, and that the Japanese forces were mostly safeguarded by the Europeans, not the Americans.

Germany, as mentioned, decided not to dispatch any armed forces. However, Germany and Japan were ultimately able to identify common aims and objectives. Prime Minister Koizumi and Chancellor Schröder met at a bilateral summit meeting in December 2004, and the two leaders decided to take joint efforts to preserve Iraqi cultural heritage and to train the Iraqi people. The two countries came to a joint decision to train Iraqi policemen. Germany was training them in the UAE, and Japan asked Germany to train Iraqi policemen who were stationed in Samawah. Japan provided technical assistance for the police training, by sending machinery and materials for personal identification. This German-Japanese cooperation over Iraqi reconstruction was a fruit of their political dialogue since December 2003, when Koizumi sent a special envoy to France and Germany. Former Prime Minister Hashimoto met with French President Chirac and Chancellor Schröder, and they devised a joint technical cooperation scheme among Japan, France and Germany. In February 2004 Yukio Okamoto, the then special aide to Koizumi on the issue of Iraq, met his counterparts in Paris and Berlin, and followed up on the December decision on technical cooperation. More concrete steps were then taken by Japan and Germany at their summit meeting.

The traditional concept of civilian power explains the effectiveness of non-military means after the actual use of force, that is, war. Those international actors who are described as civilian powers in a traditional sense tend to be 'responsive'. Just as in 1991, Europe and Japan were 'still' two civilian powers even in 2003, but this time in a rather more 'proactive' sense. There has been some European/ EU–Japan political cooperation in the wider security field. This chapter has mentioned Japan's cooperation with the Netherlands and Germany in the aftermath of the Iraq War, and with the EU in the Horn of Africa. The concept of making a 'proactive contribution to peace' increases the likelihood of domestic public approval for greater Japanese burden-sharing and enhanced military capabilities. This thereby enhances the sustained commitment of traditional civilian powers to new forms of engagement in all theatres of global insecurity. In this way, a more proactive articulation of the role of civilian power gains greater credibility and public support. It is also possible to maintain a credible distinction between civilian power and military power, and to question the primacy and legitimacy of the latter type of power.

At the time of writing, the EU and Japan are negotiating not only an EPA/FTA, but also a Strategic Partnership Agreement (SPA). EU–Japan relations will not replace any of the three fundamental pillars of Japan's foreign policy identified in the above discussion. However, EU–Japan relations will surely help to strengthen those pillars, as we have partly explained with regard to the US–Japan pillar and the UN pillar. With regard to the third, the Asian pillar, there is more for Prime Minister Abe to do, or rather not to do. The visit to the Yasukuni Shrine on 26 December 2013, just 10 days after the NSS was launched, for example, should have been avoided, at least from the perspective of 'strategic patience' (a phrase coined by Yachi, the NSC head). Japan has failed to be a regional leader and to promote regional integration in North East Asia. Hatoyama's idea of building an 'East Asian Community' did not even receive wholehearted support from his Chinese and Korean counterparts, before his resignation. Both Europe and Asia face new security challenges and can face many of them in partnership, in bilateral, regional and global contexts. However, the fact remains that they operate in two fundamentally different regional milieus. Japan can make a proactive contribution to peace and security in concert with the EU in places such as Iraq and Somalia, and can pursue a raft of global public goods in partnership with the EU in international fora. But Japan must also make a more 'proactive contribution to peace' in Asia.

Chapter 2

The EU in a Changing Global Order: Is Emergent German Hegemony Making the EU Even More of a Civilian Power?

Mario Telò

Introduction

This chapter focuses on the EU's distinctive role within the emergent multipolar order. A substantial international literature has emerged during the 20 years since the end of the bipolar order, arguing that the EU is not only a sophisticated regional association of neighbouring states, but also a very important global player, even if of an unprecedented kind, weak according to some critics and unique according to others.

This chapter aims to go beyond two opposed and oversimplified pictures of the EU's international role. Realists believe it is increasingly evident that the EU is not a fully-fledged military and political power, is superseded by NATO in the security realm, was irrelevant in the Arab Spring, the Israeli-Palestinian conflict, the Iranian controversy and the Korean crisis, and seems unable to cope with its internal complexity. The EU therefore cannot be considered a power at all: it is condemned to internal fragmentation and external irrelevance. According to the second, more idealist picture, the EU is an alternative kind of power, a post-Westphalian values-based community and a federal state in the making. On this second view, the European Union has often been described as a 'normative power' (Manners 2002), essentially characterized by a distinctive normative basis consistent with the UN Charter, asserted through 'a series of declarations, treaties, policies, criteria and conditions' (Manners 2002: 242). Against both of these views, this chapter argues that the EU is still a regional entity and an unprecedented power. The concept of civilian power[1] (Telò 2007) does apply to the EU, but with

---

1 The civilian power concept is controversial but useful when analysing certain foreign policies – such as those deployed by the EU or Japan – as it emphasizes the distinctiveness of these actors in international relations (Telò 2007: 36). Against Eurocentric concepts of 'normative power' (Manners 2002), civilian powers are firstly unable to act as classical international powers for three reasons: their decentralized institutional set, unfit to declare war; their focus on internal social welfare while defence budgets are below 2 per cent of GDP; and their history fostering demilitarized external action (Telò 2007, 2013).

some caveats: the power of all states has a normative dimension, of course; and normative features are not the very soul of the EU's influence and power. The concept of civilian power should be freed from its purely idealistic conception. The chapter further argues that growing German hegemony in the EU will have a major impact on its identity as a civilian power. The existence of German primacy in the economic realm is no longer in doubt, but superficial analyses are glossing over the political implications of this for the EU. Furthermore, this chapter posits that in avoiding a false division of the debate about Germany and the EU which separates economic and political dimensions, one cannot avoid the conclusion that Germany's rise signals a deeper process of civilian power in the making. The assertion made here is that German supremacy on the one hand confirms the impossibility of the EU becoming a 'normal' military and political power, and on the other hand, is strengthening the long-lasting alternative basis for EU external power, which includes material *and* non-material resources.

The EU as a Power

Despite the excessive dramatization of the sovereign debt crisis, the emerging 'German Europe' constitutes the largest advanced, industrialized market in the world, at €12.5 trillion in 2010, making up 30 per cent of global GDP (Damro 2011), and is also a 'trading state' (Rosecrance 1987). Until being recently overtaken by China, Germany was the biggest exporter in the world. The EU strongly influences international trade as a trading bloc (generating 20 per cent of global trade flows in 2010), and is both a leading destination for FDI and a major regulator in global competition policy (Dewatripont and Legros 2009) and standardization, a position which will be strengthened if the Merkel–Obama project for a Transatlantic Trade and Investment Partnership (TTIP) succeeds. With a population of 500 million people who are relatively well-trained and educated, the EU is still the largest Western demographic entity. The Eurozone crisis has not seriously affected the Euro's role as the US dollar's most important competitor as a global reserve currency; 18 per cent of foreign exchange reserves were held in euros in 2000, a

---

Civilian powers influence near and far abroad partners through structural foreign policies and comprehensive external relations strategies rather than through military action (Telò 2007). A civilian power *'exercises influence and shapes its environment through what it is, rather than through what it does'* (Maull 2005: 778). Harnisch and Maull concluded that the foreign policy identity of a civilian power is characterized by six elements: efforts to constrain the use of force through cooperative and collective security arrangements; efforts to strengthen the rule of law through multilateral cooperation, integration and partial transfers of sovereignty; promotion of democracy and human rights, both within and between states; promotion of non-violent forms of conflict management and conflict resolution; promotion of social equity and sustainable development; and the promotion of interdependence and a division of labour (Harnisch and Maull, 2001b: 4).

figure which rose to 25.7 per cent in 2010, with a high of 27.6 per cent in 2008. The EU is also the most significant actor in global development.

The European Neighbourhood Policy affects 17 countries belonging to the larger European region, from former members of the Soviet Union, including Eastern European neighbours and the Caucasus region, to the southern rim of the Mediterranean. Enlargement candidates and pre-enlargement partners include Turkey, Iceland, Serbia and other Western Balkan states. The EU is at the centre of the world's largest network of international arrangements and agreements of several kinds (this includes bilateral, multilateral and inter-regional arrangements, as well as Strategic Partnerships). Finally, the EU has begun more than 20 international missions of various kinds: military operations under the rubric of the 'Petersburg tasks', humanitarian missions, and peacekeeping and peace-enforcing missions – 13 of which are currently ongoing – under the umbrella of the CFSP-ESDP.[2]

The EU is a significant power because it can use its material might to change and influence other actors' decisions, even against their will. Both positive and negative measures can be adopted. Positive measures include trade agreements, cooperation agreements, association agreements, tariff reductions, quota increases, inclusion in the Generalised System of (trade) Preferences, aid provision and loan extensions. Negative measures include embargoes (bans on exports), boycotts (bans on imports), delaying the conclusion of agreements, suspending or renouncing agreements, tariff increases, quota decreases, removal from the GSP, reducing or suspending aid and delaying the granting of successive loan tranches. The EU has used all of these measures against and in support of a range of actors including states, private multinational companies, NGOs and international organizations over the past few decades.

All in all, since the end of the Cold War the EU has been able to transform itself from a regional grouping of neighbouring states, a largely economic entity, into a multidimensional global actor. However, the EU has not been able to mobilize this huge potential by integrating its domestic institutional capacities and its large array of external policies. Even the coordination of CFSP and trade policy called for in the Lisbon Treaty, now five years old, looks to be beyond the scope of the EU as things presently stand.

In comparing the capacities of the EU and the US, many observers neglect the radically different size of their respective central budgets. The EU budget remains below the Treaty benchmark of 1.27 per cent of EU GDP, which is much less than the American federal budget, which amounts to roughly 20 per cent of US GDP. (The US defence budget is roughly 740 billion dollars, which accounted for approximately 20 per cent of the total US federal budget in 2012). CFSP and ESDP missions are funded via declining national defence budgets, while the

---

2   See Article 42 (formerly Article 17) and Article 43 of the TFEU.

central administrative budget for the CFSP – despite the fact that it doubled in the last decade – only amounts to approximately €250 million a year.[3]

The Emergent German Hegemony and Its Implications for Civilian Power Europe

An important question is whether regional polities such as the EU can work better when a regional hegemon gradually emerges. Can a dominant regional power drive institutional reform and a more coherent supranational policy agenda, even within a multilateral framework which constrains to a certain extent the hegemon's own interests and objectives?

Until its reunification in 1990, democratic Germany never seemed a plausible candidate to lead the EU. However, subsequent reunification and domestic reform during the period from the Schröder/Fischer government to the two Merkel coalitions explain the large journalistic and academic literature predicting a coming 'German Europe'. Fifteen years after the first attempt at Franco-British military cooperation, it is clear that these two countries are totally incapable of building up an alternative hegemony within the EU, whose core remains the Eurozone. The project proposed at the 1998 Saint Malo meeting between Jacques Chirac and Tony Blair has failed. Nothing serious can be done by the EU at the international level without Germany. Germany is at the centre of the Eurozone, the very soul of the EU as a regional and global power. Could emergent German leadership, spreading from the economic to the political level, therefore work as the main driver of change for the still decentralized and complex EU foreign policy system? If so, what would be the foreign policy of an increasingly 'German' Europe?

Since the Schröder/Fischer government (1997–2005), Germany has actually displayed, both within the EU and internationally, an unprecedented diplomatic assertiveness:

- Germany achieved the discontinuation of the principle of parity among the four largest member states in the Council and Parliament, and the recognition of population size as the criterion for the allocation of QMV votes (starting with the Nice Treaty in 2000, and carrying through to the Lisbon Treaty in 2009).
- Germany pushed for permanent member status of the UNSC through a comprehensive and vigorous international lobbying campaign in alliance

---

3   The total amount earmarked for the period 2007–2013 was €1.74 billion. Compared with €46 million in 2003, €62 million in 2004 and 2005 and €102 million in 2006, there has been significant progress. However, the amount allocated for the CFSP is very small, compared with the €49 billion available to the Commission for external relations over the period 2007–2013 (humanitarian aid, development aid, regional cooperation, trade policy etc.) and minuscule compared with the US defence budget.

with Japan, India and Brazil (collectively, the G4), despite controversies and conflicts with other EU members over this issue.

- Germany decided to take part in the NATO military intervention in Kosovo in 1999 (benefitting, because of the intervention's humanitarian purposes, from extensive public support, including from leading public intellectuals such as Jürgen Habermas).
- In alliance with France, other member states and the European Commission, Germany opposed the Bush administration's pre-emptive war in Iraq, even at the price of the most serious transatlantic rift since 1945.

Furthermore, in the Merkel era Germany radically changed its international image from that of the 'sick member of the European economy' – then mainly opposed to the dominant Anglo-Saxon model – into Europe's economic leader. Germany became not only the first world's leading exporting economy and the first country to recover from the worst financial crisis since the Great Depression, but also the leading force within the European Council as far as anti-crisis measures are concerned. All of the main decisions between 2008 and 2012 have been taken with the main input coming from Germany (with France playing the role of junior supporting partner). These include building three financial market monitoring agencies, strengthening the rescue funds – notably the EFSF and then the ESM up to €800 billion, allowing the ECB to distribute €1 trillion to the European banks, creating a national budget surveillance system (called the 'European semester'), and finally firmly asserting, in spite of the self-exclusion of the UK, the new intergovernmental 'fiscal pact' for stability, which for the first time can enter into force with ratification by only 12 member states.

All in all, restoring the EU's economic stability, the very basis of the EU's credibility within the G20 and the globalized and multipolar world, will be achieved in proportion to a shared acceptance of the 'German model'. This provokes a large international debate about the coming 'German hegemony' and even about the transformation of the EU into a 'German Empire' (Beck 2011) with inevitable implications regarding Europe's internal legitimacy, its external image and its foreign policy.

Is the German pressure in the European Council to boost top-down European convergence and centralize economic governance paving the way for a German regional hegemony? Germany needs to achieve the following objectives in order to be recognized as a 'benevolent hegemon', according to the criteria set out in the literature:[4]

---

4 According to the liberal school, hegemonic stability implies providing 'common goods' (Keohane 2004); according to the Canadian school, hegemonic powers strongly influence the realm of ideas and perceptions, and create consensus among a large social alliance of interests (Cox 1986).

- Germany needs to disseminate its ideas and the core elements of its modernizing political and economic culture, but it needs to connect these to the EU's ideas and governance culture. Germany must emphasize not only its opposition to inflation, but also the other aspects of its successful model: industrial consensus, greening the economy, prioritization of the knowledge economy, social inclusiveness (from its welfare state to its experience expanding high wages to 18 million former East Germans) and administrative efficiency. Germany already influences the EU 2020 agenda in this direction, but the instrumental interpretation of the 'German model' as mere budgetary austerity still prevails, which negatively affects its external appeal.
- Germany must provide the EU with new 'European common goods', in the form of a sufficient Regional Fund, a banking union and eventually also Eurobonds, as key elements of strong economic governance, enhancing both growth and cohesion.
- Germany needs to support a new 'Marshall Plan' for the indebted economies of the EU periphery, so as to offset the pain of austerity policies. This could include, for example, investments in solar energy, as suggested by the European Parliament President Martin Schulz in 2012.

Germany still has a long way to go to achieve recognition as a benevolent hegemon. However, we can anticipate the eventual 'German Europe' scenario and consider its implications for the CFSP. The alternative hypothesis of an Anglo-French hegemony, in spite of the UK and France's shared identity as declining nuclear powers, looks fragile and lacking in any real economic or institutional foundation. No foreign policy leadership is possible in the EU without the backing of an institutional core based on the more highly integrated Eurozone. Experts are aware of the multiple historical, domestic and constitutional obstacles to the achievement of this leading role (Telò and Seidelmann 1996; Bava 2001; Bulmer and Padgett 2010). However, the possibility of change cannot be discounted. What impact would the emergence of a more German Europe have on EU foreign policy? Will German leadership be the driving force for the EU to translate its institutionally complex, politically divided foreign policy into a coherent, effective one befitting an independent global power?

Comparative analysis with other states suggests that old labels such as 'German Empire' or 'German power' will not be appropriate to define the unprecedented international profile a new German leadership would increasingly provide for the EU. At the institutional level, the EU would remain a multilateral entity combining supranational and intergovernmental procedures, and the institutional framework would evolve towards an enhanced role for the 'community method'; at the level of policies and identity, the model of the EU as a 'civilian power' would be strengthened rather than undermined. This deep correspondence of the EU with the new Germany has also been emphasized by a pluralist group of scholars including Czempiel (1999) Habermas (2006) and Maull (2006). They point to the weight of Germany's history, the constitutional limits imposed on it at the domestic and supranational levels, and Germany's inevitably low international profile, to suggest that the EU would adopt these German characteristics, which are also those of a civilian power.

Maull (2006) Nakamura (2013) Telò (2013) and others have underlined the similarities between Germany, Italy and Japan as losers of the Second World War. Each experienced a backlash against nationalist traditions, established constitutional provisions against war, and adopted a low-profile approach to foreign policy. More comparative research is needed to explore this convergence, but in the case of Germany, some of the recent evidence seems to confirm this analysis:

- Germany has been the leading EU country with regard to substantial national defence budget cuts, with defence expenditure currently below 1 per cent of GDP.
- Germans have been identified as 'timid Teutons' because of public opposition and government reticence towards military intervention (for example the 1991 Gulf War, the Southern Lebanon Mission of 2007); the early 1990s concerns regarding German revanchism following reunification have proved unfounded.
- The Libyan crisis of 2011 and the German abstention at the UNSC on Resolution 1973 which authorized an intervention to stop the imminent Benghazi massacre, show that Germany is ready to pay the double price of deepening the CFSP crisis and dismantling its own previous 'G4 strategy' (application to be a permanent member of the UNSC) in order to keep its international profile low and oppose the '*Europe puissance*' scenario.[5]

This analysis suggests that Germany is still far from becoming a recognized regional hegemonic power and second, that German hegemony would likely weaken the CFSP, and strengthen the civilian power thesis. Howorth has argued that a weak CFSP calls for the merging of the CFSP and NATO (Howorth 2013). This argument can be addressed in two ways. On the one hand, Germany and a 'German Europe' would be in favour, not of simply complying with but rather of transforming the nature of the alliance, and creating a 'Europeanized NATO' (Sommer 2012). Secondly, any transatlantic link under the NATO umbrella would be a conditional scenario: it seems possible with a multilateralism-friendly US administration, but not with a more unilateralist US administration, such as that of George W. Bush. Modest improvement could come as far as the rationalization of national defence budgets is concerned: the current radical shrinking of defence budgets under the pressure of the spending reviews can also be seen as an opportunity for enhanced coordination, pooling and sharing, and reducing fixed costs generated by redundant personnel, overlapping infrastructure and waste.

---

5 For a critical French perception confirming these trends, see La Documentation Française (2012).

Overall, there would be significant continuity between the identity of an emerging 'German Europe' and some of the EU's present concerns and commitments. These include Europeanization of the transatlantic alliance, balanced partnership with Russia, special relationships with strategic partners like the US (TTIP) and Japan (FTA), good relations with the BRICS, a low political and military profile, and better coordination of declining national defence budgets.

Elements of a Low-profile Civilian EU Foreign Policy

The foreign policy of the 'German EU' will rest on a distinctive balance between diplomacy and coercion, notably in making greater use of economic sanctions and peace-enforcing missions. However the EU will continue to leave 'dirty jobs' involving coercive force (like the Libya intervention) to NATO. The Lisbon Treaty paragraph on collective defence does not change this because it simply reiterates the UN Charter while recognizing the complementary role of previous military alliances such as NATO. The majority of the 21 ongoing missions are civilian or mixed, and the five military missions are designed to make the EU's civilian presence more credible.[6]

The EU's foreign policy will still be that of a regional entity coordinating neighbouring member states and slightly enhancing internal convergence. A legitimate question is to what extent the institutional dynamics of EU coordination can improve, reducing the current dependence upon member states. According to a rational choice institutionalist approach, the EU is not very much more than an instrument of the largest member states (Hill 1996).

However, historical institutionalism better explains both the EPC's origins, its transformation into the CFSP, and the evolution of the current distinctive EU approach. Is the German aversion towards military force unique within the EU? Italy and Austria share the same tragic history of self-destructive nationalism. The Iberian and Eastern European experiences of dictatorship converge in support of a reserved foreign policy. Pacifist Sweden and Finland have a long record of supporting international peace organizations such as the UN. Other European countries also have convergent historical reasons to support the adoption of a low international profile: between 1939 and 1960 all major European countries lost a war, either the Second World War or a colonial war. Civilian power is above all the typical profile of defeated or weakened powers. A comparative analysis of Italian, Japanese and German constitutions shows the impact that history has on the adoption of specific constitutional provisions, which is difficult to grasp through mere rational choice approaches. Why did others, including the winners of the Second World War, also adopt these norms? Many winners of the Second World War were losers of tragic colonial wars during the next two decades, which

---

6   In 2012, of the 21 ESDP missions eight were in Africa, six in Asia and seven in Eastern Europe.

also explains the declining international capabilities and profile of the Netherlands and Belgium and even of the UK and France (and the consequences for their attitudes to the EU). The Germans are not at all unique in wanting to adopt a low international profile.

The most efficient EU foreign policies are the external projections of internal policies (namely the democratization and free market norms embodied by the *acquis communautaire*) along with some civilian foreign policies. We have already drawn attention to the EU's market power (competition policy, trade policy, agricultural policy), but not yet to its linkage power: both horizontally and vertically, between internal policies and external policies, and beyond the traditional distinction between high politics and low politics. Horizontally, for instance, trade policy negotiations are often linked to concessions in environmental policy; cooperation in research and education (patents, Galileo and so on) is offered as part of packages including economic cooperation and political dialogue; international support for the Eurozone might be situated within strategic dialogues aimed at reform of multilateral organizations such as the IMF.

Furthermore, contrary to Eurocentric postmodern dreams, a certain degree of coercion is an essential part of the cooperative and diplomatic game. An example is provided by sanctions. The distinctive EU approach to difficult geopolitical challenges emphasizes diplomacy, supporting regional solutions, enhancing legitimacy for interventions through the UNSC, and only deploying economic sanctions having exhausted these instruments.

Notwithstanding its limitations, the external action of the 'German EU' would demand further conceptual innovation. Beyond the Eurocentric focus on the EU as a 'normative power', the world's most value-driven political entity, I propose comprehensively applying discourse analysis to EU external relations, whether actions appear based on interests, practical policies or ideas. There is no simple opposition between ideas and interests, because discourse can also be seen as a practice. Focusing on values and ideas is also a practical policy, which makes convergences with other civilian powers, such as Japan, more likely.

A New Civilian Multilateralism for the Near and Far Abroad?

Is civilian power diplomacy possible when the major global actors still see the world through a lens of hard power, or is civilian power no more than rhetoric which masks a more classical realist approach to IR? The literature is still divided regarding the features of the current multipolar system, the place of regional actors and the ability of multilateral and multilevel frameworks to shape and constrain the modern exercise of national sovereignty. Secondly, how and to what extent can EU foreign policy effectiveness, institutional efficiency and material capability be improved and adjusted to the nature of external challenges, in order to cope with a rapidly changing international context?

Within a few years, The EEAS will, at least on paper, be one of the world's largest and most relevant diplomatic services and will be challenged both in the near and far abroad. Its effectiveness will be sorely needed in bolstering an EU facing major foreign policy challenges, including:

1. Providing the 'near abroad' with a solid cooperation architecture. Offering a viable alternative to both enlargement policy and foreign policy has been an EU priority since the 1970s (for example early *Ostpolitik* and the Mediterranean partnership). In contrast with the success of enlargement policy, the multiple European neighbourhood policies are often mentioned as a case of EU foreign policy failure, despite two democratization waves and the general diffusion of EU values. In competing for influence with geopolitical and normative competitors such as Russia in the East and Islamic movements in the Arab world, the EU has been at best only partly successful. The EU has been criticized for 'realist' compromises with authoritarian regimes on the one hand, and for a lack of comprehensive and effective policies regarding the regulation of immigration and energy on the other. However, despite a series of shortcomings, there are no classical security dilemmas between the EU and its largest neighbouring partners, and the EU remains a dominant actor in its neighbourhood.

2. The European Neighbourhood Policy reflects the EU's interest in shaping the Euro-Mediterranean macro-region by using a shared institutional architecture to frame common policies. The EU is facing a difficult choice between returning to the old bilateral renationalization of policy by regional partners, or exploring a new multilateral approach to the Euro-Mediterranean macro-region. The latter should be defined by experimental forms of external governance, the cultivation of civil society networks and a new macro-regional common architecture. Such an approach could take inspiration from the conditionality approach seen in both enlargement and ENP negotiations. A regional power such as the EU has the responsibility of organizing through common principles and rules a larger territory beyond the strict borders of the actual member states: the enlargement policy (based on the Copenhagen criteria of 1993) and the European Neighbourhood Policy (since 2003) provide the toolkits for these pan-European and Mediterranean policies. In both policy fields the EU could better implement a typical civilian power approach at the macro-regional level. Many of these policies are bridging between external governance and internal governance, even if with different degrees of conditionality. These policies will be more effective if national diplomatic services greatly increase coordination with the new EEAS, even if their full integration under a supranational diplomatic core is not realistic.

3. The second challenge EU external action is facing is gradually building a 'third kind of multilateralism' beyond both its own tradition of supranational integration and the instrumental approach of other players like the BRICS

and the USA. This means combining its internal experience of a deeper and binding kind of multilateral cooperation with an inclusive policy of outreach, looking for convergence with as many players as possible, including those which are adopting a merely instrumental, ad hoc, approach to multilateral cooperation. Echoing the elements which characterize a civilian power's distinctive foreign policy action, the EU and Japan have actively defended the institutional strengthening of international organizations such as the UN, NATO and the WTO, and also actively promoted the construction of new global regimes as well as global civilian policies (Telò 2007: 54), both as a matter of principal as well as necessity. The EU and Japan's distinctive role in the international system sees their global influence flow directly from their deliberative internal orders and their historically built-up central positions in the global multilateral system. As a result both Tokyo and Brussels have a shared interest in seeing the global system evolve and adapt to welcome new emerging players.

4. To some extent, the EU is already exporting its modes of multilateral governance and aiming at strengthening the forms of international rule-based multilateral cooperation which are fundamental to its foreign policy identity. Let us look at two examples of multilateral negotiation: climate change and trade. The climate change issue is a very good case study, showing the success of building inclusive international regimes from Kyoto to Bali, but also failures, such as in Copenhagen in 2009. However, Copenhagen also shows the risk of a unilateral and Eurocentric understanding of 'binding measures' which can alienate other global players. The challenge is to combine binding multilateral regimes which are as inclusive as possible (particularly including China and the US) with self-constraining and national targets, and looking for a kind of third way between both the EU-styled and instrumental forms of multilateral cooperation. Engagement with major players abroad will only bear fruit if the EU is ready to find a compromise between its own supranational multilateralism and its partners' ad hoc, instrumental types of multilateralism. The UN Durban Conference on climate change is considered by many to be a success rather than a failure: for the first time the EU's support for a self-constraining treaty has been welcomed not just by Japan but also by the BRICS, and by the most threatened countries belonging to the G77 bloc.

5. The example of trade also reveals some distinctive features of EU diplomacy, and their complex implications for negotiations. The Commission has been granted exclusive competence in the domain of trade, and acts as the EU's representative in trade negotiations, often without consulting the EEAS and the HR. The EU deploys a controversial combination of trade bilateralism, regionalism and multilateralism. Whereas its ideology is in favour of global multilateralism and liberalization, its competition and cooperation with the US and other major trade actors foster bilateralism and its practical internal model emphasizes regionalism and inter-regionalism, including

de facto protectionism. While the model is one of diffuse reciprocity, the EU is increasingly oscillating between issue linkage and demands of specific reciprocity in its relationships with the BRICS. Issue linkage is not a distinctive feature of EU diplomacy, but the EU looks more capable than others of finding win–win solutions in negotiations: for example trade concessions in exchange for a partner's stronger commitment to common objectives related to global issues.

6. More generally, the EU has little choice but to look for multiple bridges and communication channels connecting its internal complexity to the rapidly changing international landscape. However, that does not mean simply adjusting to the views of foreign actors, because the preferences of geopolitical partners are far from being static and fixed. In other words, the EU could be more reflexive with regard to its own internal diversity, in order to improve communication channels with a heterogeneous and changing world. Is such enhanced communication possible, or is the EU an isolated entity within a multipolar world? A large literature is suggesting that, in spite of fundamental differences, even state diplomacy abroad is evolving beyond classical Westphalian forms. Pigman suggests that there are multiple post-Westphalian tendencies in world diplomacy, including in Japan: changing actors, venues, processes and functions of diplomacy, multilateral organizations, supranational polities, global firms, civil society organizations and diplomatic functions of representation and communication (including economic, military and security, and cultural diplomacy) (Pigman 2011).

7. Several observers argue that in the current post-Cold War era, the military option, outside the realm of the Petersberg tasks, is ineffective in addressing central global problems of conflict resolution and peacebuilding, as demonstrated by recent experiences in Iraq and Afghanistan in particular. In an era of globalization, nominally local challenges spill over and affect every state, fostering cooperation rather than competition. For example, even China's foreign policy has for years integrated 'multilateralism' and 'responsibility' as watchwords for resolving global challenges (Chen 2012), which may open bridges for communication and convergence in respect for a rule-based international order. Similarly, both the EU and Japan should explore windows of opportunity for constructing an inclusive, multilevel, post-hegemonic, more institutionalized understanding of multilateral cooperation.

8. However, convergence will inevitably develop alongside divergence and conflict within this multipolar and globalized world. There is no doubt that, even with the increasing institutionalization of the international landscape, the EU's longer-term understanding of diffuse reciprocity will clash with the often short-term instrumental approaches of its geopolitical partners, with regard to cooperation.

9. A third challenge relates to the EU's promotion of democracy abroad. In the EU's understanding, encouraging democracy is an essential component of its foreign policy. However, then High Representative Javier Solana's 2003 concept of 'effective multilateralism' does not sufficiently underscore the profound link between efficiency and democratic legitimacy in EU foreign policy. Realists are also increasingly likely to link democracy and foreign policy: many recent crises (for example in the Arab world and Myanmar) confirm that non-contingent legitimacy is the complement of multilateral regime-making and more effective global and regional governance (see the famous 'governance dilemma' discussed by Keohane 2004). Emphasizing the democratization dimension of EU external action is a matter not only of idealism but also of policy sustainability.

10. A values-driven conditionality may entail coercion. Inducement increases the cost of provocation and disrespect for international arrangements. If new multilateralism demands enhanced legitimacy, it will inevitably include Kofi Annan's concept of 'the responsibility to protect', which (after the controversial Libyan intervention) has to be clearly dissociated from regime change. Since high-profile incidences of genocide in Rwanda and Bosnia sparked the development of R2P, civilian powers are now expected to elaborate a more sophisticated combination of diplomacy and coercion. In contrast with the US, the UK and France, the EU strongly opposes the option of using credible threats of force, including for example air strikes, to coerce opposing states (Byman and Waxman 2002).

11. Furthermore, the international literature recognizes the growing relevance in the twenty-first century of other instruments of coercion which for many years have been available and deployed by the EU as complementary to diplomatic action: political sanctions (for example those directed against apartheid South Africa); diplomatic isolation (Austria); economic sanctions (Iraq); indirect and direct support of internal opposition to an authoritarian regime (Myanmar); support of a provisional government (Libya); and provision of legitimacy by the international community (often the UN) to humanitarian interventions. In the context of declining public support for military intervention and the resulting credibility traps, coercive threats are more complicated to use.

12. Are trade sanctions effective as a foreign policy tool? Research suggests that the legal frameworks used to design sanctions have an impact on their efficacy. Sanctions implemented under the ACP, Article 96 umbrella, which require breaches in democratic rule, good governance or human rights, prove more successful than measures adopted under the CFSP (Title V, TEU) (Portela 2010). The Council is frequently prevented from legally committing to CFSP sanctions because of the divisions among member states in challenging and controversial cases. However, in the case of sanctions justified under ACP Article 96, material and non-material consequences of the suspension of the treaty (including development aid)

and the clarity of the 'contract', make pro-democratic sanctions more effective. The procedure of QMV in the Council, the commitment of the Commission, and the proactive role of neighbouring countries explain both the enhanced efficiency and the effectiveness of using sanctions in this way. As a second step, the Petersberg tasks underline the distinction between peacekeeping and peace-enforcing missions. The former (before the conflict) imply compliance whereas the later (after the armed conflict has broken out) require deterrence from combat forces in either the short term or the long term. The EU may be forced into peace-enforcing missions in the Caucasus and the African and Mediterranean regions. Yet, despite involving the use of force, such interventions are not in contradiction with the civilian power approach – on the contrary, they only make the civilian role more credible. The increased involvement of 'military' tools, as CFSP and CSDP are integrated – for example Berlin+ missions, Crisis Management, Civilian Defence – has strengthened the concept of civilian power by broadening the toolkit of instruments which are called upon to secure the EU or other civilian power's foreign policy goals (Stavridis 2001). This has not necessarily lead to a deterioration or a 'securitization' of civilian power, as the overarching policy goals, hierarchy of concerns and the boundaries within which its security apparatus can be called upon all contribute towards maintaining an actor's international initiatives within the confines of civilian power (Tardy 2005). However, ultimately the constantly renewed balance any civilian power strikes between its civilian and military profile seems crucial. In this regard future evolutions of the EU will be determined by the relative importance and success associated with its CFSP and CSDP missions; whereas the outcome of debates surrounding the reinterpretation of Article 9 of the Japanese Constitution will impact Japan's continued profile as a civilian power.

13. The EU must also find ways to enhance its actorness both within the multilateral system and in relation to bilateral strategic partnerships. Increasing the EU's cohesion in multilateral forums is a matter of procedural identity and will depend on both internal and external factors. At the moment, direct EU representation is very limited (FAO and WTO) and the EU mostly has mere observer status within IOs, which impacts its international effectiveness. The EU treaty revisions may facilitate the objective of external coherence and member state loyalty, provided that member states display the political will to increasingly unify their external representation, at least within the IMF. Currently, the opposition of some member states to enhanced supranational external representation still prevails. The EU is a multilateral entity, and transferring its best practices of internal negotiation into the global arena should be considered a spontaneous, bottom-up contribution to global governance. Of course, if Europeans want to be more credible on the international stage, they should also address the contradiction between their own internal multilateral

practice and identity, and the overrepresentation of European states within the IMF, G20 and other multilateral bodies.

14. However, the limits on the EU are to some extent due to the resistance of the UN system, and of other international organizations, to welcoming regional entities. In spite of the EU's strong commitment to UN values and its practical cooperation with the UN, the organization's charter presents a challenge, because the recognition of the EU at the UN depends on the assent of other states and regional entities. The UN General Assembly is an intergovernmental body, and its members are states: the EU sits among the observers even though its member states provide 55 per cent of the UN's funding. The self-restraint of European states in voting reform in IOs (already begun with the 2011 IMF shares reform) could be balanced through a united representation of the EU as such within global multilateral governance institutions.

15. A further challenge relates to bilateral relations with rising powers. The Council conclusions of September 2010 focused on emerging powers and strategic partnerships, as an obvious consequence of the EU's own rising international political status. However, there is not yet sufficient focus to the EU's approach to strategic partnerships. The 10 current strategic partners should be better differentiated from each other (Japan, India and Brazil share common values with the EU to a greater extent than others), partnerships should be deeper and more inclusive (to allow issue linkages and deal-making) and there should be a more structured sense of prioritization between strategic partnerships (Grevi 2011). To answer the charge that strategic partnerships currently lack overall focus or even distinctive policy priorities, the functional potentialities and political specificities of each partnership should be better understood and more clearly articulated. To this effect, when considering the EU–Japan partnership distinctive features of importance might include, among others: its unique historical depth as one of the EU's oldest bilateral relationships; the economic significance and heft it mobilizes as it brings together two major economic powers facing comparable challenges to their respective growth models; and crucially the fact that it brings together two global actors recognized as 'civilian powers'. These and other features see the EU–Japan relationship offer a specific set of perspectives which distinguish it from other strategic partnerships, such as those developed with the BRICS. Secondly, the follow-up activities in the time between summits should be detailed, and enhanced involvement of a plurality of actors (several commissioners, several epistemic communities, networks etc.) should be encouraged. Finally, the EU's diplomatic action and also its structural foreign policy risks being affected in cases of open competition between bilateral strategic partners, regional leaders and the inter-regional partnerships set up by the EU during the 1990s: the Mediterranean partnership (1996), ASEM (1996), the 'Rio Process' (1999) and the new ACP convention at Cotonou in 2000.

Improving coordination between bilateral, inter-regional and multilateral relations should be a matter of practical governance and not of difficult treaty reform.

16. Finally, the EU's current institutional setup allows more flexibility and differentiation within the integration process, and this differentiation will require management if foreign policy cohesion is to be retained. A new treaty is not necessarily needed to strengthen a driving group of states (as in the economic governance case); the enhanced cooperation framework provides for deeper integration among at least nine member states, and is open to latecomers (TEU Title IV, Art 20 and TFEU, Articles 326/334). The divisions caused by the Libya crisis illustrate that the necessary critical mass is not yet there for enhanced cooperation on foreign policy.

Conclusion

The EU's foreign policy (and its execution by the relatively new EEAS) will be that of a uniquely sophisticated regional grouping. It will not be a copy of strategies previously deployed by other states, and it will not be the foreign policy of a federal state. The many forecasts of the EU developing into a superpower (for example Leonard 2005) have proved well wide of the mark, but recent theories of a declining and marginal EU are also inaccurate. The EU will continue to elaborate new ideas and develop different forms of experimental governance, on the international as well as the domestic level (Sabel and Zeitlin 2010).

However, the EU is not an island, and should not be approached simply as an isolated case study. Firstly, tendencies towards civilian power (in the broader and more realistic understanding presented here) matter in many relevant countries, such as Japan, Canada, Brazil, South Africa and Indonesia. Bilateral strategic partnerships, notably the one with Japan, mutually strengthen this shared approach to global challenges of the twenty-first century. Furthermore, international institutionalization matters as a powerful framework for the 'civilianization' of power. As such, the EU can combine in either a confused or a smart way a large array of soft foreign policy means of coercion. Its main realms of action are those regional and global multilateral issue-areas where a rigid power hierarchy does not yet exist: the environment, climate change, health, human rights protection, financial stability and other transnational challenges. The EU is representing the diffuse call for new forms of institutionalization of international life, which bind state behaviour without substituting for states. Without doubt, this is an important contribution to the international relations of the twenty-first century, provided that it is not identified with imposing imitations of the EU model of institutionalization on others.

The EU is also not an isolated case study because 'New Regionalism' is spreading in every continent and giving birth to a 'world of regions' (Katzenstein 2005), where pluralism and regional multilateralism are becoming ubiquitous structural forms of global governance. Within a heterogeneous global system, 'apolar' (Badie 2011) and 'interpolar' theories (Grevi 2011) are genuinely capturing emerging aspects of social reality, as are multipolar theories. Regionalism is limiting balance of power tendencies, making global governance more complex and multilevel, and multiplying the number of relevant actors. Within the emergent multi-layered global governance structure, many factors are increasing complexity, including expanding regional cooperation, inter-regional relations, multi-actor negotiations, transnational networks, and pressures for a more diffuse reciprocity. The very concept of international power (as political power plus military power) is challenged, as the attractiveness, efficiency and effectiveness of unilateralism and hard power wane in the context of a post-hegemonic world.

Finally, the EU, even more so under German hegemony, will remain an unprecedented civilian power, both by choice and by default. However, power is also changing elsewhere within the current multipolar interdependent world. Multiple and divergent forms of power are emerging in different issue-areas. Transformative powers foster transformative multilateralism. A gradual revision of the Westphalian order is occurring even if by multiple paths; this urgently requires a re-conceptualization of power and of multilateral cooperation (including more 'diffuse reciprocity' for example), rather than a postmodern dream or a U-turn back to an old form of thought and practice, based on mere power politics.

Last but not least, the European Union is not an isolated case study as far as its new diplomatic service is concerned. The EEAS is an extraordinarily relevant experiment in socialization and identity-building, of both an intergovernmental and supranational nature. If adjusted to current challenges, the European structural foreign policy may to some extent suggest and foster solutions for the twenty-first century's regional and global governance, because it anticipates tendencies which are in the process of emerging elsewhere in the world. We are witnessing the spread in every continent of several forms of new diplomacy: the interplay between internal complexity and new forms of regional integration, and between diplomacy and external coercion.

In contrast to more idealistic worldviews, a mix between *realpolitik* tendencies and a completely new context is emerging in all parts of the world, where fragmentation, interdependence and multilateralism, including deeper forms of multilateralism, matter simultaneously. Europe is an innovative part of the same planet where more traditional kinds of powers are emerging. When talking about a possible 'new multilateralism' we are not contrasting an idealized EU-styled approach to others, but drawing attention to existing similarities and exploring the possibility of a convergence scenario where the EU becomes less complex and more 'federal' (due to functional pressures towards more integration, both from within and from outside the Union), whereas other powers are becoming more responsible, complex and less classically 'sovereign'. A dialectic relationship will perhaps be possible between even diverging interests, practices and visions: this mix of cooperation and competition can, however, keep a common evolving multilateral context as a shared rule-based framework.

Machiavelli asserted that the performance of a given power depends upon the combination between *fortuna* (objective circumstances and material conditions) and *virtu* (the subjective variables of institutional and human capacities). In the current heterogeneous context, both *fortuna* and *virtu* pose substantial challenges. The best future scenario for the EU and other civilian powers would be a convergence scenario, in which the EU would forge relationships with similar powers such as Japan. But the EU can also forge relationships with previous rivals, who, thanks to various favourable internal and external trends and pressures, would allow a cooperative dynamic to prevail through a combination between traditional and contingent forms of intergovernmental cooperation, and broader, deeper, more innovative and legitimate forms of multilateral governance.

Chapter 3

The EU through the Eyes of Japan: Perceptions of the European Union as a Civilian Power

Paul Bacon and Martin Holland

Introduction

This chapter focuses on two of the three pillars of the 'EU Through the Eyes of the Asia-Pacific' research project.[1] It draws on extensive analysis of the Japanese print media, and more than 30 interviews conducted with members of the Japanese elite in 2011–2012. A very high number of EU-related news items were identified in the study, suggesting that the EU has a significant profile within the Japanese print media. A majority of news items were economic in nature, with a particular focus on the sovereign debt crisis. This is somewhat predictable, and not particularly in need of analysis. Rather, our analysis considers two other distinctive and interesting issues that emerged from the research on Japan. The first of these is exasperation within Japan (and the EU) at the slow progress towards an EU–Japan Free Trade Agreement/Economic Partnership Agreement (FTA/EPA). This exasperation was most clearly expressed in the Japanese elite interviews, but the trade negotiations also featured significantly in discussions in the Japanese print media. The second issue is that the EU was consistently perceived to be a significant civilian power, and a leader on human rights promotion, a perception that was strongly evident in both the Japanese media and elite interviews. Furthermore, the EU was perceived far more positively as a political rather than an economic actor, and, in a boost for post-Lisbon perceptions of the EU, High Representative Ashton had a generally high and somewhat positive profile in Japan, particularly in the print media.

In a much-quoted speech given in Japan in 2006, Commission President Barroso talked of the significant untapped potential of EU–Japan relations (Barroso 2006). However, the issue is, ultimately, one of frame. Perhaps Barroso's perspective is

---

1   External perceptions of the EU have been a long-standing research focus for the National Centre for Research on Europe (NCRE), based at the University of Canterbury, New Zealand. This research was carried out for the 2010–2012 research project titled 'After Lisbon: The EU as an Exporter of Values and Norms through ASEM'. For more information, please visit the NCRE project website: http://www.euperceptions.canterbury.ac.nz/lisbon/index.shtml.

excessively ambitious, or exaggerates the potential of the relationship. Perhaps we should instead be satisfied that the EU and Japan are each other's seventh and third most important trade partners respectively, and that some productive normative cooperation has been possible across a range of hard and soft security issues. An analysis of perceptions of EU–Japan relations is important, because it allows us to see how actors in Japan frame these issues themselves, both in the Japanese media and in various elite domains. Conceptually, a focus on perceptions helps to inform us about the global importance of the EU and how it is being interpreted outside Europe. And through our study, we discover that the Barroso perspective *is* in fact shared by many within Japan; although the EU–Japan relationship is perceived as important, and there is a belief that it will remain important, there is also a widely shared sense that significant potential for civil power cooperation is indeed being left untapped, unfulfilled.

It is necessary at this point to clarify the sense in which the term civilian power is used in this chapter. In one of his seminal discussions of the concept, Duchêne notes that nuclear stalemate in Europe has 'devalued purely military power, and given much more scope to civilian forms of influence and action' (Duchêne 1973: 18). Of these forms of influence, for Duchêne 'perhaps the most important' is economic (1973: 18). However, civilian powers must also be a political force for the 'international diffusion' of 'democratic standards', 'rights' and 'values' (Duchêne 1973: 19). Finally, civilian powers recognize that 'civilian standards cannot be maintained unless economic and social policies sustain the international open society' (Duchêne 1973: 19). We can therefore say that civilian powers: are committed to non-military forms of diplomacy; recognize the importance of economic power; and possess a normative agenda which includes the international promotion of human rights and democracy. In what follows, we argue that the Japanese print media and Japanese elites consistently identify these attributes in the European Union.

Methodology: Japanese Media Analysis and Elite Interviews

The project methodology involved the monitoring of three daily newspapers, from 1 January until 30 June 2011: the *Yomiuri Shimbun* (hereafter Yomiuri), the *Nihon Keizai Shimbun* (hereafter Nikkei) and the *Japan Times* (hereafter JT). The Yomiuri was chosen as representative of popular and general newspapers written in Japanese. Its circulation in 2013 was just under 10 million, which is the largest circulation for a daily newspaper in Japan (and probably in the world) (*Yomiuri Shimbun* 2013).The Nikkei was selected because it is the leading business newspaper in Japan, also written in Japanese. With a circulation of nearly 3 million copies in 2014 for its morning edition alone, the Nikkei boasts the world's largest circulation for a daily business newspaper (*Nihon Keizai Shimbun* 2014). The JT is the most popular main independent English-language daily newspaper in Japan, and has a longer history than the other two daily English-language newspapers.

A total of 1786 news items were identified across the three media sources. This in itself is a highly encouraging number, demonstrating that the EU does in fact have a significant profile within the Japanese print media; the number of items recorded was the highest for the most recent 10-country 'perceptions' study. Roughly one-half (911) of the identified items came from the business newspaper, roughly one-third (606) came from the English-language daily, and the remaining 269 items came from the popular Japanese daily. As we can see in Figure 3.1, there was considerable consistency in the monthly trends across the three newspapers for the six months analysed. This suggests both that there were concrete editorial reporting strategies being implemented at each of the three newspapers, and that our methodology and data analysis were sufficiently robust to pick up on this. (The 11 March 'triple disaster' – earthquake, tsunami and nuclear – did not have a distorting impact on this study, with March generally ranked fourth out of the six months in terms of EU news items identified.)

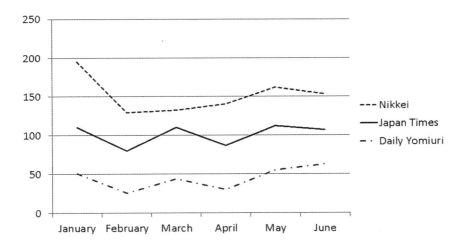

Figure 3.1 EU news items/month – all newspapers

With regard to the interview component of the project, 32 members of the Japanese elite were interviewed in 2011–2012. Four societal cohorts were identified – business, politics, media and civil society – and eight people were interviewed within each of these cohorts. Information was collected through individual, standardized, semi-structured, in-depth, face-to-face interviews that lasted for up to 40 minutes. This technique is designed to be personal, flexible, respectful of privacy and status, and generate greater openness and trust between interviewer and interviewee. Interviewees were given the option of anonymity. This methodology utilized open-ended responses – the pre-tested

18-question questionnaire featured only two structured questions. Two versions of the questionnaire were employed – one for business, political and civil society respondents, and another, slightly modified questionnaire for media practitioners. The question order rotated depending on the flow of conversation.

The sampling strategy for the 'elite' interviews involved the selection of key informants in each location across the four designated sectors. The selected elite interviewees were identified from members of national parliaments, or equivalents, representing a range of political views. Media elites were identified as the editors/ news directors and lead reporters of the reputable media outlets. Civil society elite participants were representatives of various national and international non-governmental organizations. Business respondents were identified from members of national business round-tables and other official business networks.

Similarities and Differences between Print Media and Elite Interview Findings

There was a significant correlation between the content of the print media and the views of the elite interviewees on the two issues highlighted – trade and normative power. The print media discussed trade and the FTA/EPA issue in some detail: a total of 191 articles on trade, and 122 articles on the FTA/EPA issue were found. Coverage of these issues in the print media tended to be neutral/positive, rather than negative. Overall, when all economic issues were discussed, 75 per cent of a total of 1,149 items were classified as neutral in journalistic tone. In the remainder of cases, when an evaluation was made, this was three times more likely to be negative than positive. However, if we look more specifically at just the data for trade and the FTA/EPA, in excess of 90 per cent of all such articles offered a neutral evaluation. In the remainder of cases, items were twice as likely to be evaluated positively as negatively in the trade sub-frame (12 to 6), and four times as likely to be evaluated positively rather than negatively in the FTA/EPA sub-frame (8 to 2). Thus, not only did EU–Japan trade and the FTA/EPA generate significant coverage, both were significantly more positively evaluated than economic issues in general.

If we turn to the external politics sub-frame, we can see a similar neutral/ positive evaluative profile. We found a total of 296 articles within the external politics sub-frame, and roughly 80 per cent of these items were evaluated as neutral. Of the remaining 20 per cent, 42 were evaluated positively, and 19 negatively. In other words, non-neutral items were more than twice as likely to be evaluated positively rather than negatively. In each of the three cases of trade, FTA/EPA and external politics, a significant majority of items were neutrally reported, but where this was not the case, a positive evaluation was at least twice as likely as a negative evaluation.

Elite interviewees also identified the FTA/EPA issue as one of the most important issues for the relationship, but negativity and exasperation were more evident, especially within the business cohort. The significance of the EU as a civilian power actor also came through very clearly in the interviews, but with the elite interviewee responses being more strongly and consistently positive, both about the type of civilian power actor the EU is, and the type of actor that it could and should become.

So, we can say that the print media both identify trade and normative power as important, and overall that coverage of both issues tended to be neutral/positive. We can also say that elite interviewees consistently identified trade issues and the EU's civilian power as highly significant, although the views expressed were critical with regard to trade, and complimentary with regard to civilian power.

Framing, State of the Relationship and Key Issues

The media project methodology categorized EU news reports according to five frames – economics, politics, social affairs, environment and development. The overall percentages by frame were: economy (64 per cent), politics (25 per cent), social affairs (7 per cent), environment (2.5 per cent) and development (1.5 per cent). There was an overarching consistency across the three newspapers. In every paper, the frames appeared in identical ranking order: economics generated the most items for all three papers, followed by politics, social affairs and so on. Overall, there were roughly 2.5 times as many items about economics as there were about politics, and the economic items were much more likely to focus on events *within* the EU. The political and economic frames combined dominated the other categories: the combined percentage figure for the Nikkei was 94 per cent, for the Yomiuri 89.5 per cent, and for the JT 83 per cent. As a result of this dominance of these two frames, it is necessary to move to the sub-frame level of analysis for economics and politics, in order to get a clearer sense of the content of the various EU-related items.

Six economic sub-frames were identified: business/finance, trade, industry, state of the economy, agriculture and energy. The 'state of the economy' sub-frame accounted for the largest proportion (56 per cent) of economic items, followed by the 'business/finance' sub-frame and then 'trade', which accounted for 19.5 per cent and 16.5 per cent of the economic items respectively. The main 'state of the economy' sub-frame issues discussed were the sovereign debt crisis, the state of the world economy and the Euro exchange rate. The main issues discussed within the 'business/finance' sub-frame were investment and banking, while for 'trade' the issues were the implications of the sovereign debt crisis for international trade, and the potential for an FTA/EPA between Japan and the EU.

The EU–Japan relationship was consistently regarded as important by each of the four interview cohorts, each of which also anticipated that the relationship will remain important in the future. On a scale of 1 to 5, where 1 is not important at all and 5 is very important, respondents accorded the current significance of the EU an average rating of 3.8, rising to 3.9 in the future. Only the business cohort saw the relationship becoming less important in the future, and then only by a small margin. When asked to describe the current state of the EU–Japan relationship, three-quarters of respondents conceived of it as stable. On this occasion the business cohort was a significant outlier, in viewing the relationship as stagnant, with one-half of business respondents characterizing the relationship in this way (see Figure 3.2).

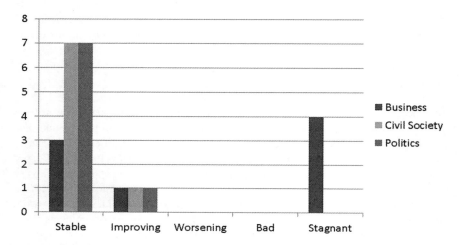

Figure 3.2 Perceived state of EU–Japan relations

Importantly, the two issues that elite respondents felt had the most direct impact on EU relations were the sovereign debt crisis and the prospects for an EU–Japan FTA/EPA. There was a widely held perception that the Eurozone crisis is one of the main reasons why the value of the yen had been so high, which in turn has made it difficult for Japan to recover economically. There was also a widely held elite perception that Japan's difficulties with regard to the successful conclusion of trade agreements are putting Japanese businesses at a competitive disadvantage.

When asked what issues should be kept in mind when Japan is developing trade or government policy towards the EU, the policy recommendations offered by interviewees were diverse, often contradictory and mostly general rather than concrete. Five interviewees felt that Japan should adopt a tough position in FTA/EPA negotiations, whilst four felt that Japan should be more flexible, and not waste this important opportunity. Other individuals argued that Japan should alternatively push for a regional trade bloc, or join the TPP. The fact that there was a rough balance between those that think Japan should be tougher, and those that think Japan should be more conciliatory in trade negotiations itself illustrates the difficulty of securing agreement. The fact that some individuals argued for trade possibilities other than those with the EU also suggests that there is a lack of clarity among Japanese elites over the way forward for Japanese trade policy in general, and EU–Japan trade relations in particular.

EU–Japan Relations: Significant Untapped Normative Potential

As well as having significant untapped trade potential, the relationship is also perceived as having significant untapped civilian power potential (Barroso 2006). Across the three newspapers we found 300 articles which associated the EU with international political activities consistent with the definition of civilian power identified above. These articles were more likely both to feature the EU as the main actor and to evaluate the EU more positively than were articles on economics. High Representative Ashton had a high profile in these political articles. Articles featuring Ashton were also more likely to feature the EU as the main actor, and to evaluate Ashton/the EU in a positive way. These 300 articles also referred to a highly impressive range of civilian power activities undertaken by the EU in a number of different countries and regions. For example, during the period of the study, the EU rigorously applied conditionality-based human rights diplomacy to its dealings with potential members of the EU such as Croatia (which has joined since the study was conducted), Macedonia, Serbia and Turkey, and to partnership countries such as Belarus and the Ukraine. The EU monitored elections in the Ivory Coast, Nigeria, Southern Sudan and Uganda, and criticized the human rights records of countries such as China, Myanmar, Pakistan and Uzbekistan. The EU frequently applied diplomatic and human rights pressure in a number of 'Arab Spring' countries, such as Egypt, Libya, Syria and Tunisia. The EU played a significant leadership role in nuclear non-proliferation diplomacy with Iran, actively contributed to the Middle East peace process, and dispensed disaster relief aid to Japan. Across all of these dimensions, and in all of these places, the significance of the EU as a civilian power was undeniable, and was strongly reflected in coverage of the EU in the Japanese print media.

This emphatic recognition of the EU as a civilian power was also evident in the elite interviews, where significant numbers of interviewees categorized the EU as a great power in the normative and diplomatic domains. Interviewees also identified the EU as a leader, and argued that the EU's leadership role is most significant in the area of human rights. For all of these reasons, across both the media analysis and elite interviews, it is clear that in Japan the EU is considered to be a significant civilian power.

Furthermore, over the last decade, Brussels and Tokyo have undertaken numerous successful joint civilian initiatives, and established bilateral dialogue forums to deal with international nuclear non-proliferation, and hard and soft security issues. These have included:

- agreeing to jointly promote the reform of the Conventional Weapons Protocol on anti-personnel landmines;

- supporting the conclusion of the Comprehensive Test Ban Treaty (CTBT);
- signing an agreement on universal adherence to the Nuclear Non-Proliferation Treaty;
- jointly supporting implementation of the principles and objectives for nuclear non-proliferation and disarmament;
- promoting the non-proliferation of nuclear weapons and the abolition of anti-personnel landmines, through joint support for the Ottawa Convention of 1997 and the November 2002 International Code of Conduct against Ballistic Missile Proliferation;
- engaging in joint peacekeeping and peace-building initiatives;
- holding European-Japanese seminars, training and workshops on post-conflict nation-building in Afghanistan, Cambodia and a number of African countries;
- holding regular joint training sessions for UN peacekeepers;
- engaging, since July 2002, in periodic consultations on terrorism and counter-terrorism cooperation;
- joint efforts to support the economic and social development of the Palestinian people, through Japan's contribution to the EU's PEGASE mechanism;
- cooperation on security, reintegration and development assistance in Afghanistan, including the establishment of a police training centre;
- close cooperation on counter-piracy for the safety of maritime navigation off the coast of Somalia and in the Gulf of Aden;
- joint promotion of Tajikistan–Afghanistan border management and cross-border cooperation in 2011/2012.

This list is drawn from Berkofsky (2007: 19), and the *Joint Press Statement on the 20th EU-Japan Summit* (Council of the European Union 2011). These initiatives were not referred to during our research project, as they pre-date it, but they nevertheless illustrate the actuality of and the potential for greater cooperation between the EU and Japan. However, although the list is quite impressive, critics would still argue that there has been no defining project or projects commensurate with the resources that both polities could potentially deploy, separately or jointly, in support of a genuinely comprehensive civilian power agenda. Here, again, from a negative perspective there is a sense that continued drift is the most likely scenario, unless decisive diplomatic initiatives are taken on both sides.

Politics: International Focus, Positive Perceptions and Greater Centrality

Turning to the political frame, in the print media the EU was perceived to be a more significant *international* political actor than a domestic one, was evaluated in a more positive light when discussed in political rather than economic items, and was more likely to feature as the main actor in political rather than economic items. The politics-focused EU stories in the print media were divided between internal and external, with the latter constituting two-thirds of the political coverage. There was thus a significantly greater focus on the EU as an international political actor, rather than on political issues within the EU. With regard to focus of the external politics news items, the most important topics were the Libyan conflict, EU–Japan relations, China, and the capture of the alleged war criminal Mladic. Other significant issues included the protests and political crackdown in Syria, and the mediation of the Israel/Palestine problem. Human rights diplomacy with Belarus, China and Myanmar also featured quite prominently, as did the ongoing Iranian nuclear impasse. Another consistent concern was the elections in Turkey, Turkey's apparent drift away from the EU, and the implications of this for EU enlargement. Finally, of course, there were numerous articles relating to EU–Japan relations in the context of the triple disaster, and ongoing negotiations concerning an FTA/ EPA between the EU and Japan. It should be noted that in all three newspapers, the EU did not feature prominently as an environmental actor (44 items) or a development actor (26 items). This is a sobering finding for those who believe the EU to be a significant environmental and development actor, and who like to imagine that it is widely recognized around the world as being so. There is a very significant gap here between the EU's self-image as a global leader on the environment and development, and the way that it is portrayed or represented in the Japanese print media.

All news items reporting the EU were analysed to determine the evaluation of the EU that they contained: neutral, positive or negative. As can be seen, all three of the monitored newspapers consistently evaluated the EU neutrally, with 76.5 per cent of all EU-related news items containing no explicit bias. Where reporting was not neutral in tone, negative evaluations were more common than positive ones, with a two-to-one ratio overall. However, it should be stressed that positivity and negativity were not equally distributed across the news frames. Importantly, items within the economic frame were nearly three times as likely to generate a negative rather than a positive evaluation, whilst those within the political frame were more than twice as likely to generate a positive rather than negative evaluation. This is an understandable finding. Many of the economic items, of course, focused on the sovereign debt crisis, and we can expect a reasonable proportion of these to be negative. So, neutral evaluations dominated, but where bias was detected the EU was consistently evaluated in a more negative manner in the economic frame, and a more positive manner in the politics frame.

High Representative Ashton: High Visibility and Positive Evaluation

The research also considered who were the visible faces representing the EU in the news media. High Representative Ashton was seen to be active in connection with a number of high-profile issues around the world. She was mentioned several times in connection with the Libyan conflict, with human rights diplomacy in Egypt, and nuclear diplomacy with Iran. She also made statements and/or engaged in human rights diplomacy with a number of countries including China, Belarus, Serbia, Taiwan, Thailand/Cambodia, Bahrain, Syria and Tunisia. In terms of degree of centrality, the EU was significantly more likely to be the main actor in items which mentioned Ashton. Overall, the EU was the main actor in 35.5 per cent of articles, but in articles that mentioned Ashton, this figure rose to 48 per cent.

With regard to items in which the EU and Ashton were mentioned, the evaluation was positive, something of a contrast to the general findings, where the EU was twice as likely to receive a negative rather than a positive evaluation. Overall, 22 per cent of items which mentioned Ashton produced a positive evaluation, as opposed to 16 per cent which produced a negative one. Thus, items which featured the EU and Ashton were evaluated positively overall and significantly more positively than items that fell within the economic frame. Baroness Ashton has achieved a reasonably high and somewhat positive profile in the Japanese print media.

Elite Opinion and EU Civilian Power

Elite interviewees associated the EU with human rights and integration, overwhelmingly perceived the EU to be a great power, and considered the EU to possess substantial economic, diplomatic and normative power, all of which are the key ingredients of civilian power. Many considered the EU to be a leader in the domain of human rights, and suggested a number of joint initiatives that the EU and Japan could pursue together in the future.

When elite respondents were asked which three thoughts came to their minds when thinking about the EU, the three most common images were: integration and community, the EU's commitment to human rights and democracy, and the sovereign debt crisis. Other prominent images included perceiving the EU as a successful peace experiment, and as a significant environmental actor. This is encouraging, because it shows that despite an understandable concern regarding the sovereign debt crisis, substantial numbers of respondents continued to associate the EU with civilian power attributes to an even greater extent.

When asked if they thought that the EU was a great power, 27 of 32 respondents replied positively, and two-thirds felt that the EU was a great economic power. One-third also felt that the EU was a normative power, and another third considered it a diplomatic power. In contrast, only two respondents felt that that the EU was a military power. We might have anticipated these findings with respect to economic and military power, but the fact that Japanese elites clearly recognized the EU as a normative and diplomatic power is welcome news. This elite view supports the finding, noted earlier in this article, that the Japanese print media frequently conceives of, and portrays the EU as, a significant civilian power actor.

When asked whether they considered the EU a leader in international politics, just over one-half of respondents felt that this was the case. What is more, there was a perception that when it does lead, the EU acts on issues that are most closely associated with civilian power, such as human rights and the environment. As noted, the EU was not often portrayed as an environmental or development leader in the Japanese print media, so it is interesting to note that the EU *was* recognized as an environmental leader by a substantial number of elite interviewees. The fact that the EU was also identified as a leader in this normative domain, as well as a great power, is further evidence of the EU's strong civilian power profile in Japan.

Although, as shown above, elite opinion on trade issues was more critical and mixed, a number of interviewees suggested joint initiatives that could form the basis for a more substantial shared civilian power agenda. With regard to the definition of civilian power offered above, elite respondents argued that there were a number of ways in which the EU acts as a civilian role model for Japan: Japan should strive to emulate EU human rights standards in general, and more specifically should redouble its efforts to abolish the death penalty; Japan should de-regulate along the lines of the EU model, and embrace ISO standards; and Japan and the EU should pursue joint renewable energy initiatives. It was also suggested that Japan should be more proactive in general on conflict prevention, bringing it more in line with EU strategy, and more proactive in particular with regard to the particular case of Somalia, where it was suggested that the EU and Japan should expand their anti-piracy cooperation to land operations. It was also suggested that in the realm of post-conflict peacebuilding, the EU and Japan should develop a joint initiative on Security Sector Reform. We can therefore see that the notion of untapped civilian power potential suggested by Barroso had strong support among many of the elite interviewees.

Conclusion: Overview of Core Findings

To conclude, we can see that the EU has a high profile in the Japanese print media, and that trade and normative issues feature prominently in this high profile. The EU's general economic profile is more likely to be evaluated negatively, and significant numbers of businessmen feel that the relationship is stagnant and possibly even in decline. Against this, however, we can say that trade ties between the two polities are significant – the EU and Japan are each other's seventh and third most important trade partners respectively. The Japanese media evaluate trade and FTA/EPA issues more positively than general economic issues, and the EU–Japan relationship is seen as important and stable by most elite interviewees.

There is also a positive perception of the EU as a civilian international political actor. In our study we identified roughly 300 newspapers articles which refer to this dimension of the EU's identity and influence. Articles on politics are more likely to feature the EU as the main actor, and are more likely to feature a positive evaluation of the EU. High Representative Ashton has a significant profile, and is also evaluated positively. The EU is identified as being active across a range of different civilian activities in a variety of different countries and regions. This finding is strongly reinforced in the elite interviews, where human rights and democracy promotion is one of the images most commonly associated with the EU. The EU is widely acknowledged as a normative and diplomatic great power, and as a leader on human rights issues. We can therefore say that there is a strong and recurring positive perception of the EU as a civilian power in both the print media and elite interviews. To this we can add an impressive list of civilian projects and initiatives prosecuted jointly by the EU and Japan.

Perhaps we should be satisfied with this state of affairs, and celebrate the fact that the EU–Japan relationship is stronger than most international relationships around the world. And yet, although relations are seen as stable and important, there is a nagging sense that they could be significantly better, and that important opportunities for trade and normative cooperation are being missed. It is clear that this perspective, most provocatively advanced by Barroso, is not isolated or exaggerated. As we have demonstrated, it is a perspective shared by those that highlight the trade significance and the normative identity of the EU so prominently in Japanese newspapers. And it is a perspective shared by most of our elite interviewees, who are alternatively frustrated at missed economic opportunities, and hopeful that there can be greater cooperation between the two polities in the future. To conclude, it is clear that the Japanese print media and elites both identify the EU as a civilian power, and recognize the need for a new chapter in EU–Japan civilian power cooperation.

PART II
Enhancing Trade Relations and Regulatory Standards

Chapter 4

Three Balancing Acts:
The EU's Trade Policy towards East Asia

Min Shu

Introduction

Trade relations between Europe and East Asia[1] have become ever more important. Bilateral trade has increased more than two and a half times since 2000, rising from less than 365 billion US dollars to more than 965 billion in 2012 (IMF 2013). Today, three Northeast Asian economies – China, Japan and South Korea – rank as the second, seventh and tenth-largest trading partners of the European Union (EU) respectively. Meanwhile, the Association of Southeast Asian Nations (ASEAN) has become the EU's third-largest extra-European trading partner after the US and China. As a whole, East Asia accounted for 27.5 per cent of EU imports and 18.8 per cent of EU exports in 2012 (European Commission 2013b). Yet despite the enormous exchange of goods and services, the trade relationship between the two sides has not been without problems. The EU's trade deficit with East Asia soared over the past decade, reaching a level of over 260 billion US dollars in 2012. Not surprisingly, dealing with such a huge trade deficit has been a very important issue for the EU's external trade strategy (European Commission 2006b).

In addition to the trade imbalance, the EU faces another important task regarding its trade policy towards East Asia. The Doha round of WTO negotiations has been dragging on for more than 13 years. Initially, the EU had been quite ambitious in pushing forward the so-called 'Singapore issues' through the multilateral platform of the WTO. The Singapore issues deal with trade rules with regard to public procurement, trade facilitation, investment rules and competition policy. They are widely regarded as the next generation of trade-related issues to be tackled in global trade liberalization. In 1996 the WTO decided to set up special working groups to study these important issues. The EU has long been a major supporter of these non-traditional trade issues, because they are the areas where the EU has maintained a comparative advantage vis-à-vis trading partners. However, the failure of the Cancun Ministerial Meeting[2] forced the EU to abandon its 'deep'

---

1   East Asia here refers to China, Japan, South Korea and the original 10 ASEAN member states.

2   The Cancun Ministerial Meeting of the WTO, held in Mexico in September 2003, was supposed to produce a roadmap for the negotiation of the Doha Development

trade agenda at the WTO (Bhagwati 2004; Dür 2008). Since then, how to revive the Singapore issues with like-minded trading partners has been another key issue for the EU's external trade strategy (European Commission 2004).

The growing influence of East Asia and the stagnant Doha round of WTO negotiations have prompted the EU to reconsider its trade policy. Over the past decade the EU has taken some major steps to reform the Common Commercial Policy. In 2006 the European Commission launched its 'Global Europe' strategy. Departing from a long-term preference for multilateral trade negotiations, it proposed to open bilateral Free Trade Agreement (FTA) negotiations with third countries and regions. ASEAN and South Korea were listed as the priority negotiation partners (European Commission 2006a: 11). In 2009 the Treaty of Lisbon came into effect. Not only has the Common Commercial Policy become an integral part of the EU's external action, but the European Parliament (EP) has been granted additional power in the EU trade policy-making process. In the following year, the European Commission released a new trade policy guideline entitled 'Trade, Growth and World Affairs', along with the initial plan for a European international investment policy.

This chapter examines these important changes in trade relations between Europe and East Asia. The aim is three-fold: first, to chart the recent development of EU-Asian trade relations; second, to analyse the institutional reforms of the Common Commercial Policy; third, to assess the challenges facing the EU's external trade strategy towards East Asia. To achieve these goals, the next section explores the evolving structure of bilateral trade between Europe and East Asia. It shows that growing trade with the Far East has not only created a large trade deficit on the EU side, but has seriously divided domestic interests within the EU. Next, the third section explores the recent reforms of the Common Commercial Policy. It discusses the 'Global Europe' strategy, the Lisbon institutional framework and the new policy guideline of 'Trade, Growth and World Affairs'. How these policy and institutional reforms have reshaped the EU's trade policy towards East Asia is the focus of the fourth section. The section details the recent trade disputes and negotiations between the two regions, and identifies three balancing acts that the EU is facing in dealing with East Asia. The final section summarizes the main findings and concludes the chapter.

Round. The meeting saw fierce debates and disagreements over the 'Singapore issues' between developed and developing countries. Developing countries formed a fairly solid coalition – the G20 – among themselves (Narlikar and Tussie 2004; Taylor 2007). Due to their opposition, the Cancun Ministerial Meeting was unable to reach any meaningful compromise on the Singapore issues.

The Evolving Structure of EU-Asian Trade

One and a half decades after the Asian financial crisis, East Asia has been playing an even larger part in the world economy. Relying on booming exports, most East Asian countries have enjoyed relatively stable economic growth despite the global financial crisis in 2008. What has been different is the changing pattern of regional production in East Asia. In the late 1980s and early 1990s, Japanese manufacturing multinationals invested heavily in Northeast and Southeast Asia. These investments created efficient regional production networks in the white goods, electronics and automobile industries (Hatch and Yamamura 1996). Centred on Japanese capital and technology, regionalized production not only contributed to the host countries' exports to the world, but also led to the healthy growth of intra-regional trade in East Asia (Tachiki 2005; Ernst 2006). As the newly industrialized economies (NIEs, including Hong Kong, Singapore, South Korea and Taiwan) climbed up the industrial ladder, they also expanded production lines to neighbouring countries and created positive externalities for the regional economy (Beeson 2007: 194). It did not take very long for Korean and Taiwanese companies to compete directly with Japanese ones for intra-regional production bases and extra-regional markets. Through this process, the 'flying geese' model of regional production is being replaced by a multi-core growth platform in East Asia (Fujita 2007).

Adding to the growing influence of the NIEs is the rise of China in the regional economy. China joined the World Trade Organization (WTO) in 2001. Its WTO membership soon attracted a rapid inflow of overseas capital. China was the world's top destination for foreign direct investment in 2003,[3] and continues to be considered one of the most attractive destinations for investment. As overseas capital poured into the country to take advantage of its cheap and disciplined labour force, regional production in East Asia went through another major transformation. Multinationals operating in the region typically used their Chinese factories as assembly lines for component products manufactured in neighbouring countries. These newly created regional value chains quickly reshaped trade patterns in East Asia. On the one hand, China began to export massively to the global market. Within a decade, Chinese exports to the world grew almost six-fold, rising from 266.1 billion US dollars in 2001 to 1,577.9 billion in 2010. With the presence of 'made-in-China' products all over the world, China has established its position as a 'world factory' for manufacturing goods. On the other hand, the intra-regional trade in component, semi-finished and finished products prospered in East Asia. Studies show that the 'fragmentation trade' – that is, the cross-border trade of component products – has increased considerably since 2000 (Athukorala 2006; Ando 2006). With the help of China's economic rise, neighbouring East Asian countries' exports have maintained robust growth (Athukorala 2009).

---

3   According to UNCTAD (United Nation Conference on Trade and Development) statistics, the inward foreign direct investment flow to China was 53.3 billion US dollars in 2003.

Changing patterns of regional production in East Asia have significantly influenced the region's trade with the EU. Between 1980 and 1990 East Asian exports to the EU market increased from 39.7 to 115.6 billion US dollars, with Japan playing a leading role throughout the decade (see Figure 4.1). The 1990s saw the growing weight of South Korea, China and ASEAN countries in the region's total exports. As Japanese exports stagnated, the annual growth rate of East Asian exports to the EU declined from 11.29 per cent in the 1980s to 7.82 per cent in the 1990s. Yet the picture was reversed in the 2000s. Not only did China quickly become the leading regional exporter to the EU, but Japan, South Korea and ASEAN members also began to export aggressively to the EU market. Japan's exports to the EU increased from 86.9 billion US dollars in 2000 to 112.4 billion in 2008. South Korea, on the other hand, more than doubled its exports between 2000 (24.6 billion) and 2008 (58.1 billion). This trend was only reversed after 2009, as the global financial crisis and the European sovereign debt crisis drained demand in the EU.

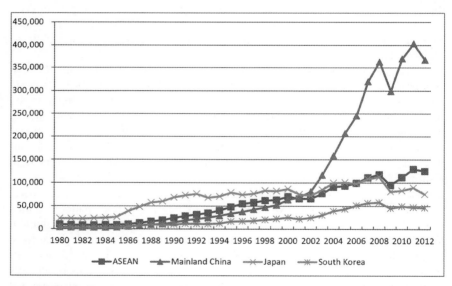

Figure 4.1 East Asian exports to the EU 1980–2012

Looking at individual ASEAN economies, their increasing exports to the European market were not very different from the regional pattern (see Figure 4.2). In particular, the exports to the EU of the five original ASEAN member states (Indonesia, Malaysia, the Philippines, Singapore and Thailand) grew in tandem with the expansion of regional production in East Asia. Singapore, one of the NIEs, had been the leading ASEAN-5 exporter throughout the 1990s. The growing clout of the Chinese economy has not altered this trend in the 2000s. The five Southeast Asian countries' exports to the EU increased more than 1.4 times between 2001 and 2010. Among the later entrants to ASEAN, Vietnam stood out for its export performance in the mid-1990s. In 2006 it overtook the Philippines and became the fifth largest ASEAN exporting country to the EU. The latest data show that Vietnam secured an even larger share of the European market in 2012. On the whole, neither the expansion of NIEs nor the rise of China altered the upward trend of export growth in Southeast Asia.

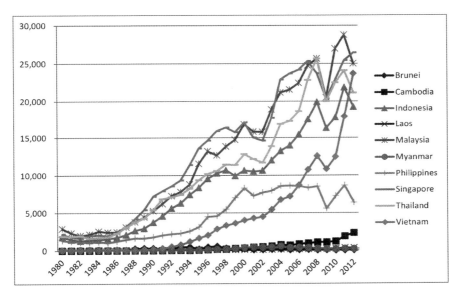

Figure 4.2 ASEAN-10 members' exports to the EU 1980–2012

As Northeast and Southeast Asian economies increased their exports to Europe, the EU experienced a rapidly rising trade deficit with the Far East. It should be noted that the EU has been in trade deficit with East Asia for most of the past three decades. The only exceptions were its trade with China in the mid-1980s, and with South Korea in the mid-1990s. In spite of being used to a trade deficit, the EU was still caught by surprise when East Asian products flooded into the European market in the early 2000s. A close look at bilateral trade data reveals that both the direction and the level of the trade deficit have changed substantially in this period (see Figure 4.3). These changes were closely related to the transformation of regional production in East Asia.

Prior to 2000 the EU's largest trade deficit was with Japan; despite some fluctuation, the EU's trade with Japan was in a deficit of around 30 to 50 billion US dollars between 1987 and 2000. The deficit amount remained stable in the 2000s. This, however, was not due to stagnated bilateral trade between the EU and

Japan. Between 2000 and 2008 the EU's exports to Japan increased by 2.04 billion US dollars whereas Japan's exports to the EU grew by 2.55 billion. The relatively mature trade relationship between the two was probably the main reason behind the stable trade deficit. By contrast, the EU's trade deficit with ASEAN and South Korea grew noticeably following the Asian financial crisis in 1997–1998. The regional financial crisis may have temporarily reduced these countries' demand for EU products. Nevertheless, the past 15 years saw the continuation of a large trade deficit on the part of the EU. Based on newly established regional production networks, South Korea and ASEAN reached trade surpluses of 22 and 38 billion US dollars respectively in the mid-2000s. The impact of the Chinese economy on the EU's external trade relations went far beyond expectations. In the same year as China joined the WTO, the EU witnessed a trade deficit of 41 billion US dollars resulting from EU–China trade. The deficit continued to grow exponentially to a record high of 247 billion in 2008. Only the global financial crisis and the European sovereign debt crisis moderated the trend after 2009.

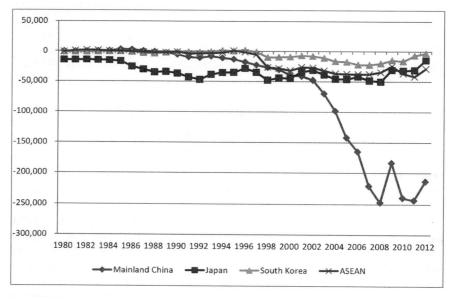

Figure 4.3 The EU's trade deficit with East Asia 1980–2012

Just as the growing trade deficit forced Europe to reconsider its trade policy, the EU found itself internally divided on how to deal with East Asia. On the one side, the protectionist member states in southern Europe demanded effective application of trade defence instruments to protect domestic producers in the EU. On the other side, the liberal member states of northern Europe insisted on an open trade policy towards East Asia. The two sides have clashed on several occasions in the past decade (Heron 2007; Luo 2007; Shu 2008), with surging exports of Chinese and Vietnamese leather shoes to the European market being one notable example.

In 2005 the European footwear industry launched a complaint against the growing inflow of leather footwear produced in China and Vietnam.[4] Upon receiving the complaint, the European Commission launched anti-dumping proceedings against the two East Asian countries. As it turned out, the proceedings were more controversial than expected. European footwear producers claimed that the import of Chinese and Vietnamese shoes had reduced their market share, increased unemployment, and imposed a serious threat to the footwear industry in the EU. In opposition, European footwear importers accused domestic producers of shifting the blame for their own lack of productivity and innovation onto outsiders. The two sides not only publicly criticized each other, but staged vigorous lobbying efforts throughout the anti-dumping proceedings. In March 2006 the European Commission proposed imposing a provisional anti-dumping duty on Chinese and Vietnamese shoes. Among the 25 member states at the time, only three voted for the proposal, 11 voted against, and another 11 abstained.[5]

The divided vote was not surprising because the footwear industry has become concentrated in a few southern European countries over the years. The European countries that no longer produce footwear came to rely on imported shoes for domestic consumption. An anti-dumping duty would increase costs for importers and lead to higher prices for retailers. These countries thus had good reason to stand for free trade and vote against the anti-dumping measures. Indeed, the liberal member states had at least twice voted down Commission proposals for definitive anti-dumping duties.[6] It was not until the European Commission decided to reduce the anti-dumping measures from a normal duration of five years to two years that the member states at last gave a green light to the Commission proposal (see Shu 2008). Still, the final vote was extremely close: of the then 25 member states, nine voted for the proposal, 11 voted against, and four abstained.

The footwear case is only one of the many trade disputes that recently occurred between the EU and East Asia. As the intra-regional value chains extend from Japan and the NIEs to neighbouring countries (Robles 2004), China and ASEAN developing economies are facing more bilateral trade disputes with the EU. These disputes indicate that the trade relations between the two regions have gone beyond the simple dichotomy of trade liberalization versus protectionism. Inside

---

4   According to an investigation by the European Commission, leather shoes produced in China and Vietnam accounted for nearly 20 per cent of EU market share in 2005. See Commission Regulation (EC) 553 (2006) (published on 23 March 2006), *Official Journal* 6 April 2006: L98, 28.

5   According to EU regulations, the Commission's proposal for anti-dumping measures can only be rejected by a simple majority of the member states (Council Regulation [EC] No 461/2004, *Official Journal* 13 March 2004: L77, 12). This means that abstention is equivalent to approval in anti-dumping votes.

6   Based on reports in the *EUobserver*, *Financial Times* and *Wall Street Journal*.

the EU, there are both liberal actors who are in favour of expanded commercial links, and protectionist forces that caution against deepened trade relations. Since the EU's growing trade deficit has diametrically opposite impacts on these two groups, they disagree on how to manage the trade relationship with East Asia. As the next section shows, such internal divisions triggered some major institutional and policy reforms to the Common Commercial Policy.

Reforming the Common Commercial Policy

The Common Commercial Policy (CCP), which regulates the EU's external trade with third countries and regions, is one of the most important policies of the EU. The scope of the CCP's mandate has expanded progressively over the past five decades. First introduced in the Treaty of Rome in 1957, it now covers a variety of trade-related issues including tariff reduction, trade defence, trade in goods and services, the commercial aspects of intellectual property, foreign direct investment, and trade in cultural, educational and health services.[7] In terms of institutional setting, the Common Commercial Policy features a sophisticated process of supranational decision-making. The European Commission enjoys the right of initiative in proposing new policies, the Council votes on the proposals following the rule of qualified majority voting for most decisions, and the EP influences the direction of policy-making under the ordinary legislative procedure.[8] The current configuration of the Common Commercial Policy has been an outcome of recent policy and institutional reforms, some of which were in direct response to the growing influence of East Asia.

On the same day (4 October 2006) the EU agreed on a definitive anti-dumping duty against Chinese and Vietnamese footwear, the European Commission adopted a new strategy for its Common Commercial Policy. The major policy paper is entitled 'Global Europe, Competing in the World: A Contribution to the EU's Growth and Jobs Strategy' (European Commission 2006a). It highlights the twin goals of maintaining internal competitiveness and opening external markets for the EU. To achieve them, the paper makes four concrete proposals. Firstly, it recommends opening trade negotiations with potential partners for a new generation of bilateral FTAs. Two major economies in East Asia – ASEAN and South Korea – are mentioned as the priorities for such negotiations. Secondly, the policy paper states that China would become 'the single greatest test' for the EU's trade policy, calling for a comprehensive trade strategy towards China.

---

7   See Article 207 of 'Consolidated Versions of the Treaty on European Union and the Treaty on the Functioning of the European Union', *Official Journal of the European Union*, 2008/C 115/01.

8   For details of the ordinary legislative procedure, see Article 294 of 'Consolidated Versions of the Treaty on European Union and the Treaty on the Functioning of the European Union'.

Thirdly, intellectual property, trade in services, foreign direct investment, public procurement and competition policy are quoted as 'new areas of growth' for the EU. Largely a re-bundling of the Singapore issues, these areas are supposed to play a major role in the pursuit of market access in third countries. Fourthly, the Commission promised a full review of trade defence instruments – that is, anti-dumping duties, anti-subsidy measures and safeguards – after a public consultation. As it turned out, the Global Europe strategy has had a profound impact on the Common Commercial Policy.

There is no doubt that the Global Europe strategy was a direct response to surging imports from East Asia. Not only did the timing of its adoption coincide with the controversial anti-dumping case against China and Vietnam, but its policy proposals sought to address the broader challenges resulting from the growing influences of East Asian economies. By the end of 2005 total East Asian exports to the European market reached 443.8 billion US dollars, more than twice as high as in 1999. Though China played a significant part in this, almost every country in East Asia exported substantially more products to the European market between 1999 and 2005 than previously (see Figures 4.1 and 4.2). The most effective way to balance out the surging inflow of East Asian products was to expand EU exports. To reach this goal, the Global Europe strategy highlighted the importance of seeking market access, negotiating bilateral FTAs and dealing with the rise of China. Curiously enough, Japan was almost absent in the Global Europe strategy. The strategy neither mentioned the EU's trade deficit with Japan, nor singled out Japan as a potential target for bilateral trade deals. Apparently, it was the emerging economies in East Asia that caught the attention of the EU in 2006.

While the Global Europe strategy was intended to respond to the trade balance crisis with East Asia, it also sought to resolve broader internal ideological and institutional divisions over commercial policy. The trade disputes between the two regions led to a fierce debate between the northern liberal and southern protectionist EU member states. Underlying the debate were the divergent interests of European producers, retailers and importers, all of whom fiercely lobbied their respective national governments. How to avoid a similar situation in the future was a second major concern of the Global Europe strategy. Two concrete proposals were put forward. First, the European Commission initiated an internal review of its trade defence instruments. Second, it promised a public consultation in relation to the internal review. In a supplementary paper to the Global Europe strategy, the European Commission called for 'a stronger partnership … between the Commission, member states, and business, based on extensive public consultation' (European Commission 2006b: 2). The public consultation, held between December 2006 and March 2007, was 'the largest ever organized on the subject',[9] attracting a large number of responses from EU domestic producers, retailers, import organizations, consumer groups and trade unions. In addition,

---

9   This is based on the self-assessment of the European Commission. See the report 'Evaluation of the Responses to the Public Consultation on Europe's Trade Defence

the governments of EU member states and third countries also participated in the consultation. In total, 542 entities submitted contributions. Notwithstanding the modest reforms that followed, the large-scale consultation opened a new era of trade policy-making in the EU. By the end of the 2000s, public consultation had become an integral part of trade policy-making in the EU.

If the Global Europe strategy was an important milestone, the Treaty of Lisbon has brought another round of institutional reforms to the Common Commercial Policy. After some initial delays,[10] the Lisbon Treaty came into force in December 2009. The Treaty has comprehensively streamlined the legal and institutional structure of the EU (Piris 2010), but as far as the Common Commercial Policy is concerned, the Treaty has made three crucial changes to existing institutional arrangements (Woolcock 2010; see also Shu 2009). Firstly, the Common Commercial Policy has been placed within the framework of EU external action.[11] This requires trade policy-making to integrate more closely the foreign policy objectives of the EU. These objectives may involve issues such as support for democracy, the rule of law, and human rights, as well as concerns over environmental protection and sustainable development. Secondly, the exclusive competence of Common Commercial Policy has been extended to the areas of trade in services, the commercial aspects of intellectual property, and foreign direct investment. These were previously identified by the Global Europe strategy as the essential 'areas of growth' for Europe. By redefining them as falling within the exclusive competence of the EU, the Lisbon Treaty enhances the EU's capacity to take action in these policy areas. Thirdly, the EP has been granted an influential role in the trade policy-making process. It is now sharing decision-making power over trade legislation with the Council under the ordinary legislative procedure. In addition, the EP has won the right to be informed about ongoing trade negotiations, as well as the power to ratify (or block) trade deals that the EU concludes with third countries and regions.

The institutional reforms made possible by the Lisbon Treaty offered a good opportunity to reform the Common Commercial Policy. The EU's external trade strategy has long been accused of having too many objectives. The so-called 'trade and ...' agenda has long characterized the CCP (Baldwin 2006). For instance, trade and development are the key themes of the EU's trade relations with LDCs (Least Developed Countries). Yet when dealing with authoritarian regimes, the EU tends to stress human rights and democratic conditionality in its trade policy.

Instruments in a Changing Global Economy', available at http://trade.ec.europa.eu/doclib/docs/2007/november/tradoc_136846.pdf, accessed on 15 June 2013.

10   The Treaty of Lisbon was initially supposed to be ratified by all the member states in 2008. However, an Irish referendum rejected the Treaty on 12 June 2008. The ratification process was completed only after a second Irish referendum approved the Treaty on 2 October 2009.

11   See Part V, 'Consolidated Version of the Treaty on the Functioning of the European Union'.

As such, the Common Commercial Policy has rarely been a pure trade policy. By aligning external trade with the wider agendas of external action, the Lisbon Treaty makes it possible for the EU to formulate a holistic trade strategy towards third countries and regions.

Such a trade strategy is assisted by the expansion of EU exclusive competences to new policy domains. Trade in services, intellectual property rights and foreign direct investment are all areas where the EU possesses comparative advantages vis-à-vis trading partners. They also reflect the EU's 'deep' trade agenda concerning the Singapore issues. Because of the exclusive competence designated by the Lisbon Treaty, the EU is now able to handle these issues on behalf of the member states.

In addition, the trade negotiation power of the EU is enhanced under the Lisbon Treaty. According to the logic of two-level games, smaller domestic win-sets often bring extra bargaining advantages (Putnam 1988). Because the EP now shares legislative power with the Council, domestic interests may choose to lobby the EP to obtain access to EU trade policy-making. The newly established approval procedure by the EP further raises the ratification hurdle for EU trade negotiations. This may help the EU to seek better deals with trading partners.

These institutional and policy changes redefine the EU's trade relationship with East Asia in important ways. Most notably, the EU can no longer treat East Asia as a single economic entity. As non-commercial goals enter the policy-making process, the EU's trade relationship with East Asia must be subject to assessment of the politico-economic situation of individual countries. Depending on the overall conditions of trading partners, the EU is obliged to adopt corresponding trade policy positions. Meanwhile, the inclusion of the 'deep' trade agenda in the Common Commercial Policy demands the EU look beyond emerging economies in East Asia, and pay more attention to matured market economies such as Japan and South Korea. After all, only such countries have the institutional capacity to fulfil the EU's ambitions regarding the Singapore issues. Last but not least, the enhanced trade negotiation capacity also puts more pressure on the EU to seek high-quality deals with long-term trading partners.

Under the Lisbon framework, the European Commission soon launched a new trade policy guideline in November 2010. The guideline is entitled 'Trade, Growth and World Affairs: Trade Policy as a Core Component of the EU's 2020 Strategy' (European Commission 2010). Its aim is to set a new trade policy agenda for the EU between 2010 and 2015. Like its predecessor – the Global Europe strategy, the policy guideline has highlighted the important role of East Asia in the globalized world economy. Firstly, it suggests that the EU should seek more bilateral trade agreements with potential partners. One month before its publication (October 2010), the EU signed an FTA with South Korea following two years of intense negotiations. To deepen the EU's trade relations with East Asia, the guideline recommends more bilateral trade negotiations with individual ASEAN countries such as Singapore, Malaysia and Vietnam. Secondly, it calls for strategic partnerships with major trading partners. In addition to Russia and the US, China and Japan are considered the EU's main strategic targets for potential trade agreements, broad regulatory cooperation and market access for European business. Thirdly, in light of the Lisbon Treaty, the guideline recasts European investment policy as an integral part of the Common Commercial Policy, and proposes that the EU 'integrate investment protection [and] investment liberalization into ongoing trade negotiations'. Fourthly, the guideline stresses the importance of consultation in the light of the new institutional role of the EP. In concrete terms, public consultation will be extended to 'all new trade initiatives with a potentially significant economic, social or environmental impact'.

In short, the EU has speeded up reform of the Common Commercial Policy in the past decade. The Global Europe strategy in 2006, the Lisbon Treaty in 2009 and the trade policy guideline in 2010 all sought to revitalize the roles that the EU had played in international trade. Under the reformed Common Commercial Policy, the policy agenda has been reconsidered, the institutional settings have been restructured, and novel forms of public consultation and impact assessment have been implemented. These policy and institutional reforms were closely related to the unprecedented challenges that East Asia posed for the EU. How these reforms transformed the EU's trade strategy towards the Far East is the focus of the next section.

Between Deals and Disputes: Three Balancing Acts

The institutional and policy reforms of the Common Commercial Policy have had a considerable impact on the trade relationship between Europe and East Asia. On the one hand, the EU has made substantial progress in pursuing FTAs with trading partners in East Asia. 'New generation' bilateral FTAs were successfully concluded with South Korea (in 2011) and Singapore (in 2012). The EU also launched FTA negotiations with Japan, Malaysia, Vietnam and Thailand. Though Japan only emerged recently as a negotiation partner, the EU–Japan FTA may possibly be the next bilateral FTA that the EU will conclude in East Asia. On the other hand, several high-profile trade disputes have put great strain on the bilateral trade relationship. In particular, as environment-friendly products such as solar panels and energy-saving light bulbs came under the spotlight, the EU experienced more frequent internal divisions with regard to the multiple implications of surging imports from East Asia. How can we make sense of these two seemingly contradictory trends in the trade relationship between the EU and East Asia?

Bilateralism vs Regionalism

First, the EU's trade strategy towards East Asia has been caught between the desire to establish region-to-region trade connections and the reality of entrenched bilateral trade relations. As the most advanced regional organization, the EU has been keen to export the European model of regional cooperation and integration to the rest of the world (Börzel and Risse 2012). Establishing region-to-region trade connections is perceived as an essential way to promote the EU model. When the EU moved away from the WTO platform in the mid-2000s, one of the alternatives was to pursue region-to-region trade liberalization. In line with the Global Europe strategy, the EU initially made it a priority to launch trade negotiations with ASEAN and Mercosur, key regional groupings in East Asia and Latin America (European Commission 2006a: 16). However, the region-to-region format of trade liberalization turned out to be very difficult to achieve. Unlike the EU, many regional groupings are based on geo-political concerns rather than economic connections (see Fawcett and Hurrell 1995). The intra-regional variations in economic development and political structure between different member states make it hard, if not impossible, for the EU to adopt a unified approach to such trade negotiations. The problem is further exacerbated by the lack of institutional capacity of these regional organizations (see Acharya and Johnston 2007).

In the case of EU–ASEAN trade talks, the four least developed member states – Vietnam, Cambodia, Myanmar and Laos – were excluded from the start of negotiations in 2007. Even so, EU negotiators found it difficult to deal with the diversity among the remaining ASEAN countries. ASEAN is still attempting to build the ASEAN Economic Community by 2015, and therefore lacked the institutional competence to coordinate activities within and between its member states. Facing these problems, the EU decided to abandon (at least temporarily) the region-to-region approach in March 2009. Later that year, it moved to pursue bilateral trade agreements with individual ASEAN economies. The bilateral approach bore its first fruit when the EU successfully concluded an FTA with Singapore in December 2012. At present, the EU is pursuing additional bilateral trade deals with three other ASEAN countries: Malaysia, Vietnam and Thailand.

The most notable bilateral trade agreement between the EU and an East Asian country is the EU–Korea FTA.[12] South Korea is the EU's tenth largest trade partner, and the EU is South Korea's fourth largest export market. Based on mature trade relations, the EU–Korean FTA was the first major achievement following the reorientation of the EU's trade liberalization strategy to bilateral platforms. The first of its kind, the EU–Korea FTA negotiation was launched in 2007, and after nearly two years' intense negotiations, a deal was finally reached on 6 October 2010. The EU–South Korea FTA is significant because the agreement is the biggest bilateral FTA ever concluded by the EU. It stipulates that the EU remove 99 per cent of its tariffs against Korean products and South Korea eliminate 96 per cent of its tariffs against the EU over a period of three years. More significantly, the bilateral FTA addresses most of the unresolved Singapore issues. After the failed Cancun Ministerial Meeting of the WTO, the EU made the decision to pursue the Singapore issues through bilateral FTAs. This approach was first announced in the

---

12   For details of the EU–Korea FTA, see 'Free trade Agreement between the European Union and Its Member States, of the One Part, and the Republic of Korea, of the Other Part', *Official Journal of the European Union*, 14 May 2011, L127.

'Global Europe' strategy in 2006. The trade policy guideline in 2010 also highlights the importance of the 'new generation of bilateral trade agreements' (European Commission 2010: 9). The EU–South Korea FTA has not only established rules concerning market competition, state aid, intellectual property rights and public procurement, but also included specific articles dealing with labour standards and environmental protection.

Encouraged by these substantial achievements of the EU–Korean FTA, the EU launched another ambitious trade negotiation with Japan in 2013 after some initial hesitation. At present, Japan is the EU's second largest trading partner in East Asia. A potential EU–Japan FTA will certainly be the next milestone towards closer trade relations between the two regions. On the one hand, Japan has been keen to reach a deal with the EU to reduce the trade diversion impacts resulting from the EU–Korean FTA. On the other hand, the EU followed its successful strategy in the Korean case, and pushed Japan hard for the removal of non-tariff trade barriers and the opening of the public procurement market in bilateral negotiations.

While the bilateral platform of trade negotiations gained support in Europe, it has not solved the long-term problem of a trade deficit between the EU and East Asia. Admittedly, two years after the conclusion of the EU–Korea FTA, the EU's trade deficit with South Korea fell from 16.7 billion US dollars in 2010 to 3.2 billion in 2012 (see Figure 4.3). A potential EU–Japan FTA may produce a similar result. Nevertheless, this reduction of the EU-Korean trade deficit resulted not only from growing EU exports to the Korean market, but also reflected weakened demand for imported Korean goods in the EU. Similar trends also shaped the

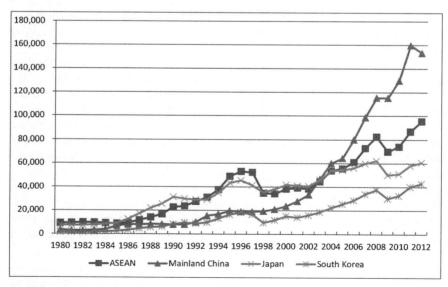

Figure 4.4 EU exports to East Asia 1980–2012

EU's trade with other East Asian economies after the outbreak of the European sovereign debt crisis in 2009 (see Figures 4.1 and 4.4). Between 2010 and 2012 the EU's trade deficits with China, Japan and ASEAN shrank by 26.2, 17.5 and 8.0 billion US dollars respectively. And yet, EU-Asian trade as a whole continued to generate a very large deficit of 260.6 billion US dollars in 2012.

Trade Protection vs Market Access

Importantly, the EU's trade strategy towards East Asia is facing a second challenge of balancing between protecting domestic producers and seeking overseas markets. Many of the trade disputes between Europe and East Asia resulted from evolving multinational production and the globalized value chains such production creates. Take the example of the EU–China trade dispute over energy-saving light bulbs. In 2001 the EU imposed an anti-dumping duty as high as 66.1 per cent against the energy-saving light bulbs made in China. The duties were due to expire in 2006, but the European light-bulb industry requested an expiry review to determine whether or not to extend the duties for another five years. In late 2006 and early 2007 the EU was trying to expand the use of green technology and improve energy efficiency in Europe. In response, the European Lamp Companies Federation issued an ambitious plan to phase out inefficient incandescent lamps in June 2007. Amid the heated debate about the future of the European lamp industry, the anti-dumping duty against energy-saving light bulbs came under the spotlight. Many demanded that the duty be abolished. However, the major light bulb manufacturers in Europe were sharply divided on the issue. On the one side, the Dutch light bulb producer Philips, together with GE and Sylvania, demanded an end to the anti-dumping duty. This was because a large proportion of their products were already manufactured in China by then. On the other side, the German light bulb producer Osram pushed for the continuation of the duty, mainly due to its smaller use of China-based production. When the member states of the EU were invited by the European Commission to cast a vote on the issue in July, 10 countries voted in favour, nine voted against and the other eight were undecided. According to media reports, Germany was one of the most vocal supporters of the duty.[13] At last, the European Commission reached a compromise solution in August 2007, recommending only a one-year extension of the anti-dumping duty so that 'EU companies can adjust to new patterns of production and trade'.[14] The duty was formally lifted in October 2008.

As a recent Commission document notes, '[t]he fundamental changes in global supply chains mean [the EU] needs to look more closely at where value is added to products and less at where exports are booked' (European Commission 2012a:

---

13   See 'EU States Divided Over Energy Saving Light Bulbs', *EUobserver*, 27 July 2007, http://euobserver.com/news/24541, accessed on 15 June 2013.

14   See the European Commission press release on 29 August 2007, IP/07/1261, http://europa.eu/rapid/press-release_IP-07-1261_en.htm?locale=en, accessed on 15 June 2013.

6). With the growing importance of regional production networks, East Asian countries have become more regularly involved in joint regional production. Intra-regional economic integration makes it more difficult for individual bilateral FTAs to resolve the overall trade imbalance between the EU and East Asia. Further complications are brought by European manufacturers, importers and retailers who have created their own global value chains that involve East Asia. In the dispute on energy-saving light bulbs, when Philips opened its Chinese factory to produce light bulbs for the European market, it effectively established a global value chain that relies on both Dutch technologies and Chinese labour. As a result, the anti-dumping duty not only hurt Chinese exports to the EU, but also reduced the profit margins of the Dutch company. The attempt to protect domestic producers turned out to be in contradiction with the interests of many EU businesses.

The recent trade dispute over Chinese-produced solar panels offers another vivid example of the dilemma that the EU faces in its trade strategy towards East Asia. In September 2012 the European Commission launched an investigation against Chinese solar panel producers for alleged product dumping on the EU market. The case was significant because the EU imported nearly 21 billion euros worth of solar panels from China in 2011. As the European Commission moved to impose provisional duties nine months later,[15] the case again seriously divided the member states. According to one *Reuters* report, 15 EU members claimed that they opposed the anti-dumping duty, six members confirmed their support, while the other six did not express a clear opinion.[16] Among the opponents of the anti-dumping duty were Germany, Britain, Sweden and the Netherlands. It was widely believed that the major concern of these countries was the potential loss of their access to the lucrative Chinese market. Indeed, soon after the provisional solar panel duty was imposed, China announced a plan to launch separate anti-dumping and anti-subsidy investigations against wines exported from the EU.[17] The Chinese market has become hugely important for the European wine industry in recent years. With an increasingly affluent middle class, Chinese imports of European wines increased by more than 300 per cent between 2009 and 2012. Imports of Bordeaux wine alone soared 110 per cent in 2011. Although the solar panel and wine cases were pursued separately by the two sides, EU officials

15   The European Commission decided to impose an initial anti-dumping duty of 11.8 per cent against solar panels produced in China, in June 2013. The duty was much lower than the 67.9 per cent that the Commission had threatened to impose. For more details, see Commission Regulation (EU) No 513/2013, 4 June 2013, *Official Journal of the European Union*, L152, 5–47.

16   See the *Reuters* report on 30 May 2013 'Chinese Media Rejects Accusation of Pressure on EU in Solar Row', http://www.reuters.com/article/2013/05/30/us-china-eu-solar-idUSBRE94S07620130530, accessed on 15 June 2013.

17   The anti-dumping and anti-subsidy investigation was formally launched on 1 July 2013. See the Chinese Ministry of Commerce (MOFCOM) Announcement Nos. 36 and 37 of 2013, http://www.mofcom.gov.cn/article/b/e/201307/20130700181495.shtml, accessed on 1 August 2013.

publicly admitted that any agreement over the solar panel case would help defuse the wine debate.[18] Once again, the EU was trapped between the twin goals of trade protection and market access in dealing with East Asia.

Economic Interests vs Foreign Policy Goals

Besides the balancing acts of regionalism vs bilateralism and trade protection vs market access, the EU's trade strategy towards East Asia is confronted with a third task: that of attempting to pursue both economic interests and foreign policy goals simultaneously. In many ways, the EU's trade policy-making has never been a purely economic issue (Baldwin 2006). Under the Lisbon Treaty, the Common Commercial Policy is for the first time formally integrated into the external action of the EU; together with development cooperation and humanitarian aid, trade policy-making is required to reflect the overall foreign policy objectives of the EU. According to Article 21 of the consolidated Treaty on European Union, such objectives may involve consolidating and supporting democracy, the rule of law, human rights and the principles of international law; preserving peace, preventing conflict and strengthening international security; fostering sustainable economic, social and environmental development; the progressive abolition of restrictions on international trade; and promoting an international system based on multilateralism and good governance. As these non-commercial policy goals are taken into account, the EU's trade relations with East Asia have shown some subtle changes.

As an institutional arrangement, the European Commission has strengthened the internal coordination between DG Trade and DG External Relations. For example, when the EU was preparing for negotiations with China on a Partnership and Cooperation Agreement (PCA) in 2006, DG Trade and DG External Relations jointly released two policy papers: one on trade and investment, and another on bilateral relations.[19] These two policy documents dealt with a wide range of EU positions on the bilateral relationship, covering not only economic and commercial topics but also political, development and environmental issues. These two documents eventually formed the bases of the EU's ongoing PCA negotiations with China.

In terms of policy orientation, the European Commission appears to have divided East Asian countries into different categories and adopted specific policy agendas towards each of them. DG Trade documents usually place China in the same category with Russia (European Commission 2010, 2012c). Just like

---

18   See the *Reuters* report on 21 June 2013 'Any China Solar Panel Pact Would Help Defuse Wine Spat: EU Official', http://uk.reuters.com/article/2013/06/21/uk-china-eu-trade-idUKBRE95K0IP20130621, accessed on 1 August 2013.

19   The two Commission documents are 'EU-China: Closer Partnership and Growing Responsibility', COM(2006) 632 final, and 'A Policy Paper on EU-China Trade and Investment: Competition and Partnership', COM(2006) 631 final.

the EU's trade policy towards Russia, the immediate goal of EU–China trade relations is to conclude a bilateral PCA. Meanwhile, Japan is often associated with the US in the EU's external trade strategy, perhaps because of the sizeable and sophisticated economic systems that the two countries possess. Based on the successful experience of the EU–Korea FTA, the EU has decided to pursue bilateral FTA negotiations with both Japan and the US. Less controversially, ASEAN countries are put into the same category of 'emerging Asia', towards which the EU has adopted a simultaneous bilateral and regional policy agenda. It is difficult to ascertain the extent to which these artificially categorized groups reflect the overall economic interests of the EU. No doubt, non-commercial factors have played a part in defining the EU's trade policy towards individual East Asian countries. Yet, East Asia has become ever more economically integrated during the past two decades. Without an economically-oriented regional policy agenda, the EU will probably face more difficulties in managing its trade relationship with East Asia.

In summary, the EU's trade policy towards East Asia has shown some noticeable changes under the reformed policy and institutional framework. A rigorous agenda was set out for bilateral trade liberalization with East Asian economies. The EU increased the use of trade defence instruments to check surging imports. Non-commercial factors were also taken into account in the trade decision-making process. Nevertheless, the EU still faces several challenges in dealing with East Asia. First, the emphasis on bilateral trade liberalization has not reduced the desirability of a regional approach. Second, the goal of protecting domestic producers has clashed with the demand for foreign investment and access to overseas markets. Third, foreign policy goals have not always been in line with the economic interests of the EU. On the whole, the EU's trade strategy towards East Asia is confronted with three balancing acts: bilateralism vs regionalism, trade protection vs market access, and economic interests vs foreign policy goals.

It is worth noting that how the EU handles these balancing acts could directly influence its trade relationship with Japan. As the EU has come to put greater emphasis on bilateral trade deals, the importance of Japan has risen considerably in the EU's trade strategy towards East Asia. Between the two sides, trade protection and market access remain the major obstacles to successful trade negotiations. Nevertheless, it is equally possible that a final trade deal between the EU and Japan would be concluded based on political rather than economic considerations.

Conclusion

One and a half decades after experiencing a regional financial crisis, East Asia has not only recovered from the crisis but has grown to play a much more important role in the world economy. Between Europe and East Asia, vibrant trade connections have led to an ever closer economic relationship. Nevertheless, the increasing exchange of goods, capital and services between the two regions has not been without tensions. With more East Asian products flooding into the European market, the EU faced unprecedented challenges with regard to its external trade policy. To deal with them, the EU has adopted three rounds of policy and institutional reform between 2006 and 2010. These reforms not only reshaped the Common Commercial Policy in a substantial way, but also redefined the EU's trade strategy towards East Asia.

This chapter shows that the growing clout of East Asia in its trade relationship with the EU has been closely related to the changing structure of regional production in the Far East. As Japan and the NIEs moved their production bases to neighbouring countries, the region's exports to Europe rose considerably. The rise of China and its importance as the assembly line for regional manufacturers further boosted East Asian exports to the EU. The result has been the rapid accumulation of a significant trade deficit on the EU side since the early 2000s. While surging Asian imports benefited European importers and retailers, domestic producers in the EU increasingly found themselves in competition with Asian products. The question of how to balance different domestic interests in Europe with a large trade deficit has emerged as a key issue for the Common Commercial Policy. As the debate continues, the EU has become internally divided between those who prefer protectionist trade defence measures and those who favour trade liberalization with East Asia.

To deal with these problems, several rounds of policy and institutional reform of the Common Commercial Policy have been undertaken. The Global Europe strategy was launched in 2006. As a major policy turn, it proposed that the EU launch bilateral trade negotiations with trading partners in East Asia. It also launched a review of the EU's trade defence instruments, with the aim of reconciling the interests of importers, retailers and producers in Europe. The Lisbon Treaty came into force in 2009, bringing with it important changes to the objectives, mandate and decision-making process of the Common Commercial Policy. Institutionally the EP has been granted co-legislative power in the trade policy-making process. Additional areas of exclusive competence such as foreign direct investment were introduced. The Common Commercial Policy has been further integrated into the external action of the EU. In 2010 the European Commission released another trade policy guideline entitled 'Trade, Growth and World Affairs'. In addition to a renewed call for bilateral FTAs and strategic partnerships with large key trade partners like Russia, China and Japan, the guideline highlights the roles of foreign direct investment in the EU's external trade policy.

These policy and institutional reforms had a substantial impact on the EU's trade strategy towards East Asia. Ever since the launch of the 'Global Europe' strategy, bilateral trade negotiations have dominated the EU's policy agenda towards Asia. Notably, the EU–Korea FTA was concluded in 2010; the EU–Singapore FTA was reached in 2012. The EU is currently involved in additional bilateral negotiations with Japan, Malaysia, Thailand and Vietnam to pursue even closer trade relations with East Asia. Together these initiatives marked a dramatic departure from the EU's long-term preference for multilateral trade liberalization through the

WTO. However, the EU continued to face serious internal divisions on how to cope with the surging imports of Asian products. In particular, trade disputes with China have not only divided European producers, importers and retailers, but also pitted EU member states against each other on several occasions. As more non-commercial objectives have an impact on the trade policy-making process after the Lisbon Treaty, the EU's trade policy towards East Asia has become more volatile. Essentially, the EU has been muddling through with regard to three balancing acts – bilateralism vs regionalism, trade protection vs market access and economic interests vs foreign policy goals – in dealing with East Asia. As the two sides of the Eurasian Continent move ever closer in economic terms, more complex and difficult challenges lie ahead.

Chapter 5

The Political and Institutional Significance of an EU–Japan Trade and Partnership Agreement

Frederik Ponjaert[1]

Introduction

The EU and Japan's vaunted status as like-minded civilian powers is systematically raised in view of their shared values, comparable political systems and overlapping societal challenges (Remacle and Ueta 2001; Vanoverbeke and Ponjaert 2007; Nakamura 2013; Keck, Vanoverbeke and Waldenberger 2013). However, the question whether such broad strategic convergences suffice to foster deeper cooperation has been a perennial one. Faced with growing competitive pressures from rising powers and the risk of marginalization (Ponjaert 2009; Vanoverbeke 2013) Brussels and Tokyo have sought to secure greater cooperation.

The Japan–EU Free Trade Agreement negotiations (JEUFTA) typify wider global trends favouring Preferential Trade Agreements (PTAs) and crystallize the issue of whether the EU–Japan partnership can tap into its unfulfilled potential (Vanoverbeke 2013: 329–38; Bacon and Kato 2013). JEUFTA is not a goal *per se* but rather a *means to an end*; it is a component of both partners' broader policy agendas, be they domestic or foreign policy ones (see Figure 5.1). To assess whether deeper cooperation is likely to occur between Japan and the EU, the following chapter will confirm the mainly domestic political-economic drivers of the current wave of PTAs, identify the respective agendas of the EU and Japan, explain the changing institutional environment, and explore the resulting politics.

---

1   The author wishes to acknowledge and thank those who through their thoughtful comments and suggestions have contributed towards the elaboration of this chapter. Special mention is to be made of this volume's editorial team, notably P. Bacon, as well as several colleagues, including J. Robberecht, H. Yoshizawa, S. Sato, S. Ahmed-Hassim and S. Ghislain.

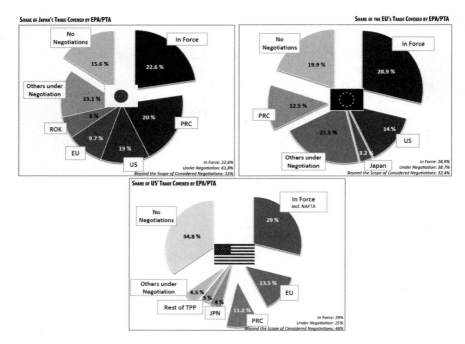

Figure 5.1 Share of trade covered by PTAs (January 2014)

The Context for JEUFTA: A Global Trend Driven by Domestic Factors

The sheer size of the economies involved makes any trade agreement between Japan and the EU of systemic importance. Together the EU and Japan represent over one third of global GDP. Although PTAs have proliferated since the 1990s (Messerlin 2012), until the early 2010s this mainly involved smaller economies (see Table 5.1). The push to see large economies conclude PTAs only started gathering steam following the 2008 economic crisis. Considering JEUFTA is part of this broader trend, one must assess whether the proliferation of such large-scale high-stakes PTAs is a reaction to inefficiencies in the global system, or the product of domestic political economies.

Table 5.1 Ongoing and concluded PTA negotiations involving the Quad (January 2014)

G20 Members	Share of Global GDP (%)	EU28	USA	China	Japan
EU28	26.6	N/A	Ongoing (TTIP)	–	Ongoing (JEUFTA)
USA	23.9	Ongoing (TTIP)	N/A	–	Ongoing (TPP)
China	9.6	–	–	N/A	Ongoing (RCEP)
Japan	9.0	Ongoing (JEUFTA)	Ongoing (TPP)	Ongoing (RCEP)	N/A
Brazil	3.4	Ongoing	–	–	–
India	2.8	Ongoing	–	Concluded	Concluded
Canada	2.6	Concluded	Concluded	–	Ongoing
Russia	2.4	–	–	–	–
Mexico	1.7	Concluded	Concluded	–	–
Korea	1.7	Concluded	Concluded	Initial stages	Ongoing
Australia	1.5		Concluded	Ongoing	Ongoing
Turkey	1.2	Concluded	–	–	–
Indonesia	1.2	Suspended	–	Concluded	Concluded
Saudi Arabia	0.7	Suspended	–	–	Ongoing
Argentina	0.6	Ongoing	–	–	–
South Africa	0.6	Concluded	–	–	–

The Global Trend towards Mega-PTAs

The long stalemate over the Doha Development Round has laid bare the multilateral trade system's inefficiencies. As the WTO proved unable to tackle new policy concerns, alternative negotiation platforms gained in prominence. The relative advantages attributed to bilateral or regional platforms are more straightforward and sheltered negotiations, a targeted approach to tariff reduction and a greater ease in broaching new topics. However, despite these efficiency claims, their perceived success rate is above all the product of a diminished patience for longstanding negotiations. The shorter political shelf-lives of PTAs means that ineffective bilateral or regional negotiations will more readily be abandoned than stalled multilateral ones.

PTAs have also been argued to be suited to broadening the liberalization agenda, since unfinished tariff cuts (UTCs), non-tariff barriers (NTBs), regulatory harmonization (RH) and joint standard-setting (JSS) are central to most PTAs. However, one cannot speak of a structural commitment, as most PTAs involve one large and one smaller country, where the former is in a privileged position to push its agenda in exchange for limited concessions (Laird 2002). The scope and efficiency of PTAs have proven highly unpredictable as they are defined by the stronger party's domestic agenda. Consequently, mega-PTAs, where none of the parties play a hegemonic role, are contingent on a fortuitous convergence in domestic agendas.

The Domestic Growth Agendas in Japan and Europe

With their focus on the nature of markets rather than merely on access to them, third generation trade agreements can impact both reform- or export-driven strategies.[2] This raises the question of how JEUFTA fits with European and Japanese agendas, and whether these agendas are compatible. A cursory overview of economic governance in Europe and Japan sees a shared concern for growth and budgetary imperatives; yet their respective long-term priorities are different (see Table 5.2). The European domestic agenda, as institutionalized in its post-crisis modes of governance (Héritier and Rhodes 2011; Rodrigues and Xiarchogiannopoulou 2014), enforces structural adjustment by way of restraint and hopes for export-driven growth. Conversely, Japan has settled on more expansionary adjustments labelled 'Abenomics', which seek enhanced competitiveness through structural reforms fuelled by consumption-friendly fiscal stimulus and monetary easing. JEUFTA dovetails with both of these agendas, and yet its expected usefulness differs. In Europe PTAs are expected to open new export markets through enforced regulatory reform (Meunier and Nicolaïdis 2006) or the fight against 'exporter discrimination' (Elsig and Dupont 2012: 501). In Japan they are a useful means of strengthening competitiveness through structural reform of production networks (Oyane 2004: 58) and the gradual removal of protective barriers in investment, services, standards and certifications (Munakata 2004). The decision to launch

---

2 Large economies can leverage PTAs to capture extra growth, either through additional exports or through efficiency gains. Later growth windfalls can arise as a result of improved domestic production born from economies of scale and heightened competition. More level playing fields for international trade also facilitate economic growth.

JEUFTA negotiations reflects a shared shift in favour of proactive trade policies; yet the respective outlooks of the EU and Japan do not coincide altogether.

Table 5.2 The EU and Japan's domestic growth agendas compared (2014)

	European Union	**Japan**
Growth Agenda	**Europe 2020 / Fiscal Compact**	**'Abenomics'**
Monetary Policy *(Instruments)*	Narrow *(Rate Cuts and Qualitative Easing)*	Expansive *(Quantitative and Qualitative Easing)*
Fiscal Policy *(Instruments)*	Restrictive *(European Semester)*	Expansionary *(Stimulus Packages)*
Budgetary Policy (*Instruments*)	Rapid Deficit Reduction *(Austerity Measures)*	Long-term Deficit Reduction *(Progressive Consumption Tax Hikes)*
Welfare Policy *(Instruments)*	Welfare Cuts *(Means Testing and Cost Reductions)*	Welfare Efficiency *(Universal Insurance and Expanded Fiscal Base)*
Trade Policy	**Global Europe (2006)**	**Extending the Frontiers to Growth through Global Linkages (2009)**
Access to Export Markets *(Underlying Focus)*	Primary Offensive Concern *(Securing the removal of discriminatory obstacles facing exports)*	Secondary Defensive Concern *(Favor targeted and managed liberalization to urge structural reforms)*
Domestic Market Reform *(Underlying Focus)*	Secondary Defensive Concern *(Ensure the preservation of the Common Market dynamics and its uniform principles)*	Primary Offensive Concern *(Securing the removal of discriminatory obstacles facing exports)*

The Agenda of JEUFTA: From Confrontation to Benign Neglect and Beyond?

A given partnership's agenda reflects the political strategies and institutional leeway of mobilized groups of domestic actors. Leading policy-makers will focus on expected contributions to the wider agenda, whereas bureaucracies will have a tendency to consider trade agendas as standalone realities. Vested interests will weigh on the proceedings in a variety of ways depending on their focus (either on economic or foreign policy interests) and their overriding outlook

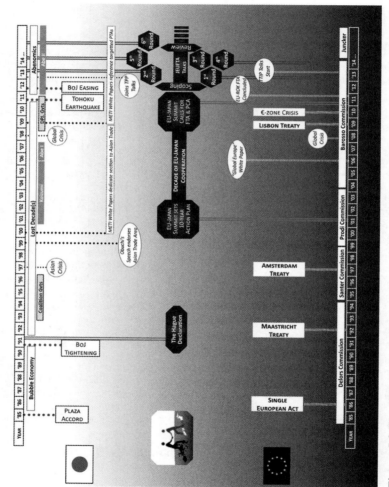

Figure 5.2 The EU–Japan partnership: a trade-centric timeline

(either offensive or protectionist). Lastly, parliamentary stances are a product of a deal's political optics, which can cultivate either benign neglect or reactive protectionism (Messerlin 2013). Jump-started in 1991 by the so-called 'Hague Declaration', the EU–Japan partnership's agenda is one of the first comprehensive bilateral relationships to see interactions between all of the mobilized actors fully institutionalized at the European level (see Figure 5.2).

Initially, bilateral contacts were born from mounting trade tensions (Ponjaert 2009: 255–6) with the initial decades characterized by recurring commercial and industrial disputes tied to Japan's massive trade surplus (Keck 2013a, 2013b). Trade and exchange rates have remained a core feature of the relationship (Bertoldi 2013), yet the 2001 '10-year Joint Action Plan' marked a shift away from conflict resolution in favour of cooperative policies and rhetorics (Rothacher 2013). The resulting 'Decade of EU–Japan Cooperation' identified a set of four shared strategic concerns[3] (Nakamura 2013: 204) and booked some notable sectoral achievements[4] (Ohta 2005a; Ponjaert 2009: 259; Hardy and Niepold: 2013). Nevertheless, as the decade came to a close both partners felt the relationship had not fully matured and further steps were needed. To this effect, an agreement was reached in 2011 on the desirability of both a Free Trade Agreement (FTA) and a Strategic Partnership Agreement (SPA).

From Scoping Exercises to Actual Negotiations

The 2001 Joint Action Plan already called for greater economic cooperation; yet because as earlier trade tensions remained in everyone's minds and years of unsuccessful talks on NTBs had drastically lowered expectations, far-reaching trade negotiations seemed uncertain. Nevertheless, JEUFTA suddenly became a possibility as two evolutions conspired to change both Japanese and European interest calculations: a strengthening of the partners' negotiation capacities, and the conclusion of the Korea-European Union Free Trade Agreement (ROKEUFTA).

The domino effect (Ravenhill 2010) set into motion by the conclusion of ROKEUFTA in July 2011 proved a major catalyst. Considering the similarities between the South Korean and Japanese economies, the obvious risk of trade diversions prompted then Prime Minister Noda to push for the opening of trade talks. The EU's reaction to the DPJ-led government's overture was initially rather cautious, as Europeans remained unconvinced by the ability of the Government of Japan (GoJ) to deliver on its promises. Ultimately, Brussels would come to strongly insist on an unusually thorough pre-negotiation phase.

---

3   (1) Promoting peace and security; (2) strengthening economic and trade partnership; (3) coping with global and social changes; (4) bringing together people and cultures.

4   For example a bilateral Mutual Recognition Agreement (MRA), a shared Trade Assessment Mechanism (TAM), a bilateral Climate Dialogue, an upswing in Science and Technology (S&T) cooperation agreements, and the Mutual Legal Assistance Agreement (MLA) which was the first legally binding agreement signed between Japan and the EU.

At the 2011 Joint Summit, two scoping exercises were launched, with a view to both clarifying the goals which were in play and assessing the GoJ's capacity to deliver on certain sensitive issues. Without even being assured that proper negotiations would follow, both parties proved remarkably committed to the process, and the scoping exercises were successfully completed in May/July 2012. Consequently, the Council green-lit official negotiations in November 2012, and JEUFTA was formally launched in March 2013. Doubts did however remain, as reflected in the EU's mandated interim assessment 12 months into the negotiations.

The first negotiation round left mixed feelings as it only confirmed the list of outstanding issues. The second round saw some progress made on public procurement, just as several industrial sectors started to express their support for JEUFTA. The third round gathered further steam as the 'two sides focused primarily on proposals for the text of the proposed pact. Topics addressed included trade in goods and services, technical barriers to trade and non-tariff measures, dispute settlement, and rules of origin' (International Centre for Trade and Sustainable Development 2013). The fourth round built on the growing momentum to broach new topics and 'fruitful discussions [continued] on areas such as trade in goods, trade in services, investment, intellectual property rights, non-tariff measures, government procurement and others' (METI/MOFA 2014) with a particular interest in eliminating NTBs in the Japanese rail sector (Messerlin 2014b) and abolishing EU tariffs on Japanese automobiles. According to Kyodo News, '[t]he two sides [had] agreed earlier to exchange proposals on scrapping or lowering tariffs at an early date. A senior Japanese government official ... said that they were striving to exchange offers by April [2014]' (*Kyodo News International* 2014). These offers were fleshed out during the fifth round, the last before the EU's mandated review at the end of the first year. Rather significantly, neither the EP nor the Council seized upon this unprecedented additional review to politicize or influence the negotiations. They simply endorsed DG Trade's expert opinion endorsing the progress made throughout rounds 1–5, and it was therefore possible to hold the sixth round in July 2014. JEUFTA's rhythm has proven comparable to other negotiations, thereby signifying continued commitment and a fairly routinized approach to the negotiations, be it with regards to the free trade agenda or its associated strategic partnership (see Figure 5.3).

The extensive scoping exercises pre-identified the key trade-related issues whereas the SPA, agreed upon in principle, ushered in a whole host of new issues which still had to be fleshed out. The FTA and SPA do make strange bedfellows, as the former is highly legal and regulatory in nature while the latter is political and principled in outlook.

The Free Trade Agenda: A Clearly Marked Path

A trade agreement will require a compact on: peak automobile tariffs, non-tariff barriers (NTB), regulatory harmonization (RH), public procurement (PP) and agriculture. With average tariffs on goods already very low, tackling NTBs is the

Number of Negotiation Rounds

	Round 1	Round 2	Round 3	Round 4	Round 5	Round 6	Round 7	Round 8	Round 9	Round 10	Rd.11	Rd.12	Rd.13	Rd.14	Rd.15	Rd.16
EU–Korea	Mar-07	Jul-07	Sep-07	Oct-07	Nov-07	Jan-08	May-08	Mar-09	Jul-09							
EU–Singapore	Mar-10	Jun-10	Sep-10	Nov-10	Jan-11	Mar-11	Jun-11	Oct-11	Jan-12	Mar-12	Jul-12					
EU–Canada	Oct-09	Jan-10	Apr-10	Jul-10	Oct-10	Jan-11	Apr-11	Jul-11	Oct-11	Mar-12	Apr-12	Sep-12	Oct-13			
TTIP	Jul-13	Nov-13	Dec-13	Mar-14	May-14	Jul-14	...									
EU–Japan (FTA)	Apr-13	Jun-13	Oct-13	Jan-14	Apr-14	Jul-14	...									
EU–Japan (SPA)	Apr-13	Jul-13	Oct-13	Jan-14	Jun-14	...										
JPN–Vietnam	Jan-07	Mar-07	Jun-07	Aug-07	Oct-07	Mar-08	Apr-08	Aug-08	Sep-08							
JPN–Swiss	Mar-07	May-07	Jul-07	Oct-07	Dec-07	Feb-08	May-08	Jun-08	Sep-08							
JPN–India	Jan-07	Apr-07	Jun-07	Aug-07	Jan-08	Apr-08	May-08	Jul-08	Sep-08	Oct-08	Jan-09	Sep-09	Apr-10	Sep-10		
JPN–Australia	Apr-07	Aug-07	Oct-07	Feb-08	Apr-08	Jul-08	Oct-08	Mar-09	Jul-09	Nov-09	Apr-10	Jan-11	Dec-11	Feb-12	Apr-12	Jun-12
JPN–Peru	May-09	Jul-09	Aug-09	Oct-09	Feb-10	Aug-10										
JPN–Canada	Nov-12	Apr-13	Jul-13	Nov-13	Mar-14	...										
RCEP	May-13	Sep-13	Jan-14	Apr-14	Jun-14	...										

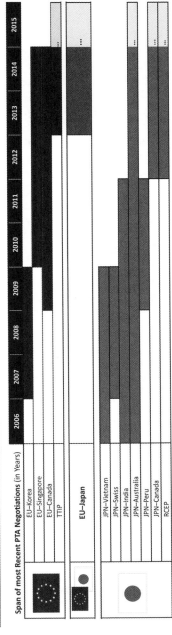

Figure 5.3 The rhythm of recent European and Japanese PTA negotiations (2014)

principled way to increase exports, which is intended to be the main contribution to the EU's domestic growth strategy. Accordingly, NTBs were thoroughly discussed during the scoping exercises and both partners decided to establish a precise list of 27 NTBs, along with roadmaps describing how to dismantle them. RH and cutting red tape are a shared concern; yet if the more ambitious 'unconditional mutual recognition' (UMR) remains an option, a broadening of the 2001 MRA seems more likely. In this respect, the strengthened legal and jurisprudential environment produced by such bilateral sectoral achievements as the MRA, the MLA or the growing number of bilateral social security agreements between Japan and European Member States is a familiar and broad enough basis for additional regulatory and legal convergence. Public procurement constitutes a more difficult chapter, as JEUFTA must tackle both the differences between *de jure* and *de facto* public procurement liberalization and the varying understandings of which products and services fall under this header. Finally, agriculture remains sensitive as it is heavily subsidized and protected on both sides. Deep liberalization is unlikely so the focus is on joint standard-setting, be it sanitary and phytosanitary measures (SPSs) or the thorny issue of regulatory competition between the 'geographical indications' system favoured by the EU and the 'trademark' system pushed by the US.

Given the results the EU secured in negotiations with South Korea, Singapore and Canada, it is a near certainty that the EU will seek comparable concessions from Japan as a bottom line. A narrower formula akin to Japanese EPAs concluded between 2002 and 2014 would not be acceptable, as it would not contribute in any significant way to the EU's growth agenda. Overall, JEUFTA's trade agenda hinges on striking a balance between advances on all non-tariff concerns listed in the scoping exercise, and tariff reductions in the politically sensitive European automotive sector.

The Strategic Partnership Agenda: An Opened-Ended Exploration

The SPA is set to cover cooperation in over 30 areas. It would see EU–Japan relations move from sectoral agreements to a comprehensive, binding and forward-looking framework. However, despite their comparable status as civilian powers, agreeing on the format and content of their political partnership has proven difficult. Opening up trade to outside considerations raises the risk of political instrumentalization and poses a range of legal and practical questions (Kleimann 2011: 10–11). Hitherto in this case hesitations are not value-based, they are the product of insufficient trust rooted in an absence of precedent and a lack of familiarity. Japanese officials have expressed unease with the exact nature of the SPA, wondering whether it is a political commitment similar to past joint declarations, or a legally binding one akin to the FTA with which it is associated. Europeans for their part are concerned with how to assuage the competitive tensions between the EEAS, which is responsible for external action's overall coherence, and DG Trade, which is charged with shepherding the FTA.

Several actors are reluctant to fully commit to a far-reaching political partnership piggy-backed onto an FTA. Both METI and DG Trade have a longstanding tradition of negotiations centred on technical discourses, focused agendas and quantifiable goals. As a result, broader political agendas are an uncomfortable fit and are often seen as a threat to the underlying trade agenda. Regardless, for historically entrenched reasons, both Tokyo and Brussels have embraced the rise of the strategic component in their increasingly comprehensive agenda.

Tokyo's frustrating experience with perceptions of 'chequebook diplomacy' during the first Gulf War crystallized burgeoning doubts about Japan's carefully crafted post-Second World War foreign policy compromise. This compromise combined a separation of politics and economics (*seikei bunri* – 政経分離) with a civilian power stance 'almost exclusively in the sense of being a non-military country focused on economic affairs' (Prime Minister's Commission on Japan's Goals in the 21st Century 2000: 10). Throughout the 1990s, innovations such as 'human security' (Remacle 2008) saw ever broader readings of Japan's diplomatic remit, without ever upsetting the foundational non-military principle. Functional links entrenched at that time, such as the instrumentalization of ODA for wider policy goals have remained ever since, yet deeper principles such as *seikei bunri* endured. The early 2000s proved a critical juncture as the Koizumi government reacted to changes in the country's regional environment by launching a fundamental reappraisal of its foreign policy principles in favour of 'a civilian power encompassing three of its principal functions: (1) engagement in security affairs; (2) involvement in global systems, particularly the international economic order; and (3) cooperation with developing countries' (Prime Minister's Commission on Japan's Goals in the 21st Century 2000: 10). This endogenous drive towards a more holistic and comprehensive international stance has accelerated as the exogenous pressures born from China's rise to prominence have increased. Both Abe governments have invested significant political capital to infuse Japan's diplomacy with a renewed sense of geo-strategic power balancing and geo-economic competitive triangulation, which has in turn further eroded the post-war compromise. The 'values-based diplomacy' introduced by Aso in 2006 made Japan more conspicuous (Fouse 2007) whereas the US-centric EPA strategy, driven forward by the Prime Minister's Office, has diluted *seikei bunri*, the Japanese separation of politics and economics. Overall, a largely normalized comprehensive foreign policy has emerged mobilizing the full range of possible instrumental issue-linkages (Hook, Gilson, Hughes and Dobson 2012: 70–74).

In Brussels, the original endogenous catalyst which floated the spectre of unavoidable interactions between politics and trade was the EC's legal incapacity under the Lomé III convention to terminate STABEX payments to Uganda, in response to gross human rights violations (Bartels 2005: 1–8). One must bear in mind that unlike a sovereign state, the EU has but limited political leeway to reinterpret its foreign policy resources beyond those set in the treaties. In the early 1990s the Chilean and Argentinian appeals in favour of human rights and democracy clauses proved further exogenous factors supporting the generalization

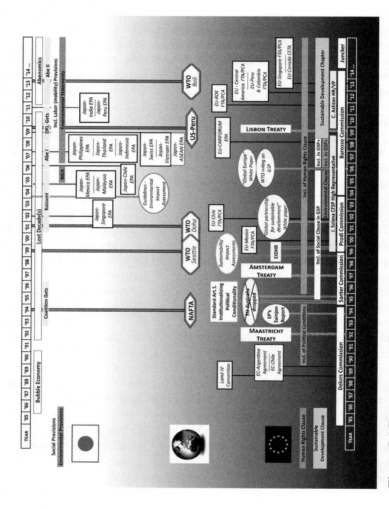

Figure 5.4 European and Japanese PTAs compared over time

of such clauses in EU agreements (European Commission 1993). Subsequently, the human rights and democracy agenda was rapidly entrenched as then Commissioner Brittan allowed trade negotiations with Australia to falter over Article 1 (Elijah, Murray and O'Brien 2000: 27) just as its inclusion was successfully secured in the EU–Mexico deal (Szymanski and Smith 2005: 183–4). Regardless of the target partner's development level or political regime (see Table 5.5) a standardized Article 1 included in the 'essential elements' has become a common basis for all of the EU's agreements.

Considering both actors' increasingly strategic motivations and the growing number of SPAs the EU has signed with both highly developed strategic partners and developing associate ones, binding agreements on fundamental rights, sustainable development and strategic cooperation cannot be discounted. This will require a whole set of new jointly managed institutional provisions geared towards trust-building, guaranteeing commitments and avoiding unwanted impositions.

The Set-Up for JEUFTA: An Experimental Institutional Framework

JEUFTA is being negotiated within an institutional environment characterized by policy paths honed over the past decade through a series of successfully concluded PTAs involving smaller partners (see Figure 5.4). Parallel institutional evolutions in Japan and Europe have sought greater efficiencies through a sharpening of bureaucratic resources, increased legitimacy through a re-balancing of leadership away from technocrats in favour of political actors, and coherence through strengthened issue-linkages.

The Reform Path Shaping Japan's Trade Negotiations

In Japan reforms launched by PM Koizumi (Shinoda 2004; Uchiyama 2010) saw a strengthening of the coordinating function of the Prime Minister's Office (PMO). Moreover, the 'new' politics ushered in by the 2009–2012 DPJ-led government continued the drift towards greater politicization. The DPJ identified 'a shift to politician-led politics from a bureaucrat-dominated one' as the first of five manifesto principles for the election (DPJ 2009). The Koizumi government's foray into intra-Asian EPAs would thus be expanded on following the DPJ's 2009 electoral victory, as their electoral programme stated they 'would promote negotiations on an FTA with the United States and advance trade and investment liberalisation' (DPJ 2009: 27). Eventually the Noda government approved the 'Basic Policy on Comprehensive Economic Partnership' which opened the way for negotiations with the EU. Subsequently, the LDP's 2012 programme stated that they would 'oppose Japan's participation in talks for any regional free trade pact if the elimination of all tariffs without exception is assumed to be an ironclad rule' (*Asahi Shimbun* 2012). However, the then freshly re-elected Prime Minster Abe (LDP) enjoyed enough political leeway to keep JEUFTA on course, while simultaneously launching the LDP's prized engagement with the TPP, by simply stating that the 'LDP had sufficient negotiating power to break through tariff abolition without exceptions'. On the whole, successive governance reforms have sought to tackle those components of Japan's 'domestic political structure discourag[ing] pro-active foreign-policy behaviour, ... most importantly the fragmented character of state authority' (Calder 1988: 528).

The increasingly presidential PMO proved instrumental in anchoring wider inter-ministry coordination. By 2004 Koizumi had ordered the institutionalization of regular meetings of the Directors-General of 14 FTA-related ministries under the Deputy Chief Cabinet Secretary, while also gathering 15 government agencies within the Council of Ministers on the Promotion of Economic Partnerships. According to Yoshimatsu (2007: 84) '[t]hese two institutions, [along with formal criteria identifying those countries/regions with which to negotiate], aimed to overcome miscommunication and bickering within the different governmental branches'. On this basis, the Council on Economic and Fiscal Policy (CEFP) under the Fukuda government drafted the '2008 Basic Policies for Economic and Fiscal Reform' identifying the EU as a negotiation target (Yoshimatsu 2012: 199). Ultimately, the 2009 METI White Paper would mark the full integration of Japan's trade policy into its wider domestic agenda, just as the DPJ-government dissolved the CEFP in favour of the more wide-ranging National Policy Unit (Yoshimatsu 2012: 210).

Alongside the PMO's near presidential leadership, both METI and MOFA were voicing more proactive stances (Yoshimatsu 2007: 84). The 2001 Central Government Reform saw the Ministry of International Trade and Industry (MITI) becoming the more all-encompassing Ministry of Economy, Trade and Industry (METI). Around this time the Ministry of Foreign Affairs (MOFA) published *Japan's FTA Strategy* (MOFA 2002) stating that 'unless we take a stance linking FTAs to economic reforms in Japan, we will not succeed in making them a means of improving the international competitiveness of Japan as a whole'. If the 2000s witnessed a continued convergence between METI and MOFA, slight variations remained. From 2000 onwards METI's annual white papers would prioritize a concerted effort in favour of Asian market integration (Yoshimatsu 2007: 85–6), whereas MOFA favoured bilateral negotiations with high political returns – for example South Korea, Mexico or Singapore.

On the whole, these institutional shifts allowed for more pro-active and less fragmented foreign policy-making, yet a preference for presidential-style solutions (Shinoda 2004) saw successive governments shy just short of creating an independent administrative authority able to promote PTAs. This stands in contrast with DG Trade's role or the one acquired in 1998 by Korea's Office of the Ministry of Trade (OMT). As a result, political decisiveness on the part of the PMO has become and remains essential to the GoJ's reinforced but not yet autonomous trade promotion machinery.

The Reform Path Shaping European Trade Negotiations

European institutional reforms have equally sought to foster greater political acumen and coherence with regards to the EU's external action (Telò and Ponjaert 2013) and economic governance (Sapir et al. 2004; Molle 2011). Growing politicization has been a long-term trend in the EU's Common Commercial Policy (CCP). First, the Amsterdam Treaty saw a strengthening of the Member States' influence through the delegation and oversight mechanisms controlled by the Council (Meunier and Nicolaïdis 1999: 499). Subsequently, the Lisbon Treaty (TFEU) would see an increase in the European Parliament's sway with regards to oversight and consent (Kleimann 2011: 13–15). As a result, if DG Trade's autonomy as sole negotiator was not significantly impeded upon, its actions were more clearly framed, as the Council retained sole control over a toughened mandate procedure, and the EP saw its oversight and consent privileges increase.

Concomitantly, the TFEU also saw DG Trade's outlook broadened, as trade policy was integrated into the EU's overall external action agenda and its remit widened as services, TRIPs and FDI became largely exclusive EU competences (TFEU, Article 207). These reforms sought to alleviate institutional and legal fragmentation. To favour its preferred comprehensive rules agenda (Woolcock 2013: 212), the TFEU abolished the three-pillar structure, according to which several types of competence had been superimposed and their related acts adopted using distinct procedures. The resulting EU with a single legal personality and a unified set of legislative procedures allowed for more coherence. While DG Trade has welcomed the broadening of its exclusive remit, the EP and Council welcomed the resulting 'mixed agreements' covering both exclusive and shared competences, seeing that as a whole they are negotiated by DG Trade yet crafted by way of the 'ordinary legislative procedure' involving all three of the EU's legislative bodies.[5]

Conceptually, the TFEU seeks to tackle a 'five-tier understanding of coherence that includes vertical, horizontal, inter-pillar, rhetorical, strategic and external engagement' (Mayer 2013: 105). Institutional provisions, notably with regards to trade, have thus been conceived of to foster positive connections in several of these tiers. The creation of the EEAS and the generalization of the ordinary legislative procedure are intended to prompt greater rhetorical, strategic and horizontal convergence. Strengthened conditionality and implementation mechanisms are set to improve vertical and external coherence. Institutional innovations championed by the EU in trade negotiations – the inclusion of an SPA; the involvement of the EEAS; increased parliamentary oversight; the inclusion of human rights and sustainable development; or formal monitoring, implementation and dispute settlement provisions – are all the product of the EU's quest to go beyond the 'consistency' – that is, absence of contradictions – called for in the Maastricht Treaty (Tietje 1997) in favour of the TFEU's goal of greater 'coherence' – that is, signifying positive connections.

---

5   The Commission, Council and Parliament.

Changes centred on strategic, rhetorical or horizontal coherence have fostered shifting power balances within the EU's internal machinery (Carta 2013). Conversely, those innovations seeking vertical and external coherence through tougher conditionality have drawn non-EU partners into a web of obligations which have proven quite controversial. Seen from Brussels obligations such as those born from 'the EU's human rights clauses and sustainable development chapters are not simply a matter of discretionary foreign policy [but] mechanisms that in theory enable [it] to comply with its [treaty] obligations' (Bartels 2012: 17). Partners, however, invariably experience these clauses as extraordinary incursions into their national sovereignty, posing unprecedented legal questions. The EU's comprehensive and integrated approach has thus compelled Japan's Cabinet Legislation Bureau to explore and clarify its understanding of the suspension clause and all associated legal obligations to make sure the agreement conforms to Japan's own internal order.

In this respect it is important to note that if the inclusion of these measures is a necessity for the EU, there is room for joint interpretation. In practice 'the EU falls short in virtually all respects of what is legally possible under these clauses' (Bartels 2012: 7) and sees their enforcement checked by so-called 'appropriate measures' where 'priority must be given to measures that least disrupt the functioning of the agreement [and where] any suspension clause would be a measure of last resort' (Bartels 2012: 7). A further reassurance is the fact that the EU has never triggered unilateral enforcement mechanisms outside of the Cotonou Agreement, and that it has developed a gradualist approach to any form of sanctions (Portela 2010). Finally, even if blanket exceptions to these clauses are unthinkable, the EU has proven amenable to a certain margin of interpretation, notably in collaboration with partners who are able and willing to argue the redundancy of certain enforcement mechanisms within the specific context of a given relationship. Overall, these caveats support a favourable reading of the EU's use of these clauses as an approach preferring constructive ambiguity (Hoffman 1995: 131) over damaging instrumentalization.

The Politics of JEUFTA: Restless Parliaments and Widening Agendas

Bearing in mind the strengthened institutional context for negotiations in Japan and the EU (see Table 5.3), the main risk is to see the human resources, policy expertise and time invested in JEUFTA progressively deployed elsewhere. As both TTIP and TPP are moving ahead, the number of mega-PTAs the EU and Japan can simultaneously negotiate remains unclear. Furthermore, in Japan a lack of manpower risks being compounded by a relative loss of expertise as the members of the negotiating team and associated working groups rotate too much, and change composition more than has been the case on the European side (see Table 5.4). This stretches civil servants too thinly and a lack of continuity can impede the socialization mechanisms which habitually contribute towards greater trust. This

Table 5.3 The improved institutional context for the negotiation of PTAs within both Japan and the EU

	Japan		European Union	
	Early 2000s	**Early 2010s**	**Early 2000s**	**Early 2010s**
Strategic Coherence	**Weak** Isolated MITI Low-profile PMO	**Strong** Presidential-Style Leadership of PMO	**Weak** Distance b/w supranational trade policy and intergovernmental CFSP	**Stronger** *(if more complex)* Creation of the High Representative and the EEAS alongside DG Trade
Vertical Coherence	**Weak** Isolated MITI + no relays to domestic implementation	**Stronger** Regular meetings of the Directors-General of 14 FTA-related ministries under the Deputy Chief Cabinet Secretary	**Weaker** Disconnect between strong legal mechanisms of the common market, and external impotence	**Stronger** Mainstreaming of the conditionality clauses, empowering the EU to act internally and externally
Horizontal Coherence	**Weak** Isolated MITI + opposition from other ministries	**Strong** 15 Agencies gathered in the Council of Ministers on the Promotion of Economic Partnerships	**Weaker** Conflicting competences and procedures between the various pillars	**Stronger** Greater remit of DG Trade and the use of mixed agreements
Rhetorical Coherence	**Weak** Isolated MITI	**Stronger** PMO/METI/ MOFA convergences BUT no autonomy in negotiations	**Strong** *(if isolated)* Clear negotiation mandate and authority for DG Trade	**Strong** *(less isolated)* Unchanged mandate for DG Trade, but inclusion of a new voice: the EEAS
Inter-pillar Coherence	N/A		**Circumstantial** Intergovernmental coordination through the Council	**Political** Unification under the Ordinary Legislative Procedure sees oversight shared by Council and EP

leaves only political arbitration as a stalemate breaker, which can alternatively come from the parliamentary or executive forces at play.

Table 5.4 Stewardship of the Japanese and European negotiating teams

JEUFTA Negotiation Round	Japanese Delegation	European Delegation
Round 1 Brussels, Belgium, 15 /19 Apr. 2013	**S.E.M Jun YOKOTA –** Chief Negotiator (MOFA – and Special Representative for JEUFTA)	
Round 2 Tokyo, Japan 24 June – 3 July 2013	**M. Hirofumi KATASE** (METI – Industrial Science and Technology Policy and Environment Bureau)	**M. Mauro PETRICCIONE** FTA Chief Negotiator
Round 3 Brussels, Belgium 21/25 Oct. 2013	**S.E.M Jun YOKOTA –** Chief Negotiator (MOFA – and Special Representative for JEUFTA) **M. Shigehiro TANAKA** (METI – Director-General, Multilateral Trade System Department)	DG Trade – Director for Asia and Latin America, Directorate General for Trade, the European Commission **M. Viorel Isticioaia BUDURA** SPA Chief Negotiator
Round 4 Brussels, Belgium 27/31 Jan. 2014	**S.E.M. Yasumasa NAGAMINE** – Chief Negotiator (MOFA – Deputy Minister for Foreign Affairs)	EEAS – Managing Director for Asia and the Pacific, the European External Action Service
Round 5 Tokyo, Japan 31 Mar. – 4 Apr. 2014	**M. Shigehiro TANAKA** (METI – Director-General, Multilateral Trade System Department)	
Round 6 Tokyo, Japan 7 June – 11 July 2014		

An Increased Role for Parliaments in Trade Agreements

The EU–Japan partnership, one between two mature democracies, has always had a vibrant parliamentary dimension (Jarzembowski 2013). Parliamentary exchanges have occurred since the 1970s and have mainly focused on two sets of issues: values and trade. Throughout the 1990s and early 2000s, as trade conflicts receded, parliamentary diplomacy and its associated resolutions were increasingly focused on values-related issues. This proved a fertile environment for far-reaching agreement between the EP and the Diet as they shared a common commitment to multi-party democracy, the rule of law and human rights. Only two points of contention would remain between both chambers: the death penalty and whaling (Jarzembowski 2013: 285). On trade, the US legislative branch has historically stood out as uniquely potent, prompting other parliaments to increase their roles in the name of greater transparency and political awareness. In this respect, European and Japanese legislators have chosen different strategies. The EP has advocated *de jure* reform of the CCP, to see it awarded a formal role as a recognized agent of any trade negotiations involving the EU (Leal-Arcas 2010). Conversely, Diet members have not sought new powers but have rather relied on more informal political levers and historically-biased electoral districting to weigh on the GoJ rather than act as an agent in the negotiations themselves. Parliamentary dynamics are therefore crucial in determining whether JEUFTA will muster the necessary political impetus to overcome existing obstacles, or whether it will come to face unsurmountable political hurdles.

Following the TFEU the EP acquired similar adoption, oversight and implementation prerogatives to the US Senate (Kleimann 2011: 4–8). The EP can now take down a trade agreement, as it did when rejecting the Anti-Counterfeiting Trade Agreement (ACTA). At the time of the TFEU's drafting, uncompromising opposition from the EP to an agreement put forward by the Commission and carried by the Council seemed a rather remote possibility, but the EP has since repeatedly proven its intentions to seek an altered power balance. The ROKEUFTA was the first agreement to arrive on the EP's docket under the new rules, and it was expected to simply endorse or reject the proposal, as this is what 'giving its consent' had meant. However, in response to intense lobbying by the European automotive sector the EP decided to vote for a second resolution including safeguards measures in the automobile sector. The EP held its ground and withheld consent until the Council caved in. Korean objections notwithstanding, a compromise had to be found, and eventually a new settlement was reached when both resolutions were ratified. The EP had won its first trade skirmish.

Reflecting JEUFTA's low political salience, the seventh European Parliament saw only 8 JEUFTA-related votes. Nonetheless, as part of its jostling with the Council, the EP was quick to organize itself on JEUFTA. It insisted on giving an opinion on the draft mandate even before the Council vote. Again, the EP was actively interpreting the TFEU in its favour by asserting an unprecedented move. The resolution's impact on the mandate itself is uncertain, but the EP's position was clearly known and an important precedent was set. It is a given that the Commission had better anticipate the EP's demands as the agreement will have to gather a majority, both in standing committees such as those for foreign affairs and international trade, and at the plenary level.

Illustration 5.1 Japanese Communist Party anti-TPP campaign poster

Meanwhile, Japan's Diet has not seen its formal oversight and adoption roles altered, but increased politicization of trade issues has seen a shift in parliamentary practices. Alternating political leadership, the relative 'bureaucratic Glasnost' brought about by the 2001 national information disclosure law (Kingston 2011: 68), the political salience of the concomitant TPP negotiations, and the political weight given to rural constituencies have all conspired to see trade agreements move up the political agenda. Trade agreements, notably the TPP, have become a wedge-issue in rural constituencies where rivals of the LDP have sought to make inroads by leveraging their opposition to any liberalization in agriculture (see Illustration 5.1). Mounting political pressures have thus prompted non-binding resolutions with an eye to influencing the negotiations. In this regard the Diet standing committee for Agriculture, Forestry and Fisheries adopted a resolution calling for:

> The Government of Japan [to exert] due diligence in dealing with bilateral and multilateral economic partnership agreements with other countries and ensures … that sensitive agriculture, forestry and fisheries products – including rice, wheat and barley, beef and pork, dairy products, sugar and starch crops – are either to be excluded from the negotiations or to be subject to renegotiation, … and the government should not hesitate to withdraw from negotiations if it judges that … five sensitive agriculture, forestry and fisheries products … could not be protected. (National Diet of Japan 2013)

Overall, the power balance between the Diet and the government has not changed, but heightened publicity and the sensitive nature of the issues discussed have seen politicking take on a more prominent role than in past trade talks.

If the EU–Japan partnership is to move forward significantly, the optics and discourses surrounding the deal will have to be precisely calibrated on either side. The contours of the overall agenda will in this regard play a key role, as this will determine which interests might be mobilized.

The Incorporation of Trade Agreements within Broader Policy Agendas

Even more than in multilateral trade talks, agenda-setting is a highly contentious stake for the executives involved as they seek to better articulate the economic relationship within the broader political dialogue, an ambition fortified in this case by the EP's 'No SPA, No FTA' stance. If both Tokyo and Brussels have repeatedly called for a deepened strategic dialogue, the many names the various negotiators have used[6] reflects a certain ambiguity regarding the dialogue's exact scope and

---

6   So far, official statements, expert commentators and the academic literature have used the following terms: Free Trade Agreement, Economic Partnership Agreement, Economic Integration Agreement, Political Cooperation Agreement, Strategic Partnership Agreement, Political Cooperation Agreement or Bilateral Framework Agreement.

format. The EU's persistence in wanting to formalize such non-trade related issues in bilateral/interregional negotiations has repeatedly baffled its partners. Often misunderstood, the EU's remarkably constant commitment (Börzel and Risse 2004: 26) to the principle and form (Bartels 2012) of human rights and sustainable development obligations has for better or worse become a structuring feature of its foreign policy.

Over time the mainstreaming of human rights and sustainable development has seen the related clauses migrate from the all-encompassing association agreements themselves to a set of relatively standardized and binding human rights and sustainable development clauses, which are included in either the 'free trade agreement' proper, or the correlated 'political cooperation agreement' (see Table 5.5). This functional separation has allowed for more flexibility and specialization in negotiations, notably with advanced economies. For example, from May 2009 until its preliminary conclusion in October 2013, Europeans and Canadians focused on the Comprehensive Economic and Trade Agreement (CETA) before seriously considering the corollary Strategic Partnership Agreement (SPA), for which negotiations were only launched in 2011, and which were tentatively concluded in the spring of 2014 (European Commission 2014). Despite the tensions surrounding the SPA's wording, and the benefits secured through CETA, it was ultimately assiduous trust-building measures and a constructive ambiguity which allowed both European and Canadian interpretations to coexist, that prompted the Canadians to accept an SPA. From the outset JEUFTA negotiations proceeded along similar lines, with a relatively strict division of labour between DG Trade and METI on the one hand, and the EEAS and MOFA on the other.

In the end, such two-track bargaining raises the question of the link between both agreements, urging leading policy-makers to guarantee overall coherence, as leaders of the executive branches on either side – that is, the Japanese PMO and the European Commission and Council – are held to make the final political arbitrations regarding the institutionalized relationship between the FTA and the SPA.

Table 5.5 The inclusion of Article 1 in bilateral/inter-regional agreements signed by the EU

Inclusion of Article 1 Issues in …		Type of Agreement	Partner Country/Region	
CONCLUDED	… the essential elements of the overall agreement	Association	Peru and Colombia	Central America
		Euro-Med Association	Morocco Egypt Tunisia Lebanon	Jordan Israel Algeria
		Economic Partnership	CARIFORUM	
		Trade, Development and Cooperation	South Africa	Cotonou
	… the FTA's preamble + the essential elements of the linked agreement	FTA + Partnership and Cooperation	Georgia	Singapore
		FTA + Framework / Comprehensive Partnership	Indonesia	Korea
		FTA + Strategic Partnership	**Canada**	
ACTIVELY ONGOING	… the FTA's preamble + the essential elements of the linked agreement	FTA + Framework / Comprehensive Partnership	Malaysia Vietnam	Thailand
		FTA + Strategic Partnership	**Japan**	**India**
	… the FTA's preamble	Standalone Trade and Investment Partnership	USA	

The Political Discourse on JEUFTA: Grappling with an Expectations Deficit and Vested Interests

The political discourse surrounding JEUFTA is understood as the sum total of the negotiation positions and political statements helping to define that which the lead agents on either side find within acceptable limits. For an agreement to be reached, and deeper forms of cooperation to be broached, JEUFTA must make these discourses converge towards a shared hierarchy of concerns and a set of acceptable institutional provisions. Said political discourse exists within a specific institutional framework which 'connect[s] the role of discourse to specific institutional settings' (Crespy 2015) reflecting the distinctive context shaping it, the specific function it is to fulfil, and the role played by individual agents (Schmidt 2008; Rayroux 2014: 229). For JEUFTA to fully realize its promise, political discourse will need to provide the impetus to overcome two specific problems: an 'expectations deficit' due to low political salience, and unevenly distributed benefits among vested interests.

The Expectations Deficit as a Dispiriting Backdrop

JEUFTA's low profile is obvious when compared to TTIP, TPP or even RCEP. Trade talks involving the US (or China) have invariably become a defining political issue. Trade liberalization with the US (Žižek 2014; Boyer 2015), or economic cooperation with China (Garcia 2010; Ravenhill 2010), have come to reflect wider geo-strategic stakes while also serving as shorthand for a politician's position on the political spectrum. The same was true in Korea, where negotiations with the US became a central point of contention, while the more discreet negotiations with Brussels did not cause any significant mobilization.

This suggests that JEUFTA will most likely be spared wider public pressure, and will continue mainly to engage experts and stake-holders. The flipside to this relatively benign environment is the absence of exogenous drivers and the resulting 'expectations deficit' (Tsuruoka 2008). The low political salience of the EU–Japan relationship causes a reversal in the traditional expectation-capability gap normally driving foreign policy forward. Typically policy-makers seek to balance the 'structural forces which keep expectations up just as they limit the growth of capabilities' (Hill 1989: 29), but the Euro-Japanese expectations deficit sees both expectations and capabilities drift downwards. This problem 'is mutual in nature [with] Japan's lack of expectations of Europe [echoing] the EU's indifference or lack of expectations of Japan' (Tsuruoka 2008: 113). Such lacklustre political optics provide few 'background ideational abilities' (Schmidt 2008: 313–14) emboldening leading policy-makers to break the status quo. Because of this, individual agents will have to mobilize their own political capital or 'foreground discursive abilities' (Schmidt 2008: 315–17) to prevail over Japan's focus on the US and Asia, its lack of understanding of EU policy-making and habitual preference for bilateral relations, on the one hand, and the

EU's relative indifference to Japan, the at times unsophisticated articulation of its principles, and the complexity of its foreign policy apparatus, on the other (Tsuruoka 2008: 115–22).

Coordinating Vested Interests: The Main Function of the Discourse

The political viability of JEUFTA's ambitions is squarely in the hands of three groups of elite agents: leading politicians, elite technocrats and mobilized interest representatives. Their level of commitment is a function of the agreement's perceived 'usefulness'. JEUFTA's political usefulness in the eyes of elected politicians is mainly determined by its perceived throughput and output legitimacy (Schmidt 2010b). The first term refers to the efficiency with which its procedures can secure its stated goals, the second refers to its impact on the political agenda it is meant to serve. In this regard the ability of leaders to associate JEUFTA with wider growth strategies on either side will be determining.

Focus among negotiating technocrats remains on the relative power balances JEUFTA could solidify. All things being equal, JEUFTA will most likely enjoy similar levels of throughput legitimacy as earlier trade agreements, the only possible spanner European and Japanese negotiators might throw into the works is if they make JEUFTA into a battleground for principled turf wars. On the European side, inter-institutional turf wars between the Commission, Council and EP are to be avoided by way of a coordinating 'trilateral dialogue'. In Tokyo, coordinating discourses are necessary to help sidestep ideological turf wars crystallized around specific value-laden clauses. Crucial in this regard will be a better understanding of the practical purpose of these clauses, and having Japanese institutions such as the Cabinet Legislation Bureau better coordinate the means and interpretations Tokyo has at its disposal to secure its internal order.

Pressure groups are singularly concerned with JEUFTA's ultimate outputs, which are largely determined by the agreed upon scope. If the FTA marshals traditional economic lobbies, the SPA mobilizes a whole new set of foreign policy ones. JEUFTA's output will therefore be a factor of its ability to coordinate these different interests. From the onset, interest groups representing stakeholders who were deemed to lose have been quite vocal,[7] and those criticisms were initially not really countered by voices from the many sectors standing to benefit.[8] Eventually a multitude of voices did manifest themselves; yet as often the case in PTAs

---

7   For instance the European carmakers association (ACEA) has pushed a relatively protectionist stance, leading some Member States with an important car industry – such as France, Italy and Germany – to take an acutely defensive position at a very early stage. The ACEA also mandated Deloitte to produce a separate impact assessment for the automotive industry which was highly critical of the FTA's potential consequences.

8   It is only after the second round that such sectors as financial and ICT mobilized in sufficient numbers to push leaders in the UK, Poland, the Baltic States and Scandinavia to write a letter calling upon the EU to show a sufficient level of ambition and commitment.

involving developed economies (Yoshimatsu and Ziltner 2010: 1080) these vested interests are alternatively geo-political, geo-economic or domestic in outlook (see Table 5.6).

The desired convergence of interests within JEUFTA will depend on the capacity of negotiations to: quarantine agriculture by dodging vexing issues with little economic return; change the defeatist discourse dominating the European car industries; clearly identify those targeted sectors set to gain the most from an agreement; and use the SPA to bind untapped constituencies to the agreement. In this regard, changes in discourse would renew a number of underutilized sectors. For example, in the environmental field, where both Tokyo and Brussels have taken on a leading role, deeper cooperation is possible only if one can move beyond the limited and 'developmentalist' clauses characterizing Japan's EPAs. A broadening of Tokyo's international environmental discourse would allow for comprehensive and forward looking initiatives besides those limited to mitigating an agreement's own environmental footprint through ODA (Yanai 2014).

Furthermore, a number of key sectors, of specific importance to highly developed knowledge economies, are still to be included in the partnership discourse in a meaningful way. For example, in the field of research and higher education, Japan's Ministry of Science and Technology (MEXT) does not even co-direct the Euro-Japanese Joint Committee on Scientific and Technological Cooperation, which itself was only launched in 2011. Such relative neglect in a series of strategic areas is rooted in both the primacy of US–Japan cooperation, as illustrated by the complete lack of a Euro-Japanese space dialogue, and the hermetic effect of the significantly more sophisticated European cooperation programmes (Ponjaert and Béclard 2010), notably those shaping the European Areas of Higher Education and Research. Changes in policy discourses seeing greater strategic openness and balance in Tokyo, and more flexibility and responsiveness in Brussels, would allow for such longstanding policy gulfs to be bridged.

Overall, if the zero-sum calculations of diverse economic interests are to be overcome, lead agents must ensure JEUFTA tackles all of these strategic issues without being taken hostage by specific interests – for example agriculture or the car industry. This will require pro-active individual agents able to produce well-calibrated coordinative discourses geared towards rallying a coalition of supportive interests. The relative opportunities associated with each interest group are a factor of its organizational and policy capacities. An impressive body of research has unpacked several of these fields with an eye on assessing their respective merits, and this book seeks to make a contribution to this body of work. Moreover, cumulative expertise built-up over the 'Decade of EU–Japan Cooperation' has equipped policymakers with the necessary insights, and prepared various targeted policy sectors for the possibility of further cooperation, so all that remains is for individual agents to find the right tone.

Table 5.6 Japanese and European vested interests with regard to JEUFTA (continued on p. 112)

(continued on p. 112)

	Japan	EU
Geo-political	**(PMO and MOFA) Proactive** *Alliance building in various global institutions* *Balancing in view of rising China* *Values-oriented diplomacy* **(PMO) Fluctuating** *Continued if a bit waning following change from DPJ to LDP govt. and the return of a US-centric outlook*	**(EEAS) Proactive** *Alliance building in various global institutions* *Build an Asian Presence* **(EEAS and EP) Reactive** *Preserve the EU's established 'normative' diplomacy*
Geo-economic	**(METI) Proactive** *Domino effect – i.e. Counteract trade divergences caused by ROKEUFTA* **(PMO) Positive** *Political hedging faced with increasing Chinese assertiveness*	**(DG Trade and Council) Proactive** *Domino effect – i.e. TPP/RCEP* **(Commission) Proactive** *Enforce the EU's regulatory diplomacy* **(Council and Commission) Reactive** *Assess whether new export markets are opened*
Domestic	**(PMO) Proactive** *Instrumentalization of precisely calibrated PTAs to foster domestic reform agenda* **(METI) Proactive** *Driven by autonomous alter ego – i.e. DG Trade* **(MOFA) Positive** *Political Prestige expected from a proactive Foreign Policy* **(Keidanren) Positive** *Including proactive car and electronics sector and rather passive service and financial sectors*	**(EEAS) Proactive** *Need to be seen making headway with major powers* **(DG Trade) Proactive** *PTAs are its main source of autonomous action* **(BusinessEurope) Positive** *Services and investment are dominant voices* **(DG RTD and EAC) Positive** *Desire to build on existing collaborations* **(EP) Indifferent** *But remains sensitive to trigger issues*

	Japan	EU
Domestic (continued)	**(JETRO) Positive** *Desire to build on existing collaborations* **(Diet) Indifferent** *Focused on TPP and RCEP* **(MOF) Indifferent** *Reflects unexpected relative passivity of financial sector* **(MAFF) Relative support** *Easier negotiations for Agriculture, Fisheries and Forestry* **(Cabinet Legislation Bureau) Defensive** *Unsure of the FTA/SPA unintended impact on internal order* **(MOJ) Defensive** *Fears intended impact on internal judicial order*	**(Council) Defensive** *A divided Council is necessarily cautious* **(DG Agriculture and DG Fisheries) Defensive** *Remain within limits of concessions made to other partners* **(Environmental NGOs) Hostile** *Incredulous that sustainable development clauses will make a difference* **(ACEA) Protectionist** *Protect European car market*
Relatively Untapped	**(MEXT)** *Higher education is completely absent and scientific cooperation remains marginal* **(Trade Unions)** *Only involved in the Dialogue on Social and Employment Issues, which involves a topical conference every two years* **(NGOs and Civil Society)** *Annual Civil Society Dialogue has failed to produce issues of joint mobilization* **(Competition Policy)** *Focus on NTBs and investment has seen competition relatively ignored*	**(DG ECHO)** *Focused on intra-institutional competition with EEAS* **(DG Industry and SMEs)** *Marginalized by large MNEs* **(DG Energy)** *Inertia caused by uncertainties in future energy policies on either side* **(ETUC)** *Only involved in the Dialogue on Social and Employment Issues, which involves a topical conference every two years* **(NGOs and Civil Society)** *Annual Civil Society Dialogue has failed to produce issues of joint mobilization* **(DG Competition)** *Focus on NTBs and investment has seen competition relatively ignored*

Conclusion

Considering the aforementioned cumulative expertise and shared values between the EU and Japan, the difficulties facing policy entrepreneurs seeking to coordinate emerging issue-linkages comes to some as a surprise. This chapter has sought to unpack the context, institutions, politics and discourses surrounding JEUFTA to better grasp which obstacles these two civilian powers must overcome to see their strategic partnership deepen. In the end, these strains are not wholly unexpected as they are tied, respectively, into Japan and the EU's international environments and actorships. Though both powers remain committed to the slightly tautological goal of 'actively promot[ing] the "civilising" of international relations' (Harnisch and Maull 2001b: 3) and largely conform to the six characteristics of a civilian power (Maull 2001: 124–6), a relative drift has occurred, as both have sought to integrate their fragmented political authority within more comprehensive strategies.

Confronted with distinct geo-strategic environments and different path-dependent experiences of kerbs on sovereignty, a growing disparity has emerged between European and Japanese perceptions of the suitability of the diplomatic toolbox at their disposal. Essentially, both actors can draw on three types of instruments to promote strategic partnerships and desired forms of governance (Börzel 2009: 5): political dialogue geared towards social learning and persuasion; conditionality seeking to alter cost-benefit calculations through new incentives or constraints; and assistance seeking to build capacity. As a partnership between two highly developed economies the third instrument offers but few prospects, whereas the inadequate results of the 'Decade of EU–Japan Cooperation' have shown the limits of the first. This leaves only constructive and jointly agreed upon conditionality as a possible instrument to foster progress. The required joint decision-making that political conditionality would imply will prompt Tokyo and Brussels to break the expectations deficit spiral and establish positive linkages which are able to foster new forms of cooperation. To do so a new shared discourse on the relationship's revised priorities must be jointly forged which in turn will involve strengthened institutions which are able to provide the necessary stability and trust to allow for constructive ambiguity. Such an approach to negotiations preserves 'a penumbra of ambiguity [and flexibility] around the enterprise, so as to keep [all lead agents] hoping that the final shape will be closest to their own ideal, and to permit broad coalitions [of vested interests] to support the next move[s]' (Hoffmann 1995: 131).

Beyond the necessary decisions to be made by technocrats calculating JEUFTA's various material consequences, political leaders face an irreducible choice: remain within the current framework of remote political dialogue, thus abandoning the ambition to forge a comprehensive, binding and forward-looking partnership, or jointly devise new and acceptable institutionalizing arrangements which are able to juggle the internal conflicts facing Brussels and Tokyo, while also adjudicating between the different incomparables the agreement would unlock.

Chapter 6

Food Fights or a Recipe for Cooperation? EU–Japan Relations and the Development of Norms in Food Safety Policy[1]

Gijs Berends[2]

Norms in Food Law

Food safety policy may carry the connotation of a dry and expert-run specialisation, but under this technocratic veneer many a battle between policy-makers, scientists, consumers and traders takes place. Food safety rules aspire to safeguard consumers against harm. They serve to protect human life and health. But food safety regulations require agreement on what exactly is harmful. The results of scientific inquiry are widely used to determine policy, but research is not without problems. Science is not always clear, and findings take time to verify conclusively. Even if the science is convincing, it might clash with consumer perceptions of safety. There are numerous examples of consumers being sceptical of established views (as with genetically modified organisms, or GMOs, for example) and these citizens demand from politicians that they show understanding. As a result, the desire not only to be safe but also to feel safe will have an impact on political decision-making.[3]

At the same time, food safety rules cannot be too restrictive. Restrictions may lead to higher production costs which in turn could trigger price increases to levels that citizens can ill afford or are not willing to accept. Excessive regulations may also impede trade in foodstuffs. All countries import food and some are import-dependent. Countries cannot therefore wall off their markets with prohibitive safety rules. What is more, when countries team up to create markets where goods flow freely, there will be pressure to have a uniform set of rules. It is undesirable to have widely diverging safety regulations in a customs union or in an internal market. Some fear that such a quest for uniformity will lead to a race to the

---

1 I would like to thank Paul Bacon, Carla Boonstra and Megumi Kobayashi for their support and for their comments which helped me to much improve the first draft.

2 Gijs Berends is an official at the European Commission and was posted to the Delegation of the European Union to Japan from 2008–2012. The views expressed in this chapter do not necessarily correspond to those of the European Commission.

3 Being safe versus feeling safe would be *anzen* versus *anshin* in Japanese.

bottom; others believe the outcome will be acceptable. Either way, the pressure for harmonisation may infringe on established safety parameters. Similarly, if exports contribute heavily to the economy, there will be pressure to interact with trading partners and find ways to smooth the flow of goods. Finally, there can be friction between traditional culinary practices and food safety. Modern rules may clash with local customs in slaughter or food preparation and this can lead to intense, emotional debates. Human health, science, consumer perceptions of risk, food security, food prices, trade in goods, and traditional practices all have influence on food safety policy. In the interaction between these forces, norms – defined here as principles and institutions – are born. This chapter seeks to understand whether the same norms have emerged in Japan and the EU. Do these norms survive when there are trade disputes between the two parties? Do Japan and the EU influence world-wide norm-setting by virtue of being 'civilian powers', and if so, do they do this together?

Development of Norms in the Food Safety Systems of the EU and Japan

European Union

In the early days of EU integration, when Member States had separate and at times very different food laws, products were regularly blocked from crossing borders for not complying with domestic legislation. But were such restrictions justified or desirable when the EU treaties professed to seek free movement of goods? The European Court of Justice, in what is now the well-known and pivotal case of *Cassis de Dijon*, decided that provided a product has been lawfully produced and marketed in *one* Member State it could be put on the market of *another* Member State. The profound implication of this decision was termed the principle of *mutual recognition*. It holds that a divergence in standards cannot constitute an obstacle to free movement of goods. Foodstuffs produced under a light regulatory regime may then have advantages over those produced under a heavier regulatory burden. Was it therefore not sensible to create EU-wide legislation that could do away with these differences in standards?

This is why early on politicians expressed the ambition to create a single market. One way to create this market was to harmonise legislation. This is not easy, as Member States would have to accept that their national legislation might be superseded by EU-wide legislation. Furthermore, which legislation would need to be harmonised; would it make sense in every area or only if there is some overriding interest? As it turned out, harmonisation measures in food law developed in a piecemeal fashion, and without the benefit of an overall framework.

This situation proved untenable when the BSE crisis broke out in 1996. It started when the public became aware that BSE could be transmitted from cattle to humans. The ensuing food scare blew away consumer confidence and citizens' belief in the regulatory competence of the European Union. Investigations into the crisis turned up some unpleasant conclusions: science was not free from outside influence, the public had not been properly informed, too many mistakes were made, and there was an ad hoc, rather than conceptual, approach to regulation (Vos 2000). With these criticisms in mind, the EU set out to revamp its food safety system. A General Food Law (GFL) was adopted in 2002 which established or codified the principles and institutions that would guide the EU's new safety system, bringing food law under a single framework.[4] Arguably, the most important principle under the GFL is the separation of those who assess risk and those who take decisions on the basis of that assessment. This separation serves two purposes. First, it helps to avoid any political influence. Second, it cements the recognition that 'scientific risk assessment alone, cannot, in some cases, provide all information on which a risk management decision should be based, and that other factors ... should legitimately be taken into account including societal, economic, traditional, ethical and environmental factors and the feasibility of controls' (Article 19 of the General Food Law, European Parliament and Council of the European Union 2002). A new institution emerged – the European Food Safety Authority (EFSA) – to take up the role of risk assessor.

But what to do when the assessment provides no clear-cut outcome on whether something is harmful? For this, the General Food Law lays down the so-called 'precautionary principle'. This principle holds that if 'the possibility of harmful effects on health is identified but scientific uncertainty persists' the EU may adopt provisional restrictive measures (Article 7). There has been much debate on this principle. It pitted those who think government should not be too inclined to create a risk-free society against those who believe that the government ought to protect its citizens even if there is no certainty of risk.

While the GFL confirmed the goal of smooth trade in goods, it prioritised food safety as the guiding principle for policy-making. To this end, the responsibility to put safe food on the market came to lie with the business operator. The law also called for transparency, arguing that consumers, NGOs and trading partners in third countries should be informed when there are grounds to think there is a risk to health. Importantly, the GFL established the Rapid Alert System for Food and Feed (RASFF). This network ensures that information about 'a direct or indirect risk to human health deriving from food or feed' is flagged for relevant authorities not only in the EU but also in third countries (Article 50).

At the risk of simplification, one could summarise by saying that the new norms that emerged from the revamping of the food safety system consisted of a handful of principles (decisions based on science, separation of risk assessment and risk management, the precautionary principle, the need for transparency, putting consumer protection first and making business operators responsible for safety) and three institutions (an overarching framework legislation in the form of the General Food Law, the European Food Safety Authority and the RASFF).

---

4 Some say it established for the first time food law as an autonomous branch of EU law (Holland and Pope 2004).

Japan

Modern food law in Japan has a different history. The free movement of goods, a desire to harmonise legislation and the principle of mutual recognition have not had much relevance. Japan also does not export very much food. By 2010 its food self-sufficiency rate hovered around 40 per cent, which means Japan imports 60 per cent of what it consumes. Consumers seem not to have much faith in the quality and safety of all these imported products. Surveys often show that Japanese tend to be less trustworthy of food products than citizens in Western countries. When in 2009 the New York-based advertising agency JWT published an anxiety index, Japan topped the rankings. JWT's survey showed that the anxiety drivers included food safety and the 'quality of products imported from China' (*Yomiuri Shimbun* 2009). For many a decade food safety was regulated under the Food Sanitation Act. Adopted in 1947, it survives until this day, even if it has been subject to successive amendments through new provisions on additives, labelling, hygiene and so on. The law was essentially the sole instrument governing food safety – until 2001.

On 10 September 2001 the first case of BSE was detected in Chiba Prefecture. Like in the EU, this finding propelled a reform of Japan's food safety system. The ensuing crisis and the plummeting trust by consumers led to much soul-searching. When a committee (the Commission on Investigation and Examination of BSE Issues) investigated how this food scare came about, it blamed the authorities for their lack of crisis consciousness, their opaque decision-making, their reliance on industry-oriented policies, the poor cooperation between the Agriculture Ministry (MAFF) and the Health Ministry (MHLW), and, most damagingly, for drafting policies that did not reflect scientific opinion.[5]

This verdict called for a legislative overhaul and an entirely new law – the Food Safety Basic Law – was drafted to co-exist with the Food Sanitation Law. Similar to the EU equivalent, its most important stipulation was the proposal to separate risk assessment and risk management. This meant the establishment within the cabinet office of what became the Food Safety Commission (FSC). Science-based policy-making was promoted (Article 11) even if policy-makers were also instructed to compose policies that reflect public opinion (Article 13). The public was granted the right to make its views heard in official consultations but in parallel, and maybe somewhat patronisingly, the public was also tasked to endeavour 'to improve their own knowledge and understanding of food safety' (Article 9). The new law prioritised safety – rather than food security or the health of Japan's food industry – and responsibility for ensuring food safety was imposed on business operators. The investigative committee also proposed that the new law include the precautionary principle, although the law remains vague on this, even

---

5   Takahashi (2009) has made a valiant effort to map Japan's food safety system. See http://www.ab.auone-net.jp/~ttt/index.html (last accessed 14 October 2014).

if it does say that under certain conditions measures can be taken without a proper risk assessment (Article 11).[6]

Even if these changes were profound, dissatisfied consumers continued to call for greater government action in securing food safety.[7] Prime Minister Yasuo Fukuda (in office from September 2007 to September 2008), was receptive to such demands. His willingness to act was cemented by the *gyōza* (dumpling) food scandal in which some frozen *gyōza* imported from China in late 2007/early 2008 were found to contain high levels of the pesticide methamidophos. Consumption of the dumplings caused several people to fall ill and resulted in a massive drop in trust in food coming from China. Although it later turned out that a disgruntled worker had tampered with the dumplings, the incident happened to come on top of a series of indigenous food safety scandals. These included respected Japanese companies using expired ingredients, or manipulating the expiry date or the place of origin on labels. As a consequence, consumer faith in the food safety system was low and consumer anxiety mounted. This national mood gave PM Fukuda the necessary momentum to establish the Consumer Affairs Agency (CAA) within the Cabinet Office. The agency was given direct jurisdiction over food labelling legislation and the organisation was expected, through the collection and analysis of information about harmful events and incidents, to intervene and streamline government reaction to food scares. It also has the right to recommend legislative action and take up risk communication in times of emergency.

The similarities between the revolutions in the food safety frameworks of the EU and Japan are striking. Despite different histories, the EU and Japan both dramatically changed their systems after a BSE crisis. Investigations revealed similar faults and deficiencies. The BSE crises presented opportunities to clean up systems that had respectively grown stale, and to churn out fresh and modern norms. Both parties overhauled their food safety systems, drafting an overarching framework law, separating risk assessment from risk management, moving away from trade and industry-based systems to consumer oriented systems, and backing increased transparency. As some Japanese commentators note, these commonalities were partly due to Japan having purposefully followed the steps the EU had taken since the outbreak of the BSE crisis in 1996.

Yet there are still differences between the two. The EU has elevated the precautionary principle into law, whereas Japan did not go that far. There are also differences in the institutional setting. The EU's policy-making process can be defined as multi-level governance whereby Member States, their scientific bodies, the European Commission and the European Food Safety Agency all interact, but where the WTO and international standard-setting organisations such as CODEX,

---

6   This exclusion is somewhat surprising as in 1997, under a WTO dispute settlement case, Japan tried to use the precautionary principle to argue that it was justified in requiring that US exporters test each variety of fruit before export so as to avoid 'coddling moths' settling as a pest in Japan.

7   This paragraph can also be found in Berends (2013).

the OIE and the IPPC are also essential given the EU's role as a major trader in food products (Ansell and Vogel 2005). By contrast, Japan's regulatory process remains more of a national affair. But within that 'single' level of governance, there are many actors: not only the Food Safety Commission, but also the Consumer Affairs Agency (CAA) are tasked with analytical assignments, and MAFF, MHLW and the CAA are all three involved in the legislative process.

EU–Japan Relations: Trading Food and Barbs

Italian, Spanish and French food establishments are ubiquitous in Japan. Similarly, the number and popularity of Japanese restaurants in Europe have increased remarkably in recent years. Both Japan and many EU Member States can rely on a rich culinary tradition and can pride themselves on exerting a disproportionate influence on world cuisine. Does this also mean that they are powerful trading partners?

The EU has been a considerable exporter of fresh and processed food to Japan. In 2002–2009 the EU exported roughly €3.9 billion per year and in 2012 exports went up to as much as €5.3 billion. This is a fair amount even if Japan is not a top-five export market for the EU. France is the largest food exporter, responsible for more than €1 billion worth of produce, followed by the Netherlands, Germany, Italy and Ireland. The top 10 EU exports that make their way to Japan include pork, wine, alcohol, cheese, water, olive oil, chocolate and others.

In comparison, Japan has been a minor player on the European market. Between 2002 and 2009 exports hovered around €147–157 million per year. An uptick in Japanese exports in recent years brought the figure up to €180 million per year between 2010 and 2012. Japan ships sauce, fish products, tea and vegetables to the EU. Altogether these exports constitute around 0.3 per cent of all EU food imports.[8] Japan exports to other countries but is not a food exporting giant. It exports so little partly because Japan's self-sufficiency rate is low. Local producers and food operators have little problem in finding a domestic market for their produce and the need to access foreign markets has been limited. More importantly, farmers have little incentive to lure foreign consumers as they have been well-protected by subsidies and tariffs (Boonstra 2013). But change is looming. Japan's ageing and declining population forces operators to look out for outside markets to sustain demand. Furthermore, the rise in prosperity in eastern Asia has meant that consumers there have started to be able to afford Japan's high-priced, high quality products. The more recent phenomenon of Japan engaging in trade negotiations with partners that are competitive in agriculture also has some explanatory power. Once such trade agreements enter into force, producers need to find new markets in the face of an inevitable increase in imports of foreign products.

---

8   All figures come from Eurostat. Statistics exclude fishery products.

When two countries sell goods to each other, trade predicaments can emerge swiftly and unexpectedly. In what should be a classic example, we could look at the egg. The EU prohibits the washing of eggs. Japan is a proponent of egg-washing. The EU claims that washing an egg could force micro-organisms to enter the shell. Japan claims that it would clean the egg and remove micro-organisms. There is no foul play and there are no mean intentions. There are just diverging views. How can the EU and Japan solve such problems? The instruments at the disposal of authorities range from sending an inquiring email to a full-fledged dispute settlement case under the WTO. But it usually starts with a meeting. The moment a trade irritant emerges, the parties sit down and try to understand what the problem is, exchange views, and get a feeling for how serious the problem is, how justified the barrier is, and whether a quick fix can be arranged. If this quick fix does not come about, then the frequency of meetings increases, and depending on the severity of the dispute, the level of intervention rises. Higher-level officials will get involved, possibly up to ambassadorial, ministerial or prime-ministerial level, through letters, meetings, visits or phone calls.

Meetings are also institutionalised. The EU and Japan used to have what was called a Regulatory Reform Dialogue and a High Level Trade Dialogue, to discuss regulatory misunderstandings, incompatibilities, irritants or disputes. These dialogues have now been superseded, given the launch of the negotiations for a free trade agreement. Trade negotiations offer a platform to negotiate both tariff reductions and non-tariff barriers. Institutionalised meetings can also develop an international dimension. WTO members meet in the Sanitary and Phytosanitary (SPS) committee. During such rounds, the troubling issue can be raised in informal bilateral talks. If the issue is serious then it can be tabled in the plenary session in front of all the other members. One alternative is to prevent an irritant from arising. Most countries are members of international standard-setting bodies that help bring uniformity in, or at least common understanding of, food rules. Both Japan and the EU bring considerable expertise and a fair number of specialists to meetings on food standards (CODEX), animal health (OIE) and plant health (IPPC).

In more Machiavellian fashion, officials could try and find trade-offs. The desired outcome in one pending issue could be linked to progress in another. Finally, the most serious form of intervention would be if one party takes recourse to the WTO dispute settlement mechanism. Even if WTO members take this avenue ever more often, it is generally a measure of last resort. It is the start of what journalists often like to call a trade war. Normally – but there are of course exceptions – WTO members opt for dispute settlement if the economic interests are high, their legal case is strong, and if the costs of damage to a political relationship do not outweigh the gains of winning a dispute. If one scans the WTO portal on the disputes by subject, one is struck by the number of food-related matters.

So do Japan and the EU have many trade irritants or conflicts? Normally, obstacles to trade are divided into tariff barriers and non-tariff barriers. Let's first look at tariffs. In Japan the average applied tariff for agricultural goods in 2012 was 17.5 per cent. This can be compared with the overall average of 6.3 per cent for goods in general. In 2011 the EU's agricultural products were subject to an average rate of 15.2 per cent, considerably higher than tariffs for non-agricultural products, which average 4.1 per cent (WTO 2012). These averages fail to show that some individual sensitive products face even higher tariffs, at times so high that trade becomes prohibitive. Many gains can therefore be made through tariff negotiations, but tariff averages such as these do not qualify as exceptional.

What about non-tariff barriers? Japan has raised very few problems about market access in the EU. This does not mean that Japan does not care or is being kind to the EU. The lack of conflict is a function of the fact that Japan does not export much to the EU. The EU, in contrast, sells a fair amount to Japan and consequently has a list of complaints. Many of these are long-standing matters. For one thing, EU business operators do not understand why Japan does not allow certain additives even if they are widely used in both the EU and the US. Similarly, they complain that there is no dedicated approval system for food enzymes, which hinders their use in products that could otherwise be sold. Business also believes that Japan should introduce maximum permissible levels for a pathogenic bacterium called *listeria monocytogenes* for foods that do not support the growth of the bacteria. Japan currently practices zero-tolerance across the board. Finally, business operators have complained about lengthy approval procedures and say that it took 19 years of negotiations to export Spanish oranges due to Japanese fears over the Mediterranean fruit fly pest. This is not an exhaustive list but it goes to show that European businesses face hurdles. Still, it is far from making EU–Japan food safety relations conflictual. In the last 20 or so years neither party has launched a dispute settlement case against the other in the WTO. The EU only occasionally makes use of the WTO SPS plenary session to call into question the practices of Japan, and Japan rarely does so with regard to the EU. At the end of the day, in an otherwise relatively calm trading relationship, there have in recent years only been two salient food disputes.

Can the EU and Japan Solve Trade Irritants? Two Case Studies

The Fukushima Accident and Contamination of the Food Chain

The Great East Japan Earthquake unleashed a tsunami that disabled the cooling systems at the Fukushima Dai-ichi nuclear power plant, which led to the nuclear drama that gripped the world. In the wake of this drama, the Fukushima accident caused a food scare that was remarkable for its magnitude. As a result, for the first time Japanese food faced a host of restrictive measures imposed by its trading partners.

The first finding of contaminated food kick-started a process characterised by a high level of regulatory complexity. What are acceptable levels of contamination? Who should do the testing and how? What should happen to contaminated food?

What kind of restrictions ought to be imposed? How long should these restrictions remain in force? In the course of around 24 months following the accident, the Japanese government undertook more than 300,000 samples. A great variety of food products were prohibited from being marketed, including milk, vegetables, fruits, rice and beef. Food scares such as foot-and-mouth disease, BSE or avian influenza tend to be product-specific. But when radioactive substances are released there are almost no boundaries to the range of products within the affected area that can be affected.[9]

It took some time before the administration put in place a functioning system. Above all, it had to make a decision on what exactly would be subject to restrictions. If one finds contaminated spinach in a village in Fukushima prefecture then what should one do? Is it better to limit restrictions to spinach or to all products in that area? Should the restriction be limited to the village or to a zone around the village or maybe the entire prefecture? The Japanese authorities ultimately decided that it would take only the product in question off the market and that the restriction would be limited to small administrative units (towns or municipalities) provided that this unit could demonstrate its ability to manage the restriction. Japanese authorities believed that they had managed to prevent any unsafe food from entering the market, and consequently dangerous food could not be exported either. The Japanese government hoped that its trading partners would put their trust in the adequacy of the system and align with the Japanese restrictions.

But Japan's trading partners were not willing to fall in line. Some countries like China, Taiwan, Russia and South Korea simply imposed blanket bans on a (in some cases large) number of prefectures. The EU also did not simply accept that exports should be able to continue as before. Instead, it demanded that for products coming from 12 prefectures, each consignment of food be accompanied by a declaration that would attest that the foodstuff in question did not contain contamination above the maximum permissible levels. Initially the authorities had to sign off on this declaration. The EU measure somehow was comparatively relaxed – nothing was banned – but at the same time it was onerous for exporters. Food products that had not been found to be contaminated, coming from a prefecture with few other findings of contamination, would still need to abide by this legislation.

Japan and the EU did align on what they thought should be the maximum permissible levels of contamination. Due to the Chernobyl crisis the EU Member States had already experienced what panic a nuclear predicament could trigger. Post-Chernobyl, the EU agreed on acceptable levels of contamination, as shown in Table 6.1, that still apply to some products that up to this day require certificates.

---

9   The following paragraphs rely on or can be found in Berends (2013).

Table 6.1 EU – maximum permissible levels of caesium in Bq/kg

Goods from EU			Goods from third countries		
Infant food	Dairy	Other foodstuffs	Liquid foodstuffs	Milk/infant food	All other products
400	1,000	1,250	1,000	370	600

Source: Council of the European Communities (1989).

What happened with these levels when the troubles in Fukushima became known to the outside world? The EU decided not to apply them. Instead it decided to align with the levels set by Japan. This was interesting because Japan's levels were less lenient, initially they were only provisional, and they were not set with European conditions in mind.

After Japan set its own levels on a provisional basis in the days following the accident, the health minister then turned to the Food Safety Commission for a risk assessment. The FSC's subsequent scientific advice held that a consumer should not face lifetime radiation exposure of more than 100mSv. This was useful to know but how was this figure to be translated into acceptable contamination levels for daily intake? An essential assumption that MHLW officials subsequently made was that 50 per cent of a person's intake could be contaminated and in the case of infants the entire intake could be contaminated. When the MHLW sent its proposals for consultation to the radiation council of the science ministry MEXT, its reaction was one of scepticism. Council members did not feel that the assumption of daily intake contamination was realistic. Despite the criticism, the MHLW went ahead and roughly one year after the Fukushima accident the health minister decided to adopt levels that were 5 to 20 times stricter, as shown in Table 6.2.

Table 6.2 Japan – maximum permissible levels of caesium

Provisional levels from 17 March 2011		Levels applicable from 1 April 2012	
Category	**Levels in Bq/kg**	**Category**	**Levels in Bq/kg**
Vegetables, grains, meat, eggs, fish	500	Food (including processed dairy)	100
Drinking water	200	Infant food	50
Milk	200	Drinking water (including tea)	10
Dairy products	200	Milk	50

Source: Ministry of Health, Labour and Welfare (2012).

One interesting aspect of the revision was that the health ministry never claimed that the original, provisional levels had been unsafe. But it felt that stricter levels would reinforce the 'peace of mind' of consumers. With that consideration, the ministry responded to the debate about whether *anzen* (safety) or *anshin* (peace of mind) should steer policy. The former is about science and about established parameters. The latter is a subjective condition. The difference between the two sets of limits shows that in times of crisis science and consumer perceptions policy can get mixed up.

If these strict levels already caused Japanese to scratch their heads, why did the EU follow? The EU argued that because products not allowed on the Japanese market could not be exported either, it was 'appropriate, in order to provide consistency between the pre-export controls performed by the Japanese authorities and the controls on the level of radionuclides performed on food and feed originating in or consigned from Japan at the entry into the EU, to apply the same maximum levels' (European Commission 2011d: 1). In other words, the EU risk managers did not rely on their own risk assessor, the EFSA, but made decisions for reasons of 'consistency'.

In the meantime Japan's business operators still faced EU restrictions on their exports, and Tokyo officials were keen to change this. They took three kinds of actions. First, they were as transparent as possible. At the Ministry of Foreign Affairs daily press conferences were held to inform the diplomatic community about the nuclear crisis, and food safety was a staple of these information sessions. Japanese diplomats all over the world were instructed to inform their host countries of the measures that Japan was taking and how the safety system was performing. Furthermore, officials gave explanations in Geneva at the plenary session of the WTO SPS committee. Secondly, Japan tried to persuade its partners that food was safe. It held promotional events all over the world. The Prime Minister invited ambassadors to Japan to a reception with food from disaster areas. And in contacts with third countries, it tried to convince interlocutors that restrictions were not needed because unsafe food would not be exported. But this approach backfired. As it happened, contaminated feed had been fed to cattle, and contaminated beef was sold and distributed all over Japan. This unfortunate turn of events forced the then Foreign Minister Mr Matsumoto to instruct his ministry to refrain from claiming the safety of Japanese foods. Thirdly, Japan exerted pressure. It arranged bilateral meetings, visits, intervention by ministers and even the Prime Minister to give political backing to Japan's desire to see the restrictions alleviated.

At the time of writing, the EU measures have been somewhat softened. Instead of asking for a declaration for all food products coming from the 12 prefectures, a positive list has been established for the prefectures – with the exception of Fukushima – which means that only the listed products need to be accompanied by declarations that would attest to their safety. Others products are free to be exported without constraints.

Mad Cows and Angry Exporters

The magnitude of the BSE crisis was such that the international standard-setting body the World Organisation for Animal Health (OIE) drew up special recommendations on the conditions under which trade in beef and other bovine products could take place safely. It categorised the risk by classifying countries into three classes: undetermined, controlled or negligible. The OIE gave its blessing to trade in products coming from countries in the latter two categories.[10] Today 20 EU Member States have been designated as 'controlled risk' and five as 'negligible risk'. Japan itself is also classified as 'controlled risk'.[11] One would therefore assume that Japan would open its market again for European beef. But it has not done so. Why not?

Japan first of all decided it wanted to make its own risk assessment and did not want to live by the OIE categorisation alone. It devised a procedure under which countries could apply for the resumption of beef imports: (a) applicants would fill in detailed questionnaires. These included questions on relevant legislation, measures taken by the applicant to prevent an epidemic, its surveillance measures of BSE and so on; (b) the Japanese authorities would review the replies and ask additional questions where necessary; (c) consultations between the two parties would take place, after which (d) Japan would send inspectors for on-site investigations; (e) a dossier would then be submitted to the risk assessor – the Food Safety Commission; (f) the FSC would report its assessment to the risk manager, the Minister for Health, Labour and Welfare, who (g) would then take a decision on resumption of imports.

This procedure was uncontested by the EU. The SPS agreement under the WTO allows a country to undertake its own risk assessment. But EU exporters did deplore that the application procedure turned out to be unnecessarily restrictive. First, the procedure was considered cumbersome. Some applicants thought their submission of publicly available information to the OIE already covered many of the questions raised by the Japanese authorities. Secondly, they questioned the relevance of some of the queries. But thirdly, above all, the length of time it took for the Japanese authorities to move from one step to the next was considered discouraging. It took no less than two years from on-site investigations in France and the Netherlands – the frontrunners in the application process – to the submission of dossiers to the Food Safety Commission for risk assessment. Member States found this all the more hard to swallow given that the US and Canada had been granted access already in 2006. Whether or not this amounted to discriminatory treatment, European applicants feared that a larger and larger share of the Japanese market would be lost.

---

10 The EU28 and Japan are members. Decision-making lies with OIE members themselves.

11 At the time of writing, Japan was awaiting an OIE assessment to reclassify it as a 'negligible risk' country.

What could the EU then do? The EU adopted a three-pronged approach. First of all, the applicant Member States followed as diligently as they could the application procedure. Questionnaires were sent in, additional questions were answered, on-site visits were arranged. Secondly, in parallel the EU launched bilateral interaction, both at EU and Member State level. Letters were sent, meetings were held, the issue was put on bilateral regulatory dialogues and high-level interventions gave the process political backing. Furthermore, during WTO SPS committees the EU held talks with Japanese delegates and tabled the matter during the plenary sessions. Thirdly, the EU anchored the trade irritant in the talks about the possible opening of free trade negotiations. After all, why would the EU launch negotiations with Japan if the Japanese authorities could not agree to lift trade barriers on products that the EU considered safe?

Did all this result in a desirable outcome? At the time of writing, Japan had opened up its market, under certain conditions, to bovine products from France and the Netherlands. Other countries' applications, like those of Ireland, Poland (both applications are now being assessed by the Food Safety Commission) and Sweden (still in the questionnaire phase) are still pending.

Are the EU and Japan Setting Norms for the Rest of the World?

Are Japan and the EU 'civilian powers' because they influence world-wide norm-setting? One would have to proceed carefully before drawing any strongly-worded conclusions. There has been little research done on this question when it comes to food safety. All the same, we can consider four lines of reasoning to see if European and Japanese norms have an impact on the rest of the world.

First, we can look at past food scares and whether the experience in addressing these crises has imparted lessons to other actors. The BSE crisis in the EU was so severe that its regulatory response was inevitably scrutinised by other countries that faced an outbreak. A case in point was Japan's reaction to its own BSE scare, which bore a strong resemblance to that of the EU. It is not by accident that the Japanese Food Safety Basic Law stipulated many of the same principles as those found in the EU General Food Law. Similarly, the Japanese response to the Fukushima accident, and its impact on the food chain, will provide ample food for thought for any country that wishes to prepare itself for a nuclear accident and the potential contamination of food.

Secondly, any impact on food safety norms depends on the trading clout of the EU and Japan. Japan is not a major exporter, but imports 60 per cent of its food. The EU is the world's largest exporter of food and its second largest importer. It has a clear benefit in ensuring that its food is accepted by its trading partners. What is more, because the EU is an importing giant – it offers a market of 500 million consumers – there is an incentive for third countries to align with EU legislation as it helps facilitate exports to this desirable market. This is why some Chinese food laws can be found to resemble EU rules.

Thirdly, the presence of Japanese and European experts in the global standard-setting bodies such as the OIE, the IPPC and Codex Alimentarius are an indicator of potential influence. Both Japan and the EU are well represented and are active participants in the debates on how to harmonise food rules globally. The secretariats of all three bodies are housed in Europe, although this does not necessarily mean that the norm-setting bodies produce EU-type norms. Many Asian officials that participate in these deliberations are educated in the US. Emerging countries dominate the secretariat of the IPPC. And the weight of the US is seen as predominant overall in international food norm-setting institutions.

Fourthly, the EU and Japan have influence on their neighbours. The EU continues to enlarge, and candidate countries need to align fully with EU food law. In addition, the EU is negotiating a series of trade agreements with neighbouring countries in the Mediterranean and Caucasus regions. Part of these talks concerns legal approximation, which is an exploration of whether the EU's neighbours can align with EU law. In the case of its neighbours, Japan has no such leverage. But the large number of Japanese food companies established in China and South Korea abide by Japanese standards. What is more, the EU sees 'signal value' in Japan's position. Once Japan, with its high and sophisticated standards, opens its markets to European products, such as beef, other countries in the region, like South Korea, are more likely to mirror that decision.

This is not to say that the EU and Japan actually team up to develop global food norms. If the EU and Japan would have been the world's top food exporters (as they are in the car sector), then there may have been more incentive to do so. Yet there are some telling signs of cooperation. The EU and Japan signed an agreement on Japan's participation in the RASFF. It allows Japan to gain real-time information on alerts and notifications of potential safety problems with food that is traded between the two parties. In addition, the Tokyo-based Food Safety Commission has signed a Memorandum of Cooperation with the Parma-based European Food Safety Authority, and the two institutions have set up an annual dialogue. Finally, now that negotiations for a free trade agreement have been launched, a chapter on food safety issues is being discussed.

Conclusion

At the outset of this chapter four questions were listed to guide this paper. Do Japan and the EU live by the same food safety norms? Do these norms survive when there are disputes between the two parties? Do Japan and the EU influence world-wide norm-setting, and if so, do they do this together?

Food safety norms in the EU and Japan have much in common. In both parties, the BSE crisis propelled systemic reform. Food laws urge policy-makers to make policy based on science. Risk assessment and risk management are separated. Food safety prevails over industry-oriented concerns. And business operators are responsible for putting safe products on the market. There is a premium on transparency and the public is expected to involve itself in the decision-making through consultation processes. Some differences are also evident. The EU enshrined the precautionary principle into law, but legal provisions in Japanese legislation fall short of doing that. The EU comes to its decisions through a complex interplay of Member State authorities, European decision-making and international bodies. Japan has a more domestic focus but a variety of institutions is involved in decision-making.

Do these norms survive when the going gets rough? This chapter gave special attention to the two most salient trade irritants between the EU and Japan: post-Fukushima radioactive food contamination and BSE. In the case of Japan, one could argue that the country did not buckle under pressure when its strict regime caused trouble for business operators and its trading partners. But this is not to say that science reigned. After all, the science that underpinned the health ministry's decision to impose very strict levels of maximum permissible radioactive contamination was contested by its own science ministry. The ministry admitted that feeling safe was as important as being safe. Similarly, in the case of imports of beef from the EU, risk assessment and risk management were properly separated, and the risk assessment was based on science. But what is the usefulness of a science-based decision when the risk assessment is delayed by years? In the case of the EU, its restrictions on potentially contaminated exports from Japan were science-based in the sense that the there was no dispute that radiation could be harmful. But on the question of acceptable levels of contamination, the EU did not perform a risk assessment by itself and EFSA, the risk assessor of the EU, did not get involved. Instead, the EU followed Japanese levels, even if these were much stricter than those set by the EU after Chernobyl, and even if the science behind these new levels was not without controversy in Japan. This alignment took place not because science dictated it so, but for the more prosaic reason of 'consistency'. This all goes to show that scientific concerns do not monopolise decision-making.

As civilian powers, do Japan and the EU influence the development of global safety norms? There is little evidence that the EU and Japan team up to impose their norms on the international community. There are signs of cooperation, but these do not constitute an attempt to force joint norms upon third parties. This is not surprising, as for the moment Japan is too small an exporter to create an incentive for both parties to collaborate to that extent. But one should not underestimate what it means if both the EU and Japan have similar norms. The overhaul of the food safety system in both parties has led to a similar outcome. Japan seems to have closely followed the EU in its reaction to the beef crisis. The free trade negotiations and the cooperation between Japan's Food Safety Commission and the European Food Safety Authority may bring further convergence. This is important, because even if the EU and Japan are not actively teaming up to convert the rest of the world to their norms, other countries can find inspiration in these food safety systems. The reaction from Japan and the EU to the BSE crisis and the Fukushima accident will be studied by other countries who hope to avoid having to face a similar predicament. The EU and Japan import great quantities of food and therefore offer an incentive for supplier countries to align with their safety norms. And both parties have an impact on their neighbours, for instance through the allure of possible membership in the case of the EU, or in the case of Japan, through the large number of Japanese operators in neighbouring countries. The relationship between the EU and Japan in food safety is not very conflictual and cooperation is not extensive; but the fact that both have produced a similar safety system will reverberate across third countries.

PART III
Promoting Environmental, Economic and Energy Security

Chapter 7

Environmental and Energy Policy: Learning and Cooperation between the European Union and Japan

Miranda A. Schreurs

Introduction

In many respects the environmental programmes, laws, and institutions found in Europe and Japan are similar. As advanced industrialized states, they have experienced many of the same pollution problems and environmental concerns. They have introduced many similar laws to deal with these problems, learning from each other's experiences, scientific insights and policy solutions, yet are also distinct in their approaches to environmental protection and energy policy (Jörgens et al. 2014).

Combined, the European Union (28 member states), the European Free Trade Area (Iceland, Liechtenstein, Norway and Switzerland) and Japan account for about 33 per cent of the global economy. Their economic and energy policy choices have influence that extends far beyond their own borders. They are major importers of energy, food and raw materials and thus have a significant global environmental footprint. They are also major exporters and their products are consumed around the world. The more energy and resource efficient their production processes and products become, the better it will be for the entire globe.

In many areas, these 32 European states and Japan are environmental leaders. In the Environmental Performance Index, which provides a ballpark estimation of a country's environmental performance, they hold 21 of the top 25 best performing country rankings (for 2012, Switzerland ranked number 1, France 6, the United Kingdom 9, Germany 11, and Japan 23) (Yale University 2012).

Given the size of their domestic markets and the global reach of their industries, they can influence product standards globally. In making decisions for higher levels of energy efficiency in product design, stringent targets to lower greenhouse gas emissions, ambitious goals for renewable energy development, and strong conservation policies, they can also provide examples for other countries to consider. Just as Japan and the European Union have learned much from each other in their policy development, other countries also watch and sometimes adopt ideas based on what these major economies do. Thus, the importance of the policy choices they make in the future in relation to the major environmental challenges facing the planet, including biodiversity loss, tropical rainforest depletion, ocean acidification, climate change, resource exhaustion, toxic and nuclear waste, and plastic and other wastes.

This chapter is concerned with understanding how Europe and Japan have influenced each other's environmental and energy policy decisions. It also considers how they have and could work more closely together in the future to address pressing global environmental challenges.The chapter begins with a brief discussion of cross-societal learning before turning to an historical overview of some of the first steps at pollution control and nature conservation in Europe and Japan in the nineteenth and early twentieth century where there are clear signs of Japan, in particular, studying and learning from European experiences. This is followed by an examination of some of the learning that occurred between Europe and Japan as they struggled to deal with the pollution caused by rapid economic development, where there was a considerable cross-national exchange of ideas. Several more in-depth and recent examples of cases where Europe and Japan have learned from each other on environmental or energy issues are also discussed. As can be seen from these examples, learning is occurring in both directions. Some of the examples are cases where Europe has learned from Japan, others where Japan has learned from Europe, and others where Japan and the European Union have cooperated to pursue global norms they both deem to be important. There is much need for states like Europe and Japan to act as global leaders because they have the capacity and know-how to do so. To what extent they will choose to act together as leaders in the years to come remains to be seen.

Cross-Societal Learning

Europe and Japan have a long history of cross-societal learning in relation to environmental issues. Early examples of such learning began with the formation of national parks, sanitation legislation and conservation measures in the latter half of the nineteenth and into the first half of the twentieth century. Beginning in the 1960s, focus shifted to finding solutions to the pollution caused by industrialization. Since then there has been a relatively rapid spread of environmental protection norms, policies and practices addressing issues related to sustainability, climate change, biodiversity preservation, ocean pollution, consumption, recycling and alternative energy. Europe and Japan have entered into many bilateral and international environmental agreements and have frequently partnered to address major global challenges, even though there are still deep disagreements between them on some issues. Still today there continues to be much environmental information exchange and debate about policy priorities and measures, as Europe and Japan confront the many global environmental problems facing the planet.

Traditionally, the member states of the European Union and Japan have both looked more to the United States than to each other for cues. Yet in the areas of environment and low-carbon energy, Europe and Japan have strongly influenced each other in terms of policy ideas and priorities. At times this has been positive learning – borrowing ideas about best practice in energy efficiency promotion or renewable energy development. At other times it might be thought of as negative lesson learning, such as after the Fukushima nuclear accident when Europe recognized the need to reassess its own approach to nuclear energy. Europe and Japan frequently find themselves in competition but also learn from each other's mistakes and successes. They have also cooperated on global environmental issues in an effort to promote multilateral problem-solving and good governance norms in the environmental sector. Given their status as leaders in many environmental areas, Japan and Europe can strongly influence global environmental norms when they choose to do so.

There are many factors that have driven such cross-societal learning (Keck et al. 2013). At times it stems from the desire to learn from a recognized leader in the field who has experience with problem-solving. This may be important when a policy problem emerges and results in a search for solutions. An example of this would be in relation to air pollution control measures taken in Japan in the 1970s, which were observed in Germany and perceived as a model to learn from as Germany struggled to address its own air pollution problems (Weidner 1996). Alternatively, it may be triggered by a kind of regulatory competition and a desire to gain a leadership role or advantage. A state can benefit by being in the lead with its environmental standards as it can set the rules of international competition. Much like companies, states may compete to be in the lead in policy design (Jänicke 2005; Vogel 1995). Europe and Japan have been in a kind of competition with one another in efforts to obtain high levels of energy efficiency in their products, and market superiority. Europe and Japan have also cooperated on global environmental issues in an effort to find multilateral solutions to large challenges facing the planet and also to promote good governance norms in the environmental sector.

Early Interactions on Sanitation and Pollution Control

Environmental policy learning is something that has been occurring between Europe and Japan for centuries. The Industrial Revolution transformed the relationship between humans and the environment. The advent of the steam engine, railroads and automobiles made travel faster and the transport of goods easier. The discovery of electricity brought light into homes and city streets. The invention of the telephone revolutionized communications. Factories made mass production of goods possible. The Industrial Revolution gave humans unprecedented abilities to harness nature and use its resources to improve their quality of life. Yet, for much of the next two centuries after the start of the Industrial Revolution in Europe, industrial pollution became increasingly worse, partly because so little was done about it. Pollution was viewed as an unavoidable externality of development. Factories pumped huge quantities of smoke, dust and pollutants into the air and dumped waste into waterways and on land. Forests were cut down for agricultural development, the establishment of highway and railroad infrastructures, and the building of new communities and industrial facilities. The prevailing view was that natural resources were there for humans to exploit to improve their economic condition. With the Meiji Restoration, Japan followed this European quest for modernization and quickly moved to introduce railroads, steel plants, petrochemical industries and the other signs of what was then thought to be an advanced civilization. It did not take long for Japan to start suffering from many of the pollution problems facing Europe. The air was thick with smoke from the burning of coal, rivers were foul with pollution, and waste was dumped into the oceans.

During the nineteenth century, protests against the worsening pollution began in both Europe and Japan. Great Britain, where the Industrial Revolution began, led the world in the introduction of pollution control measures. After numerous earlier failed attempts, the British Parliament approved legislation in 1853 aimed at reducing the level of smoke emitted by coal-burning furnaces, and in 1863 issued the Alkali Act requiring factories to remove 95 per cent of the hydrochloric acid emitted in the production of soap, glass and textiles. A second Alkali Act was passed a decade later; it required industries to apply the 'best practicable means' to address pollution problems. Water pollution was addressed when the stench of the River Thames, which had basically become an open sewer, was so bad that it made it almost impossible for Parliament to conduct its business. In 1876, Parliament approved the Rivers Pollution Prevention Act (Jacobson 2002: 84). Germany followed on the heels of Great Britain. In 1877 Prussia forbade the use of rivers for the dumping of sewage and introduced licensing requirements for polluting firms as a way of addressing air pollution (Wey 1982).

The fifth article of the Charter Oath of 1868 of the Meiji government stated that 'Knowledge shall be sought throughout the world so as to strengthen the foundations of imperial rule'. This led to the Iwakura Mission, about 100 individuals sent to Europe and the United States to learn from the West. This included areas of health, and the German concept of hygiene, *Gesundheitspflege*, was introduced to Japan and translated into Japanese as '衛生' (*eisei*) (Lee 2008). Europeans were also brought to Japan to help modernize the country. One was engineer William Kinninmond Burton who was invited to become a sanitary engineer and professor at Tokyo Imperial University. From his arrival in Japan in 1887 and for the next decade he worked on introducing water filtration and sewerage systems to Japan (Joyce 2006). Japan was in the middle of a cholera epidemic at the time, with reports of over 100,000 deaths in 1886 alone (Hayami 1986: 305). Europe had experienced similar cholera outbreaks and had started introducing sewage systems and treatment plants. This knowledge could thus be brought to Japan. In 1922 a sewage treatment plant was built in Tokyo (Mikawajima) and treatment plants followed in the next decades in Nagoya, Kyoto and other major cities (Asai n.d.). These early examples suggest that even when communication means were limited and the time required to travel distances was great, Europe and Japan were consciously learning from and assisting each other with serious pollution problems.

Cross-Societal Exchanges and Environmental Civil Society

There has also been considerable learning and exchange going on at the level of environmental civil society, and this for the better part of the last century. Both in Europe and Japan concerns about the loss of natural resources, rural landscapes and historical monuments gave birth to conservationist and preservationist movements and the beginnings of environmental non-governmental organizations (NGOs).

Private voluntary organizations for protection of open spaces began to form in Europe in the middle of the nineteenth century. In Great Britain the Commons, Open Spaces and Footpaths Preservations Society was formed in 1865; Mrs Robert W. Williamson established the Royal Society for the Protection of Birds in 1891 and four years later the National Trust was established to preserve places of historical interest and natural beauty. In Germany state governments sponsored the formation of nature-conservation agencies in response to the growth in nature tourism caused by urbanization and the growth of railroads. In 1914 the Deutscher Bund Heimatschutz (The Association for the Protection of the Homeland) formed as a network of local conservation and historical preservation associations. Japan's largest environmental group based on membership, the Wildbird Society (Nippon Yachô no Kai), was formed in 1934. It was clearly influenced by the bird watching societies that had formed in England (Schreurs 2005).

There are also signs of direct learning between Europe and Japan in relation to conservation initiatives. In 1896 the Reverend Walter Weston, an Englishman, wrote a book, *Mountaineering and Exploration in the Japanese Alps* (a name given to the mountains of central Japan by the Englishman William Gowland in his 1888 Japan Guide). Weston is credited with popularizing mountaineering in Japan (although the mountains he climbed had been scaled and formally consecrated decades earlier by the Buddhist monk Banryu). He was also instrumental in founding the Japan Alpine Club (Sutherland and Britton 1995). There are also more recent examples of cross-societal influences shaping the development of environmental civil society in Japan. The Dutch Prince Bernhard, for example, used the occasion of the Tokyo Olympics to invite Japan to form a branch of the World Wide Fund for Nature (WWF) (WWF 2014).

Through branch offices of various international environmental groups, such as WWF, Greenpeace and Friends of the Earth, Japanese and European environmental groups have also exchanged experiences and cooperated on campaigns. There are, however, major differences between the size and influence of environmental NGOs in Europe and Japan. Environmental groups remain relatively small and weak in Japan compared with Europe. In Europe NGOs receive substantial funds for their operations from public sources (although some groups such as Greenpeace do not accept government funds). They often have tens to hundreds of thousands of members, relatively large staffs and, due to their size, the ear of policy-makers.

Efforts to form a Green Party in Japan are also clearly influenced by the successful experiences of the green parties in Europe, and especially the Green Party in Germany. Various efforts to launch an environmental party in Japan have been undertaken. The most recent followed the Fukushima nuclear accident when in 2012 Japan Greens (緑の党) was established on the back of predecessor initiatives. The party remains small and its future remains uncertain, but it is clear that there is an interest in trying to import European successes with Green parties to Japan. A comparison of civil society groups in Europe and Japan shows that ideas and concepts travel. In the case of civil society activities, the learning appears to be going on in a more unilateral direction, passing from Europe to Japan. This may reflect both institutional factors that have inhibited the development of a strong civil society in Japan and cultural factors that may favour more local forms of association in Japan rather than the larger national and international networks that are common in Europe.

Cross-Societal Learning in the Establishment of Institutions for Environmental Protection and Pollution Control

The 1950s and 1960s were periods of rapid economic growth in Western Europe and Japan. Because of the importance placed on economic development, much like in earlier periods, industrial pollution was treated as a nuisance that simply had to be tolerated. But pollution became increasingly severe as the costs in terms of human suffering and loss of life, ecological destruction and economic loss mounted. Slowly, in the late 1960s and into the 1970s, environmental protection began to be recognized as a national government responsibility in Europe and Japan.

In Japan outbreaks of Minamata mercury poisoning, *itai-itai* disease, asthma from air pollution, and a long campaign fought by victims and their families with the support of outside experts for the rights of victims, forced the government to make pollution control a national priority. In response to the severe pollution and the suffering of thousands of victims, framework environmental regulations began to be introduced. The first major step was the Pollution Control Basic Law of 1967, which was strengthened through amendments in 1970. At this time over a dozen laws and amendments addressing air and water quality, nature conservation and noise pollution were passed. An Environment Agency was also established.

In Europe, which was suffering from its own severe pollution problems, pressures for change were building as well. Great Britain, suffering from severe air pollution incidents, such as the killer smog in London in 1952, which led to an estimated 4,000 deaths, was also under pressure to act. Parliament passed Clean Air Acts in 1956 and 1968 and the Control of Air Pollution Act in 1974. Sweden, suffering from acid rain caused by coal burning in England, Germany and Poland, led the way with the establishment of an Environmental Protection Agency in 1967. Sweden also initiated and hosted the 1972 United Nations Conference on the Human Environment (the Stockholm Conference) to focus global attention on the deteriorating state of the global environment and the problems of pollution, resource depletion, species loss and acid rain. A group of Japanese lawyers working on behalf of pollution victims introduced the idea of recognizing environmental protection as a natural right. Influenced by developments in Japan, Sweden, Britain and the United States, as well as at the international level, Germany created an environmental division in the Ministry of the Interior in 1971, and an Environment Agency in 1974. In 1971 Germany introduced a national environmental programme addressing numerous pollution issues. France established its Ministry of the Environment and the Protection of Nature in 1971. The similarity in timing of the major policy initiatives in Europe and Japan is striking and suggests that there was considerable cross-societal borrowing of policy ideas and approaches.

At this time, the European Economic Community (EEC, the predecessor to the European Union) was still relatively small. The EEC had only six members until Denmark, Ireland and the United Kingdom joined in 1973, raising the number to nine. Environmental protection was not yet a major topic for the EEC. Yet with attention to environmental matters growing within its member states and internationally, and with an interest in harmonizing the environmental laws of its member states to reduce internal trade barriers, the European Economic Community also launched its first environmental action programme in 1973. Its focus was on water protection and waste. A second programme was launched in 1977 with a broader focus on nature conservation.

European Interest in Japanese Approaches to Air Pollution Control

Various examples of the European Union or its member states turning to Japan for environmental policy ideas are observable. In the early 1970s Japan was one of the most polluted places on the planet. Yet its aggressive introduction of environmental pollution control laws transformed conditions so that by the end of the decade Japan was becoming a model for other societies. Europe, which had long been the source for environmental ideas for Japan, began to look with interest to Japan for inspiration in how to deal with major pollution problems.

Sulphur oxides from the burning of coal have long been known to cause health problems and local acidification. It was not until the 1960s and 1970s that the scientific community began to appreciate that sulphur emissions could be transported long distances and fall to the ground in the form of acid rain or snow, thereby causing damage to forests, water systems, buildings, monuments and other infrastructure. Acid rain became a major issue of concern in Europe in the 1970s and 1980s.

Given that in Japan there were dramatic drops in sulphur oxide emission levels during the 1970s, Europe began to look towards Japan. Japanese efforts to reduce sulphur oxide emissions were in significant part successful because of fuel switching, the use of desulphurization technology and the extensive use of voluntary agreements between industry and local governments regarding pollution control. Furthermore, the Pollution Victims Compensation Law introduced in 1973 provided an added incentive to reduce pollution levels, as companies had to pay into a system to support the medical bills of air pollution victims living within designated pollution zones. During the 1970s Japanese industries invested heavily in pollution control technologies and became world leaders in the use of desulphurization equipment.

When Germany and Europe began experiencing damage to their forests as a result of acid rain, pressures to control air pollution grew stronger. As Japan was far more advanced than Germany in its air pollution control at this time, Japanese pollution control techniques and policies began to be studied in Germany (Schreurs 2002). Eventually, in 1983, the German Diet passed the Large Combustion Plant Ordinance (*Grossfeuerungsanlagen-Verordnung* (GFAVo)), which established stringent sulphur dioxide emission controls for large polluters. The following year the European Community introduced a similar directive.

The Top Runner and Energy Efficiency Programmes of Europe and Japan

Another example of Europe taking ideas from Japan is the Top Runner programme, introduced by Japan in 1999 as a means to promote the development of more energy-efficient appliances. The programme is credited with speeding the introduction of more energy-efficient models into the market. Essentially, the programme takes the standard of the most efficient product on the market and makes that the standard that the entire industry must meet within a given time frame, usually four to eight years. It has done this for over 20 different product groups ranging from various electrical goods (for example refrigerators, washing machines, television sets) to vehicles (passenger cars and freight) to heating and cooking stoves and vending machines. Firms that fail to meet the new standards are penalized by having their failure reported. Products that meet the standard get a Top Runner label. The programme has resulted in something similar to a race to the top – a race to be the best.

In November 2005 the new coalition government in Germany announced the promotion of a European 'Top Runner programme'. The inspiration came from Japan via a proposal produced by Greenpeace for a national top runner programme. Although the proposal adapted the concept of the Top Runner programme to the German and European situations, it clearly was inspired by the Japanese model (Nordqvist 2007). With the European Union having adopted an energy efficiency goal of 20 per cent by 2020 (compared with each member state's 2005 energy efficiency levels) and the reality that implementation has been problematic, any measures that might help to reach the goal are being given renewed attention.

In 2011 the German Federal Environment and Economics Ministries published a joint concept paper outlining how the top runner approach could be further developed at the EU level. The concept paper argues that as is the case in Japan, the EU should take the most efficient products of a group as the base reference and make this standard the minimum efficiency standard for the future. In addition, energy consumption labelling should be implemented and extended to a wide range of product groups. This and a series of other proposals were forwarded by Germany to the responsible EU Commissioners and represent the position that Germany took in relation to the implementation and development of the EU framework directive on ecodesign and energy consumption labelling (Federal Environment Ministry 2014). In the meantime the German Energy Agency (DENA) has launched a website focused on the European Top Runner Strategy, referring to the European Union's coordinated group of regulatory measures to systematically increase the energy efficiency of products (Germany Energy Agency 2013).

The Collaborating Centre on Sustainable Consumption and Production, together with the Federal Environment Agency (Umweltbundesamt) and the Wuppertal Institute for Climate, Environment and Energy also issued a paper, 'Resource Efficiency: Japan and Europe at the Forefront'. The paper begins with the comments:

> Both Germany and Japan have been among the leaders in the field of environmental technologies, and both are currently pursuing advancement in strategic issues of resource management. One of the objectives of the German government's sustainability strategy of 2002 is to double raw material productivity by 2020 compared to the reference year of 1994. The Japanese strategy aims at improving resource productivity by forty per cent by 2010 (compared to 1990). The 3R initiative as well as Japanese governance structures are of interest to German resource efficiency efforts for two reasons: firstly, national policy can benefit and learn from exchange of experiences between the two countries. Secondly, the German EU/G8 presidencies in 2007 offered a favourable opportunity for exploring and expanding international cooperation mechanisms and mutual policy learning, especially as Japan took over the G8 presidency following Germany in 2008. (Federal Environment Agency 2008)

The study highlighted other programmes of potential interest to Europe in addition to the Top Runner programme. These included the Eco Town Programme, which seeks to reduce resource use through intelligent waste management systems within specific regions; a law requiring green public procurement to support the use of eco-friendly products; and Japanese approaches to the measurement of material flows (material flow analysis or accounting).

Europe Learning from Japan's Experiences with a Catastrophic Accident: The Fukushima Nuclear Crisis

Sometimes the learning between Europe and Japan is stimulated by crisis experiences. This is the case with the Fukushima nuclear accident. The inundation of the reactors at the Fukushima Dai-ichi Nuclear Power Plant by the tsunami waters and the subsequent loss of electricity that led the cooling systems to shut down triggered the world's second worst nuclear accident after Chernobyl. The fact that the accident occurred in a technologically advanced democracy like Japan had major ramifications for nuclear policy in Europe. It led to decisions by a number of European member states to abandon or reduce their dependence on nuclear energy.

The report of the German Ethics Commission for a Safe Energy Supply (2011: 10–11) discussed the various lessons learned from Japan's nuclear catastrophe:

> The accident in Fukushima has shaken people's confidence in experts' assessments of the 'safety' of nuclear power stations ... Even citizens who do not reject nuclear power categorically are no longer prepared to leave it to committees of experts to decide on how to deal with the fundamental possibility of an uncontrollable, major accident ...

> ... The risks of nuclear power have not changed as a result of Fukushima; the perception of those risks has ...

> ... firstly, [there is] the fact that the reactor accident occurred in a technologically advanced country like Japan. In view of this, the conviction that such an event could not occur in Germany, is waning ...

> ... secondly, [there is] the impossibility even weeks after the accident of predicting an end to the catastrophe, of assessing the final extent of the overall damage or of conclusively defining the geographical region affected. The widespread view that the extent of the damage due even to major incidents can be adequately determined and limited in order to be weighted up [or compared], in a scientifically informed process, against the disadvantages of other sources of energy, is becoming considerably less persuasive ...

> ... thirdly, [there is] the fact that the accident was triggered by a process which the nuclear reactor was not 'designed' to withstand without sustaining damage. This fact casts a light on the limitations of technological risk assessments. The events in Fukushima have made it obvious that such assessments are based on certain assumptions, for example about earthquake resistance or the maximum height of a tsunami, and that reality can prove these assumptions wrong.

In response to the Fukushima nuclear accident, the German government reversed a decision it had made in October 2010 to extend the allowable operation time of Germany's nuclear power plants. A decision to speed up a nuclear phase out that had already been agreed upon in 2001 was also made. Under the laws passed in the summer of 2011, Germany is to phase out the last of its nuclear power plants in 2022 (Schreurs 2013a; Mez 2012). Several other European countries also decided to abandon nuclear energy after the accident. This was the case in Italy where there was a public referendum in which an overwhelming majority of the population voted against nuclear energy; Switzerland, which decided to shut down its nuclear industry when the contract for the youngest of its nuclear power plants ends in 2034; and Belgium, which has also announced its intent to shift away from nuclear energy. France decided not to abandon nuclear energy but to work to cut its dependency on nuclear energy as a result of the Japanese catastrophe (Schreurs 2013b).

Not all European countries responded similarly to Japan's nuclear accident, however. Great Britain has announced its intentions to continue with nuclear energy, and Poland and the Czech Republic have both expressed interest in building new power plants. Thus, at the European level, the focus has been more on improving safety measures. The European Commission issued a proposal for an amendment to the Euratom Directive on the nuclear safety of nuclear institutions. The proposal begins with a discussion of the implications of what happened in Japan for the EU:

> The accident at the Fukushima Daiichi nuclear power plant (NPP) in 2011 resulted in significant environmental, economic and social damage, and raised concerns about possible health effects in the affected population in Japan. Although triggered by an earthquake and tsunami of an immense magnitude, investigations of the causes of the accident reveal a range of foreseeable factors which combined to produce a catastrophic outcome. The analysis of the Fukushima nuclear accident reveals quite substantial and recurring technical issues as well as persistent institutional failures similar to the ones from the post-accident evaluations of the Three Mile Island and Chernobyl nuclear accidents decades ago. This latest nuclear accident once again undermined public confidence in the safety of nuclear power; and particularly so at a time when the use of nuclear power is being debated as a possible option to meet global energy demands in a sustainable manner. The Fukushima nuclear accident renewed attention on the paramount importance of ensuring the most robust levels of nuclear safety in the EU and worldwide (European Commission 2013f).

The proposal then goes on to list the steps the EU has taken in response to the events in Fukushima: EU-wide comprehensive risk and safety assessments (stress tests) related to extreme natural events challenging the plants' safety functions; an EU-wide peer review process that led to a series of recommendations and an action plan; and legislative review. Finally, proposals for an amendment to the safety of nuclear plants directive were presented (European Commission 2013f).

Japan Learning from the EU: Renewable Energy Development

In the wake of the nuclear crisis, Japan too has been keenly studying European approaches to renewable energy development. Due to the shut down for safety checks of the nation's nuclear power plants and the local opposition that has prevented many plants from reopening, Japan is in a quite desperate energy situation. Pressured by a public that has become wary of nuclear energy, the government began to consider ways to promote renewable energy, a vastly underdeveloped resource in Japan. Both civil society groups and government officials have been eager to better understand European development of renewable energy. Dozens and possibly hundreds of government, academic, and civil society groups have made special visits to Europe to meet with European energy experts and learn from European experiences with renewable energy development.

The European Union has been strongly promoting renewable energies. Renewable energy amounted to 11.9 per cent of EU-27 gross electricity consumption in 1990, 13.8 per cent in 2000, and 19.9 per cent in 2010.This rapid expansion has been driven by a series of directives and measures adopted at the national level by member states. In 2001 the European Community issued Directive 2001/77/EC with a goal of reaching a 21 per cent share of renewable energy in the EU's electricity mix by 2010. In March 2007, the EU Council established new climate and energy targets; these were codified in EU Directive 2009/406/EC. The directive set three main targets for 2020: a 20 per cent reduction of EU greenhouse gas emissions compared to a 1990 baseline or 30 per cent if other major emitting countries commit to comparable action; a 20 per cent share of renewable energy in the EU's primary energy mix (covering transport, heating/cooling and electricity) and enhancing energy efficiency by 20 per cent compared to 2005 levels in each of the member states. Interim targets were also established for meeting the renewable energy goal. Each member state was expected to have obtained 25 per cent of the target between 2011 and 2012, 35 per cent between 2013 and 2014, 45 per cent between 2015 and 2016, and 65 per cent between 2017 and 2018.

Most European member states have implemented feed-in-tariffs to support the introduction of renewable energy. The feed-in-tariff models vary considerably in terms of their conditions and levels of support but work on similar principles. They require grid operators to purchase renewable energy and provide suppliers of renewable energy with fixed prices for specific lengths of time.

After the Fukushima nuclear accident Japanese experts studied the European feed-in-tariff models and made proposals to the Japanese government for the introduction of a Japanese feed-in-tariff system. The Japanese government introduced a feed-in-tariff system, with some of the highest support rates for renewables (especially photovoltaics) in the world, in June 2012. The programme has had considerable success in terms of rapid capacity expansion in photovoltaics since its introduction. Japan is now ranked number five in the world in terms of installed capacity with about 10 GW as of mid-2013 (Germany has 35 GW and is ranked number one in the world). It has been less successful in stimulating investment in wind power.

Japanese Learning from the EU's Problems with Feed-in-Tariff Designs

Renewable energy promotion has not always followed a smooth trajectory in the European Union. In Spain, a leader in Europe in the installation of solar photovoltaics and wind power, overly favourable feed-in-tariff rates for photovoltaics made renewable energy such an attractive area for investment and led to such rapid capacity expansion that the state determined it could not continue to support the programme and thus pulled the plug on its feed-in-tariff programme.

In Germany, after the Fukushima nuclear accident, there was a rapid expansion of renewable energy capacity. Because of the way the feed-in-tariff was designed and the exclusions that were given to large energy-intensive industries, the cost of the feed-in-tariff is largely born by households and small- and medium-sized firms. This fee comes in the form of a feed-in-tariff surcharge. In 2005 the surcharge was only 0.6 euro cents per kilowatt hour, but in 2013 the amount had jumped to 5.3 euro cents per kilowatt hour and in 2014 it hit 6.2 euro cents per kilowatt hour. Because renewable energy is more established in the market, the feed-in-tariff levels will be reduced and new design elements will be introduced that slow the rising costs to consumers without preventing the further growth of renewables. Eventually the feed-in-tariff will be phased out as renewable energy becomes more market competitive.

Japan has been watching these trends, and has already begun the process of adjusting its own feed-in-tariff support levels, especially for large-scale photovoltaic systems. As a first step, one year after the programme was introduced, the support level for photovoltaics was reduced by 10 per cent. Here too there are clear indications of cross-societal learning going on.

EU–Japan Bilateral Cooperation

Various institutions have been developed to encourage EU–Japan cooperation on environmental matters. These are certainly additional channels for promoting exchange of ideas and joint activities. Olena Mykal has traced EU–Japan environmental cooperation to the 1970s and focuses special attention on how, due to Japan's embrace of a concept known as comprehensive security and the EU's positioning of itself as a civilian power, environmental protection quickly entered EU–Japan security dialogues (Mykal 2011).With the 1991 Hague Joint Declaration on Relations between the European Union and its member states and Japan, Japan and the EU agreed to cooperate on 'transnational challenges, such as the issue of environment, the conservation of resources and energy' (EEAS 1991). In subsequent yearly meetings, various issues were discussed at various lengths, including forest conservation, acid rain and climate change, and information was exchanged on various environmental issues, like waste management and toxic chemical classification. At the 16th EU-Japan Summit that convened in Berlin in June 2007 both sides agreed to work on a UN post-2012 framework for climate change that ensures the participation of all major emitting countries. They also agreed on the importance of having a 2050 goal to halve global greenhouse gas emissions and supporting developing economies in addressing climate change. The European Commission and Japan also meet for High Level Consultations on the Environment (Delegation of the European Union to Japan 2014).

The 21st meeting was held in Tokyo in November 2013. At the meeting there was discussion of the importance of cooperating to achieve the Millennium Development Goals and coordinating contributions to global discussions about post-2015 goals. This includes addressing climate change (with a focus placed on phasing down reliance on hydrofluorocarbons, which have a particularly high global warming potential), and improving the liberalization of electricity markets, nuclear regulatory frameworks (especially nuclear safety) and energy research.

The EU-Japan Centre for Industrial Cooperation, a non-profit created in 1987 by the European Commission and Japan, and with offices in Brussels and Tokyo, has also focused some attention on environmental and energy issues. The centre has held joint seminars on energy efficiency in buildings, on power sector transitions, on the Doha Climate negotiations, energy efficiency in industry through corporate networks, energy security and sustainability challenges, trade in legal timber and EU–Japan–Iceland cooperation on geothermal energy, among many other issues.

EU–Japan Cooperation in International Agreements

Yet another avenue where Europe and Japan work together is in the context of global environmental negotiations. Japan, the EU and its member states are parties to many of the same global environmental agreements. In many areas, Europe and Japan have also been drivers in pushing for stronger global environmental agreements. In a number of instances Europe and Japan have cooperated to support an international agreement that the United States failed to enforce, an interesting display of what Yves Tiberghien has referred to as the Minervan powers exerting influence over the shape and influence of international agreements and institutions (Tiberghien 2013). Two examples of this are the cases of the Convention on Biological Diversity and the Kyoto Protocol.

Biological Diversity and the Biodiversity Convention

There have been considerable divisions among countries over how biological diversity should be protected and genetically modified organisms regulated.[1] In the mid-1980s the United States proposed a comprehensive global treaty to conserve biological diversity. International negotiations began in 1991, and an international agreement on biodiversity preservation was formed at the United Nations Conference on Environment and Development (UNCED) in Rio de Janeiro in June 1992. Surprisingly, given its early role in initiating the idea for such a global agreement, the United States did not sign the agreement in Rio de Janeiro. The agreement received wide-scale support and 150 countries, including Canada, Japan, the European Community and all of its member states, signed. The Biodiversity Convention entered into force in December 1993 after obtaining the requisite number of signatories.

The Biodiversity Convention is intended to slow species extinction through conservation practices and the promotion of economic development based on sustainable use of ecological systems. The richest areas in terms of biological diversity tend to be in developing countries where many species have yet to even be identified and documented.

The Biodiversity Convention has led to the development of an information base on biological diversity and national biodiversity strategies and action plans and indicators for measuring trends in biodiversity. Under the George H.W. Bush administration, the United States failed to sign the convention due to the pharmaceutical industries' concerns about the convention's provisions dealing with biotechnology regulations and intellectual property rights. Also problematic for the Bush administration was the equity regime's focus on equity and just compensation as this could mean large transfers of funding and know-how to developing countries. While Bill Clinton took a different stance on the agreement and signed it in 1993, the convention was never brought before the full US Senate for a vote, and thus has never been ratified. Opposition to the convention in the US Senate stems from concerns about ownership of intellectual property, financial and technological transfer demands, and property rights issues.

In this instance, Japan and the European Union chose to move forward in cooperating with other states to ensure the agreement's success. In the meantime they have developed national strategies on biological diversity. The European Union adopted a goal of halting biodiversity loss within its member states by 2010. A major element of the EU's strategy was enhancing the development of indicators and monitoring techniques related to biodiversity conservation and making these open to the public. Japan's National Strategy on Biological Diversity was released in 1995. It did not have a concrete goal to halt biodiversity loss by a particular date

---

1   The following three sections, on the Biodiversity Convention, the Cartagena Protocol on Biosafety, and Global Climate Change, draw heavily on Schreurs (2012).

but promoted monitoring, research and surveys, the strengthening of protective measures, and the addition of new protected and conservation areas. The Japanese government also established new funding institutions and mechanisms to support conservation efforts in developing countries. At the 2010 Nagoya Conference of the Parties to the Convention on Biological Diversity several new goals were established, including cutting by at least half the loss of natural habitats, expanding nature reserves to 17 per cent of global land area by 2020 (up from about 13 per cent today) and expanding marine reserves from 1 per cent to about 10 per cent of the world's seas. Countries are also required to draw up national biodiversity preservation plans. Finally, new rules on how countries should share benefits derived from genetic resources were established.

The Cartagena Protocol on Biosafety

A provision of the Biodiversity Conservation called for an assessment of the need for a protocol on biosafety. Throughout the 1990s, as new technologies developed, scientists, NGOs and developing countries began to express their worries about potential human and environmental harm from genetically modified organisms. These actors called for an international agreement that would lay out safety rules governing bio- and genetic engineering. European nations began to add their voices to the calls for a biosafety protocol. In 1995 an ad hoc Working Group on Biosafety was set up by the conference of the parties to the Biodiversity Convention. After four years of contentious negotiations, the Cartagena Protocol on Biosafety, a supplement to the Biodiversity Convention, was agreed upon (Cosby and Burgiel 2000). It went into effect in 2003. The protocol gives member states the right to signal if they are willing or opposed to the import of genetically-modified products. They must communicate their concerns, and the basis for those concerns, through the Biosafety Clearing House.

Japan, the EU and all EU member states have ratified the Cartagena Protocol. In Europe, where public distrust of genetically-modified organisms is strong, there was powerful public demand for the Cartagena Protocol and acquiescence on the part of the agricultural industry, which has not been widely involved in testing or manufacturing GM products. In contrast, the United States, Canada, Australia and Argentina have not ratified the agreement due to the very strong opposition coming from their agricultural lobbies and a lesser level of concern shown by their publics. Japan was a member of the 'compromise group' (Japan, Norway, Switzerland, Mexico and South Korea) in the negotiations. This group supported trade in genetically modified organisms, but recognized the need for safety restrictions as demanded by developing countries and the United States.

Global Climate Change

The United States was initially a supporter of establishing an international agreement to address global warming. The United Nations Framework Convention on Climate Change (UNFCCC) as negotiated at the UNCED in 1992 recognized global climate change as a serious problem and called upon the developed nations, which are responsible for the majority of the anthropogenic greenhouse gases that have accumulated in the atmosphere, to take action first to reduce their emissions and to provide financial and technological assistance to developing countries in addressing the impacts of climate change. Canada, Japan, the United States and the European Community all signed the agreement in Rio de Janeiro and ratified it in the following one and a half years.

The UNFCC established a Conference of the Parties that was given the mandate of formulating a protocol that would spell out specific measures to be taken to protect the planet from global warming. After five years and considerable disagreement, the European Union, the United States and Japan negotiated the Kyoto Protocol. By the end of the difficult negotiations the United States had agreed to reduce its greenhouse gas emissions by 7 per cent of 1990 levels by 2008–2012. The European Union accepted an 8 per cent reduction with differentiated targets for each of its then 15 member states. Under pressure as the host nation to the negotiations, Japan agreed to a 6 per cent reduction target.

The Kyoto Protocol, however, was never presented to the US Senate for ratification because of strong opposition there to the agreement on the grounds that it did not ask developing countries to participate in sufficiently meaningful ways. Opponents argued that it would cost the US economy too much to implement and would put US industry at a competitive disadvantage with industries in developing countries. Initially, individual EU member states, EU delegates and Japan tried to persuade the United States back into the agreement with suggestions of further compromises. After it became clear that the United States was not planning to change its position, the EU and Japan decided to move forward in their efforts to win sufficient support for the protocol to become binding even without US participation. After some initial wavering, Canada and Russia agreed to cooperate. The Kyoto Protocol came into force in 2005 largely due to joint Japanese and European Union efforts. Japan has not, however, been willing to support a second phase of the Kyoto Protocol as pushed for by the European Union, instead supporting an inclusive global agreement. The future shape of a global climate agreement remains, however, unclear.

Conclusion

Competition and cooperation have helped Europe and Japan become increasingly effective at dealing with conventional pollution problems. They have clearly influenced each other's environmental and energy policy trajectories. They have also worked together to promote some key global environmental agreements. As economically strong states with high education levels and strong environmental capacities, they also have a responsibility to take on leadership roles in relation to the many global environmental challenges still facing the planet: resource depletion, climate change, biodiversity loss, overfishing, excessive consumption and resulting waste, plastic islands in the world's oceans and radioactive waste disposal.

The European Union became increasingly assertive in its environmental foreign policy in the 1990s due to a combination of factors. In the 1990s several states with strong domestic environmental movements joined the European Union (Austria, Finland, Sweden). Public opinion was also strongly pro-environment. Compared with the 1970s, the European Union also gained new competencies, strengthening its ability to play a leadership role. It is also significant that due to its own experience gained from harmonizing environmental regulations across its member states, the EU has an appreciation for multilateral solutions to problems. There are also strong traditions of consultative decision-making among business, government and NGOs in Europe. Finally, Europe is eager to be a global player, and environmental protection is an area where it feels it has an advantage and can take on such a role.

In response to its efforts to lead internationally on the environment, Europe has set out on a course of structural transformation. It has established goals to reduce its carbon dioxide emissions by 80–95 per cent of 1990 levels by 2050, to sharply improve energy efficiency and expand renewable energies. It has developed new sustainability indicators and resource efficiency policy strategies and biodiversity protection measures. There are, of course, many obstacles that still need to be addressed or overcome – such as different perspectives of member states on nuclear energy and carbon capture and sequestration. Nevertheless, there is a relatively solid understanding that Europe's future must be one based on a model that is low resource and energy intensive and protective of natural ecological systems.

In Japan the implications of the Fukushima nuclear disaster are still unfolding. Already, however, paths of change are evident. It is likely that Japan will reduce its reliance on nuclear energy and develop more renewables. Energy conservation measures that have been taken in response to the shortages of electricity tied to the shutting down of most of the country's nuclear capacity in the years following Fukushima are making Japan once again a global leader in energy efficiency processes and technologies. Thus, for somewhat different reasons, Europe and Japan are likely to be leaders in the next stages of the development of green economies. This is likely to lead them into further situations of both competition and cooperation.

Chapter 8

Sympathy or Self-Interest?
The Development Agendas of the European
Union and Japan in the 2000s

Bart Gaens and Henri Vogt

This chapter compares the evolution of the development policies of the European Union and Japan since the turn of the millennium. The analysis focuses on how official development activities play into the ambitions of both of these self-proclaimed civilian powers to increase their regional and global presence. The ultimate question thus concerns the extent to which the fusion – or should we rather talk of fission? – of instrumental and idealistic development policies differs in the case of those two actors, and what the consequences of these differences are.

A comparison of the two cases has a triple advantage. First, it will yield new insights into the different paths and outcomes that ensue from two seemingly similar ideational approaches to aid. Both the European Union and Japan are 'soft powers' with limited military capacities, and both have aimed to apply development assistance to achieve similar goals, but their respective trajectories in terms of aid policy are often remarkably divergent. Second, comparing the European experience with an Asian model will shed new light on the 'Western paradigm' of Official Development Assistance (ODA). Third, the comparative method potentially reveals prospects for enhanced future cooperation in the development sector between the EU and Japan.

Since the Treaty of Rome development policy has composed an essential part of the process of European integration. The EU has also actively contributed to the formulation of global development paradigms, from the development idealism of the 1970s, through the scepticism and structural adjustment policies of the 1980s and 1990s, until today's focus on the Millennium Development Goals (MDGs) and comprehensive human development framework. Japan, by contrast, has had a much lower profile in the field of international development policy, but similarly to the EU it has also increasingly focused on the MDGs and human security. In both cases, it is obvious that development actorness has not only been based on altruistic considerations, but has been a vital tool of foreign policy. Approaches to aid therefore also elucidate how these two actors define their self-interest and how they see themselves as global players.

The chapter begins by reviewing the most important features, current trends and recent changes in the development policies of these two actors. The analysis

then turns to comparative observations, concentrating on global civilian power
discourse and image, security and trade issues, and the respective regional roles
of Japan and the EU. The chapter concludes by identifying possible convergences
and potential opportunities for future cooperation.

The Rationales of EU Development Policy

Development policy has been significant for the process of European integration
from the very beginning, originally because of the colonial legacy of *les six* (the
founding members of the EU) and of their need to solve the 'problem' of their
overseas colonies. With time the policy has become a crucial building block of
the Union's self-understanding and image: in its rhetoric of the 2000s the Union
has constantly boasted that it is the number one donor in the world – and indeed
it is, if the member states' ODA flows are also taken into account. In 2012 the EU
member states' net ODA totalled 64.9 billion US dollars[1] (including approximately
17.6 billion in aid channelled through the Union), which was equivalent to 0.3 per
cent of these countries' GNI. The respective figures for the United States, clearly
the world's number two donor, were 30.5 billion and 0.19 per cent (OECD 2013a).

For the EU, development policy has served, and still serves, at least three
main purposes. First, the Union has acted as a donor in its own right. The African,
Caribbean and Pacific countries (ACP) have traditionally been the main target of
this, and the European Development Fund (EDF) its main financial instrument; the
so called Cotonou Agreement has regulated the relations between these groups of
countries since its signature in June 2000 and will do so until its expiration in 2020.
The Union's efforts to assist the democratization processes of its neighbouring
regions and the establishment of the current comprehensive global development
paradigm have made it more difficult than before to unequivocally delineate the
boundaries of this donor role. The role is now more diverse than, say, 20 years ago.
The EDF is by no means the only source of EU development funding; considerable
amounts of money are also delivered through the European Neighbourhood Policy
and the Development Cooperation Instruments.[2]

---

1   Of this amount, the 15 EU members that are also members of DAC covered 63.7
billion. This was equivalent to 0.42 of these countries' GNI.

2   The 10th EDF for the years 2008–2013 was 22.7 billion euros, of which 97 per
cent was allocated to the ACP countries (the 9th EDF, 2000–2007, was 13.5 billion euros).
The assistance commitments for the European Neighbourhood Policy Instrument (ENPI)
in 2007–2012 were 10.9 billion euros and the allocations for the Development Policy
Instrument 16.9 billion euros for the same period. The ACP countries are afraid of further
losing the special status they enjoyed for decades under the new Lisbon Framework, where
bilateral relations are taken care of by the EEAS and not by a development DG (see, for
example, Bartelt 2012). The Cotonou Agreement, which has been revised several times
already (the most recent revision is from 2010), is much less 'economic' and much more

Second, the EU has sought to coordinate the aid policies of its member states. Most of them have deemed it necessary to maintain an independent development aid policy of their own, parallel to that of the Union. This has been justified in the name of efficiency and complementarity: many member states enjoy a natural advantage in terms of cooperative networks in receiver countries, stemming from their colonial histories. The Nordic countries, for their part, have believed that their non-colonial past has guaranteed them particular credibility and goodwill among the partner states. In this respect, the Lisbon Treaty did not change the division of labour between the member states and the Union itself. The Treaty states that EU development policy and member states' development policies should 'complement and reinforce each other' (Article 208; Stocchetti 2013: Ch. 2.2). It is noteworthy that in terms of actual financial flows, bilateral aid of the member states tends to be larger than the aid coordinated through the EU. To give an example of a close-to-average member state, Finland's total disbursed ODA in 2011 was 1.013 billion euros (ca. 0.5 per cent of GNI), of which 155 million was channelled through the EU (including 48.6 million allocated to the EDF), whereas bilateral and regional development assistance was 242 million.[3]

Third, and most importantly for this chapter, the EU has sought through development policy to increase, more or less consciously, its norm-setting power and general influence in global affairs. In many respects, the Union has certainly succeeded in this effort, but its development partners have also occasionally interpreted the gap between the Union's rhetoric and deeds as prime examples of Western double standards. This naturally entails potential negative consequences to Europe's overall soft power both globally and with respect to regional cooperative frameworks.

In the EU's recent documents guiding its development activities, this third aim manifests itself in terms of a strong adherence to *international society*, primarily discernible through the United Nations system; in this society norm-enforcement by external actors appears ever more possible.[4] For example, 'The European Consensus on Development' of December 2005, the most important development policy document in the 2000s, starts off with a strong commitment to the UN Millennium Development Goals and global poverty eradication: 'The primary and overarching objective ... is the eradication of poverty in the context of sustainable development, including pursuit of the Millennium Development Goals' (Article

---

political than its predecessors, the Yaoundé and Lomé Conventions, primarily because many of the economic issues now fall under the WTO regime.

3   Other significant disbursements included humanitarian aid (91.4 million euros), support for development cooperation with NGOs (92.4 million) and non-country-based development aid (46.7 million). www.formin.fi, accessed 11 June 2013.

4   In other words, the basic values of that society increasingly seem to follow the principles of a solidarist, as opposed to pluralist, take on the world, to use the terminology of the English School. Through its development policy, the European Union naturally contributes to the habitual redefinition of these values.

5). Moreover, the document emphasizes the importance of good governance and the 'objectives agreed at the UN major conferences and summits'. Since the mid-2000s this UN-friendly rhetoric has not changed much. In a 2011 Commission communication, 'Increasing the Impact of EU Development Policy: An Agenda for Change', these objectives have basically been reproduced, though with a stronger emphasis on a differentiated treatment of partner countries. The two cornerstones of the policy are to promote 'human rights, democracy and other key elements of good governance' and 'inclusive and sustainable growth for human development' (European Commission 2011e: 4).

Coherence and Differentiation

The European Union has been well aware of the looming risk of double standards in its external relations, and the critical reactions that these can provoke in partner countries. It has therefore invested a lot of energy in efforts to improve the coherence between its various policies over the past decade. This has happened both vertically, by seeking to better coordinate policies with the member states, and horizontally between the various institutions, policy sectors and directorates of the Union itself. Because of its potentially altruistic nature, development policy has often been at the core of these efforts. The most important conceptual innovation in this respect has been the notion of *policy coherence for development* introduced by the European Consensus. Newer development documents are full of references to the notion (for example Article 12 of the 2010 version of the Cotonou Agreement).

In the Union's institutional reforms of the late 2000s, the goal of coherence also played a crucial role. The 2009 Lisbon Treaty sought to bring all the Union's external activities, including development policy, under the same umbrella. Development policy shall now be conducted within the framework of the principles and objectives of the Union's external action, and 'the Union shall take account of the objectives of the development cooperation in the policies that it implements which are likely to affect developing countries' (Article 208). The Treaty also established the European External Action Service, launched in January 2011, and the post of the High Representative for Foreign Affairs that were also thought to guarantee better coherence between the various EU external policies.

In reality, however, achieving policy coherence for development has proved very difficult, and these institutional reforms have possibly even had a negative impact on it. Through its regional units and delegations in partner countries, the EEAS deals with a great number of development issues. It does this in the context of the Union's overall foreign and security policy agenda, but its range of concrete carrots or sticks to back up its objectives is fairly limited. Development issues 'proper', and the main financial resources in the form of the EDF, remained primarily within the Commission and its Directorate General for Development and Cooperation – EuropeAid. Within the overall institutional infrastructure in Brussels it has become weaker than its predecessor DGs, however. It is still premature to say what the long-term impacts of these institutional changes on development policy will be (see, for example, Balfour and Raik 2013).

Many, if not most, EU policy sectors include a potential development dimension, but three of them seem particularly relevant in terms of coherence: trade, security and sustainability (writ large). Figure 8.1 highlights that in development rhetoric and jargon, and perhaps also in reality, these can be understood in terms of a multidimensional nexus, which also comprises an analytical distinction between altruism/idealism and interests. The *Agenda for Change*, for example, notes that security, development and democracy are 'intertwined' (European Commission 2011e: 3) and, as was noted previously, growth must be inclusive and *sustainable*.

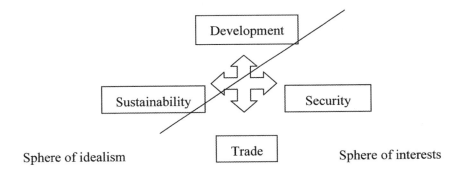

Figure 8.1 The development nexus

Trade policy, one of the EU's central fields of activity, composes possibly the most crucial dimension in this context; *aid for trade* has prevailed as a paradigmatic slogan of the 2000s. Even a superficial reading of trade policy documents makes it clear that the language is clearly different from the 'pure' development documents, which indeed seem to include an element of altruism; it is obvious that in terms of policy coherence attitudes even within the Commission still need some streamlining. For example, in the Commission Communication 'Trade, Growth and World Affairs', perhaps the most important recent (2010) document related to the EU's role as a trade actor, the attitude of defending one's own interests is strongly at the forefront. The rhetoric is occasionally almost fierce:

> The EU will remain an open economy but we will not be naïve. In particular, the Commission will remain vigilant in defence of European interests and European jobs. It will fight unfair trading practices with all appropriate means. (Ch. 1)

In spite of this outspoken defence of Europe's own interests, the document also emphasizes coherence with respect to global development objectives.[5] This drive for policy coherence should be reconcilable with the need for *differentiated*, context-specific treatment of individual partner countries:

> EU trade policy is helping the poorest economies by also providing generous unilateral trade preferences. More generally we are employing a carefully differentiated approach depending on the level of development of our partners. We are paying systematic attention to coherence with development policies, such as poverty eradication. (Ch. 1)

It seems that it is precisely the idea of *differentiation*, within the context of coherence, that has now assumed the status of an overarching principle on both sides of the development–trade nexus. For example, in another important recent Commission document, entitled 'Trade, Growth and Development' (2012a) differentiation is justified by reference to the fact that partner countries increasingly experience divergent development outcomes, from economic success stories to failed-states, and that 'the notion of developing countries as a group is losing its relevance as a result' (p. 2). What is also important in this logic is that it is primarily trade that has made the positive development path possible; therefore trade, and liberalized trade, is needed even more than before. In practice, the implications of differentiation can vary significantly: from mixing policy instruments differently to drastic rechanneling of development assistance. Some countries may no longer even be eligible for development aid in the first place (ECDPM 2012).

This differentiated treatment does not appear to be too popular among the Union's partners, particularly within the ACP group. At the ACP Summit in December 2012, for example, the Heads of State of these countries were explicitly critical of the approach, expressing their 'concern regarding the notion of differentiation, which if applied as graduation may lead to significant reduction in allocation of EDF resources' (Sipopo Declaration, Article 15). From the ACP's point of view, the problem is apparently that the EU itself can define what 'differentiation' means, to whom certain policy measures apply, and what forms of assistance a partner country needs. New conditionalities can be applied even more easily than before.

In the context of EU development policy, the nexus between development and trade – and efforts to bring about coherence in terms of differentiation – has primarily materialized through the efforts to reach a decision on the bilateral Economic Partnership Agreements introduced in the Cotonou Agreement and drafted according to the principles of the WTO. The EU has negotiated regionally with six groups of countries, but only one of these negotiation processes has been completed successfully, that with the Caribbean countries. The main

---

5   It is often also the notion of *complementarity* that figures in the discourses on the linkages between trade and development.

problem appears to be that the EU demands very far-reaching reciprocity in trade liberalization, whereas the ACP countries find it justified that a part of their domestic production remains protected from complete trade liberalization.[6] From the latter's point of view, the question is thus of justice and continuity in terms of development assistance. In the above mentioned Sipopo Declaration, the ACP Heads of State thus addressed this message to the EU:

> ... we recall that the key objectives of the trade and economic cooperation is to transform ACP's economies, improve competitiveness, promote sustainable development and thereby reduce poverty with a view to its eradication and to increase our States' share of world trade. (Article 34)

On a positive note, as Silke Trommer (2013) convincingly shows, trade policies within the context of EPA negotiations can potentially also involve the society at large. Within the West African region that Trommer studied, we can even observe participatory trade politics, with positive implications for development objectives. Allowing civic actors to be part of the EPA negotiation process has strengthened the region's knowledge base and thus made it better equipped to challenge the views of its negotiation partner.

Japanese Development Policy in the 2000s

Similarly to the EU, Japan has regarded Official Development Assistance as a prime strategic tool in its foreign policy. ODA has become an increasingly important component in Japan's recent efforts to redefine its place in East Asia as well as globally, particularly in light of the growing power of China. Not unlike the EU, Japan aims to develop its international role from a 'great economic power without military might' towards becoming a 'global civilian power' with enhanced diplomatic, economic, commercial and security-related interests.

Historical Background and Japan's ODA Today

Japanese ODA started in 1954, when the government decided to join the Colombo Plan for Cooperative Economic Development in South and Southeast Asia by offering technical assistance. Financial aid in the form of yen loans started in 1958 followed by grant aid in 1968. Financial aid throughout the 1950s and 1960s went hand in hand with war reparations: Tokyo signed reparation and economic cooperation agreements with the Philippines, Vietnam, Burma and Indonesia.[7]

---

6   Trade relations between the EU and the ACP countries are currently conducted under interim EPAs.

7   China never demanded war reparations, and renounced its demand for reparation in 1972.

In the 1970s and 1980s Japan's rapid economic growth was accompanied by strongly increasing ODA. Its economic advancement in other parts of Asia and its dependence on the import of natural resources from other Asian countries resulted in boosted aid as compensation for the unfavourable effects of Japanese trade and as a tool to improve the country's image abroad. Partly as a result of the economic regionalization process, aid, and in particular infrastructure development, became a necessary and useful tool for Japanese companies to penetrate local markets (Watanabe 2005: 4). The strength of this trend became strongly visible after the stronger yen and more expensive exports as a result of the 1985 Plaza Accord necessitated the relocation of production to other parts of Asia. Furthermore, the principle of 'tied loans' – the provision of aid linked with the duty to procure Japanese goods and services – played an important role in integrating the neighbouring countries with Japan's own economy (Hook et al. 2012: 216).

Shortly after becoming the world's largest donor in 1989, the government released a first strategic document in the form of the ODA charter of 1992. The main principles underlying ODA would be the promotion of environmental protection, the prevention of the application of ODA for military purposes, and the transition to market-oriented economic systems in conjunction with democracy and basic human rights and freedoms. Human-centred development and the enhancement of individual welfare also appeared as key concepts. The publication of the Charter and the strategization of ODA also meant that Japan shifted from 'the principle of request' (*yôseishugi*) to 'policy dialogue' and a more pro-active approach in determining aid targets. The successor to this document was the updated 2003 Charter, which added the perspective of 'human security' and 'fairness' in relation to gender issues and the gap between rich and poor. The charter reveals a stronger emphasis on Japan's national interests, and a focus on Asia as the main context of Japanese security and prosperity. The poverty reduction dimension also featured more prominently in the revised charter, especially in the light of the MDGs.

Japan was the world's largest donor throughout the 1990s, only to be overtaken by the US in 2001. Japan is currently in fifth position among the OECD's DAC (Development Assistance Committee) members in terms of net ODA, after the United States, Germany, the United Kingdom and France. In 2012 Japan contributed 10.6 billion USD. In relative terms, however, Japan's development contributions are fairly modest. Japan's ODA per GNI (Gross National Income), for example, continues to drop, from 0.20 per cent in 2010 to 0.17 per cent in 2012 (and 0.23 per cent in 2002), falling progressively further behind the UN target of 0.7 per cent and well below the DAC average of 0.43 per cent. Japan is placed in twentieth position among the 24 DAC countries with respect to ODA/GNI, just ahead of the EU countries hardest hit by the financial crisis, namely Greece, Italy and Spain, and of East Asian neighbour South Korea (OECD 2013a). Japan's ODA per capita is also relatively low at 87 USD per person per year (MOFA

2012: 52).[8] Nevertheless, on the bright side, Japan is still the world's number two provider in terms of gross ODA.[9] Japan's gross ODA equalled approximately 18.6 billion USD in 2012 (OECD 2013a). Due to the repayment of loans by recipient countries, Japan is by far the country with the greatest difference between gross and net ODA.[10]

Key Features of Japan's ODA

Japan's ODA is often said to be based on its own historical experiences. Just as Japan focused its post-war development on rebuilding its economy, Japanese ODA centres on infrastructure development and capacity-building in order to help recipient countries to develop a market economy. The starting point has been that developing countries have to take the initiative and be responsible for their own development (OECD 1999: 14). Supporting 'self-help' efforts of developing countries (*jijo doryoku shien*) is therefore a core philosophical underpinning, enshrined in both the ODA Charters of 1992 and 2003. Japan sees its own model of offering comprehensive support to developing countries' self-help efforts as a valuable public good that Japan can contribute to the international community. As the 'Commission on Japan's Goals in the 21st Century' argued, Japan is critical of purely humanitarian and idealistic goals, and a narrow focus on poverty reduction through humanitarian aid. These efforts need to be complemented by concrete medium-term economy-building measures. In other words, 'you can give fish to hungry people, but unless you teach them how to fish for themselves, they will never be able to provide for their own needs' (Prime Minister's Commission on Japan's Goals in the 21st Century 2000). One result of the focus on self-help is that Japan has been wary of debt cancellation, and instead opted for debt relief grants to countries incapable of repayment (OECD 1999: 19).

Japan's preference for loans over grants is also said to be rooted in the country's own experiences. Between 1953 and 1967 Japan took 34 loans with the World Bank, fuelling Japan's economic growth. All loans were paid back by 1990 (Watanabe 2005: 3). Loans represented 55 per cent of total bilateral aid in 2002, and 47 per cent in 2008, by far the highest amount in all of the DAC countries (OECD 2004: 11; OECD 2011: 48). Consequently, as loan repayments accumulate, Japan needs to increase its ODA budget in order to maintain the level of net flows. The volume of loan repayments from recipient countries basically

---

8   This compares to 99 USD for the US, 159 USD for Germany, and 485 USD for Sweden.

9   Gross ODA: the total amount disbursed over a given accounting period. Net ODA: the gross amount less any repayments of loan principal or recoveries on grants received during the same period.

10   According to the OECD definition, loans have to include a grant element of at least 25 per cent. In 2010 Japan's bilateral ODA loans had an average grant element of 75 per cent (DAC definition).

explains why Japan has dropped from its position as the world's top donor since 2002.[11] Furthermore, the dominant presence of loans lowers the overall grant element of ODA, recommended by the OECD to be 86 per cent or higher. In 2008/2009 the grant element of Japan's total ODA amounted to 85.8 per cent, the lowest of the DAC countries.[12]

Japan has occasionally used ODA conditionality to influence the behaviour of recipient countries. Japan's ODA charter stipulates that 'full attention should be paid to efforts for promoting democratization and the introduction of a market-oriented economy, and the situation regarding the protection of basic human rights and freedoms in the recipient country'. Though direct interventions in governance are few, Tokyo has used ODA as a diplomatic weapon on a number of occasions. Between 1995 and 1997 Japan froze grant aid to China due to the country's nuclear testing (OECD 1999: 70). Aid to Myanmar was suspended after the military coup of 1988, although limited economic assistance resumed the following year (Howe and Jang 2013: 135; Edström 2009: 30).

Nevertheless, a third key feature deriving from Japan's own history is the relative reluctance to interfere in the internal affairs of recipient countries. Japanese wartime expansionism in East Asia is still a sensitive issue. Japan has thus tended to decouple political ideology and economic exchange (*seikei bunri*, Hook et al. 2012: 75). Rather than using aid as a stick, it has aimed to apply it as a carrot especially in countries where Japan's perceived self-interests are at stake (Hook and Zhang 1998: 1062). In Myanmar, for example, since the early 2000s Japan has tried to reward promises to implement reforms with aid, and aimed to provide humanitarian assistance as well as advice on economic and political reforms in order to achieve change in the country. As such, Japan has tried to find a middle way between the Western sanctions-oriented approach and the non-interference principle adhered to by Asian countries such as China. The European and US approach is marked by sanctions and pressure for reform, whereas Chinese and ASEAN engagement policies provide assistance without pushing for reforms.

Japan's focus of development assistance on Asia is logical given its location and history. In 2002 74 per cent of its aid went to the region. China in particular was a priority recipient between 1979 and 2006, mainly in the form of ODA loans. After the start of the 'mutually beneficial relationship based on common

---

11   Loan repayments can even result in the net loan flow to developing countries turning negative. In 2010 Japan's gross loan aid amounted to 8,324 million, but the amount recovered was 7,850 million, leaving net disbursements at 474 million. However, net loans take into consideration principal repayments, not interest repayments. If taking into account interest repayments, Japan's net cash flow on ODA loans was even negative, meaning that there is a net transfer of resources from developing countries to the donor country (Tew 2013: 7).

12   The DAC average is 96.1 per cent (MOFA 2012: 221).

strategic interests'[13] in 2008, aid has been limited to promoting non-governmental exchanges and to dealing with common challenges such as pollution and communicable diseases (MOFA 2012: 107). In 2010, for example, Japan's net disbursement of aid to China was negative, as Japan recovered close to 1.2 billion USD in loans from China (MOFA 2012: 170). Now that more Asian countries are graduating from developing-nation status, Japanese aid to Asia has been on the decline. Currently over half of Japan's gross ODA (53 per cent in 2010) is disbursed to Asia, whereas approximately 15 per cent goes to the Middle East and North Africa, and 12 per cent to Sub-Saharan Africa (MOFA 2012: 50). During the past decade, net Japanese aid to South and Central Asia and to Sub-Saharan Africa has gained markedly in importance.[14]

Japan's belief in the concept of 'human security' is a more recent feature. It appeared for the first time in a UN document in 2005, though its roots can be traced back to the 1994 Human Development Report of the United Nations Development Program (UNDP) (Minami 2006: 44). Japan has been attaching importance to the concept since 1998, when then Prime Minister Obuchi used the concept to launch Japanese assistance efforts in East Asia after the Asian Financial Crisis. The concept was concretized through the 2003 report by UN High Commissioner for Refugees Ogata Sadako and Nobel laureate Amartya Sen. Human security was defined as being driven by the top-down approach of 'protection', and the bottom-up dimension of 'empowerment'. The concept has, however, been criticized for being vague vis-à-vis the responsibility to protect principle. Unlike other countries such as Canada and Norway that have emphasized the 'Freedom from Fear' aspect, Japan has centred on 'Freedom from Want', a broader concept that focuses more on hunger, disease and natural disasters as threats to human security (Howe and Jang 2013: 126).

Like any other donor, Japan aims to create synergies between aid and economic cooperation, on the one hand, and the promotion of national interests, on the other. As noted above, national interest featured more prominently in Japan's ODA Charter of 2003. The DAC 2004 peer review critically pointed out the risk that narrow national interest supersedes the primary development objective of benefiting the recipient country and emphasized the need to mainstream the goal of poverty reduction (OECD 2004). Japan's strong confidence in ODA's utility for national interests rather than altruistic reasons was illustrated in a 2006 speech by Minister for Foreign Affairs Asô Tarô who quoted the Japanese saying 'sympathy is not for others' sake' (*nasake wa hito no tame narazu*), adding that 'charity is a good investment'.

---

13   A joint statement aiming to re-launch Sino-Japanese relations in a comprehensive way and on an equal footing. The statement was an outcome of Prime Minister Abe's efforts in 2006–2007 to improve relations between both countries.

14   Net aid to South and Central Asia increased from 19.2 to 35.3 per cent between 2000 and 2010, whereas the share taken up by aid to Sub-Saharan Africa in total ODA almost doubled, from 16 to 35.1 per cent (OECD 2012: 278).

Since the early 2000s ODA has been seen as underpinning Japan's efforts to pursue 'enlightened national interest' (*hirakareta kokueki*[15]), in contrast to its pursuit of 'isolated national interest' before the Second World War. Prime Minister Obuchi's 'Commission on Japan's Goals in the 21st Century' advocated a broader 'civilian' dimension in international relations, in order to make the pursuit of Japan's interests and global public interests mutually overlapping. According to the Commission's final report, Japan 'must not be afraid of debating the merits of policies openly in terms of national interest'. Japan has transformed from an economic power without military might to the prototype of a 'global civilian power'. Together with engagement in security affairs and involvement in a changing global economic order, cooperation with developing countries through ODA is one tool to advance this new international role.

Comparative Observations

Both the European Union and Japan can be seen as 'aid superpowers'. EU institutions alone disburse substantially more net ODA than Japan, but in terms of gross ODA, both actors are practically equal.[16] It goes without saying that, when including the total aid provided by EU member states combined, the EU remains by far the world's largest ODA donor. Of the EU members, Germany, the UK and France have been bigger individual donors than Japan. It also needs to be kept in mind that as an aid donor Japan is punching far below its weight in terms of ODA per GNI or ODA per capita. Europe's colonial heritage and the traditional internationalism (or idealism?) of the continent's social democratic parties, often dominant within national polities, are possibly the most plausible explanations for this difference in the intensity of development engagement.

The profiles of the EU and Japan as donors show a number of similarities. The aim to be a global civilian power characterizes both of them. By emphasizing civilian and 'soft' strengths rather than military means both seek to exert influence in the international community and shape the global agenda. This notion of 'civilian power' has in turn shaped development policy. In both cases the objective to become prototypical global civilian powers materializes through a focus on the Millennium Development Goals. In the EU's rhetoric since 2000, the MDGs have figured as the fundamental starting point to which a broader human development perspective has been added, including social and gender issues, sustainability and security; in relative terms the emphasis on democratic values was somewhat stronger in the 1990s than now. Japan's conceptual formulations have been marginally different, with its strong advocacy of the human security

---

15 Literally meaning 'open national interest'.

16 In 2011 EU institutions disbursed net aid to the amount of 17.4 billion USD compared to 10.8 billion for Japan. As for gross ODA, the figures were 18.3 billion USD for EU institutions, and just under 20 billion for Japan (OECD 2013a).

approach since 1998. This must be seen in the context of the country's attempts to focus aid more on 'human-centred development' after the Asian Financial Crisis of 1997–1998, and place more emphasis on social development, poverty and institutional and governance issues. Japan has repeatedly been criticized for insufficiently concentrating on social sectors including health and education, and on cross-cutting issues such as poverty, gender and governance (OECD 1999).

Both actors also strongly emphasize the long-term benevolent influences of trade. Aid is therefore often understood in terms of economic cooperation promoting liberalized trade and building up functioning market economies, while at the same time achieving development goals. Often, however, the (short-term) potential economic benefits of trade tend to override the more noble (long-term) objectives of aid policies. The EU's difficulties in bringing the EPA negotiations to conclusion clearly show how strongly the Union is willing to defend its own economic interests – even at the risk of losing reserves of goodwill among its global partners. For resource-poor Japan, development assistance has always served domestic economic and industrial needs. Current aid to Myanmar provides an example. Japan disburses aid in order to increase Yangon's electricity generation. This aims to supply power to a Japan-led Special Economic Zone close to Thilawa Port, which is destined to attract major Japan manufacturing companies in the future (Kakuchi 2013).

In spite of these similarities, external perceptions of the EU and Japan as aid donors diverge widely. The respective development policies of these two actors have shaped their general image in the world, and the ways in which partner countries perceive the ambitions of these self-proclaimed global civilian powers. Development assistance is closely tied to the peculiarities of a country's international reputation – and thereby concrete influence in world affairs.

The global image of the European Union remains complicated, notwithstanding the official propaganda with which the Union has sought to justify its development activities over the past few decades (Vogt 2006). 'The world's number one donor' keeps on emphasizing its developmental benevolence, and it seems to believe that other actors indeed see it that way. But several studies indicate that the distinct actorness of the EU is vague among lay audiences outside Europe; foreign perceptions of the European polity still tend to be nation-state-based (Lucarelli 2011: 154). By contrast, the elites of partner countries do have an understanding of the Union, but the ultimate interpretations of it vary greatly, between geographic regions in particular.[17] In those countries, predominantly in Africa, where the EU does play a significant donor role – sometimes the economies of these countries are completely dependent on European aid – many of the elites see the Union as a benign master rather than a benign partner – and this 'masterness' is obviously not positive. In Asia, by contrast, the EU simply appears to be an economic giant, not

17 The EU is seen, above all, as a successful example of regional integration, a champion of multilateralism, an environmental powerhouse and a peace-maker (Lucarelli 2011: 155–6).

particularly different from the other main economic actors (Chaban et al. 2013). It also seems that on international political stages such as the UN, the EU qua EU has not been able to attain an ambience of goodwill. A widely spread sense in the global South remains that the Union primarily seeks to advance its own interests rather than acting for the sake of all humankind or those most in need (Smith 2013).

In contrast to the EU, Japan does not have a strong global image as an aid donor. When looking at DAC peer reviews, however, it is clear that Japan's development model is distinct and is often criticized for that reason. As argued by Lancaster (2010: 32), Japan clearly falls short on both quantitative and qualitative measures of model aid policy, because of the country's low emphasis on grants and on social aid, and high priority given to economic infrastructure and to middle-income countries.

In addition to external images, EU and Japanese aid models show wide discrepancy in terms of sectoral focus and importance attached to aid conditionality. Japan's bilateral aid has been overwhelmingly oriented towards the economic sector. In 2010 47.5 per cent of Japan's bilateral ODA was disbursed in the fields of transport, communications and energy, whereas social and administrative infrastructure accounted for just 22.5 per cent. EU institutions as well as individual EU member states display the opposite trend, giving precedence to social and administrative infrastructure.[18]

Aid conditionality also sets the two actors apart. The EU has explicitly tied its aid to political conditions, and has habitually initiated consultations if the partners have not met the required conditions, in spite of the general doubts of their usefulness (for example, in the 2000s with Côte d'Ivoire, Haiti, Liberia and Zimbabwe). In the Cotonou Agreement, for instance, the 'political dimension' is fundamentally based on the principles of democracy, human rights and good governance – and on both sides' adherence to these principles. Japan in turn has tried to find a 'middle way' between the 'hard' Western sanctions-based approach and the non-interventionist principle followed by many Asian countries. The Japanese strategy has been based on providing aid as a positive instigator of change, driving economic reform in order to achieve progress towards democracy in the recipient country. In Myanmar, for example, Japan has espoused engagement, applying humanitarian assistance and direct aid support as an incentive for democratic change. In contrast to the EU's approach based on restrictive sanctions, Japan has generally stuck to the idea that a continuous aid relationship is vital to achieving change.

Nevertheless, a cautious trend towards convergence can be detected in both actors' development policy during the 2000s. This trend is particularly clear in geographical focus, targeted income range of recipient countries, and increasing attention paid to poverty alleviation. Japan has traditionally focused on its 'near-abroad', and at present over half of the country's ODA still goes to the region.

---

18   EU Institutions: 10 per cent to economic infrastructure and almost 40 per cent to social and administrative infrastructure (statistics provided in OECD 2012: 276).

However, as traditional Asian development partners have reached a level on which they are no longer eligible for direct economic assistance, South Asia and even more so Africa are currently gaining in importance. Japan's more proactive policy for Africa is also the result of a clear strategic policy choice, revealing an attempt to catch up with China's strong presence on the continent. It is telling that Japan's PM Abe Shinzô pledged 3.2 trillion yen in aid to Africa over the next five years at the June 2013 Tokyo International Conference on African Development (TICAD).

The EU's attention has been traditionally geared towards Africa, and given that Africa's development is finally showing truly positive signs, the strategic importance of the continent for Europe may even increase in the future. Slightly less than half of all DAC-EU countries' net ODA goes to Sub-Saharan Africa (OECD 2012: 278). Simultaneously, however, the Union's 'near-abroad' – the Balkans, former Soviet Union countries and the Mediterranean shore – has assumed an increasingly important role within the Union development agenda. Asia has also clearly been gaining in importance recently: over 20 per cent of EU institutional assistance now goes to Asian countries, and the major donors – Germany, France and the UK – have significantly increased their aid flows to the region.[19]

The EU has sought to concentrate its ODA on the least developed countries. In 2010, for example, the 'least developed' and 'other low-income' countries received approximately the same amount of aid directly from the Union as the middle-income countries (around 5.5 billion USD). Japan's focus on the other hand has for a long time been not on least developed countries (LDCs), but rather on middle-income countries (MICs). Only due to international pressure has Japan gradually shifted its focus in recent years more towards lower-income countries (LICs) and LDCs; the share of ODA allocated to these countries is already higher than in the case of the EU.[20]

The focus on poverty alleviation, including extreme poverty and even humanitarian crises, is another area in which we can see indications of convergence. The EU has been a leading force in the realization of the MDGs, and the Union's institutions disburse almost 20 per cent of total ODA in humanitarian aid. Japan, by contrast, only dedicates approximately 5 per cent of total ODA to humanitarian aid, but the introduction of 'human security' in Japan's development philosophy since the Charter of 2003 has helped to add the dimension of poverty to an approach traditionally focused on economic growth (OECD 2011: 28). Attention to basic human needs and emergency aid has increased, mainly through the extension of grants and technical cooperation (Howe and Jang 2013: 131). An increased focus

---

19   See the statistics provided in OECD (2013b: 5).

20   In 1999–2000 Japan's aid to LDCs and LICs constituted 38.2 per cent, whereas aid to MICs accounted for 61.8 per cent. A noticeable change has occurred since then, since in 2009–2010 75.3 per cent went to the former category, and 24.7 per cent to the latter (OECD 2012: 277). As the DAC-EU countries currently disburse 59.3 per cent to LDCs and LICs, this reveals a clear trend towards convergence.

on the fight against poverty and on social infrastructure may be a result of foreign pressure (*gaiatsu*, Lancaster 2010).

An explicit articulation of national interests – or regional interests, in the case of the EU – in the framework of aid policy also seems to increasingly unite these two actors. Regarding the EU and its trade and development nexus, formulations referring to enlightened self-interest now appear somewhat stronger and more common than in the 1990s; 'enlightened' could often be translated simply into 'mutual'. Perhaps this is related to the fact that it seems to have become more acceptable to emphasize national interests within the EU after the integration enthusiasm between 1989 and 2004.[21] More generally, it seems evident that the extent to which the EU can exploit its active development policies for advancing its interests in other policy fields or for increasing its overall power in world affairs has proved highly limited. But this is not only because of the lack of policy coherence, the absence of a single voice for European foreign policy or even the primacy of commercial interests over idealistic development goals. It is also partially a result of the newness and uniqueness of the Union as a foreign policy actor which makes it difficult for others to relate themselves to it.

For Japan, the use of ODA to advance national interests remains at the core of foreign policy.[22] Nevertheless, 'national interest' is re-defined as 'enlightened', in essence similarly to the EU: as Japan's peace and prosperity are linked with global peace and prosperity, using ODA to tackle global, common interests will also serve Japan's national interests and underpin its active international role.[23] Nevertheless, especially since the latter half of the 2000s, Japan has clearly used 'strategic ODA' more to cater to national security interests in its region, in particular in view of China's more assertive geopolitical stance. In 2012, for example, the DPJ government officially 'strategized' ODA by announcing plans to provide patrol boats to other coastal nations. In one such instance, Japan announced an agreement with the Philippines to enhance cooperation on regional security, providing the Philippine coast guard with 12 patrol boats (Bergenas and Sabatini 2012). In further efforts to balance an increasingly strong Chinese presence in East Asia, Japan has also been looking to increase economic assistance and maritime cooperation with Sri Lanka.

---

21   For a fine critical account of the importance of national interests within today's EU, see Menasse (2012).

22   A recent speech by Minister for Foreign Affairs Fumio Kishida illustrates this well. He declared that 'Japan will utilize official development assistance (ODA) and its overseas diplomatic missions in order to incorporate the vitality of other countries' (28 February 2013).

23   See, for example, 'Enhancing Enlightened National Interest: Living in Harmony with the World and Promoting Peace and Prosperity – ODA Review Final Report' (June 2010). Cf. Lancaster (2010: 42).

Final Remarks

In spite of their active roles as aid donors, the general image of both the European Union and Japan has remained contested, or even controversial. Development partners throughout the world still seem to believe that Japan and the EU only seek to maximize their own, more or less short-term political and economic interests through development policies. These views are obviously not ungrounded: one of our most important points has been that the logic of self-interest clearly has the upper hand over the logic of altruistic idealism, and that this trend is even more clearly pronounced now than in the 1990s. The gap between real developmental instrumentalism and professed idealism is clear in the case of both Europe and Japan, but is perhaps more visibly present in the case of the EU, as the EU has tended to emphasize its role as a global normative player. The question is not only of trade: Japan increasingly utilizes aid as an integral part of its regional security policy, whereas for instance in the Union's Cotonou cooperation, security issues are clearly more prominent on the agenda than during the original negotiations in the late 1990s.

The EU's and Japan's development models vary widely in terms of approach, means and targets. Nevertheless, during the past decade a trend towards some sort of convergence has emerged as a result of shifting external influences and a changing international environment. Perhaps because of pressure from actors such as the EU, Japan's focus on economic infrastructure is increasingly complemented by attention to social issues, human security and humanitarian aid. Japan's approach to conditionality, emphasizing engagement and giving precedence to carrots over sticks can be seen as a valuable alternative to the sanctions-based Western approach.

The tendency towards convergence potentially offers new opportunities for cooperation, especially in the light of the ongoing free trade negotiations between Japan and the EU. The increased attention that the EU and Japan are paying to Africa can provide a chance to collaborate, striking a balance between humanitarian, governance and social issues on the one hand, and economic growth emphases on the other. In addition, both actors share a common interest in counterbalancing the strong Chinese presence in the continent. Cooperation between the EU and Japan could potentially result in new, effective aid projects that combine the goals of growth and poverty reduction, say, in African rural development. Japan can offer its expertise in concrete economy-building and productivity-promoting measures based on its guiding philosophy to strengthen the partner country's self-help efforts, while collaboration with the EU can help in tackling issues related to governance and administrative infrastructure.

The EU and Japan are occasionally seen as possible examples and trailblazers, whose institutional and political principles and practices are worth copying. Japan's own evolution from an aid receiver to a key global donor, for example, can serve as a model for contemporary emerging economies. Japan's aid to China during several decades, especially through ODA loans, can be regarded as an example of how aid is a valuable tool to help drive economic growth in a third country in a way that is also highly beneficial to the donor country itself. As for the EU, its 'model power' may have waned somewhat during the current economic crisis, but it is still the world's most successful example of regional integration. The African Union has been explicitly drafted with the European prototype in mind. Continuous aid flows from Europe to Africa will hopefully play an important role in guaranteeing that the current boom in many African countries will not prove to be a transient phenomenon.

Chapter 9

Saving the Kyoto Protocol: What Can We Learn from the Experience of Japan–EU Cooperation?

Hiroshi Ohta and Yves Tiberghien

Introduction

The great saga of the Kyoto Protocol began with abundant hope in 1997, suffered a near-death experience in 2001, and a resurrection to great fanfare in 2002–2003. This was followed by a gradual demise after the Bali conference in 2007, and a hard blow delivered by Japan in December 2011 (Harrison and Sundstrom 2010; Ohta 2000, 2009). The Kyoto Protocol was a historic milestone, the first binding international treaty involving all developed countries, and even developing countries as future participants, with a clear commitment to the reduction of greenhouse gas emissions (GHGE) and a reversal of the gloomy trend towards global warming. The treaty that was signed in 1997 in the historical capital of Japan committed the EU (with 15 members at the time) to reduce its GHGEs by 8 per cent from the 1990 level by 2012, while it committed the US and Japan to reduction targets of 7 per cent and 6 per cent, respectively. In real terms, the target meant a 31 per cent reduction for the US from its business-as-usual trend (United States Department of State 2002) and a 15 per cent reduction for Japan. For Europe, the target was not entirely trivial, but was comparatively easier to achieve in the light of structural shifts in the energy sector away from coal in eastern Germany and the UK. Most importantly, the Kyoto Protocol was an institutional trailblazer that set in motion a host of innovations (especially in Europe), such as the carbon trading market, the clean development mechanism (CDM), new monitoring mechanisms, and experimentation to encourage alternative energies and developments with regard to carbon taxes.

However, there was trouble from the start. The Kyoto Protocol was dead on arrival in the US Senate, and the Bush administration quickly withdrew from the Treaty after taking office in early 2001. Given that the US was responsible for 36 per cent of emissions by Kyoto Annex I countries (developed economies) and 23 per cent of worldwide emissions based on 1990 data (IEA 2010), the US withdrawal was a bombshell. Yet after months of uncertainty, European countries and Japan decided to hold together and push the Kyoto ratification over the hump during the 2001–2003 period (Ohta 2009, 2010; Schreurs and Tiberghien 2010;

Tiberghien and Schreurs 2010). By later joining forces to lobby Russia, they succeeded in gathering together enough countries, responsible for a sufficient fraction of worldwide global emissions, to enable the Kyoto Protocol to be legally implemented. This was a crucial and symbolic moment. The assurances of EU support for Russia's entry into the World Trade Organization (WTO) actually pushed the Russian government to proceed with the ratification of the Kyoto Protocol. Following Russia's ratification in November 2004, the Kyoto Protocol came into force on 16 February 2005. With the help of Russia, Annex I nations who decided to share the burden of emissions reductions represented 37 per cent of global GHGEs (IEA 2010). Standing against the United States and Australia, they drove the Kyoto ratification and implementation process against huge odds.

Unfortunately, ratification was one thing and implementation was another. The EU kept pushing forward the implementation battle through its domestic measures, and Japan also made some effort, while avoiding more painful measures such as a carbon tax. However, the global negotiations for a post-Kyoto treaty that began in earnest in Bali in 2007 proved to be even more painful for the saviours of the Kyoto Protocol. At the critical summit in Copenhagen in December 2009, neither was present in the room when the final deal was negotiated: instead, negotiations saw the US square off with the newly formed BASIC axis (Brazil, China, India and South Africa). The EU and Japan did not manage to get much traction with their more ambitious agendas, that called for large cuts by 2020 or 2050 (20–30 per cent for the EU, and 25 per cent for Japan from the 1990 baseline). Things did not improve much at Cancun in December 2010, Durban in 2011 or Doha in 2012. In fact, after a blunt statement by Japan that continuing Kyoto made no sense in December 2010, Canada withdrew entirely from the old Kyoto Treaty in 2011. The EU was left alone and without much support.

Despite this disappointing outcome, EU–Japan efforts to push Kyoto in 1997 and to save it in 2002 were significant milestones. Why did the EU and Japan do this, despite great pressure not to from the US and from their own economic interest groups? In this chapter we argue that Japan–EU cooperation was not driven by economic calculations, realist counter-hegemonic moves or even purely normative concerns. Japan and the EU always aimed to include the US and, while sensitive to NGO pressure, always retained a high degree of political autonomy in designing their strategy. Instead, we argue that the roles played by the EU and, surprisingly, Japan can only be understood by looking at the role of political leadership in the context of domestic audiences. In the EU a logic of mutually reinforcing competitive leadership between key states such as Germany, the Netherlands and the UK on the one hand, and the EU Commission, the European Parliament (EP) and the Council of the European Union on the other, resulted in a strong and resilient position on climate change. Similarly, this chapter argues that the critical role played by political leaders, including Noboru Takeshita, Ryutaro Hashimoto, Keizo Obuchi and even Junichiro Koizumi, made a key difference to Japanese behaviour. Only decisive political leadership in response to receptive public opinion could tilt the balance of interests in favour of Kyoto ratification and partial implementation.

The rest of this chapter proceeds in five steps. The first part outlines the EU and Japanese contributions to Kyoto. The second explains the causal story rooted in domestic political leadership within these two polities. The third analyses the shifting positions within Japan after 2006, leading to significant fluctuations. The fourth turns to post-2007 international events and the great defeats suffered by the EU in its attempts at continued normative leadership. Finally, the conclusion discusses the lessons from EU–Japan cooperation experience, its limits, and the possibility that EU–Japan experience could extend to include China.

The Japan–EU Contribution to the Kyoto Protocol

Clearly, the footprints of Japan–EU cooperation are all over the Kyoto Protocol and the path it has followed in its development since the early 1990s. European ideas and Japanese leadership were all critical during the Kyoto summit in 1997. While it was in fact the EU that pushed the frontiers and acted as a global climate entrepreneur, partners such as Japan played an important role. When it comes to climate issues, the EU has been called a climate superpower; and its environmental reach has been a defining feature of its rise as a global actor (Bretherton and Vogler 2006; Reid 2004; Schreurs and Tiberghien 2010). The EU has acted both as a normative leader and an institutional entrepreneur. Numerous scholars have argued that the EU has established a strong identity as a civilian power (for example Duchêne 1973; Telò 2007). Strong action on climate change is not just a focal point for coordination among different actors within the EU, and one of the issue-areas where integration is still progressing, it is also an important facet of the EU's growing 'green civilian power' (Brande 2009). As such, the EU has elevated the issue to one of moral duty; it has sought to lead by action and speech, hoping to name and shame other major countries into action. The EU commitment to cut emissions by 20 per cent from 1990 levels by 2020, and a conditional 30 per cent reduction pledge, contingent on the cooperation of other countries, falls within this civilian power leadership approach.

As a first mover in serious climate change action, the EU has played a key role in building the Kyoto institutions, but also in developing the first Exchange Trading System (ETS), the most complete emissions monitoring system (EC Directive 2003/87/EC, implemented in 2005), carbon taxes in many countries, and advanced energy saving methods (Schreurs and Tiberghien 2010). The EU had hoped that its advantages as an institution-shaper would enable it to call the shots with regard to Kyoto II. It did not anticipate that this situation would also create incentives for the US and other countries to bypass the Kyoto framework and seek alternative frameworks, where North American advantages in science and private sector entrepreneurialism would come to the fore.

Although Japan has been a more reluctant and internally divided player than the EU, it has played a key role at critical moments, providing an important technical, political and symbolic contribution to international efforts against climate change. In 1997 Japan was initially reluctant to play an active leadership role. One of the immediate reasons for this was the economic cost of achieving the substantial carbon dioxide (CO_2) reductions targets proposed by the EU, the Alliance of Small Island States (AOSIS) and environmental NGOs. Japan's hesitation in taking a leading role also stemmed from domestic policy differences between the Environment Agency (now the Ministry of the Environment, or MOE) and the Ministry of International Trade and Industry (MITI) (now the Ministry of Economy, Trade and Industry, or METI).

Ironically, however, the US breakaway from the Kyoto Protocol framework encouraged a rebuilding of EU–Japan cooperation and allowed the EU to intensify its diplomatic efforts toward Japan (and Russia). During the resumed sixth Conference of the Parties (COP6) in Bonn in July 2001, the EU compromised with Japan particularly on 'sinks', or the sequestration of CO_2 through additional activities such as forest management, afforestation and reforestation. As a result, Japan could allocate a greater reduction allowance for 'sinks' than it had initially planned as a part of its national strategy. Japan eventually ratified the Kyoto Protocol in June 2002, right after the EU ratification. Furthermore, the EU also arranged a similar deal with the Russian Federation on forest sequestration so as to promote Russia's ratification.

Throughout the evolutionary development of the climate change regime consisting of the UN Framework Convention on Climate Change (UNFCCC) and the Kyoto Protocol, Japan has consistently played the role of 'support state' (Chasek et al. 2010). In this sense, Japan has maintained a multilateral posture on the issue of global climate change. Towards the end of the UNFCCC talks, Japan's win-set was enlarged through strong political leadership, political enthusiasm and the active participation of environmental NGOs. With favourable domestic political circumstances, the Japanese negotiating team had the room to manoeuvre to contribute substantially to the successful conclusion of the UNFCCC. Thus, Japanese negotiators, together with their European counterparts, played a significant role in finally persuading the United States to adopt the convention.

Since 2006 the Japanese contribution has followed more of a seesaw process. After siding with the US in opposition to the EU's strong posture at Bali in 2007 (in the early days of the Fukuda administration), under the Hatoyama administration in 2009, Japan swung back behind a proactive climate agenda similar to that of the EU, and even considered a carbon tax and other strong measures. That strong political posture later dissolved and was replaced with the more realist position taken in December 2010 at Cancun and reinforced by the March 2011 Fukushima disaster. However, Japan remains a leader in new energy development and advanced green technology. It has huge potential to push the technological frontier.

Breaking Coalition Deadlocks: The Crucial Role of Political Leadership

Climate change politics is an arena where the interplay between domestic politics and international politics is particularly salient, making Putnam's two-level game model useful (Putnam 1988). In this context, domestic politics includes '(political) parties, social classes, interest groups (both economic and noneconomic), legislators, and even public opinion and elections, not simply executive officials and institutional arrangements' (Putnam 1988: 432). The dynamics of the domestic arena can tightly constrain the international behaviour of actors in the global game.

In most countries the game of climate change is particularly thick and constrained. It includes powerful economic interests, bureaucratic interests across several ministries, public opinion and a lively and globally-connected civil society. Such a thick and uncertain domestic terrain offers space for political entrepreneurs to shape the outcome and tilt the balance of domestic interests one way or the other (Kingdom 1984; Tiberghien 2007; Walker 1974, 1981). For example, the outcome of bureaucratic politics hinges on the relative strength, or the presence or absence, of political leadership. Strong political leadership may make it possible to overcome bureaucratic turf wars between economic and environmental bureaucrats in favour of the environment.

Multi-Level Reinforcement of Political Leadership in the EU

Why did the EU take it upon itself to lead in the domain of climate change? Schreurs and Tiberghien have argued that EU actions can be explained through a process of competitive multi-level reinforcement among the different EU political poles within the context of decentralized governance (2010). Initially, a group of pioneering states such as the Netherlands, Germany and the UK (often under pressure from green political parties) pushed for stronger environmental leadership. In response to this initial trigger, and seeing that climate change was salient for public opinion across the EU and offered a promising avenue for projecting a new EU identity, EU-level institutions such as the Commission and the EP lobbied for both more authority and stronger policy action. This upward cycle of mutually reinforcing leadership within a quasi-federal system has been triggered by and been dependent upon strong public support and normative commitment. Thus, climate change has emerged as an issue-area where the EU seeks to offer powerful global leadership, not only for substantive reasons (concerns for the climate *per se*), but also because the climate debate is a proxy battle with regard to issues such as the growing integration of the EU and the future division of power within the evolving EU. The climate change battle is taking place within the context of a broader renegotiation of power relations within the European Union, and critical debates over the growth of a genuine EU identity. That is why even latecomers like France joined the upward leadership competition under Nicolas Sarkozy after 2007.

The Japanese Case: Unusual Political Leadership as the Key Variable[1]

Both signing on to and ratifying Kyoto were not obvious moves for Japan. Domestic opposition was fierce throughout, and the process was always on the edge. For example, Japanese industry and economic bureaucracies argued that the 1990 base-year for the allocation of emissions reduction was not fair since Japan had already achieved large energy efficiencies to overcome two major oil crises in 1973–1974 and 1979–1980. Moreover, the use of 1990 as a base year meant that the actual Kyoto target would be around 13–14 per cent below the business-as-usual trend line. How could the Japanese government overcome resistance from the strong coalition between industry and the economic ministries, especially the Ministry of Economy, Trade and Industry (METI), which had been criticizing the 'unfair' allocation of emissions reduction rates between the EU and Japan?

It is plausible to emphasize the importance of 'embedded symbolism', in which the Kyoto Protocol has become a symbol of Japanese leadership and contribution in solving such a pressing global problem as climate change (Tiberghien and Schreurs 2010). Kyoto is the name of one of the old capitals of Japan and at that time was the only Japanese name attached to any international treaty. There is no doubt about the symbolic importance of the use of the name 'Kyoto'. Yet this account still cannot fully explain the reasons why the efforts to arrest global warming have become a viable foreign policy option for Japan, even at the expense of its most crucial bilateral relationship with the United States, and also with costs to Japan's domestic material interests, as mentioned above.

Instead, the puzzling Japanese behaviour can only be understood with a focus on political entrepreneurship. The period from the UNFCCC's first Conference of the Parties (COP1) in Berlin in 1995 to COP3 in Kyoto in 1997 is characterized by relatively strong political leadership and enthusiasm for a successful conclusion of the Kyoto Protocol. Ryutaro Hashimoto, an influential policy broker, was the Japanese Prime Minister at the time. He took charge in the final stages of negotiations at the Kyoto Conference in December 1997. At this point, the EU, the US and Japan had agreed to reduce GHG emissions below the 1990 level by 8, 7 and 6 per cent, respectively, by 2012. Although the divisions between various Japanese bureaucracies remained, they all wanted a successful conclusion of the Protocol. Above all, environmental NGOs were eager to support governmental efforts, although they were dissatisfied with policy targets set by the Japanese government and by the lack of a dynamic leadership.

But the domestic space for political entrepreneurship to break coalitional deadlocks at home peaked under Hashimoto and Obuchi. Koizumi managed to retain some autonomy, but never controlled his party (the LDP). Subsequent governments led by Abe (2006–2007), Fukuda (2007–2008) and Aso (2008–2009) were weak and were forced to conform to the positions of dominant interests. This

---

1   The following account is based on several previous studies by one of the authors (Ohta 1995, 2000, 2005a and 2005b).

led to a period of muddling through in the domestic implementation of Kyoto and the next phase of international negotiations.

The distinguishing characteristics of the periods before and during COP6 at The Hague in November 2000 were an absence of political leadership and the further diminishing of political enthusiasm from Japan. Some of the most prominent Japanese political leaders on the issue of climate change had died or left office, notably former Prime Minister Noboru Takeshita, former Prime Minister Keizo Obuchi and former Prime Minister Hashimoto. Their departure from the political scene appeared to be detrimental to the maintenance of dynamic political leadership towards climate change at both the domestic and international levels. Furthermore, the erosion of popular support for the LDP in the late 1990s and the early 2000s, which failed to give the public decisive political solutions or remedies for the long-term economic recession, unseated many 'greenish' parliamentarians. The lack of political leadership, together with political indifference surrounding climate issues, resulted in increased political clout for the main bureaucratic branches that formed the Japanese negotiating team at COP6. Japan belonged to the 'Umbrella Group' (UG) of Australia, Canada, Iceland, New Zealand, Norway, the Russian Federation, Ukraine and the United States. The Umbrella Group first emerged at COP3 in 1997, and took a position distinct from the EU and others (Yamin and Depledge 2004: 45).

However, in 2001–2002, after some initial hesitation, Prime Minister Koizumi still played an important role in throwing Japan's lot behind ratification. At a Japan–US summit meeting held at Camp David on 30 June 2001, Koizumi stated that his Cabinet gave one of the highest priorities to environmental policies and noted that Japan would like to cooperate with the EU, US and the rest of the world in dealing with global warming. For this endeavour, the Prime Minister also stressed the importance of 'the spirit of the Kyoto Protocol', which includes binding numerical targets, different treatment towards developing countries and flexible measures (Hamanaka 2006: 89).

2006–2012: Puzzling Japanese Gyrations

While the pathways followed by the EU (which was firmly supporting Kyoto and ambitious targets for a successor to Kyoto) were relatively stable after 2006, Japan's position shows the most dramatic change. Japan remained officially on board with Kyoto, but adopted the minimalist position pursued by the US for the future agreement. This changed radically in 2009 with a new party (Democratic Party of Japan, or DPJ) and a new prime minister (Hatoyama) aiming to reclaim leadership in this issue-area and follow a line not far removed from that of the EU. Then again, this position weakened due to strong domestic lobbying in 2010 and was formally abandoned in 2011 after the Fukushima disaster and the temporary stoppage of most nuclear reactors. At the international negotiation meetings in Cancun (2010), Durban (2011) and Doha (2012), Japan did not support the EU's call for an extension to Kyoto, and instead argued that Kyoto without the US or China had no meaning.

In the wake of the Kyoto ratification in 2002 Japan made significant initial efforts toward implementation, particularly in terms of energy efficiency and industrial innovation. However, Japan has also avoided taking the painful measures necessary to reach its target of 6 per cent below 1990 levels, and has mostly been slacking on climate change policy since 2005. As a result, CO_2 emissions in 2007 were 9 per cent above 1990 levels, and 15 per cent above the target. This trajectory suddenly changed with the August 2009 general election in Japan, which swept aside the conservative LDP government. The emergence of a new centrist/social democratic majority led by the DPJ was the most profound electoral change since 1955. The DPJ attempted to tilt policy-making toward a social-democratic orientation and a new foreign policy that explicitly presented the European Union as a model for Asia and sought a 'more equal' US–Japan relationship. On the climate change front, the DPJ took a revolutionary turn as well. In early September 2009 Prime Minister Yukio Hatoyama made a conditional public pledge to cut emissions by 25 per cent from 1990 levels by 2020, representing a 34 per cent cut from 2007 levels, despite fierce opposition from industry and widespread disbelief among think tanks and bureaucrats. The pledge was conditional on other major players (that is, the United States and China) also making similar efforts. The commitment was publicly repeated in Prime Minister Hatoyama's speech at the United Nations General Assembly, and on13 March 2010 the Cabinet approved a bill that would turn this pledge into law if approved. This public pledge marked a major new change in Japan's climate change policy from the recent decade. Japan's alliance with the EU at the forefront of major action against climate change also marked a major shift in global governance coalitions.

The most influential consideration that determines Japan's climate change policy at home and abroad has been Japan's energy policy. The Fukushima nuclear accident brought into sharper focus for many the risk of Japanese energy policy being so heavily biased in favour of nuclear energy, while neglecting renewable energy. This bias has been a factor in Japan's fluctuating commitment to Kyoto since 2006. In connection with both climate change and energy policy, METI's 2006 *New National Energy Strategy* set itself very ambitious targets. The Strategy targeted an improvement of at least 30 per cent in energy efficiency by 2030, a reduction of Japan's dependence on oil as the primary energy source to lower than 40 per cent by 2030 and, above all, a decrease in oil dependency by the transportation sector by 80 per cent by 2030. Meanwhile, overseas natural resources development would be encouraged to ensure the development by Japanese developers of 40 per cent of total oil imports by 2030, and nuclear power generation would be increased to the level of 30 to 40 per cent or more by around 2030 (METI 2006). Despite the future plan for the expansion of new energy technologies, the role assigned for renewable energy sources was very limited as the report failed to mention them as one of the components for the Japanese energy strategy. Furthermore, in June 2010 the Cabinet adopted the Basic Energy Plan. Accordingly, 70 per cent of sources for electricity generation would be non-fossil fuels or 'zero emissions' by 2030; the share of renewable energy and nuclear energy would be 20 and 50 per cent, respectively (METI 2010a). To this end, five additional nuclear power plants were to be built by 2020 and another nine by 2030 (METI 2010b).

This energy strategy, however, had to be fundamentally revised due to the series of severe accidents in the Fukushima Dai-ichi Nuclear Power Plant on 11 March 2011, when a 9.0 magnitude earthquake struck off the coast of Sendai, Japan, and huge resulting tsunamis swept away and destroyed important facilities and equipment, including the emergency core cooling system (ECCS). The damage done by the earthquake and ensuing tsunamis forced Tokyo Electric Power Co. (TEPCO) to decommission four nuclear reactors in the Fukushima Dai-ichi nuclear power complex. According to the Nuclear and Industrial Safety Agency (NISA), the level of the Fukushima nuclear incident was elevated to scale seven, the same level as the 1986 Chernobyl incident.

In the wake of the Fukushima accident, Prime Minister Naoto Kan sensed a shift in public opinion on nuclear energy policy. Kan, who had barely avoided a non-confidence motion with his last-minute promise of resignation after the enactment of a bill on renewable energy, began to advocate for denuclearization (*datsu-gempatsu*) – though he later toned it down by proposing a policy that pursued 'nuclear power reduction' (*gen-gempatsu*). Without any legal basis, he ordered the shut-down of the nuclear power plant at Hamaoka in Shizuoka Prefecture and pushed a bill to promote renewable energy through the Diet. On 26 August the Special Measures Law on Procurement of Renewable Energy Sourced Electricity by Electric Utilities, a Japanese version of Germany's Renewable Energy Law, was passed through the Diet. However, it is uncertain how serious Kan's successor, Yoshihiko Noda, and now Shinzo Abe of the LDP, will be in promoting renewable energy under this new law, let alone with the problem of regional monopolization of both power generation and the grid by the 10 electric power providers.

It is reasonable for Japan to point out that the Kyoto framework is neither fair nor effective since the largest emitters, China and the United States, are absent. However, Japan has not articulated its own proposal for international collective action (Luta 2011); instead, from Copenhagen (COP15) through Cancun (COP16) to Durban (COP17) to Doha (COP18), it has continued to insist on 'the establishment of a fair and effective international framework in which all major economies participate and on the agreement on ambitious targets by all major economies'. Since there is no prospect of the larger emitters such as China and the United States committing to international efforts until 2020 (the 'Durban Platform'), Japan appears to have gone its own way in departing from the Kyoto process – for example in the direction of bilateral commitment schemes.

We can now identify a set of plausible explanations for why the Japanese government has recently been inflexible and tenacious in maintaining its adamant position in international negotiations, firmly refusing to accept a second commitment period to the Kyoto Protocol. This Japanese governmental position stems from its 'addiction' to nuclear energy, its half-heartedness about the promotion of renewable energy, and the strong opposition of vested interests to the introduction of the 'cap-and-trade' system. Furthermore, the worldwide economic recession has accelerated the Japanese government's relinquishing of its prior role in leading international negotiations on climate change. Without dynamic political leadership, we cannot expect Japan to undertake a proactive role in international collective action to mitigate global climate change, though Japan could contribute to bilateral mitigation schemes and aid with adaptation efforts.

Copenhagen: Normative EU Leadership Hits the Wall

While the EU and Japan (with initial Canadian support, and later Australian support) were effective in carrying the international agenda and moral high ground in the 1990s and early 2000s, that was clearly no longer the case by the late 2000s. One key factor is the changing international landscape: the international climate game shifted from a normative game to a much more high-stakes strategic game between key players within a rapidly changing global balance of power. As the negotiations heated up for a successor to the Kyoto Protocol after 2012, it has become indispensable that the largest players, namely the US and China, be included. In 1990 the EU (27) still represented nearly 20 per cent of global emissions and the US 23 per cent, while China was only at 10 per cent. By 2008 everything had changed: China had moved to the top spot, responsible for 23 per cent of global emissions (and over 25 per cent in 2010), while the US remained significant at 19 per cent. As for the EU, its share had fallen to 14 per cent and Japan to below 4 per cent (from 5 per cent in 1990) (IEA 2010).

In this context, China and the US together represent nearly 43 per cent of worldwide emissions and cannot be ignored. The EU and Japan count for less than 18 per cent and are unable to leverage this into global leadership. To make matters worse, climate change has become a key bone of contention in the zero-sum confrontation between the US and China. The US sees China as a free rider and a threat, since China is likely to become the largest economic power in the world sometime between 2016 and 2018. China, for its part, perceives the US as the chief obstacle to public good provision and a threat to China's right to development. This standoff paralyses global climate negotiations.

This changing international context became apparent to the EU at Bali in 2007, but reached a critical level at Copenhagen in December 2009. The meeting ended in failure, with delegates unable to draft a new treaty and only able to acknowledge a very rough and imprecise statement issued by the US and the four BASIC emerging powers. The Copenhagen failure highlighted two key weaknesses for the EU's global leadership on climate. The first was the growing internal divisions within the EU itself on this issue. Since 2008–2009, a growing gap appeared between the lofty global voice of the EU and the messy politics of implementation. In particular, the EU exhibited a deep East–West cleavage between its emerging and developed economies; growing German resistance on automobile emission targets; the presence of Mediterranean free-riders Italy, Portugal, Greece, Spain (with a late change of direction thanks to rising wind power in the case of Spain); conflicts over nuclear energy that pitted France against Germany and others; and tensions over an integrated energy policy in the face of predominant national and private interests.

But the most glaring failure of the EU approach has been its inability to engage and coax the other key actors in climate change politics, namely the US and China (with India and Brazil as secondary actors). The paramount strategic priority for the EU was to prevent the formation of a China–US alliance (let alone a US–BASIC compromise) and to find ways to actively engage either or both of the US and China. This goal failed, demonstrating that the EU's normative and legalistic approach could not attract coalition partners.

The main cause for this failure lies in the EU's very institutional structure: the EU's open multi-polar governance in the arena of climate change, and the EU's vertical partition of governance according to issue-areas prevented the EU from engaging in truly strategic discussions with either the US or China. The only way to make China or the US move on climate change is to propose grand bargains that cut across a large array of issue-areas (for example trade, foreign policy questions, energy and so on). But the EU Commissioners or EU Presidency dealing with climate change have no ability to engage in such wide-ranging and significant strategic bargaining. More generally, the EU's key weakness in the global arena is its lack of integration on foreign policy, particularly foreign policy with great powers such as the US, China and Russia. The divided voices of European countries and their lack of realist capacities prevent the EU from engaging in strategic interactions.

The lack of European unity is critically damaging in trying to engage with China. China approaches climate change negotiations as one issue-area in a larger strategic game, where it is negotiating its peaceful rise. China will engage in strategic bargaining on climate change, but only within a framework that facilitates its long-term development and growth. The Chinese negotiators have indicated for at least two years their readiness to engage with the UN framework and the Kyoto framework, often supporting Europe in principle. But they are only at the stage of staking a position for intense multi-issue bargaining. Europe is unable to sit down with China and engage in this intense bargaining.

Japan's abrupt shift did put Japan on the EU side of the table at the Copenhagen conference in December 2009, but the EU's lack of foreign policy integration prevented it from seizing the opportunity. Japan played a strong, positive role at the conference, combining its 25 per cent pledge with the largest pledge of financial aid to developing countries of any country ($15 billion over three years, half of the grand total promised by the OECD). Yet Japan and Europe found themselves isolated and side-lined, and individually so, instead of supporting each other.

Copenhagen marked the limits of the European focus on normative and institutional leadership. In the context of a diminishing European share in global greenhouse gas emissions and at a moment when crucial trade-offs have to be negotiated, it has become crucial to engage in real negotiations with the US and China. While the EU has shown its ability to generate a process of positive leadership reinforcement within its policy process, its lack of foreign policy integration has prevented it from engaging in real bargaining with the US, China and other emerging powers, reflecting Duchêne's concern that Europe's influence and ability to diffuse civilian standards would ultimately depend on its functional effectiveness (Duchêne 1973).

Conclusion: The Lessons of the Kyoto Saga for EU–Japan Leadership

The EU and Japan did enjoy a period of substantial civilian power environmental cooperation and leadership, and played a remarkable role in the establishment of a credible institutional framework to fight climate change. They also managed to save the Kyoto Protocol and ensure its entry into force despite the US decision to withdraw in 2001. And by and large, both the EU and Japan have made some serious efforts to implement Kyoto (the EU more so than Japan). This chapter has demonstrated that the actions of these two actors were not the result of pure realist or normative concerns, but the result of political strategic calculations in the context of public arenas. National leaders chose climate change as an arena where they could build their reputations, engage with domestic public opinion, shift political coalitions, stake a claim in future institutional arrangements, and project a new global identity. These actions relied on political legitimacy and the constant investment of political energy. As a result, Japanese commitment wavered under weaker prime ministers, who were less able to resist domestic economic and bureaucratic interests. Likewise, internal divisions started to weaken the EU in the late 2000s, and its inability to link climate with a broader raft of important strategic issues weakened its bargaining power with the US and China.

What is the legacy of EU–Japan leadership, and what are the future prospects for global climate politics? It is definitely a mixed picture. While generating new global institutions, this non-hegemonic pathway may have reached its ultimate limits in an issue-area loaded with such high stakes and intertwined with the rivalry for global leadership between the US and China. Taking up the mantle of normative and institutional leadership was probably useful in the early stages of the game, as it did define the agenda and pushed the frontier. But what is needed now is a big tent game of genuine global governance, where the EU and Japan are able to engage the interests of the US and China. The EU as an integrated entity has to overcome internal divisions, and create a coherent negotiating position vis-à-vis the US and China. In order for Japan to re-emerge as an international leader in global climate politics it is indispensable to redirect its energy policy toward a much more ambitious renewal path under decisive political leadership. It is unfortunate, however, that the prospects for Japan's comeback as a leader in international negotiations on climate change is very bleak at this moment since the current Abe administration has been preoccupied with Japan's economic recovery from the 'two decades' of recession, and also with its conservative political agenda of revising Article 9 of the Japanese Constitution, aiming at making Japan a credible player in the international security arena. Nevertheless, we can find a faint glimmer of hope in China. Despite its huge contributions to global carbon emissions, China has given some early, positive indications that it is willing to engage with the Kyoto framework and to support international efforts to tackle climate change. It may well be that a positive EU–Japan–China engagement holds the key for the advancement of global climate governance.

PART IV
Protecting Political, Food and Health Security

Chapter 10

EU–Japan Relations:
Civilian Power and the Domestication/
Localization of Human Rights

Paul Bacon

Introduction

In a seminal early discussion of the concept of civilian power, Duchêne famously argued that it is in the interest of the EU 'as far as possible to *domesticate* relations between states, including those of its own members and those with states outside its frontiers' (1973: 19–20). Civilian powers, on his view, should aim 'to bring to international problems the sense of common responsibility and structures of contractual politics which have in the past been associated almost exclusively with "home", and not foreign, that is, *alien* affairs' (1973: 20). Duchêne strongly believed that Europe 'must be a force for the international diffusion of civilian and democratic standards' (1973: 20).

We are entitled to ask who or what is being domesticated by whom, whose concept of home and alien is being invoked, and who is defining civilian and democratic standards. Human rights issues have been a point of contention between the EU and Japan, with the EU placing persistent pressure on Japan to abolish the death penalty, or at the very least establish an official moratorium. The European idea that EU–Japan relations might be transformed to reflect European values and priorities creates tension between the two polities. To adapt Duchêne's language, the EU attempts to diffuse its own human rights standards to Japan, and to domesticate its relations with Japan by ensuring that Japan reconfigures its domestic political arrangements to conform to European 'domestic' civil standards. However, Japanese and non-Japanese authors (Funabashi 1993; Maull 1990) have also defined Japan as a 'civilian power', and so a question arises as to how to mediate between the civil standards to be found in both polities.

This question brings into play the work of Acharya, and his notion of localization (Acharya 2004). Acharya argues that much scholarship on norm diffusion is founded on moral cosmopolitanism, and aims at conversion to and acceptance of 'universal' norms, rather than focusing on possible areas of legitimate contestation between universal and local norms. The norm diffusion literature, he argues, gives primacy to international prescriptions and sets up an implicit dichotomy between 'good' global or universal norms, and 'bad' regional or local norms. For moral cosmopolitans, norms making a universalistic claim about what is good are considered more desirable and more likely to prevail than norms that are localized or particularistic. However, Acharya argues that many local beliefs are themselves part of a legitimate normative order, which will in practice condition the acceptance of foreign norms (2004: 244)

Acharya argues that it is better to avoid this excessive emphasis on the 'universal' and pursue the objective of norm localization. To localize something is to invest it with the characteristics of a particular place. Acharya defines localization as 'the active construction (through discourse, framing, grafting and cultural selection) of foreign ideas by local actors, which results in the former developing significant congruence with local beliefs and practices' (2004: 245). Localization is not simply a matter of identifying pre-existing congruence between universal and local norms, but rather a constructivist notion of a dynamic social process through which parties might redefine their values, priorities and identities, which might in turn entail convergence between 'universal' and 'local' beliefs and shared practices. This chapter argues that it is more helpful and legitimate to look at ways in which Japan can and does localize 'universal' norms, rather than casting the discussion in terms of Japan being 'domesticated' and required to conform to civil standards established and dictated by Europeans.

The EU has recently attempted to develop a more effective approach to the promotion of human rights and democracy, and has lately come to recognize that it is strategically wiser to present its own values not as European values but as universal values. As a result, the EU now commits itself to promoting the universal standards which are to be found in the UN's global human rights legal framework, and dedicates itself to the implementation of this framework. However, the EU has also recognized that it needs, as a matter of practical priority, to consolidate consultations with local civil societies, notably on policy initiatives and human rights dialogues, and expand the practice of working on human rights issues through local human rights working groups (Ashton 2011b: 6–7).

Adapting Acharya's language, we can therefore say that the EU, in its recent pronouncements if not yet practice, has become more sensitive to the idea of localization. The EU has recognized the need to seek and to adopt local advice, to consult with local publics and expert communities, to see where the potential points of contact between universal and local norms might lie. This chapter attempts to identify what a tailored EU Japan strategy, sensitive to the issue of localization, might look like. It is argued that the EU should continue to pursue its abolitionist agenda, but that greater relative emphasis should be placed on other Japanese human rights issues where there is a greater chance of success, and where there is already a local dialogue within Japan for the EU to join or to influence.

The EU's New 'More Effective' Approach to Human Rights and Democracy

Over the last two years the EU has attempted to develop a more effective approach towards the promotion of human rights and democracy. The first part of the chapter traces the development of this attempt through an analysis of three landmark EU human rights documents that have been published during that time. These documents have called for a general renewal of the EU's external policy, and emphasized the need for a more localized, tailored, bottom-up, country-specific approach, working closely with and drawing on the expertise of local human rights groups. The documents have each also called for the development of cross-cutting worldwide campaigns on specific human rights themes, and specifically identified the administration of justice, or judicial reform focusing on the right to a fair trial, as an important human rights issue. The documents also each strongly recommended that the EU should use the standards established in the major international human rights treaties as benchmarks. The second part of the chapter draws out the implications of these recommendations and provides a framework for a localized, tailored human rights strategy for Japan. Drawing on the work of the UN Human Rights Committee, it is argued that in Japan there should be less preoccupation with death penalty issues, and that greater relative emphasis should be placed on issues relating to the administration of justice. This is because abolition of the death penalty is unlikely in Japan, but reform of the criminal justice system is rather more possible.

The High Representative's Joint Communication

In December 2011 Baroness Ashton, the High Representative of the European Union for Foreign Affairs and Security Policy, presented a Joint Communication to the European Parliament and the Council, entitled *Human Rights and Democracy at the Heart of EU External Action: Towards a More Effective Approach*. She argued that action was needed in a number of areas, including external delivery mechanisms, arguing that '*a bottom-up, tailored, country-based approach, coupled with cross-cutting worldwide campaigns on specific themes*' would be better for achieving the EU's human rights and democracy-related objectives (Ashton 2011b: 7, my emphasis).

The Communication argued that the general objectives of the EU's human rights and democracy policy are valid, but that it is necessary to match these general objectives to realities on the ground in particular countries. This more nuanced, differentiated strategy is more likely to get results than what is referred to as a 'one-size-fits-all' approach:

> Tailor-made country strategies should be part of the EU's overall strategy ... That is not to say that the EU should not, for example, condemn the use of the death penalty in a country that continues to apply it, *rather that this should*

not be the sole focus of EU human rights work when other areas might deliver change. (Ashton 2011b: 8, my emphasis)

It is argued below that the EU has indeed pursued something of a one-size-fits-all approach towards Japan, and that other issues are arguably just as important as, if not more important than the death penalty, and easier to make progress on. The Communication notes that '*the EU considers that respect for the rule of law, including access to justice and the right to a fair trial, is essential for the protection of human rights and democratic principles*'(Ashton 2011b: 7, my emphasis). Baroness Ashton further identifies three themes that the EU should focus on for the next three years, one of which is '*judicial reform focusing on the right to a fair trial*' (Ashton 2011b: 8, my emphasis). The Communication therefore emphasizes the need for renewal, the need for country-specific strategies, the need for cross-cutting themes, and the significance of judicial reform and the right to a fair trial. Finally, the communication identifies the significance of the work already done by the UN:

> The Universal Declaration of Human Rights sets international standards for all UN Member States. Every UN Member State is a party to at least one of the six major human rights treaties that the Universal Declaration has inspired, with 80% of states having ratified four or more. *A global legal framework therefore exists: the real challenge lies in ensuring its implementation.* (Ashton 2011b: 5, my emphasis)

The Council of Ministers' Strategic Framework

In June 2012 the Council of Ministers published an *EU Strategic Framework*, and an EU *Action Plan on Human Rights and Democracy*, which called for the mainstreaming of human rights in all EU external policies. The 2012 Strategic Framework and Action Plan are both very clearly inspired and informed by the 2011 Joint Communication. The Strategic Framework document commits the EU to the promotion of the civilian and democratic ends mentioned by Duchêne, and reconfirms the importance of the existing global framework (Council of the European Union 2012b: 1). Article 21 of the Treaty on European Union reaffirms the EU's determination to promote human rights and democracy through all of its external actions, and claims that promoting and speaking out on human rights and democracy is a joint responsibility of the EU and its member states. In the Strategic Framework, it is argued that the EU will promote human rights in all areas of its external action without exception, and integrate the promotion of human rights into trade and investment. The Strategic Framework identifies several EU human rights priorities, including the death penalty and the administration of justice. More specifically, it is argued that:

The death penalty and torture constitute serious violations of human rights and human dignity. *Encouraged by the growing momentum towards abolition of the death penalty worldwide, the EU will continue its long-standing campaign against the death penalty.* The EU will continue to campaign vigorously against torture and cruel, inhuman and degrading treatment. (Council of the European Union 2012b: 3, my emphasis)

And that:

The fair and impartial administration of justice is essential to safeguard human rights. *The EU will step up its efforts to promote the right to a fair trial and equality before the law.* (Council of the European Union 2012b: 3, my emphasis)

The Strategic Framework document further insists that 'the EU will place human rights at the centre of its relations with all third countries, including its strategic partners' (Council of the European Union 2012b: 3), which include, of course, Japan, and will 'raise human rights issues vigorously in all appropriate forms of political dialogue, including at the highest level' (Council of the European Union 2012b: 3). Furthermore, while the EU retains a firm commitment to the fact that its human rights policy is based on universal norms, '*policy on human rights will be carefully designed for the circumstances of each country, not least through the development of country human rights strategies*' (Council of the European Union 2012b: 3, my emphasis). These commitments in the Strategic Framework are entirely consistent with Acharya's notion of localization.

The Council of Ministers' Action Plan

The Action Plan, whose purpose is to provide for the implementation of the Strategic Framework, contained the following recommendations with regard to localization:

- Work closely with human rights NGOs in host countries.
- Ensure effective support to civil society organizations.
- Consolidate consultations with civil society, notably on policy initiatives and dialogues on human rights.
- Expand the practice of working on human rights issues through local human rights working groups.
- Promote improved access by local human rights defenders to the UN and regional human rights protection mechanisms.
- Continue to develop tailored, local human rights country strategies, assess lessons learnt, and identify best practice.

- Ensure that the human rights country strategies are taken into account in human rights and political dialogues at all levels (Council of the European Union, 2012a: 1–10).

The Action Plan also emphasizes the importance of targeted campaigns on the death penalty and issues relating to the administration of justice.

Having just given an overview of the High Representative's Joint Communication, and the Council of Ministers' Strategic Framework and Action Plan, it is worth briefly re-capitulating some of the key points contained in the three documents. Each of the documents called for renewal, each supported the idea of localized, tailored, bottom-up, country-specific strategies and cross-cutting themes, and each emphasized the importance of both the death penalty and the administration of justice. Each document also emphasized that it is necessary to target a number of different issues in combination. In some countries, abolition of the death penalty might be unlikely, and in such cases it would be more practical to shift relative focus to other issues.

The Death Penalty and Japan

Capital punishment is legal in Japan. Between 1946 and 1993 Japanese courts sentenced 766 people to death, 608 of whom were executed. The death penalty is ordinarily imposed in cases of multiple murders involving aggravating factors. In Japan the courts follow guidelines developed during the 1983 trial of Norio Nagayama, a 19 year old from a disadvantaged background, who committed four murders. The Supreme Court of Japan, in imposing the death penalty, ruled that the death penalty may be imposed in consideration of the degree of criminal liability and balance of justice, based on a nine-point set of criteria. Though technically not a precedent, the 'Nagayama standard' has been followed in all subsequent capital cases in Japan. The criteria are:

1. Degree of viciousness
2. Motive
3. How the crime was committed; especially the manner in which the victim was killed.
4. Outcome of the crime; especially the number of victims.
5. Sentiments of the bereaved family members.
6. Impact of the crime on Japanese society.
7. Defendant's age (in Japan, someone is a minor until the age of 20).
8. Defendant's previous criminal record.
9. Degree of remorse shown by the defendant. (Schmidt 2002: 54–5)

Those on death row are not classified as prisoners by the Japanese justice system, and the facilities they are held at are not referred to as prisons. Inmates lack many of the rights afforded to other Japanese prisoners. The nature of the regime they live under is largely up to the director of the Detention Centre at which they are held, but it is usually significantly harsher than in normal Japanese prisons: inmates are held under solitary confinement and are forbidden from communicating with their fellows; and prison visits, both by family members and legal representatives, are infrequent and closely supervised.

Executions are carried out by hanging in a death chamber within the Detention Centre. When a death order has been issued, the condemned prisoner is informed on the morning of his or her execution. The prisoner's family and legal representatives are not informed until afterwards. At the end of 2012 133 people were awaiting execution in Japan, the most since 1949 (*Agence France-Presse*, 29 December 2012).

The situation in Japan has fluctuated markedly in recent years, but there is little chance of an official moratorium or abolition of the death penalty. The Democratic Party of Japan (DPJ) was in power for three years between mid-2009 and late 2012, and is generally less supportive of the death penalty. The DPJ only carried out two executions in its first two and a half years, and there were two periods of de facto moratorium when the DPJ was in power, the second of which lasted 20 months. In 2012, however, the DPJ oversaw seven executions. This did little for levels of political support for the DPJ, and the general election, held on 16 December, was emphatically won by the Liberal Democratic Party (LDP), which is generally highly supportive of the death penalty.

From Figure 10.1 we can see that after a comparative lull between 2001 and 2005, the number of executions rose significantly in the following four years. The number of executions declined again during the first three years of DPJ rule, including a 20-month de facto moratorium, but increased significantly again in 2012, in election year.

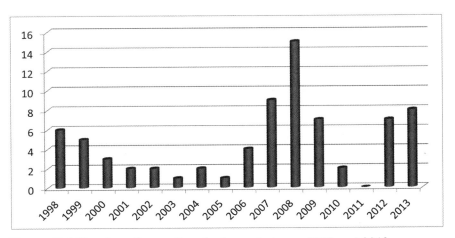

Figure 10.1 Number of executions in Japan between 1998 and 2013

Japanese politicians and bureaucrats claim that more than 85 per cent of the Japanese public support the death penalty, and use this fact to justify their retentionist stance in dialogue with UN human rights monitoring bodies. This perception, that support is so high, makes it politically costly to consider abolition, and offers an easy excuse to continue with executions. The DPJ was prepared to uphold a de facto moratorium during the middle of its term of office: two DPJ Ministers of Justice acknowledged that there was a significant international trend towards abolition, and that this was one of the main reasons why they refused to authorize executions. However, the DPJ eventually came under strong pressure from the LDP, Ministry of Justice bureaucrats and the public in 2012, in the build-up to the general election, resulting in the resumption of executions.

The de facto moratorium was a significant achievement, but is also the high-water mark of what is currently achievable in Japan on the death penalty, given the fact that the LDP is back in power. LDP Justice Minister Sadakazu Tanigaki authorized a total of eight executions during 2013, and at the same time made it clear that he has no plans to review the current system. Even though he acknowledged the international trend towards abolition, Tanigaki insisted any debate over capital punishment should be based on Japan's 'domestic situation', including public sentiment and maintaining public order, rather than movements beyond Japan's borders (*Japan Times* 2013a).

We can therefore see that a more differentiated and localized human rights strategy is necessary for Japan. Rather than positioning itself as the representative of an external international trend, the EU needs to identify and work with local Japanese human rights defenders. This approach should still include the death penalty, but should not focus exclusively or excessively on it. There are other human rights issues in Japan, including issues relating to the administration of justice, which are arguably more important than the death penalty, and on which there is greater possibility of movement by the Japanese government. These issues are taken up in the next section.

The UN Human Rights Committee: Japan's Major Human Rights Issues

Earlier in this chapter three recent EU documents on human rights and democracy were discussed. The 2011 Joint Communication, the 2012 Strategic Framework and the 2012 Action Plan all *explicitly* recommended that the EU should, in its development of human rights policy, draw on and benchmark to standards established in the work of the UN, both in international human rights treaties and in the UN human rights bodies that monitor them.

As we have seen, the same documents also note the need to use these benchmarks to engage with local civil societies and human rights NGOs. In what follows we look at the human rights problems identified by the UN Human Rights Committee, and identify both the most important problems and those on which there is already significant dialogue and debate within Japan. According to the logic of localization, the EU is likely to have more success by sponsoring actors participating in local debate, who best represent EU human rights priorities.

The following section draws extensively on the work of the UN Human Rights Committee, which has focused on human rights and the death penalty in Japan in impressive detail. The UN Human Rights Committee is the monitoring committee for the *International Covenant on Civil and Political Rights*. States-party to this Covenant are required to submit initial and periodic reports to the committee. Japan's *Fifth Periodic Report* was considered during the 94th session of the Human Rights Committee, in October 2008. This section of the chapter draws on criticisms that were made of Japan's record in the *Concluding Observations* of the Human Rights Committee. It focuses on the sections of the *Concluding Observations* that focus on the death penalty and the administration of justice in Japan's criminal justice system. For each article of the *Concluding Observations*, *subjects of concern* and *recommendations* are listed. The *Concluding Observations* document features 34 articles in total, but here we focus on subjects of concern raised in articles 16–21, which relate to the death penalty and the administration of justice.

In Article 16 the Committee reiterates its concern that the number of crimes punishable by the death penalty in Japan has still not been reduced, and that the number of executions has steadily increased in recent years. It is also concerned that death row inmates are kept in solitary confinement, often for protracted periods; are executed without prior notice being provided before the day of execution; and, in some cases, at an advanced age or despite the fact that they have mental disabilities. The non-use of the power of pardon, commutation or reprieve, as well as the absence of transparency concerning procedures for seeking benefit for such relief, is also a matter of concern. These practices are in contravention of Articles 6, 7 and 10 of the *International Covenant on Civil and Political Rights* (hereafter ICCPR) (UN Human Rights Committee 2008: 4–5).

In Article 17 the Committee notes with concern that an increasing number of defendants are convicted and sentenced to death without exercising their right of appeal; that meetings of death row inmates with their lawyer in charge of requesting a retrial are attended and monitored by prison officials until the court has decided to open the retrial; and that requests for retrial or pardon do not have the effect of staying the execution of a death sentence. These practices are in contravention of Articles 6 and 14 of the ICCPR (UN Human Rights Committee 2008: 5).

In Article 18 the Committee notes that police functions of investigation and detention are formally separated under the Act on Penal Detention Facilities and Treatment of Inmates and Detainees. However, the Committee is concerned about aspects of the substitute detention system (*Daiyo Kangoku*), under which suspects can be detained in police detention facilities for a period up to 23 days to facilitate investigations, without the possibility of bail and with limited access to a lawyer especially during the first 72 hours of arrest. This increases the risk of prolonged interrogations and abusive interrogation methods with the aim of obtaining a confession. These practices are in contravention of Articles 7, 9, 10 and 14 of the ICCPR (UN Human Rights Committee 2008: 5).

In Article 19 the Committee notes with concern the insufficient limitations on the duration of interrogations of suspects contained in internal police regulations; and the exclusion of counsel from interrogations on the assumption that such presence would diminish the function of the interrogation to persuade the suspect to disclose the truth; and the sporadic and selective use of electronic surveillance methods during interrogations, frequently limited to recording the confession by the suspect. It also reiterates its concern about the extremely high conviction rate based primarily on confessions. This concern is aggravated in respect of such convictions that involve death sentences. These practices are in contravention of Articles 7, 9, and 14 of the ICCPR (UN Human Rights Committee 2008: 5–6).

Finally, under Article 21 the Committee is concerned that death row inmates are confined to single rooms during day and night, purportedly to ensure their mental and emotional stability; and that lifetime prisoners are sometimes also placed in solitary confinement for protracted periods of time. It is also concerned about reports that inmates may be confined to protection cells without prior medical examination for a period of 72 hours initially which is indefinitely renewable; and that a certain category of prisoners are placed in separate 'accommodating blocks' without an opportunity to appeal against this measure. These practices are in contravention of Articles 7 and 10 of the ICCPR (UN Human Rights Committee 2008: 6).

We have now discussed in some detail what the UN Human Rights Committee identifies as some of Japan's most pressing administration of justice and death penalty-related problems. The final section of the chapter investigates ways in which the EU could distinguish due process issues from death penalty issues, and looks briefly at the more specific possibilities for EU human rights diplomacy that are opened up by this distinction.

Towards a Localized Human Rights Strategy for Japan: Separating Death Penalty and Administration of Justice Issues

It is difficult for any Japanese government to go further than adopting a de facto moratorium on the death penalty, and this important issue is a sticking point for EU–Japan relations. If Europeans adopt a zero-sum approach to debates about the death penalty then it could be difficult to make real progress. It could be argued that the EU has attached too much symbolic importance to the abolition of the death penalty, viewing it as a non-negotiable 'litmus test', to the detriment of other political and human rights objectives that could reasonably be argued to be at least as important. The EU should focus more attention on administration of justice issues, where Japan does have standards that are significantly lower than those that might be expected of a G8/OECD country, and of a country that wishes to be recognized as a civilian power.

It is morally justifiable and strategically useful to separate death penalty issues from administration of justice issues. In an ideal world one might hope that all of the recommendations enumerated by the UN Human Rights Committee on the death penalty and the administration of justice could be accepted by the Japanese government. In most foreseeable Japanese political climates, however, it would be difficult for any incumbent party to deliver abolition or an official moratorium without risking political suicide. The EU needs to appreciate this, and develop a localized, tailored human rights strategy that is sensitive to the real constraints that any Japanese government will actually face.

This chapter suggests a more flexible and nuanced approach to criminal justice issues, and discourages a disproportionately symbolic focus on the death penalty. The death penalty is a legitimate subject of concern for the EU. However, the Japanese government would find it easier to agree to many of the smaller, more detailed, less politically sensitive and incremental human rights recommendations which are identified in Tables 10.1 and 10.2. Death penalty and administration of justice issues *can* be separated, and this separation provides the EU with a more realistic framework within which to conduct its human rights diplomacy in Japan.

The preceding discussion identified subjects of concern; Tables 10.1 and 10.2 identify and list some of the most important recommendations which were made in the *Concluding Observations*. The recommendations are separated into two categories – the death penalty and administration of justice – and within these categories, the issues are provisionally ranked in descending order (with the most important issues placed at the top of each list).

The two categories of death penalty and administration of justice clearly overlap, but they are also separable. Developing human rights strategy in this way unbundles key death penalty and administration of justice issues into smaller, more achievable recommendations and targets. The Japanese government is not being presented with human rights demands that it cannot meet, but is instead presented with opportunities to co-operate over smaller, often shared human rights objectives that are not as politically sensitive.

As noted, the Japanese government is already engaged in dialogue with UN monitoring bodies and local actors over some of these issues, and it has already begun to implement reform in some areas. More detailed work needs to be done to identify the most important issues from these lists on which the EU and its supporters should focus, through intensive consultation with local civil societies and human rights NGOs.

Table 10.1 Recommendations related to the death penalty in Japan

1.	Abolition of the death penalty.
2.	Official moratorium on death penalty.
3.	Unofficial moratorium on death penalty.
4.	Significant reduction in number of executions.
5.	Reduction in number of executions.
6.	Public informed of the desirability of abolition.
7.	Persons at an advanced age or with mental disabilities not to be executed.
8.	Minors not to be executed.
9.	Pregnant women not to be executed.
10.	Powers of pardon, commutation and reprieve to be genuinely available to those sentenced to death.
11.	Mandatory system of review in capital cases.
12.	Suspensive effect of requests for retrial or pardon in capital cases.
13.	Strict confidentiality for all meetings between death row inmates and their lawyers concerning retrial.
14.	Inmates on death row and their families to be given reasonable advance notice of the scheduled date and time of the execution, to prepare themselves for this event.
15.	Solitary confinement should remain an exceptional measure of limited duration.
16.	Maximum time limit for solitary confinement.

Source: These Death Penalty issues have been drawn from the Concluding Observations of the UN Human Rights Committee (2008), separated from administration of justice issues, and itemized in descending order of priority.

Table 10.2 Recommendations related to the administration of justice in Japan

1.	Substitute detention system to be abolished.
2.	Pre-indictment bail system to be introduced.
3.	Right of confidential access to legal aid from the moment of arrest and irrespective of the nature of their alleged crime, for all suspects.
4.	Right of confidential access to a lawyer during the interrogation process for all suspects.
5.	Right of all suspects to have counsel present during interrogations, to prevent false confessions and ensure the rights of suspects.
6.	Strict time limits for interrogation of suspects, and sanctions for non-compliance.
7.	Systematic use of video recording devices for entire duration of interrogations.
8.	Role of police during criminal investigations is to collect evidence for the trial rather than establishing the truth.
9.	Silence of suspects not considered inculpatory.
10.	Courts to rely on modern scientific evidence rather than confessions made during police interrogations.
11.	Right of confidential access to all police records related to their case for all suspects.
12.	Right of confidential access to medical treatment for all suspects.

Source: These Administration of Justice issues have been drawn from the Concluding Observations of the UN Human Rights Committee (2008), separated from death penalty issues, and itemized in descending order of priority.

It is not being suggested that this discussion can be linked in any direct or systematic way to the negotiations that started in 2013 between the EU and Japan over an FTA/EPA and a political framework agreement. Whilst it is highly likely that there will be a human rights clause or clauses in any eventual agreement, it is equally likely that any references to human rights will be generic and non-specific. It has proved difficult enough for both sides to agree to start trade negotiations, without adding the additional complication of linking trade in specific or demanding ways to political or human rights objectives. It would therefore be a major (but welcome) surprise if any eventual agreement went significantly beyond the expression of a general commitment to human rights. Human rights conditionality may have worked with regard to EU enlargement and relations with some neighbourhood partners, but is unlikely to work to anything like the same extent when the EU negotiates with Japan. In a sense, this is liberating, because it frees the EU to concentrate on promoting human rights without worrying about the precise ways in which human rights pressure plays into and affects trade negotiations. It instead creates an opportunity for the EU to focus more actively and sincerely on its human rights objectives with regard to Japan, and become more closely involved in supporting and sponsoring local human rights defenders.

Indicatively, we can identify five issues from the two lists on which, from an EU perspective, there have been promising local developments in the last five years. We can address the first three of these simply by referring to the Japanese government's response to the list of issues raised by the UN, in Japan's *Second Periodic Report* under the *Convention Against Torture* (UN Committee Against Torture 2011). In that report, the Japanese government listed improvements that had been made since 2008 in the management of time limits and conditions for interrogations (UN Committee Against Torture 2011: 24–5), and there has also been a trial period where parts of police interviews have been recorded in more than 719 cases (UN Committee Against Torture 2011: 24). Japan's report also contained a commitment to keep solitary confinement as an exceptional measure of limited duration, and discussed new measures which had been undertaken to maintain this (UN Committee Against Torture 2011: 41). These three issues are cases where the Japanese government has recognized the validity of the criticisms which have been made of it through the UN reporting process, and has attempted to introduce reforms to meet the objections. It is important to note that whilst it is welcome that progress has been made, there is still some way to go, even on these specific issues where the government has acknowledged criticism and sought to make improvements.

The Japanese government report denies the request that death row inmates and their families be given reasonable advance notice of their execution, stating that 'if inmates sentenced to death are notified of their execution before the day of the execution, their peace of mind may be negatively affected and the notification could rather inflict excessive pain, etc.' (UN Committee Against Torture 2011: 41). However, a recent survey has indicated that death row inmates in Japan do not agree, and want to be told of their execution in advance, instead of on the day they are to be hanged. The survey was carried out by Mizuho Fukushima, deputy chairwoman of the nonpartisan Parliamentary League for the Abolition of the Death Penalty, from September to November 2012. Of the 78 inmates who replied, 51 said they wanted to know ahead of time that they would be put to death, with opinions varying from a day to a month in advance. Many said they wanted the chance to say goodbye to loved ones (*Agence France-Presse*, 29 December 2012). This is an interesting example of local Japanese actors disagreeing with and seeking to overturn the conventional wisdom of the government and the Ministry of Justice, and is another type of activity that the EU should be seeking to recognize and support.

Finally, the Japanese government's report claims that it is not appropriate to adopt an immediate moratorium on executions because 'the majority of citizens in Japan consider that the death penalty is unavoidable for extremely malicious/ brutal crimes' (UN Committee Against Torture 2011: 8–9). This claim is made on the basis of a government survey which has been carried out approximately every five years since 1956 by the Cabinet Office. According to the most recent 2009 survey, 86 per cent of respondents favoured retention of the death penalty, and these results have been interpreted by the Japanese government, politicians and courts as the 'voice' of the Japanese public.

However, recent research (Sato 2013: 51) has suggested that these survey results should be treated with 'extreme caution' for a number of reasons. There has been a decline in the response rate for the survey, and abolitionists are generally less likely to reply. Particular cohorts which possess the highest number of abolitionists, such as young men, are less likely to reply and are therefore under-represented in the survey results (Sato 2013: 38, 40). Finally, and most importantly, it is claimed that the questions in the survey are framed and phrased in such a way that they make it more likely that respondents will express a preference for retention of the death penalty. If a fairer survey methodology is used, it can be demonstrated that over half of respondents (55 per cent) are actually undecided or do not have a strong opinion on the death penalty (Sato 2013: 43). This is a very important finding, because it potentially removes the central plank of the government case for retention: the 'fact' of unambiguous public support for the death penalty. This is an interesting example of a Japanese academic disagreeing with and seeking to overturn the conventional wisdom of the government and the Ministry of Justice, and is another example of the type of activity that the EU should be seeking to recognize and support.

Conclusion

Of the 28 issues identified above, the EU Delegation in Tokyo should, in partnership with local civil society actors and human rights NGOs, identify those issues which are most important, and those on which progress would be most likely, and target resources to them. Some promising areas for progress have been briefly identified above, and further opinion polling needs to be carried out in order to provide support for challenges to the findings of the Cabinet Office polls. It is also probable that sophisticated deliberative polling exercises would show that the Japanese public would be highly critical of some of the problems which exist within their criminal justice system if they knew more about them. Key issues should be identified in partnership with Brussels as well as local actors, and funding support sought though instruments such as the European Instrument for Democracy and Human Rights (EIDHR), which is tasked with funding the human rights initiatives of local NGOs. The suggestions mentioned above are all consistent with a strategy of localization – engaging with local actors to construct consensus on shared values.

This chapter sought to locate credible choices for an EU human rights strategy for Japan within a coherent framework which is consistent with and develops the logic found in the three recent EU human rights documents. The approach developed above takes universal values from the international human rights treaties, recognizes the significance of administration of justice issues in Japan, identifies a country-specific set of priority issues relevant to Japan, and suggests ways of gaining support for them in a more subtle, selective way which is sensitive to the local Japanese context.

Chapter 11

The EU, Japan and the Balkans: Cooperation for Post-conflict Nation-building

Dimitar Bechev

The violent conflict that tore apart Yugoslavia in the 1990s is rightly viewed as a significant event in both post-Cold War European and global affairs. The disintegration of the multi-national federation and the ensuing bloodshed on the very borders of the fledgling European Union (EU) came as a stark reminder of the tremendous conflictual potential of ethnonationalism, in a region that had enjoyed half a century of relative calm. That fact alone put the Yugoslav war of succession, which for a variety of reasons gained currency as 'the Balkan War', at the centre of worldwide attention, despite the fact that several other conflicts of comparable or greater proportion were raging at the same time, such as the civil war in Algeria, the Rwandan genocide or the devastating violence in DRC. For nearly a decade, from 1991 all the way to the NATO intervention in Kosovo (April–June 1999), the former Yugoslavia topped the international agenda. It encapsulated issues and concerns with broader significance such as the true meaning of the right to self-determination, the place of human rights and humanitarian intervention in international society, the role of the UN and NATO in the post-Cold War world, and the future of US leadership in world affairs. Many of those questions, heavily coloured by the experience in the Balkans, lingered on well into the 2000s – even if international attention shifted away into the Middle East in the wake of the 9/11 attacks in the United States. It is not uncommon these days, for instance, to draw comparison between Bosnia and the war in Syria when international intervention is at issue.

This special place occupied by the former Yugoslavia along with its Balkan neighbours, otherwise a European subregion of marginal significance, has drawn in international players such as the EU and Japan. For all the differences between the two, they have both contributed, in different ways, to the area's pacification, reconstruction, democratic development and (re-)integration into the global economy. While it is absolutely certain that the respective capacities of the EU and Japan to catalyse transformation in the region have been vastly disparate, unequal and therefore hard to compare, it is also true that the kind of engagement both pursue in relation to the conflict-scarred part of the Balkans mirrors a shared self-conception both polities have of themselves as civilian powers. What is more, despite the varying expectations as to the roles they were to play, both Japan and the EU stepped into the region in the mid-1990s, in the wake of a massive intervention reliant on US hard power whose outcomes were cemented with the 1995 Dayton Peace Accords. In their different ways, the EU and Japan employed a range of soft instruments including financial assistance and worked via an assortment of multilateral mechanisms.

However, as the post-conflict phase drew to a close in the 2000s divergences became increasingly visible. While Japan continued with the role of a junior partner in a broad-based coalition of good international citizens, largely under UN colours, the EU graduated, thanks to its enlargement policy and the nascent peacekeeping and civilian missions, into the primary political anchor for the region. This divergence highlights both geographical realities – the EU's immediate proximity to the Balkans – but also variance in terms of foreign policy outlook. Whereas Japan has by and large stayed in the habitual civilian power mould and at times sought commercial gains, Europe has sought to re-invent itself as a more rounded foreign policy actor relying on a combination of soft- but also hard-power resources to wield influence over an extensive periphery.

The EU and Japan as Civilian Powers: The Balkan Angle

Because the EU and Japan's convergent approaches to the Balkans are connected to self-identification as civilian powers it is worthwhile to consider the concept in a little more detail. First proposed by Duchêne (1973) with a focus on the then European Community (EC) role in global affairs, the notion has sparked off and fuelled numerous theoretical battles in both European Studies and the broader field of International Relations (IR). One of the best attempts to unpack the concept and divide it into elements with direct applicability to the study of specific cases belongs to Mario Telò (2007). He distinguishes three dimensions of civilian 'power-ness':

1. The expansive force and attractiveness of peaceful coexistence and cooperation between neighbouring states, as confirmed by the success of the European project, ... its widening and deepening, and the spread of similar regional organizations in the rest of the world.
2. The renewed distinctiveness of the European socio-economic 'model' within the partially globalized economy. ...
3. The network of external relations of the EU and its Member States with regions and states all over the world and with international organisations. (Telò 2007: 1–2)

In other words, civilian power is as much about the underlying values and ends (peace built upon integration, interdependence, a healthy balance between economic openness and social cohesion) as about instruments and means (institutionalized cooperation, sharing sovereignty, trade liberalization, economic and developmental assistance, encouragement of trans-border civil society, extending the rule of law, amongst others).

Many academics and pundits have written extensively about the EU's exceptionalism in a world populated by bellicose emergent powers and indeed the US, reliant as it is on its military primacy in the conduct of foreign relations. However, although it is fair to say that the EU, an international body combining both intergovernmental and supranational elements, exemplifies and in many respects sets the 'gold standard' for civilian power, it is by no means alone.

Ever since the end of the Cold War scholars have drawn civilian power parallels between Japan and Germany, and Japan and the EU (Maull 1990). Indeed, since 1945 Japan has shared a similar trajectory with Germany, which is in many respects the keystone of the overall European construct. Maull proposes a definition of his own which tries to capture both the experience of Germany (and perhaps Western Europe more broadly) and Japan. It is particularly useful in trying to come to grips with the concept and, in doing so, escape as much as possible from EU-centric bias, in order to introduce in a more meaningful way the Japanese experience in the latter part of the twentieth century and beyond. In addition, Maull lays a particular emphasis on means which open avenues for comparison. To him, the three pillars of civilian power include:

1. the acceptance of the necessity of cooperation with others in the pursuit of international objectives;
2. the concentration on non-military, primarily economic, means to secure national goals, with military power left as a residual instrument serving essentially to safeguard other means of international interaction; and
3. a willingness to develop supranational structures to address critical issues of international management. (Maull 1990: 92–3)

The extent to which this and other definitions elucidate the role that the EU and Japan play in global politics is explored at length in some of the foregoing chapters. Focusing on the Balkan case makes a contribution in several additional interrelated ways.

First, the violent disintegration of the former Yugoslavia questioned the relevance of civilian power for addressing the most pressing challenges of the post-Cold War world. What seemed at the time to be the inexorable rise of ethno-nationalism in the formerly communist world placed the bar quite high for a nascent EU whose core strength was, and still is, linked to the forces of market integration. In a similar vein, Japan – with its commitment to multilateral action through the UN – could do little to address the conflicts in Bosnia and Kosovo that occupied the global headlines. Granted, the expectations vis-à-vis the EU were infinitely greater. Everyone remembers, to this very day, the ill-conceived 1991 pronouncement of Luxembourg's Prime Minister Jacques Poos that the 'hour of Europe' had arrived. Yet the outbreak of ethnic violence did sweep aside the notion that a peaceful age of international cooperation was dawning, to the equal detriment of both the EU and Japan.

Second, the violence in the former Yugoslavia was contained only after the US exercised hard power and prompted several interventions via NATO (Macedonia, 2001; Bosnia, 1994–1995; Kosovo, 1999). Under US leadership, NATO played a fundamental part in the maintenance of stability in wider Southeast Europe, including the management of the volatile Greek-Turkish relationship, and of Albania, Romania and Bulgaria, all of which were co-opted into the Partnership for Peace programme as early as 1994. All in all, regional order was established and cemented by the Transatlantic Alliance and was, at least initially, little more than an extension of the 'unipolar moment'. As elsewhere, Europe but also Japan was left, figuratively speaking, to 'do the dishes'. Post-conflict reconstruction initiatives such as the 1999 Stability Pact (a German initiative, with Japan as one of the donors) were filling niches, playing a complementary role to the indispensable leadership provided by the then Clinton administration.

Third, the 2000s marked a transition where the EU assumed a much more central role in the region. The turnaround had to do with the development of the European Security and Defence Policy (ESDP) post-1998 as well as the launch of enlargement towards Southeast Europe with the crucial summits in Helsinki (December 1999) and Thessaloniki (June 2003). At first glance, such a development towards strengthening Europe's role should have given a breath of fresh air to the notion of civilian power. The EU was given a chance to Europeanize the region, applying its very own toolbox and ensconcing its foundational values of interdependence, democracy and pooling of sovereignty. Such contentions, however, appear less tenable taking into account that the Balkans was in fact a testing ground for the Union developing a military capacity – starting with the Concordia mission in Macedonia (2003). Put differently, the main lesson learned in the region has been that the civilian vision is limiting and inadequate, especially if the Union aspires to be a credible actor in both its wider regional setting and on a global scale. Japan arrived at a similar turning point when its Self-Defence Force was deployed in Iraq in 2004, in the aftermath of the US-led military intervention against Saddam Hussain.

Fourth, and perhaps most important, the concept of civilian power obscures the power relationship between the EU and the Balkans (Bechev 2012). At the end of the day, Brussels has graduated since the late 1990s into being the key order-builder in Southeast Europe. The enlargement machine has transformed the former Yugoslavia and its neighbours into a part of the EU's 'near abroad' or, to use a historical reference, a marche in the 'neo-medieval empire' (Zielonka 2006) that is today's Europe. The main game in this European periphery has been governance through expansion. To the extent that the process is peaceful and relies on the functional, economic and diplomatic instruments at the EU's disposal, one could argue that it doesn't stretch too far the civilian power concept. But civilian power overlooks the centre–periphery dynamic at play as well as the interests that underscore the EU's involvement in the region. In many respects it is Japan, rather than the EU, which remains true to the civilian concept in its dealings with the

Balkans. In doing so, it is filling gaps in the EU's order-building policy, much as the EU was doing in the Clinton years.

In conclusion, one could say that the nature, dynamics and intensity of EU–Japan interaction and cooperation in the Balkans have very much been reflective of the role played by the EU in the region. This role, in turn, has been shaped by a host of variables including: the situation within the region itself, the evolution of EU integration, especially concerning areas such as security and defence and enlargement policy, and the twists and turns in the transatlantic relationship. The EU–Japan story in the Balkans has gone through three main stages mirroring Brussels' relationship with the region. The following sections present an overview.

Stage I: A Region in Flux (1989–1995)

The collapse of most communist regimes in Europe (1989–1991) and the turmoil sparked off by the disintegration of Yugoslavia resulted in pressure for EU involvement in Southeast Europe. Just as in Central Europe, newly democratizing countries' elites, whether belonging to the opposition or the post-communist establishment, saw the Union as an indispensable anchor for political and socio-economic transformation. In the former Yugoslavia, separatist republics such as Slovenia and Croatia solicited support from the EU and individual member states in recognizing and supporting their cause. Once hostilities broke out in 1991 the Union was also looked upon as a potential peacemaker. Not to forget that this period coincided with the Maastricht Treaty negotiations which paved the way to the CFSP driven by the ambition that the newly formed EU should assume a much greater political role. Of course, such hopes were soon frustrated. The inability and unwillingness of the EU to intervene in the Bosnian war, which claimed in excess of 100,000 lives between 1992 and 1995 showed the impotence of the policy swept aside by divisions among the then member states. Successive mediation efforts co-piloted by the EU and the UN, most notably the Vance-Owen plan of 1993, ended in failure. Ultimately it was military intervention directed by the US that helped contain the violence and impose the Dayton Peace Accords. Though the treaty was formally signed in Paris, it was clear that Europe was the junior partner in the American-led effort to pacify Bosnia and more broadly the former Yugoslavia.

Japan played a modest role in this initial period. First, it supported transition in Romania and Bulgaria through its overseas development aid (ODA), much like in the rest of Central and Eastern Europe (CEE). Second, high-profile diplomats were involved in the multilateral efforts to find a solution to the Bosnian crisis. One was Yasushi Akashi who became the UN Secretary-General's Special Representative for Yugoslavia in December 1993. Akashi came under a great deal of criticism over the 1995 genocide at Srebrenica. The negative publicity associated with such criticism was one of the reasons that Japanese governments focused on the Balkans in disbursing ODA (Huliaras 2007: 22). Later, Sadako Ogata, head of the UNHCR, played an important role in drawing attention to the plight of

Kosovar Albanians. Beyond the UN framework, Japanese foreign ministers and high-ranking diplomats were active in other multilateral bodies which at one point or other addressed the situation in the former Yugoslavia, such as the G7. One of the motivating factors underlying Japanese diplomatic engagement with the conflict-ridden Balkans was the country's bid to join the UN Security Council as a permanent member. As the war in the former Yugoslavia was a paramount international issue in the first post-Cold War decade, Japan's involvement, to the point of activism, was a must.

In summary, Japan adopted a dual approach: a bilateral policy of assisting reform in post-communist countries and a contribution to multilateral efforts to contain violence in Yugoslavia. It was mostly driven by political considerations, not the pursuit of economic opportunities as elsewhere in Eastern Europe. But, to be sure, Tokyo's capacities were limited. Not being part of NATO and lacking the capacity and ambitions to be a mediator, Tokyo was involved at a much lower level compared to the EU. For instance, in the 1990s the region attracted 1–2 per cent of Japan's overseas development and humanitarian assistance budget. Yet it is fair to say that both actors ended up playing, in their different ways, supportive parts in the broad Western coalition assembled and led by Washington for bringing an end to the war in Bosnia as well as in other parts of the former Yugoslavia.

Stage II: The Interregnum (1995–2003)

The second period, which was defined by the 1999 intervention in Kosovo, brought about incremental changes with respect to the division of labour within the Western coalition. Most importantly, the EU, in an attempt to draw lessons from the Bosnian debacle, broadened its commitment. That implied the gradual withdrawal of the US, becoming visible in the wake of the 9/11 attacks and the renewed focus on the so-called greater Middle East, as well as a greater share of the responsibility for the Balkans passing to the EU. Bulgaria and Romania submitted membership applications and were given a green light to start accession talks at the Helsinki Summit (December 1999). In the former Yugoslavia, Macedonia and then Croatia became the first two countries to sign Stabilisation and Association Agreements (SAAs) with the Union, a stepping-stone to full-fledged candidacy. The St Malo summit between UK Prime Minister Tony Blair and French President Jacques Chirac laid the foundations of the ESDP, adding a military dimension to the EU's foreign policy. Clearly, the Balkans would be the key testing ground.

Despite the slow transition towards EU leadership and although the US again proved its indispensable role, the dominant approach to the region in the period at hand relied on multilateral engagement involving the international community at large. The most direct example was the Peace Implementation Council (PIC) overseeing the application of the Dayton Accords in Bosnia, where Japan joined as a member from its very inception. Another good illustration is the Stability Pact for Southeast Europe, originally an initiative of the German Presidency of the

EU Council, whose purpose was to bring together a vast coalition of countries, international organizations, financial institutions and so on to co-ordinate the reconstruction endeavour following the war in Kosovo. Japan was an integral part of the international coalition as well as the donor conferences to kick-start the pact. In other words, a US which was on its way out and an EU which was on its way in sought to enlist a broad coalition of partners and allies in a collective effort, with Japan being an obvious choice.

That highlighted the value of Japan as a weighty member of the international community, which had a track record of involvement in Southeast Europe, a staunch commitment to multilateralism, and particular strengths in channelling humanitarian assistance and development aid to both post-conflict and transition countries. Again, the period largely confirmed the trends established in the 1990s. Romania and Bulgaria attracted the lion's share of Japan's bilateral programme funding – mainly in the form of low-interest loans, while the former Yugoslavia and Albania were recipients of various grants allocated to reconstruction and peace-building projects. In other words, in the Western Balkans Japan's role was overtly political, while in the eastern parts of the region, where EU integration had advanced much further, the focus was economic in character, with heavy emphasis on infrastructure development and facilitating trade relations with Japan itself. In all fairness, problems associated with conflicts and deficient governance prevented the inflow of Japanese FDI, as was occurring in the Czech Republic, Hungary and Poland. Unlike the Balkans, those countries were able to attract investment in sectors such as automobile construction and electronics, benefiting from their quick integration into the EU and swift incorporation into the manufacturing and supply chains centred on Germany and other parts of Western Europe. This is not to suggest that the Balkans were less prominent in Japan's outreach to post-communist Europe. Huliaras (2007: 23) notes that the amounts disbursed by 2004 were hardly insignificant. Together with contributions to various multilateral vehicles, financial assistance to Southeast Europe totalled some USD 1.4 billion (JPY 150.9 billion).

Stage III: The EU as Hegemon (2003–)

The last decade of the EU's presence in the region has been defined by the upgrade of ambitions. The EU has evolved from a junior partner in a US-led effort at stabilizing and pacifying the Balkans, into a central actor whose strategic objective is enlargement to include the area, accompanied by 'member state-building', to use think tank vocabulary. The coming of age has been a gradual process marked by the phasing out of the Stability Pact and a focus on the so-called Stabilisation and Association Process (SAP), essentially a pre-accession format emulating the experience of Central and Eastern Europe (CEE). In June 2003 the EU Council meeting in Thessaloniki made a commitment to bring in Western Balkans countries as future members, a decisive step forward in the Union's policy which had hitherto been more reactive. The Thessaloniki vision came to partial fruition with the start of membership talks with Croatia in 2005 leading to accession eight years later, with Montenegro (negotiating accession since June 2012), Serbia, Macedonia and Albania further back in the queue. In Bosnia and Kosovo, the post-conflict phase is still a page to be fully closed – given the continued presence of UN-mandated missions such as the Office of the High Representative (OHR) and UNMIK (largely downsized compared to the early 2000s).

Like most EU member states, Japan recognized the independence of Kosovo very early on. The decision was taken in March 2008, weeks after the Pristina parliament issued the declaration of independence. That was a clear sign that Japan continued to abide by Western policy in the region. The decision did not spur a major domestic debate and was viewed at the time as a routine step along a well-established path. Back in 2006 Japan had already extended recognition to Montenegro, which separated from Serbia following an EU-supervised referendum. At this stage several commentators noted that the once independent Kingdom of Montenegro had declared war on Japan back in 1904, out of solidarity with its imperial patron Russia, and even sent volunteers to Manchuria. As Montenegro was excluded from the 1905 peace treaty signed with St Petersburg, the establishment of diplomatic relations in July 2006 was a de jure termination of a 101-year-long state of war.

Japan's Actions in the Balkans

The EU's efforts at stabilizing and integrating the Western Balkans have opened opportunities for various projects, both at the national and cross-border level. The same could be said about the accession of Bulgaria and Romania in 2007 which enlarged the political and economic remit of the Union all the way to the Black Sea. Japan continues with policies inherited from previous times in pursuit of both political and, in part, economic goals. It is beyond the scope of this chapter to provide a detailed overview of the projects and initiatives undertaken by various Japanese governmental agencies – for example the Japan International Cooperation Agency (JICA). Yet it is worthwhile to identify the main areas of Japanese involvement in order to understand Japan's approach to the Balkans and its relationship with the EU, the lead player.

Human Security and Post-Conflict Reconstruction

This is largely an extension of Japan's self-image as a civilian power. Indeed Tokyo has been one of the promoters of the concept of human security in multilateral organizations and in post-conflict reconstruction. From the provision of funds for demining in post-1995 Bosnia and Herzegovina, to giving grants to Serbian municipalities in northern Kosovo, Japan has consistently sought to add to efforts at overcoming the legacies of conflict. Japan's involvement is not fundamentally different from that of bilateral donors in EU member states, and Switzerland and Norway. While EU programmes such as CARDS (2000–2007) and subsequently the Instrument for Pre-Accession Assistance (IPA) target major institutional reforms, especially those linked with the adoption of the *acquis communautaire*, Japan has shown a clear preference for more locally-based initiatives. In that sense there is a clear division of labour. But unlike Western donors operating programmes in the field of post-conflict rehabilitation with a view to enhancing human security, Japan has a preference for working with municipal authorities, rather than the NGO sector (Huliaras 2007: 20–21). In that sense it exhibits a more traditionalist, hierarchical attitude to assistance. The other defining feature of Japanese projects is that they seek to be perceived as politically neutral and equidistant from all parties. Japan focused on material assistance as opposed to more overtly politicized activities such as working with political parties or activists. In 2003, for instance, the Japanese government donated 93 buses to the municipality of Belgrade.

Economic Development

As already pointed out, the improvement of regional infrastructure – in post-conflict areas but in fact mostly outside the former Yugoslavia – has emerged as a top priority. Through various soft loans Japan has made a key contribution to the enhancement of the road, rail and maritime infrastructure across Southeast Europe. These are the largest projects undertaken in the region, with JICA in the lead. A good example is the construction of a new container terminal at the port of Burgas in Bulgaria, by the Japanese companies Penta Ocean and Mitsubishi JV. Completed in 2009, the project was financed by a JPY 14.3 billion loan (USD 188 million) from the Japan Bank for International Cooperation (JBIC). (However, in 2011 the Bulgarian government cancelled a second loan worth JPY 37 billion to complete two new terminals at Burgas and Varna.) The Romanian government also received a JBIC loan, to the tune of JPY 47.6 billion, for the rehabilitation of the railway link between Bucharest and the port of Constanta on the Black Sea. The railway is part of the Paneuropean Corridor IV – so it is an instance of Japan assisting EU-driven policies for connecting CEE with the rest of the EU to advance market integration, also in the interest of Japanese trade. JBIC also funded, through a loan worth JPY 12.8 billion, a section of Sofia metro's first diameter that was completed in 2009. As in the Burgas port case, the tender was won by a Japanese contractor (the Taisei Corporation). Over the years Croatia has attempted to follow the example of Bulgaria and Romania and attract Japanese funding for the port of Rijeka, one of its main gates to the Adriatic.

Promotion of FDI and Trade

This is the least important plank of Japan's policy in Southeast Europe, though one of understandable significance for the region, which, thanks to EU influence, gradually opened itself to the global economy in the 1990s and 2000s. As noted, the Balkans continue to lag behind Central Europe (Kawai 2006). Trade volumes between Southeast Europe and Japan remain very small in contrast to ODA, which accounts for a significant share of overall inflows to some countries. Yet there are a handful of green shoots that highlight the importance of Japan as a geo-economic and thereby civilian power, not solely as an advocate of human security. One concerns investment in the nascent automotive industry, following in the footsteps of the Central European investments. Romania is the frontrunner with Koyo Seiko Co. (since 2006 JTEKT), a subcontractor for Honda and others, which set up shop in 1998, followed by YKK, Sumitomo Wiring (SEWS-R) and the Yazaki Corporation. Yazaki, which supplies cables for Ford, opened a EUR 30 million plant in the Bulgarian town of Yambol in 2006, followed by a second operation in nearby Sliven. Similarly, in 2002 Daido Metal acquired a plant manufacturing roller bearings in the Montenegrin coastal town of Kotor. Panasonic commenced the production of lighting equipment in northern Serbia in 2010. Other prominent investment projects in Serbia include Japan Tobacco International's USD 35 million privatization of Senta Tobacco in 2006, starting production two years after, and Asahi and Mitsui's JPY 1 billion (USD 10.7 million) yeast-producing facility at Svilanica. The common denominator in all such investments is the opportunity to produce low-end, labour-intensive components in countries enjoying unrestrained access to the larger EU market, where the cost of labour is still low. It is only more recently that Japanese companies started diversifying their interests – for example Toshiba's talks with the Bulgarian government regarding the possible construction of a solar plant, in line with the country's programme to promote and develop green energy following EU rules.

Although Japan is present in the region's economy and is a significant dispenser of development assistance, FDI and trade remain limited. It is mostly the larger countries, which are in addition more advanced in their integration into the EU, such as Romania, Bulgaria and, lately, Serbia which are benefitting from Japanese interest.

Conclusion

The economic crisis sweeping across the globe and affecting Europe hit the peripheral economies of Southeast Europe, which are dependent on investment and trade with the Eurozone, particularly hard (Bechev 2012). The lack of growth and the stalled development perspective have prompted governments and businesses to look beyond Europe for new markets and investment opportunities. Japan has thus far been an outlier in the process, with China drawing much more attention, from both officials and the media. The China hype actually obscures the fact that Japan and Korea have been in the region longer, both diplomatically and as economic players, and have developed more multifaceted approaches, combining trade, development assistance and even soft power (via scholarships, cultural exchanges and so on).

In the Balkans, Japan has clearly benefitted from the EU's expansion into the region translating into a more stable political and business environment. The EU might hold the key to the future too. A renewed push for trade liberalization via a comprehensive EU–Japan FTA/SPA will surely have major implications for countries across Southeast Europe, both inside the Union or aspiring to join it. The type of relationship Brussels and Tokyo develop in the Balkans is, in the final analysis, an outcome of their interaction at the bilateral and global level.

Chapter 12

Global Governance of Dual Use in Biomedical Research: Cooperation between the EU and Japan on How to Minimize or Prevent Misconduct and Misuse

Yasue Fukuda

Introduction

Dual use, when it involves biomedical or life science research, presents the following problem: technology and the knowledge derived from research can be used for the good of society or for ill, depending on the intention of the user (Selgelid 2009a; Forge 2010). Discoveries resulting from biomedical or life science research have various public health benefits, but if used improperly or maliciously, they can endanger people's health, the environment and public safety (Selgelid 2009b). The main purpose of this chapter is to address the international challenge of cross-border risk posed by dual use governance, which is now an explosive political issue.

The accidental creation and diffusion of microbial pathogens can lead to cross-border environmental pollution, the outbreak of disease, the illegal production of biological weapons and even the threat of bioterrorism. An increase in the level of global terrorism, as evidenced by the events of 9/11, coupled with scientific reports stating that genetic engineering can enhance the harmful consequences of pathogens, has resulted in the threat of bioterrorism becoming an important area of research (Fraser and Dando 2001). In 2004 an advisory report entitled *Biotechnology Research in an Age of Terrorism* (also known as the Fink Report) was published by the US National Research Council, and this resulted in the creation of the National Science Advisory Board for Bio-defense in the USA. Bioterrorism should not simply be viewed as affecting individual cities or countries, but as a problem with global reach. It is, therefore, essential that much greater importance be attached to political action in response to unexpected events, and that international public health policies developed in the EU or at international organizations like the WHO, the IBRD, and the OECD focus on the prevention of bio-risk.

This chapter examines how to minimize or prevent misconduct and the misuse of biological research, as both are necessary for good global governance. Firstly, the chapter explores the background to dual use governance, explaining how and why bio-risk management has been formulated in Europe, Japan and at a global level. A second issue is whether to practice research control upstream, that is, evaluate and respond to research plans at the pre-evaluation stage; or downstream, by evaluating how research is to be used. Thirdly, the chapter discusses the design of bio-security strategies and dual use governance systems in the EU and Japan, and raise some questions about the nature of international cooperation. Finally, it concludes by attempting to outline what kind of risk management system and dual use governance may be necessary for the prevention of bio-risk across borders in the future, particularly with regard to political cooperation and policy networking between the EU and Japan.

Design of Strategies and Governance Systems Related to Bio-safety and Bio-security in the EU

Established in 1975, the European Committee for Standardization (CEN; Comité Européen de Normalisation) has concerned itself with the standardization of risk management for biomedical research in research institutes in Europe since 2004. CEN is a non-profit organization responsible for the standardization of technical guidelines and regulations in Europe. The anthrax attacks in the US in 2001 raised the spectre of worldwide bioterrorism (Bhattacharjee 2009). As a result of this, a plan for global health safety and security was launched by an international partnership the same year, to strengthen responses to threats from biological, chemical and nuclear terrorism (Harling 2002). That year the European Commission established the Health Security Committee as an organization to promote information sharing, cooperation and coordination between member states in their efforts to combat threats such as the intentional release of pathogens and the cross-border spread of new strains of influenza (European Commission 2009a).

Also in 2001, the BICHAT cooperation programme (Preparedness and Response to Biological and Chemical Agent Attacks) was launched by member states to prevent and respond to biochemical attacks (Tegnell et al. 2002). Through the various guidelines published, the European Commission called on health authorities within individual member states to introduce health security measures to assist with early detection, including effective surveillance and information relay systems. These would detect infectious disease outbreaks and counter bioterrorism and the intentional release of biological agents. In 2003 the European Council adopted the 'EU Strategy against the Proliferation of Weapons of Mass Destruction' to combat such proliferation (Council of the European Union 2003), and then subsequently ratified a Joint Action in support of the Biological and Toxin Weapons Convention (BTWC) (Council of the European Union 2008). In 2005 the EU established the European Centre for Disease Prevention and Control (ECDC) in order to strengthen health defence in Europe and to develop a surveillance network and early warning system for infectious diseases in the region.

In 2009 the European Commission instituted an action plan for security against chemical and biological agents as well as radioactive materials (European Commission 2009b). As part of this initiative the European Commission set up an inter-university network seeking to take a comprehensive approach to addressing bio-security risks and threats, whether they occur naturally or by design. In 2011 the European Commission put forward a proposal to the European Parliament and the European Council on serious cross-border threats to health, and stepped up its response to public health emergencies (European Commission 2011c). At the global level, the EU and Japan have been cooperating closely with the US, Mexico and Canada as well as the WHO to respond to and prevent potential health threats. The EU and Japan are also part of a global strategy called the Global Health Security Initiative.

There are two main methods of preventing or reducing the risk: bio-safety, which is concerned with the correct handling of biological materials, and bio-security, which refers to regulatory frameworks to control the flow of information pertaining to biological agents and also to the actual cross-border movement of pathogens and toxins. It is essential that scientific researchers engaged in areas of biomedical research such as virology, neuroscience, immunology, toxicology and drug delivery technology bear in mind the potential bio-security and bio-safety implications of their research.

Military research for both offensive and defensive purposes raises various issues related to dual use. For example, research on exposure to pathogens could have defensive military uses, such as reducing the harm caused by biological weapons, but at the same time there is the danger that discoveries could lead to offensive uses, such as genetic alterations that expand the infection route (for example bird-to-bird infection expanding to bird-to-mammal infection), resulting in the creation of powerful biological weapons.

Researchers should be able to communicate with each other and openly share information and research. This is the basis for the existence of an international scientific community; this is how scientists are supported and science that benefits international society is promoted. Scientists who publish their research on a worldwide basis, in journals or on websites, help the scientific community to develop ways to mitigate hazards. We have to ask how the international community can best address the potentially malicious use of such research.

Evaluating Biomedical Research and Research Ethics: Criteria for Evaluating the Funding of Dual Use Research

The European Commission has established standards for evaluating the social and ethical implications as well as the scientific merits of proposed research projects through the 7th Framework Programme, which the EU has used to allocate funding for scientific research. The applicants' research plans are subject to an individual evaluation that includes an ethical component, and dual use issues are considered as part of this process. According to the European Commission, potential misuse of research refers to (1) research involving agents or equipment that could be directly misused for criminal, terrorist or unethical military purposes, (2) research which creates knowledge that could be used for criminal, terrorist or unethical purposes and (3) the application and development of surveillance technologies (European Commission 2013f: 18).

Applicants and research participants go through a rigorous bio-security pre-evaluation, and are required to be fully aware of both the direct risks and the risks to society as a whole. They also have to put appropriate bio-safety and bio-security measures in place and provide training in these precautionary procedures. Applicants are also required to include independent specialists with knowledge of dual use and bio-security in their project management teams. The EU has designed a framework which it uses to systematically address the issue of dual use of scientific research at the funding stage. There were 274 applications for EU funding for research projects on bio-security between 2007 and 2011. Of those, 131 projects were subject to ethical screening, and 87 of these needed further in-depth national re-evaluation. With some modification, this system of evaluation has been adapted by Japan, whose experiences with dual use problems are considered in the next section. The criteria for deciding whether a particular piece of research has dual use implications or not are unclear, and EU–Japan cooperation in this field should be enhanced.

Design of Bio-security Strategies and Dual Use Governance in Japan

For the past 30 years Japan has been developing a legal framework for bio-safety and bio-security policy. After ratifying the Biological Weapons Convention (BWC) in 1982, Japan enacted the BWC Implementation Law the same year. The law prohibited the manufacture, ownership, transfer and receipt of biological or toxic weapons, with transgressors to be subject to criminal penalties. Under this law the development, manufacture, stockpiling, acquisition and ownership of biological agents and toxins are limited to peaceful purposes, and those who handle these materials are under an obligation to report doing so to the authorities. Communicable disease control surveillance began in Japan in 1981, with functions including (1) detecting and reporting pathogens, (2) reporting information on patients and patient numbers and (3) forecasting communicable disease outbreaks (IASR 2010). There was no legal basis for this mechanism at the time, but this was attained in 1999, with the passage of the Law Concerning the Prevention of Infections and Medical Care for Patients of Infections. The mechanism called for a stronger surveillance system to collect and disclose information on infectious diseases, to take reports from doctors as a method of monitoring the status and trends of infectious diseases, and to conduct surveys into their causes.

Pressure within Japan to strengthen measures against bioterrorism by non-state actors increased after an extremist cult, Aum Shinrikyo, attacked the Tokyo subway system with poisonous gas in 1995, killing 13 people and injuring many more. This cult also attempted to develop anthrax and botulinum. In 1997 the Japanese government started using the Wide-area Information-exchange System for Health, Labour and Welfare Administration (WISH) to collect and share pathogen detection reports from regional health institutes and quarantine stations. WISH is an online system set up by the Ministry of Health, Labour and Welfare (MHLW), and is accessible to national and local governments, as well as concerned institutions such as regional health institutes, quarantine stations and health care centres.

Japan joined the International Convention for the Suppression of Terrorist Bombings in 2001, prompting it to revise its BWC Implementation Law and impose punishments on those who illegally use biological weapons or diffuse toxins and biological agents. An updated version of the Law Concerning the Prevention of Infections and Medical Care for Patients of Infections was promulgated in 2006 and came into force in 2007. This revision resulted in a new system governing the establishment of control systems for pathogens and other proscribed biological agents, to prevent the occurrence and spread of infectious diseases resulting from bioterrorism and accidents.

In Japan the MHLW bears overall responsibility for implementing measures against infectious diseases, with support from the National Institute of Infectious Diseases (NIID), the National Center for Global Health and Medicine (NCGM) and the National Institute of Biomedical Innovation (NIBIO). At the regional level, the prefectures and large cities implement and oversee measures against infectious diseases, with approximately 500 local health care centres around the nation. There are also infectious disease information centres at the prefectural level that collect and analyse data. The NIID compiles, analyses and evaluates data from the local infectious disease information centres and sends feedback information out to the entire nation.

In May 2006 the online pathogen detection and reporting system merged with several other systems, including an infectious disease outbreak trend survey system which collected information on patients and patient numbers, to form an institution called the National Epidemiological Surveillance of Infectious Diseases (NESID), which allows data to be centrally managed using only one database for the first time. Data reported by regional health institutes since 1980 has been stored and updated in a pathogen detection and information system, created as a subsystem of NESID. Thus surveillance systems have been developed at both the regional and national levels.

In Japan a three-tiered system of government operates. Firstly, the national level, secondly the regional or district level, consisting of 48 prefectures, and thirdly, the local government level in each prefecture. Infectious Disease Surveillance Centers are installed in local health laboratories or similar institutions. In all prefectures, cities which contain a health centre or a prefectural infection information centre basically act as district information centres. Information from all prefectures in Japan is collected, analysed and sent to each prefectural

Infectious Disease Surveillance Center. The NIID collects reports of detection of infectious agents from prefectural public health centres and also reports incidents of infectious diseases from sentinel clinics throughout Japan. This information is made accessible to the public. In case of occurrence of an epidemic or outbreak of an infectious disease, epidemiological investigations will be carried out, and the information exchanged with infectious disease surveillance organizations in other countries.

At the moment the chain of command to be employed during an emergency is unclear and could lead to confusion. It is extremely difficult for the Prime Minister's Office to exercise control over the response to an outbreak or a pandemic. In order to remedy this situation, onset planning survey committees responsible for controlling infection at district level will be established in all prefectures and report to the onset trend survey plan committee at central level. This is operated by the MHLW, who will conduct infection surveillance investigation and initiate disease limitation strategies. The Ministry of Foreign Affairs provides infection information overseas for Japanese citizens traveling abroad and also to Japanese embassies and foreign local authorities all over the world. However, given the problems presented by globalization mentioned above, we cannot say that the precautions against infectious disease at country level are sufficient. More non-governmental actors need to become involved.

According to the amended Infectious Diseases Control Law, pathogens are classified into four different types for the purposes of risk management. The classification is based on infectiousness and severity of risk to public health. Depending on these two criteria, the prohibition of importation and possession, permission, notification and regulation of standards compliance are required. Under this law, very strict penalties, including prison sentences and heavy fines, were established to prevent bioterrorism (Okuzumi et al. 2007). Japan also revised its Foreign Exchange and Foreign Trade Act in 2009 to promote international peace and safety, strengthening controls on the types of materials which could be taken out of the country by individuals or exported by businesses. The law covered biological and chemical agents (such as samples for R&D), the leaking of technical information through the sharing of USBs or other media, the export of substances and mechanical devices that could be used for weapons or have military applications, joint research with parties outside Japan, as well as research data and technical instruction. Therefore we can see that Japan has built a legal system governing dual use and bio-security, which focuses on the issue of exports to third countries. It is possible, however, that the new laws and regulations may slow the pace of research that would help in the fight against bioterrorism, and that they may infringe on freedoms of research and education. The issue is how best to instil the bio-security concept into education and research in order to prevent harmful use, without placing excessive restrictions on legitimate scientific research.

Bio-security Training for Scientists in Japan

The Third Science and Technology Basic Plan, which was published in 2005, was intended to 'make Japan a nation that can take pride in its social security and public safety' (JSPS 2006: 3). Since then Japan has responded to bio-security issues using the Council for Science and Technology Policy's strategy of promoting science and technology for safety. Since the plan was implemented in 2006 Japan has aimed to use science and technology to counter terrorism and protect civil society from biohazards, including terrorist misuse of science and technology. Japan has aimed to match the needs of science and technology for countering terrorism and contributing to public safety, and to share knowledge and technology for these purposes.

Medical and public health laboratories in universities and research institutes are practising risk control, which includes setting up frameworks designed, for example, to prevent the loss, theft or misappropriation of microbial pathogens and the intentional release of biological agents, the export of technology and the spread of information. Among other initiatives, NPOs and research organs are holding workshops to raise awareness of the problem of dual use and bio-security in the academic community. The NIID, moreover, holds bio-security awareness events, while some universities provide training and offer awareness-raising sessions on bioterrorism and bio-security, focusing on the BWC and the dual use problem. Joint research between Japanese and British universities is taking place on the issue of dual use training.

On the issue of biomedical research ethics in Japan, clinical trials on the effectiveness and safety of pharmaceuticals and medical devices are subject to the force of law if they are for human use and if the developers are required to seek approval. In other research, however, although guidelines have been established, they have no legally binding force. Universities also face other problems with regard to research ethics. For example, while education in bioethics is offered at about 70 per cent of universities as part of their curriculum, only 10–20 per cent offer training in bio-security and dual use (Minehata and Shinomiya 2010). Steps need to be taken to enhance the effectiveness of dual use education, to ensure that it influences the actions of researchers and research institutes.

Examination of the Code of Conduct for Scientists in Japan

A code of conduct for scientists has been in operation in Japan since 2006. The updated Code of Conduct for Scientists published by the Science Council of Japan (SCJ 2013) consists of sections on: the Responsibilities and Conduct of Scientists, Continuous Professional Development, Accountability and Disclosure, Research Activities, Establishing Sound Research Environments, Compliance with Laws and Regulations, Consideration for Research Subjects, Relations with Others, Rejection of Discrimination and Avoiding Conflicts of Interest.

The code focuses primarily on preventing misconduct by scientists and protecting the rights of research subjects, and does not explicitly address dual use. However, following the 2005 Inter Academy Panel (IAP) statement on bio-security, the SCJ came out in support of the statement and Japan also started to debate scientists' responsibilities in biomedical research. A study group set up by the SCJ in 2011 to address the problem of dual use in science and technology pointed to the need for an updated version of the code. Consequently, the Code of Conduct for Scientists was revised in 2013, to refer to the issue of dual use: 'scientists shall recognize that there exist possibilities that their research results contrary to their own intentions, may be used for destructive actions, and shall select appropriate means and methods as allowed by society in conducting research and publicizing the results' (SCJ 2013).

In most cases scientists are not aware that their own research has a double-sided nature and may harm society depending on how it is used (Minehata et al. 2013). One of the roles of the Code of Conduct is to make scientists aware that there are ways of using their research that they never intended, but which could harm society. Another advantage of the Code of Conduct is that it reminds scientists of their social responsibilities and seeks to ensure that their work serves a positive social purpose. Furthermore, when scientists follow the code for themselves, the scientific community can regulate itself without excessive outside interference, making it possible for scientists to fulfil their social responsibilities while their freedom of research is protected. On the other hand, the Code of Conduct is not binding, making it ineffective in some ways. Solving this problem requires designing a system that will promote the practice and implementation of the code. One means of doing this is to incorporate ethical evaluations regarding dual use as a consideration for funding purposes, such as those which have been adopted in the EU.

EU–Japan Collaborative Research into Health and Dual Use Issues

The 16th EU–Japan Summit was held in June 2007. It was agreed at the summit to pursue dialogue on human security, focusing on its concrete implementation across a wide range of issues, including infectious diseases. Furthermore, through the 7th Framework Programme (FP7), the European Commission decided to set aside a 6.1 billion euro budget to be spent on collaborative research around the world. Health issues on which the EU and Japan engage in collaborative research include: (1) enhanced health promotion and disease prevention, (2) providing evidence of best practices, (3) public health measures, (4) a special focus on life-style and (5) intervention with regard to mental health.

Japan and the EU signed an agreement on cooperation in science and technology in 2009. As an outcome of the 18th EU–Japan Summit in Tokyo, the two parties pledged to strengthen cooperation on the mitigation of chemical, biological, radiological and nuclear risks, and enhance the coordination of joint projects. A national contact point for the EU Framework Programme in Japan was established to facilitate participation of Japanese entities in EU research programmes. Furthermore, exchange of researchers between the EU and Japan will be increased in future. Further joint partnerships between the EU and Japan are likely to result in higher quality dual use governance systems. By supporting medical research through EU–Japan research partnerships, for example FP7, CONCERT-Japan and Horizon 2020, the EU and Japan will be cooperating in order to address the issue of dual use of global medical research. The successor to the FP7, Horizon 2020, will focus on the fight against crime and terrorism, by conducting research through engagement with citizens and elected representatives to take interactive counter-terrorism measures. It will thus contribute to the prevention and response strands of counter-terrorism strategy.

Towards the Future: The Roles of the EU and Japan in the Governance of Biomedical Research

While it is important to prevent the misuse of biomedical or life science research, regulations which simultaneously remove the motivation to carry out legitimate research activities are not desirable. Biomedical research has many stakeholders including researchers, universities, non-governmental organizations, policy-makers, funders and enterprises. The diffusion of microbial pathogens, whether by intention or by accident, is a safety and security problem with significant social and economic implications. Furthermore, it is not necessary to establish large institutions in order to create biological weapons, and current technology is not able to effectively detect the diffusion of microbial pathogens, meaning that these are among the most difficult types of weapons to control. Furthermore, since researchers have an increasing number of opportunities to carry out research in other countries, the technological knowledge resulting from research does not stay within national borders, which makes any one nation's research regulations insufficient to deal with dual use.

I recommend that bio-safety and bio-security systems set up to deal with the issue of dual use should incorporate elements of both hard and soft law. One disadvantage of hard law solutions involving stricter and more complex international regulation is that they can hinder research that would otherwise improve public health globally (Kuhlau et al. 2008). On the other hand, systems requiring the public disclosure of detailed research methods and materials carry the risk that information on how to develop and produce biological weapons might become available to extremist cults or terrorist organizations.

The issue of dual use in biomedical research poses two questions according to the precautionary principle (Richardson 2009; Kuhlau et al. 2011): how will biomedical research be used in the future, and if it is misused, how should risk be managed? Too much regulation slows down the medical research needed to prevent and treat illness, and risks delaying the development of preventive and therapeutic medicines. What type of control system would promote medical research for the good of society? The international cooperation that the EU and Japan have shown in these fields could point the way to a form of global governance regarding dual use in medical research.

By strengthening the joint development of dual use and ethics training programmes, the EU and Japan can raise awareness among scientific researchers in the domestic sphere about the potential risks of their research to society. If the EU and Japan were to create a further cooperative mechanism that lets them learn best practice from each other, this could contribute to better global governance of medical research. Such a system should concern itself with the transparency of international research, the traceability of researcher data and the information control process. Introducing ethical research evaluations concerning dual use to the process of joint international funding would serve to raise researchers' awareness of their responsibilities, and give them an incentive to act ethically. Whatever the precise details of the legislation or guidelines, it must be remembered that governance of biomedical research is crucial to determining how to prevent improper or malicious uses without discouraging beneficial research. There must be a balance between research freedom and risk management, and as open, advanced and complex societies, and responsible civilian powers, it is incumbent upon the EU and Japan to work together to investigate the best way to achieve this balance.

Although the demand for global public goods, such as prevention of the spread of infection and prevention of international terrorism, is high and urgent, the burden is not shared appropriately and this raises the problem of the 'free rider' who enjoys these public benefits gratuitously. However, supporting vulnerable states and regions is indispensable for global security, and if some countries are allowed to avoid their responsibilities, the efforts of all other countries will be diminished. Considering that the cost of stopping the propagation of 'global public wrongs' is ultimately lower than not stopping them, it is efficient and rational to support vulnerable states and actors. Therefore, the EU and Japan are taking on a global responsibility when they act together to combat infectious diseases, and are therefore contributing to global public ethics. The EU and Japan could and should, as responsible civilian powers, present a global standard on dual use research, including ethical review boards to design and implement research projects. It is necessary and possible to conceive and implement international systems for the eradication of infection, using EU–Japan cooperation as the basis for a global model.

Chapter 13

Accountability and the Governance of Food Safety Policy in the EU and Japan

Koji Fukuda

Introduction

With the rapid spread of globalization, food safety governance has become a global issue, and has finally been recognized as a serious problem which must be dealt with by the international community working in unison. Recently food safety has become one of the most hotly debated issues arising from Japan's participation in the TPP (Trans-Pacific Partnership) negotiations, and the EU–Japan talks on an EPA (Economic Partnership Agreement). For Europe and Japan, the many stakeholders involved means it is necessary to consider the issue from the viewpoint of public health and consumer protection as well as economic interests.

This chapter considers whether, in order to safeguard human health and enhance consumer protection in international and domestic public policy processes, accountability and traceability must be strengthened in food safety policy. Governance of international food safety partly operates as a global regime, through international institutions such as the World Health Organization (WHO), the Codex Alimentarius Commission and the EU, leading to potential deficiencies in accountability, transparency and legitimacy.

For Japan, globalization has led to food being imported for human consumption as well as animal feed. The country's food self-sufficiency rate is relatively low, and it relies heavily on imported food. When Japan imports food from a country with less strict safety standards, various questions are raised concerning the presence of 'post-harvest' agricultural chemicals, the official status of these chemicals under Japanese law and, in the case of the USA and Canada, the issue of genetically modified food. Japanese people seem to be particularly sensitive to these issues, partly due to a series of problems with imported food products in recent years. There have been cases of toxic contamination of frozen foods, and various cases of mislabelling designed to disguise the country of origin.

This chapter will attempt to compare the food safety policies of the EU and Japan, summarize and analyse their experiences of food safety policy, and consider the issue of accountability. The reason why it is useful to make comparisons between the EU and Japan is that the governance system and food safety policies of the EU are being used as models for Japan to a remarkable extent. For example, the Food Safety Commission currently established by the Japanese Cabinet Office is based on the EU's European Food Safety Authority. In addition to imitating such institutional designs, many specific Japanese food safety policies are derived from the food safety policy of the EU. Bearing the above concerns in mind, the purpose of this study is to consider the following questions: first, how can accountability, responsibility and legitimacy in the food safety policy process be guaranteed, and how would the governance of food safety in the EU and Japan be affected by reforms? Second, how have mechanisms of accountability evolved in Europe, and to what extent are concerns regarding both accountability and the differences between food safety regimes between member states legitimate? Third, what kind of systems should be introduced in Japan to ensure food safety, particularly as far as the methods, evaluations and procedures involved in trans-border cooperation are concerned?

Globalization and Food Safety

In the past 20 years food imports to Japan from the USA, the EU and China have been increasing rapidly, while Japan has increased exports of non-food items such as automobiles, machinery and other high tech goods. This imbalance has led a large proportion of the Japanese public to express fears regarding both the safety of imported food and the country's long-term food security. According to data supplied by the Japanese Ministry of Agriculture, Forestry and Fisheries (MAFF), the food self-sufficiency rate (SSR) of Japan decreased by one third between 1970 and 2012, to the relatively low level of 40 per cent (calorie based) and 69 per cent (production based). This compares unfavourably to many European countries where the SSR is between 70 and 80 per cent, and particularly to France, where the SSR is 120–130 per cent (Eurostat 2011). In contrast, the Japanese have to buy most of their agricultural products from foreign countries.

Since the 1970s the process of 'fast-foodization' has threatened Japan's traditional food culture, and globalization has created a conflict between business interests and food safety. Dealing with this issue successfully implies a commitment on the part of bureaucracies to widen political accountability so that people feel that they are involved in decisions which affect their lives. As Richard Mulgan observed, 'the mounting demand for accountability is a symptom of a growing public anger at individuals and institutions that are supposed to pursue the public's interests but refuse to answer the public's questions or accept their directions' (Mulgan 2003: 1). He also pointed out problem areas such as 'declining public trust' and 'increased public risk in areas such as food safety and pollution' (Mulgan 2003: 1–2), and suggested 'new channels of accountability', such as official information legislation, more active parliamentary committee systems and new investigative agencies as possible solutions, further emphasizing the need for accountability in decision-making and the internationalization of public policy (Mulgan 2003: 2).

In Europe food regulation has been carried out for the last 45 years at a purely national level, with food safety standards being left to the discretion of individual countries. When we discuss safety standards for food, it is important to have a definition of 'food' common to all EU member states. One criterion of the European Commission definition of safe food is that it be neither harmful to human health nor unsuitable for consumption by people. Therefore, it is necessary to consider the long-term effects, especially the accumulative effects, which food has on the human body, and also to consider the possibility of negative effects on the next generation. Food regulation needs to be designed and implemented from both a scientific and a socioeconomic viewpoint. In the case of the EU, there is also a common agricultural policy, which ensures that food, including agricultural products, moves across EU borders, and that common food safety standards are enforced. Since the BSE crisis in Britain in 1996, the establishment of common safety standards at the EU level has been called for in no uncertain terms. The necessity for such reforms was clearly demonstrated during the subsequent global BSE crisis, which disproportionately affected OECD countries which had a history of 'bad governance' concerning food safety.

International Cooperation on Accountability and Food Safety Issues

Accountability and Food Safety Governance

In its attempts to safeguard human health and enhance consumer protection, food safety governance is complicated by the fact that it is both an international and a domestic public policy, and must therefore cover the entire food product chain 'from farm to table' (European Commission 1997: 8). There are a myriad of stakeholders, including farmers, feed manufacturers and relevant authorities in international institutions, nation-states and third countries. As far as food safety policy issues are concerned, how can we best ensure that politicians and bureaucrats act in the best interests of the public and are ultimately accountable for their actions? This question can best be answered by considering it from a variety of viewpoints. How should food safety be most effectively managed and administered? What might be the ideal form of policy-making and implementation? How does the relationship between governments, parliaments and bureaucracies affect the introduction of new food safety legislation?

Accountability must be regarded as a responsibility for any person who seeks public office and the accompanying authority to exercise administrative power (Harlow 2002: 8–9). In a representative democratic system, being answerable to the people usually involves being accountable to parliament. It is therefore essential for bureaucracies to keep honest and accurate financial accounts which allow the citizenry to consider the appropriateness of their financial decisions, and judge the fairness of the allocation of resources. Despite its humble origins, the term 'accountability' has become indispensable when debating public policy issues. The definition of the word has been expanded by social scientists to such a point that it is now an extremely imprecise and wide-ranging term which is causing confusion through overuse. Nevertheless, the notions of accountability and traceability must be strengthened in food safety policy areas. The development of the concept of accountability in the EU between its formation and the present day can be summarized as in Table 13.1.

Table 13.1 The modern understanding of accountability in the European Union

Level	Accountability Stages	Measures and Institutions
Political	Policy Accountability	Direct election of European Parliament A committee of independent experts consisting of Euro MPs Parliament Policy Evaluation DGs of the European Commission
Political and administrative/managerial	Programme Accountability	Programme Evaluation Project Evaluation DGs of the European Commission
Administrative/managerial	Performance Accountability	Performance Evaluation Administrative Inspection European Court of Auditors DGs of the European Commission
Administrative/managerial	Process Accountability	European Ombudsman European Court of Auditors OLAF, EFSA DGs of the European Commission
Administrative/managerial	Legal Accountability	ECJ European Court of Auditors Eurojust, OLAF, EFSA DGs of the European Commission

Sources: Stewart (1984: 17–18) and Fukuda (2009: 237).

This brings us to the present day situation, where 'policy accountability', which stresses the responsiveness of government to the public, or 'political responsibility' holds sway. The notion of political/democratic accountability in turn differs from that of managerial accountability, in that the latter is hierarchical and internal to the organization, though usually supported by external audit agencies (Fukuda 2009: 249). Legal accountability and process accountability are concerned with 'input legitimacy', while performance accountability is concerned with 'performance measurement' and 'output legitimacy' (Lord 2004: 131–2). Food safety problems have always existed, but they have been compounded recently by a general increase in economic activity, and further complicated by globalization.

Food Safety and International Administrative Cooperation

The international food safety system operates as a global regime through international institutions such as the WHO, the WTO and the EU. Nowadays, when various products may be sourced in one country, processed in another and sold in yet another, it is extremely difficult for individual governments to supervise or inspect the entire process. It therefore seems obvious that some form of supranational regulating authority must be created to supervise food safety on a global level. Considering the recent increase in Genetically Modified Organism (GMO) food production, perhaps such an authority should have responsibility for grains, pulses and vegetables, as well as processed food products. Due to the fact that scientific opinion varies from country to country, certain post-harvest chemicals and additives used in the livestock industry (such as antibiotics in beef cattle) are frequently approved in some countries but banned in others. The British BSE crisis in particular demonstrated that supranational regulation is essential for the meat industry world-wide. Supranational food safety regulation would mean greater standardization, and stop unscrupulous governments using food safety arguments as artificial trade barriers. Regulations have an important role in guaranteeing public health as well as ensuring economic growth. We shall see that the BSE crisis can be viewed as a turning point in the history of food safety policy. Greater accountability of public policy governance, consistent at both international and domestic levels, will be demanded by citizens in the future.

The BSE Crisis and Food Safety Control at the EU and Member State Level

The BSE crisis goes back to 1986, and over the last 40 years food safety legislation has evolved separately in the EU member states, reflecting their varying social, political and economic situations as well as their diverse levels of scientific and medical development. Since its inception, European food legislation has come under several different policy umbrellas, and has been linked to the Common Agricultural Policy (CAP) or internal market policy. While there were various praiseworthy initiatives for food legislation in the early days of the EU, such as the eradication of food shortages and the maintenance of food price stability, the issue of food safety was not considered to be in need of EU-level legislation. With the formal discovery of BSE in the UK and Ireland, BSE subsequently became a major disaster in the 1990s, when the link between BSE in cattle and the human variant of the disease (New Variant Creutzfeldt-Jakob Disease (CJD)) was confirmed. Yet before analysing how the various authorities involved responded to the disaster, let us consider for a moment the basic history of food safety policy since the formation of the EU, and its legal basis. In July 1997 the Santer Commission decided to set up a multidisciplinary Scientific Steering Committee to discuss and coordinate the multiple problems of various scientific committees concerning health and consumer safety issues (Christian 1999: 329), in order that the latest scientific knowledge be applied to the food safety policy area in future (European Commission 1997). If this system had been in place in the early 1990s when the BSE problem appeared, then surely a full-blown crisis would have been prevented.

But, perhaps predictably, the British government at the time, supported by several agricultural pressure groups representing the livestock industry, denied the existence of a public health problem. It was clear that the systems in place in the early 1990s were insufficient to guarantee food safety on a pan-European level. Action on food safety was usually taken too late because of the lack of reliable information from member states. Most member states tended to be reluctant to inform the European Commission when there was bad news for political and trade-related reasons, and in particular because they feared that their products might be banned. For example, in 1999 the Belgian government failed to inform the Commission about an outbreak of dioxin poisoning in the country's chickens for six months after first discovering the problem. Clearly it was unrealistic to expect member states to inform the Commission voluntarily and promptly whenever they had a food crisis on their hands.

As a result, BSE, which had looked like it was under control, began to rage again in several European countries in the Autumn of 2000. Once it had crossed the Channel, it quickly spread throughout the European mainland, resulting in panic and political turmoil. Infected bone-meal powder was exported to EU members such as France, Portugal and Ireland, and diseased animals were subsequently discovered in those countries. In France BSE-infected meat was actually found on supermarket shelves. Since the incubation period was known to be very long in humans, anything between five and 20 years, and possibly longer, even a small number of fatalities was a cause for widespread concern, indicating a possible major public health disaster in the future. A food safety time-bomb appeared to be ticking.

In Germany the BSE affair prompted a political crisis in November 2000, when the Schröder administration was heavily criticized for its perceived ineptitude in the handling of the issue. When diseased cattle were detected in Germany, public confidence in the administration was lost and both the Minister of Agriculture and the Health Secretary felt duty-bound to resign to take responsibility for the disaster (Tyshenko and Krewski 2010) To be more specific, the BSE disaster could have been avoided if the UK Treasury (the Finance Ministry) had made adequate funds available to compensate the farmers whose livelihoods were threatened by the crisis, and specifically by the ban on sales of animal feed and beef products. Such compensation would have been much cheaper than the sums which the UK government eventually agreed to award to victims of the disease. The death toll from CJD in the UK reached 100 in May 2001, the vast majority of cases being recorded in England itself. Tragically, the average age of the victims was only 24. In addition to the human cost, the financial cost was now enormous, taking into account the huge damage to the livestock industry and hefty compensation payments to the victims.

Food Safety Policy in Europe and the European Food Safety Authority

The European Commission has only ever introduced two directives on food safety, both times at the request of member states. The first came in 1989, with a directive on products to be used in livestock breeding, and the second in 1993, with a directive on products derived from animals, which was designed to be applied to non-EU member states. It is highly unusual for the EU to pass directives explicitly designed for adoption by third countries. In 2000 the European Commission adopted a 'White Paper on Food Safety' which called for the launch of a food safety legislative action programme and the creation of a European Food Safety Authority. The White Paper also established the following basic principles:

> feed manufacturers, farmers and food operators have the primary responsibility for food safety; competent authorities monitor and enforce this responsibility through the operation of national surveillance and control systems; and the Commission concentrates on evaluating the ability of competent authorities to deliver these systems through audits and inspections at the national level. (European Commission 2000: 8)

The establishment and maintenance of a food safety law at EU level which would protect human health and safeguard consumer interests to a high degree was characterized by some diversity in its objectives. Countries which had been involved in health scares tended to focus on trade issues (i.e. ending bans) while countries which had imported dangerous or potentially dangerous goods were more interested in the food safety issue (i.e. maintaining bans or introducing other sanctions). In spite of this, on 28 January 2002 the European Parliament and Council of Ministers adopted Regulation 178/2002 (EC), which laid down the general principles of food law, and established the European Food Safety Authority (EFSA) in 2002 (European Parliament and Council of the European Union 2002). Food safety in Europe would henceforth be ensured by a two-tier system (or 'decision trap' system) as legislation and safeguarding authorities now existed at both the EU level and the member state level. As far as the setting up of new food safety authorities was concerned, France, mindful of the high percentage of its GDP which derives from its agricultural sector, set the ball rolling in July 1998 with the formation of the Agence nationale de sécurité sanitaire de l'alimentation. The UK, where the BSE crisis had originated, followed suit by creating the new Food Standards Agency (FSA). Germany was not far behind, setting up the Bundesinstitut für Riskobewertung (BfR) in December the same year.

At the supranational level, the EU created the European Food Safety Authority (EFSA), a body which would be independent from other EU institutions, in 2002. This decentralized agency was set up to provide the food safety information which the Commission and the member states need when they, within their respective spheres of competence, adopt binding measures. This type of co-ordination agency is often involved in decision-making in the EU. Such organizations are usually established to include provisions concerning legal control. Their own suppliers of information are not limited to units of the national administration but also include international organizations and nongovernmental bodies (Bergström and Rotkirch 2003: 28–34). Both administration and co-ordination agencies are charged with the adoption of the rules needed for implementation of the regulations.

The major priorities of the new EFSA were to introduce a system of food safety risk evaluation, and to increase public knowledge of food safety by publicizing the results of the evaluations. The role of EFSA was defined in the context of the process of risk analysis, comprising risk assessment, risk management and risk communication (European Commission 1997: 19–23). EFSA is required by EU General Food Law to 'meet the fundamental principles of independent excellence and transparency', and 'demonstrate a high level of accountability to the European institutions and citizens in its actions' (European Commission 1997: 16).

The duties of the EFSA are:

1. to be guided by the best scientific knowledge
2. to be independent of industrial and political interests
3. to be open to rigorous public scrutiny
4. to be scientifically authoritative
5. to work closely with national scientific bodies (EFSA 2004).

The EFSA regulations were designed to help improve the accountability of the European Commission as it grapples with the improvement of food safety. The fact that EFSA could communicate directly with the public on the food safety issues within its responsibility was a good example of this policy in action. Furthermore, the Commission enhanced its own responsibility for risk management and ensuring that food safety regulations were enforced on an everyday basis. The Commission also assumed the power to take restraining measures and make emergency plans whenever an 'urgent alarm' was raised about pollution in animal feed or a new food risk became known. This warning system works based on 'EU food safety law' (Regulation (EC) No 178/2002). The precautionary principle is not defined in the EC Treaty, but 'the scope of this principle is far wider and also covers consumer policy and human, animal and plant health'. The European Court of Justice delivered BSE judgments on 5 May 1998, which introduced the precautionary principle into EU case law.

Food Safety Policy in Japan and the Food Safety Commission

In the early 2000s the EU and the WHO warned that there was a danger that BSE infected cattle would be discovered in Japan and the Scientific Steering Committee (SSC), which advises the European Commission on issues related to BSE, unofficially alerted the Japanese Government and the MAFF (Ministry of Agriculture, Forestry and Fisheries) in December 2000 about the need for an evaluation system in Japan. The likely number of expected cases of BSE-infected cattle in Japan had been computed on the basis of the amount of 'cattle bone powder' exported from the UK to Japan. It was predicted that Japan would face a crisis on a par with those experienced in France or Germany, but probably not a catastrophe comparable to the British BSE outbreak. In its provisional report on BSE in June 2001, the European Union introduced a four-stage evaluation designating system, indicating the level of seriousness of BSE infection in 50 countries, ranging from Level One (Slight Danger) to Level Four (Maximum Danger). The death toll in France from the human version of the disease known as New Variant Creutzfeld-Jacob Disease (NVCJD) then stood at three, small by UK standards but alarming for the public and for the livestock industry across Europe. While the UK was the only country to be designated Level Four, Japan was designated Level Three, alongside France and Germany. The Japanese government had not been expecting a designation as high as this and, considering it to be excessively harsh, the MAFF immediately sent an official to Brussels to request that Japan be removed from the list. Japanese politicians and bureaucrats in the relevant ministries tend to be extremely sensitive to food safety issues because the agricultural vote-catching machine produces a disproportionately high number of Diet members representing rural areas. With their rural power bases, these politicians combine with the powerful and well-funded farmers' pressure groups and the MAFF itself to produce an extremely strong agricultural lobby, sometimes referred to as the 'iron triangle'.

In September 2001, three months after the damaging report was released, the first BSE-infected cattle were officially discovered in Chiba Prefecture near Tokyo. An ad hoc consultative agency consisting of MAFF and the Minister of Health, Labour and Welfare (MHLW) submitted an investigation examination committee report on BSE problems in April 2002 in response to this development. This report proposed organizational controls such as a risk analysis system for food safety, and pointed out the necessity for new legislation. The Codex Commission, the food standard planning and implementation organization established jointly by the FAO and the WHO, had in 1999 already recommended countries to adopt a food safety risk analysis system consisting of three elements: (1) risk evaluation, (2) risk management and (3) risk communication.

The ministerial conference on food safety administration compiled a report entitled 'The Future of Food Safety Administration' in June 2002. This report recommended the adoption of a new governance system for food safety policy and the setting up of a Food Safety Commission within the Cabinet Office, a mechanism equivalent to the EU's EFSA. Risk assessment and risk management would henceforth be designated the responsibility of the Cabinet Office's Food Safety Commission, and come under the jurisdiction of the MAFF and the MHLW. The discovery of BSE-infected cattle in Japan, SARS in China and bird influenza in Vietnam forced Japan to recognize that Japanese food safety did not exist in a vacuum, but was connected to other world food safety issues. The MAFF and the MHLW, which are especially concerned with food safety administration in Japan, would jointly share responsibility for the handling of future crises. With a view to protecting public health, the Japanese government set up the aforementioned Food Safety Commission in the Cabinet Office in July 2003, based on the EU model. The Commission was designed to evaluate the level of risk and to communicate such information directly to the public. It was made up entirely of experts in the natural sciences, and was independent of organizations with responsibility for risk management such as the MAFF, the MHLW and the Consumer Affairs Agency.

The duties of the new Commission were:

1. to offer opinions to the Prime Minister;
2. to conduct assessments of the effects of food on health;
3. to make recommendations to relevant ministers through the Prime Minister's Office about policies to be implemented concerning food safety, on the basis of the results of the above mentioned assessments;
4. to monitor the implementation of policies introduced on the basis of the results of the assessment;
5. to examine and deliberate on important matters regarding policies to be implemented for ensuring food safety, and to give opinions to the heads of related administrative bodies if necessary;
6. to conduct scientific research and studies necessary to perform the duties of office cited in items 2 to 5;
7. to plan and implement systems for the mutual exchange of information and opinions among persons or parties concerned with executing the duties cited in items 2 to 6;
8. to coordinate the various duties conducted by related administrative bodies regarding the mutual exchange of information and opinions among persons or parties concerned with ensuring food safety (Food Safety Basic Law in Japan 2003, Article 24, Food Safety Commission of Japan 2003).

Risk analysis procedures are defined within the framework of the Codex Commission, which discusses food safety regulatory measures and standards for contaminants, based on the risk assessment results decided at joint meetings of FAO/WHO food additive experts. As mentioned above, risk analysis consists of three steps: risk evaluation, risk management and risk communication. In order to maintain the confidence of the general public, it is essential for food safety policy-makers to bear in mind the importance of accountability, responsibility and legitimacy. I would like to recommend the following as being necessary to ensure good governance of food safety:

a. conducting risk assessment on food in a scientific, independent, and fair manner;
b. making recommendations to relevant ministries based upon the results;
c. implementing risk communication among stakeholders such as consumers and food-related business operators;
d. responding appropriately and promptly to food-borne accidents and emergencies.

A recent example of EU–Japan co-operation regarding food safety concerns the EU's Rapid Alert System for Food and Feed (RASFF), which is designed to analyse and evaluate food safety risks. Since March 2011, when the nuclear accidents occurred in Fukushima, the RASFF has been analysing the radiation levels in food and feed imported into the EU from Japan, particularly from Fukushima Prefecture, and evaluating the possible food safety risks. The fact that the RASFF can now also be accessed over the internet using a version called 'iRASFF' means that information can be shared internationally for the global public good much more rapidly and cost-effectively than before. Further EU–Japan co-operation related to food safety, involving the setting up of new safety systems along the same lines as RASFF/iRASFF, will be essential during the ongoing EPA and FTA negotiations, which are currently taking place.

Towards the Future: Learning Lessons from Europe's Food Safety Experience

It was clear that much greater levels of accountability and transparency would be essential if the EFSA system were to work effectively and prevent crises such as the BSE and dioxin disasters from happening again. The recent history of food safety problems demonstrates the need for independent and impartial scientific advice, and the difficulties involved in securing such advice. Although it is neither possible nor advisable to translate the European model directly into a framework for Japan or other parts of the world, there are certainly lessons to be learned from Europe's food safety experience. Legislative authorities and administrative organs in Japan and other non-EU countries would be well advised to take the European BSE experience and subsequent food safety legislation into account when designing their own food safety protection systems in the future. It will be particularly useful to analyse the European situation in terms of accountability and responsibility, and to take account of the paramount importance of keeping the public informed about the medical facts and the measures being taken to rectify the situation.

The governments of EU member states derive their legitimacy from general elections. The European Commission, however, has no such readily visible form of legitimacy in the eyes of the European public. Therefore, a high degree of accountability is essential when the Commission introduces legislation which supersedes that of member states' own parliaments. Food safety is an issue which affects people's daily lives, and one in which people take a great deal of interest; it can therefore be said to act as a testing ground for EU accountability. If the general public were to perceive the Commission as acting in an unaccountable or undemocratic manner as regards food safety legislation, it would be highly damaging for the long-term future of the entire EU project, and might undermine the prospects of further enlargement and integration. The accountability of Ministers or Commissioners to the European Parliament is only one way in which transparency needs to be demonstrated. The constitutional and administrative systems will also require extensive reforms in order to achieve a satisfactory level of openness. The EU is preparing the way by seeking to achieve greater accountability and political responsibility to its citizens and to allow greater access by the media.

Legitimacy and transparency are widely accepted as requiring some multilateral authorization, preferably from international institutions. With regard to food safety, a mixed system of accountability has begun to develop, involving procedures and policies at both international and national levels. The effectiveness of decisions taken by international institutions depends on their implementation by individual states or collaboration with willing states. In the European Union, one important lesson has been learned from the BSE crisis, namely the need to move in the direction of a 'mixed' or 'fusion' system of democratic accountability within a pan-European framework (Menon and Weatherill, 2002: 113–16). The Japanese government, for its part, will face pressure from consumers who are opposed to the deregulation of food safety, which the TPP and the EPA both demand, as Japan is heavily dependent on imported agricultural products for human consumption and other foodstuffs such as animal feed. This pressure has increased recently due to a series of well-publicized health scares concerning the safety of a wide range of products imported from China, notably tea, eels, rice and vegetables that have been contaminated with pesticide.

I recommend that the following steps be taken in the interests of food safety in Japan:

1. An international institution which sets global standards for crop safety and regulates the use of chemicals in agriculture should be established to address regulatory, policy, and implementation issues with the EPA and the TPP. This institution should have the authority to limit exports

or order compensation payments to be made to consumers (under some kind of Product Liability Law) if a food company violates health and safety legislation.

2. The exporting country's government and companies should be required to supply information with regard to exported crops, feed or food. The importing country's government and companies should be responsible for disclosing this information to the consumer.

3. Constitutional and administrative systems may require transparency to an even greater degree than that demanded from third parties. The reliability of the information presented by third parties should be assessed by a peer review body, and a surveillance system should be introduced. Communicating with stakeholders is important and 'risk communication can be used for targeting both output and input legitimacy' (Rudloff and Simons 2006: 161).

We have seen that accountability in public policy governance which is consistent at both national and supranational levels is clearly essential. Furthermore, experience has shown that high level food safety protection is best assured when the national government and supranational authorities work in close cooperation with each other and effectively operate as a single body. Although the interlocking nature of such a hybrid or 'fusion' system may appear over-complicated at first, its positive benefits in terms of European governance have provided a sense of hope that the European regulatory framework is on the right track (Fukuda 2003: 61–2). The system seems to provide an excellent model for successful global governance, not only for EU member states but also for other countries such as Japan, who will be able to use the EU's experience to provide much greater accountability to their citizens in the future, and can learn from the EU's example.

Bibliography

Acharya, A. (2004) 'How Ideas Spread: Whose Norms Matter? Norm Localization and Institutional Change in Asian Regionalism', *International Organization*, 58(2), 239–75.

Acharya, A. and Johnston, A.I. (eds) (2007) *Crafting Cooperation: Regional International Institutions in Comparative Perspective*, Cambridge: Cambridge University Press.

ACP Heads of Government and State (2012) *Sipopo Declaration: The Future of the ACP Group in a Changing World: Challenges and Opportunities*. Accessed at: http://www.safpi.org/publications/acp-sipopo-declaration.

Advisory Panel on Reconstruction of the Legal Basis for Security (2014) *Report of the Advisory Panel on Reconstruction of the Legal Basis for Security*, 15 May, Tokyo: PMO.

Agence France-Presse (2012) 'Japan Death Row Inmates Want Prior Warning', 29 December.

Alesina, A. and Perotti, R. (1996) 'Fiscal Adjustments in OECD Countries and Macroeconomic Effects', National Bureau of Economic Research Working Papers, 5730. Accessed at: http://www.nber.org/papers/w5730.pdf.

Ando, M. (2006) 'Fragmentation and Vertical Intra-Industry Trade in East Asia', *North American Journal of Economics and Finance*, 17(3), 257–81.

Andrews, D.M. (ed.) (2005) *The Atlantic Alliance Under Stress: US-European Relations After Iraq*, Cambridge: Cambridge University Press.

Ansell, C. and Vogel, M. (2005) 'The Contested Governance of European Food Safety', Institute of Governmental Studies, UC Berkeley Working Papers. Accessed at: http://www.regulation.upf.edu/ecpr-05-papers/cansell.pdf.

ANSES (2010) *Agence nationale de sécurité sanitaire de l'alimentation, de l'environnement et du travail*. Accessed at: http://www.anses.fr/fr.

Asahi Shimbun (2010) 'Strong Support for Death Penalty', 9 February.

—— (2012) 'Editorial: DPJ, LDP Should Articulate Their Positions on TPP', 4 December.

Asai, Y. (n.d.) 'Sewerage in Tokyo', Staff General Affairs Section, Bureau of Sewerage, Tokyo Metropolitan Government. Accessed at: http://www.asianhumannet.org/db/datas/11_anmc21_sche/1%20Sewerage%20in%20Tokyo.pdf.

Ashton, C. (2010) *Annual Report from the High Representative of the Union for Foreign Affairs and Security Policy to the European Parliament on the Main Aspects and Basic Choices of the CFSP 2010*. Brussels: General Secretariat of the Council.

—— (2011a) *Annual Report from the High Representative of the Union for Foreign Affairs and Security Policy to the European Parliament on the Main Aspects and Basic Choices of the CFSP 2011*. Brussels: General Secretariat of the Council.

—— (2011b) *Human Rights and Democracy at the Heart of EU External Action: Towards a More Effective Approach*, Joint Communication to the European Parliament and the Council, Com (2011) 886, 12 December, Brussels: European Commission.

Athukorala, P. (2006) 'Product Fragmentation and Trade Patterns in East Asia', *Asian Economic Papers*, 4(3), 1–27.

—— (2009) 'The Rise of China and East Asian Export Performance: Is the Crowding-Out Fear Warranted?', *World Economy*, 32(2), 234–66.

Bacon, P. (ed.) (2010) *Reflections on Life: European and Asian Perspectives on Capital Punishment*, Tokyo: European Union Institute in Japan at Waseda University.

Bacon, P. and Hobson, C. (2014) 'Human Security Comes Home: Responding to Japan's Triple Disaster', in P. Bacon and C. Hobson (eds) *Human Security and Japan's Triple Disaster*, Abingdon: Routledge, 1–21.

Bacon, P. and Kato, E. (2013) 'Potential Still Untapped: Japanese Perceptions of the European Union as an Economic and Normative Power', *Baltic Journal of European Studies*, 3(3), 59–84.

Badie, B. (2011) *La diplomatie de connivence*, Paris: La Découverte.

Baldwin, M. (2006) 'EU Trade Politics: Heaven or Hell?', *Journal of European Public Policy*, 13(6), 926–42.

Balfour, R. and Raik, K. (2013) 'Equipping the European Union for the 21st Century: National Diplomacies, the European External Action Service and the Making of EU Foreign Policy', FIIA Report, 36, Helsinki: The Finnish Institute of International Affairs.

Barroso, J.M. (2006) 'EU-Japan: A Mature Relationship with Untapped Potential', Speech to the Tokyo Chamber of Commerce, 21 April 2006. Accessed at: http://www.eu-un.europa.eu/articles/en/article_5918_en.htm.

Bartels, L. (2005) *Human Rights Conditionality in the EU's International Agreements*, Oxford: Oxford University Press.

—— (2012) 'Human Rights and Sustainable Development Obligations in EU Free Trade Agreements', Legal Studies Research Paper Series, 24, Law Faculty, Cambridge University.

Bartelt, S. (2012) 'ACP-EU Development Cooperation at a Crossroads? One Year after the Second Revision of the Cotonou Agreement', *European Foreign Affairs Review*, 17(1), 1–25.

Bava, U.S. (2001) *West German Realpolitik: Unification, EU and European Security, 1949–1995*, New Delhi: Kanishka.

Bechev, D. (2011) *Constructing South East Europe: The Politics of Balkan Regional Cooperation*, London: Palgrave Macmillan.

—— (2012) 'The Periphery of the Periphery: The Western Balkans and the Euro Crisis', European Council on Foreign Relations Policy Briefs. Accessed at: http://ecfr.eu/page/-/ECFR60_WESTERN_BALKANS_BRIEF_AW.pdf.

Beck, U. (2011) 'Créons une Europe des citoyens!', *Le Monde*, 27 December.

Beeson, M. (2007) *Regionalism and Globalization in East Asia: Politics, Security and Economic Development*, Basingstoke: Palgrave.

Berends, G. (2013) 'Safe to Eat? Food Safety Policy and Radioactivity in the Market Place', in D. Al-Badri and G. Berends (eds) *After the Great East Japan Earthquake: Political and Policy Change in Post-Fukushima Japan*, Copenhagen: NIAS Press, 149–70.

Berends, G. and Kobayashi, M. (2012) 'Food after Fukushima: Japan's Regulatory Response to the Radioactive Contamination of Its Food Chain', *Food and Drug Law Journal*, 67(1), 51–64.

Bergenas, J. and Sabatini, R. (2012) 'Japan Takes the Lead in Coordinating Security and Development Aid', *World Politics Review*, 1 August. Accessed at: http://www.worldpoliticsreview.com/articles/12220/japan-takes-the-lead-in-coordinating-security-and-development-aid.

Bergström, C.F and Rotkirch, M. (2003) 'Decentralized Agencies and the IGC: A Question of Accountability', *Swedish Institute for European Policy Studies (SIEPS) Reports*, 1(14).

Berkofsky, A. (2007) 'The EU and Japan: A Partnership in the Making', European Policy Centre Issue Paper, 52.

Bertoldi M. (2013) 'Forty Years of EU-Japan Relations: Were They Driven by Trade and Exchange Rate Concerns?', in J. Keck, D. Vanoverbeke and F. Waldenberger (eds) *EU-Japan Relations, 1970–2010: From Confrontation to Global Partnership*, London: Routledge, 184–214.

Bhagwati, J. (2004) 'Don't Cry for Cancun', *Foreign Affairs*, 83(1), 52–63.

Bhattacharjee, Y. (2009) 'The Danger Within', *Science*, 323(1), 1282–3.

Blanchfield, M. (2014) 'The EU-Canada Trade Deal Talks Hit Snag over Human Rights Issues', *The Huffington Post Canada*. Accessed at: http://www.huffingtonpost.ca/2013/10/08/eu-canada-trade-deal_n_4065145.html?just_reloaded=1.

Boonstra, C. (2013) 'Rebuilding Farming in Tohoku: A New Frontier for Japanese Agriculture', in D. Al-Badri and G. Berends (eds) *After the Great East Japan Earthquake: Political and Policy Change in Post-Fukushima Japan*, Copenhagen: NIAS Press, 129–48.

Börzel, T. (2009) 'Transformative Power Europe? The EU Promotion of Good Governance in Areas of Limited Statehood', Paper prepared for the ERD Workshop *Transforming Political Structures: Security, Institutions and Regional Integration Mechanisms*, 16–17 April, Florence.

Börzel, T. and Risse, T. (2004) 'One Size Fits All? EU Policies for the Promotion of Human Rights, Democracy and the Rule of Law', paper prepared for the *Workshop on Democracy Promotion*, 4–5 October, Center for Development, Democracy and the Rule of Law, Stanford University.

—— (2012) 'From Europeanization to Diffusion: Introduction', *West European Politics*, 35(1), 1–19.

Brande, E.V. (2009) 'Green Civilian Power Europe?', in J. Orbie (ed.) *Europe's Global Role: External Policies of the European Union*, Farnham: Ashgate, 157–80.

Bretherton, C. and Vogler, J. (2006) *The European Union as a Global Actor*, London and New York: Routledge.

Bridges, B. (1993) *Japan: Hesitant Superpower*, Conflict Studies, 264, London: Research Institute for the Study of Conflict and Terrorism.

Brown, L. (1990) 'The Illusion of Progress', in L. Brown (ed.) *State of the World 1990*, New York: W.W. Norton and Company, 3–16.

Bull, H. (1982) 'Civilian Power Europe: A Contradiction in Terms?', *Journal of Common Market Studies*, 12(2), 149–64.

—— (2002) *The Anarchical Society: A Study of Order in World Politics* (Third Edition), London: Macmillan.

Bulmer, S., Jeffery, C. and Padgett S. (eds) (2010) *Rethinking Germany and Europe: Democracy and Diplomacy in a Semi-Sovereign State*, Basingstoke: Palgrave Macmillan.

Byman, D. and Waxman, M. (2002) *The Dynamics of Coercion: American Foreign Policy and the Limits of Military Might*, Cambridge: Cambridge University Press.

Cabinet Secretariat, Japan (2013) *National Security Strategy*, 17 December. Accessed at: http://www.cas.go.jp/jp/siryou/131217anzenhoshou/nss-e.pdf.

Calder, K. (1988) 'Japanese Foreign Economic Policy Formation: Explaining the Reactive State', *World Politics*, 40, 517–41.

Carta, C. (2013) 'The EEAS and EU Executive Actors within the Foreign Policy-Cycle', in M. Telò and F. Ponjaert (eds) *The EU's Foreign Policy: What Kind of Power and Diplomatic Action?*, Farnham: Ashgate, 87–104.

CBC News (2001) 'British Residents Fear Mad Cow Stockpile Sites', 31 May. Accessed at: http://www.cbc.ca/news/world/story/2001/05/28/madcow_010528.html.

Chaban, N., Elgström, O., Kelly, S. and Yi, L.S. (2013) 'Images of the EU Beyond Its Borders: Issue-Specific and Regional Perceptions of European Union Power and Leadership', *Journal of Common Market Studies*, 51(3), 433–51.

Chasek, P.S., Downie, D.L. and Welsh Brown, J. (2010) *Global Environmental Politics* (Fifth Edition), Boulder, CO: Westview Press.

Chen, Z. (2012) 'International Responsibility, Multilateralism, and China's Foreign Policy', in M. Telò (ed.) *State, Globalization and Multilateralism*, London and New York: Springer, 79–98.

Christian, J. (1999) 'Good Governance through Comitology?', in J. Christian and E. Vos (eds) *EU Committees: Social Regulation, Law and Politics*, Oxford: Hart Publishing, 311–38.

Christopher, L. (2004) *Democratic Audit of the European Parliament*, New York: Palgrave Macmillan.

Copenhagen Economics (2009) *Assessment of Barriers to Trade and Investment between the EU and Japan*, prepared for the European Commission, DG Trade, under framework contract (TRADE/07/A2). Accessed at: http://trade. ec.europa.eu/doclib/docs/2010/february/tradoc_145772.pdf.

Cosby, A. and Burgiel, S. (2000) 'The Cartagena Protocol on Biosafety: An Analysis of Results', IISD Briefing Note, Winnipeg: International Institute for Sustainable Development. Accessed at: http://www.iisd.org/pdf/biosafety.pdf.

Council of the European Communities (1977) *Council Directive 77/504/EEC on Pure-bred Breeding Animals of the Bovine Species*, Brussels: European Economic Community.

—— (1988) *Council Directive 88/146/EEC Prohibiting the Use in Livestock Farming of Certain Substances Having a Hormonal Action*, Brussels: European Economic Community.

—— (1989) 'Council Regulation (Euratom) No 2218/89 of 18 July 1989 Amending Regulation (Euratom) No 3954/87 Laying Down Maximum Permitted Levels of Radioactive Contamination of Foodstuffs and of Feedingstuffs Following a Nuclear Accident or Any Other Case of Radiological Emergency', *Official Journal of the European Communities*, L211, vol. 32, 22 July.

—— (1993) *Council Directive 93/42/EEC concerning Medical Devices*, Brussels: European Economic Community.

Council of the European Union (2003) *Fight against Proliferation of Weapons of Mass Destruction: EU Strategy against Proliferation of Weapons of Mass Destruction*, Brussels: Council of the European Union.

—— (2008) *Council Joint Action 2008/307/CFSP of 14 April 2008 in Support of World Health Organization Activities in the Area of Laboratory Bio-safety and Bio-security in the Framework of the European Union Strategy against the Proliferation of Weapons of Mass Destruction.*

—— (2011) *Joint Press Statement on the 20th EU-Japan Summit*, 28 May. Accessed at: http://www.consilium.europa.eu/uedocs/cms_data/docs/pressdata/en/er/122305.pdf.

—— (2012a) *EU Action Plan on Human Rights and Democracy*. Communication 11855/12, Luxembourg: Council of the European Union.

—— (2012b) *EU Strategic Framework on Human Rights and Democracy*. Communication, 11855/12, Luxembourg: Council of the European Union.

Cox, R. (1986) 'Production, Power and World Orders', in R.O. Keohane (ed.) *Realism and Its Critics*, New York: Columbia University Press, 204–53.

Crespy, A. (2015) 'Studying European Discourse', in K. Lynggaard, I. Manners and K. Lofgren (eds) *Research Methods in European Studies*, Basingstoke: Palgrave Macmillan (forthcoming).

Czempiel, E.O. (1999) *Kluge Macht: Außenpolitik für das 21. Jahrhundert*, München: C.H. Beck.

Damro, C. (2011) 'Market Power Europe', paper delivered at the 2011 European Union Studies Association conference. Accessed at: http://www.euce.org/eusa/2011/papers/2j_damro.pdf.

De Onis, J. (2008) 'Brazil's Big Moment: A South American Giant Wakes Up', *Foreign Affairs*, 87(6) (Nov/Dec 2008), 110–22.

De Waal, S.C and Robert, N. (2005) *Global and Local: Food Safety Around the World*, Washington, DC: Center for Science in the Public Interest. Accessed at: http://www.cspinet.org/new/pdf/global.pdf.

Delegation of the European Union to Japan (2014) 'Environmental Cooperation'. Accessed at: http://www.euinjapan.jp/en/relation/trade/current/environment/.

Democratic Party of Japan (DPJ) (2009) *Minshuto Seiken Seisaku* [DPJ Manifesto], Tokyo: Minshuto Honbu. Accessed at: http://www.dpj.or.jp/special/manifesto2009/.

Derbyshire, D. (2001) 'CJD on Increase as Human Death Toll Passes 100', *The Telegraph*, 31 May.

Deudney, D. and Ikenberry, G.J. (1999) 'The Nature and Sources of Liberal International Order', *Review of International Studies*, 25(2), 179–96.

Dewatripont, M. and Legros, P. (2009) 'EU Competition Policy in a Global World', in M. Telò (ed.) *The European Union and Global Governance*, London: Routledge, 87–102.

Drifte, R. (1996) *Japan's Foreign Policy in the 1990s: From Economic Power to What Power?*, London: Macmillan, in association with St Antony's College, Oxford.

Duchêne, F. (1972) 'Europe's Role in World Peace', in R. Mayne (ed.) *Europe Tomorrow: Sixteen Europeans Look Ahead*, London: Fontana, 32–47.

——(1973) 'The European Community and the Uncertainties of Interdependence', in M. Kohnstamm and W. Hager (eds) *A Nation Writ Large? Foreign Policy Problems before the European Community*, London: Macmillan, 1–21.

Dür, A. (2008) 'Bringing Economic Interests Back into the Study of EU Trade Policy-Making', *British Journal of Politics and International Relations*, 10(1), 27–45.

ECDPM (2012) 'Différenciation dans la coopération ACP-EU: Implications du Programme pour le changement sur le 11ème FED et au-delà', *Document de réflexion*, 134.

Edström, B. (2009) 'Japan and the Myanmar Conundrum', Institute for Security and Development Policy ASIA Paper. Accessed at: http://www.isdp.eu/images/stories/isdp-main-pdf/2009_edstrom_japan-and-the-myanmar-conundrum.pdf.

Elijah, A., Murray, P. and O'Brien, C. (2000) 'Divergence and Convergence: The Development of European Union-Australia Relations', CERC Working Papers, 3, Melbourne: Melbourne University.

Elsig, M. and Dupont, C. (2012) 'The European Union Meets South Korea: Bureaucratic Interests, Exporter Discrimination and the Negotiations of Trade Agreements', *Journal of Common Market Studies*, 50(3), 492–507.

Ernst, D. (2006) 'Searching for a New Role in East Asian Regionalization: Japanese Production Networks in the Electronics Industries', in P.J. Katzenstein and T. Shiraishi (eds) *Beyond Japan: The Dynamics of East Asian Regionalism*, Ithaca, NY: Cornell University Press, 161–87.

Ethics Commission on a Safe Energy Supply (2011) *Germany's Energy Turnaround: A Collective Effort for the Future: Ethics Commission for a Safe Energy Supply*, translated by Daniel Bullinger, commissioned by Greenpeace Germany. Accessed at: http://stophinkley.org/EngRevu/ENERGY%20TURNAROUND. pdf.

European Centre for Disease Prevention and Control (2005) 'About Us'. Accessed at: http://www.ecdc.europea.eu/en/aboutus/Pages/AboutUs.aspx.

European Commission (1993) 'Commission Answer to Written Parliamentary Question, Number 617/93', *Official Journal of the European Union*, C264/42.

—— (1997) *Communication from the Commission on Consumer Health and Food Safety*, 30 April. Accessed at: http://ec.europa.eu/food/fs/sc/comec1en.pdf.

—— (2000) *White Paper on Food Safety*, Brussels: European Commission.

—— (2004) *Singapore Issues: Clarification of the EU Position*, 31 March, Brussels: European Commission.

—— (2006a) *Global Europe, Competing in the World: A Contribution to the EU's Growth and Jobs Strategy*, Brussels: European Commission DG Trade.

—— (2006b) *Global Europe: A Strong Partnership to Deliver Market Access for EU Exporters*, Brussels: European Commission DG Trade.

—— (2009a) *Communication from the Commission to the European Parliament and the Council of 24 June 2009 on Strengthening Chemical, Biological, Radiological and Nuclear Security in the European Union: an EU Action Plan*, European Commission Communication, 273, Brussels: European Commission.

—— (2009b) *Background on the Health Security Committee and the Early Warning and Response System Authorities*, 13 August, Brussels.

—— (2010) *Trade, Growth and World Affairs: Trade Policy as a Core Component of the EU's 2020 Strategy*, Brussels: European Commission DG Trade.

—— (2011a) *Public Consultation on the Future of EU-Japan Trade and Economic Relations – Report*, Brussels: European Commission DG Trade.

—— (2011b) *Public Consultation on the Future of EU-Japan trade and Economic Relations – List of Contributors*, Brussels: European Commission DG Trade.

—— (2011c) *Proposal for a Decision of the European Parliament and of the Council on Serious Cross-Border Threats to Health*, European Commission Proposal, 866, Brussels: European Commission.

—— (2011d) *Implementing Regulation (EU) Number 351/2011 of 11 April, Amending Regulation (EU) No 297/2011 Imposing Special Conditions Governing the Import of Feed and Food Originating in or Consigned from Japan, Following the Accident at the Fukushima Nuclear Power Station*, Brussels: European Commission.

—— (2011e) *Increasing the Impact of EU Development Policy: An Agenda for Change*. Communication from the Commission, Com (2011) 637 final, 13 November, Brussels: European Commission.

—— (2012a) *Trade, Growth and Development: Tailoring Trade and Investment for Those Countries Most in Need*. Communication from the Commission, Com (2012) 22 final, 27 January, Brussels: European Commission.

—— (2012b) *Impact Assessment: Japan-EU Trade Relations*, Brussels: European Commission DG Trade.

—— (2012c) *External Sources of Growth: Progress Report on EU Trade and Investment Relationships with Key Economic Partners. Commission Staff Working Document*, Brussels: European Commission DG Trade.

—— (2013a) *Ethics for Researchers, Facilitating Research Excellence in FP7*, Brussels: European Commission. Accessed at: http://ec.europa.eu/research/participants/data/ref/fp7/89888/ethics-for-researchers_en.pdf.

—— (2013b) *ASEAN: EU Bilateral Trade and Trade in the World*, Brussels: European Commission DG Trade.

—— (2013c) *Press Release – Gute Fortschritte bei zweiter Runde der Handelsgespräche EU-Japan*, Brussels: European Commission DG Trade.

—— (2013d), 'Challenge and Opportunity: Starting the Negotiations for a Free Trade Agreement between the EU and Japan', Speech by Commissioner De Gucht at the EU-Japan Business Summit, 25 March, Brussels: European Commission DG Trade.

—— (2013e) *First Round of EU-Japan Trade Talks a Success*, 19 April, Brussels: European Commission. Accessed at: http://europa.eu/rapid/press-release_MEMO-13-348_en.htm.

—— (2013f) *Draft Proposal for a Council Directive Amending Directive 2009/71/EURATOM Establishing a Community Framework for the Nuclear Safety of Nuclear Installations*, Com (2013) 343 final, 13 June, Brussels: European Commission.

—— (2014) *Statement: EU-Canada Strategic Partnership Agreement*, 24 March, The Hague. Accessed at: http://europa.eu/rapid/press-release_STATEMENT-14-80_en.htm.

European Committee for Standardization (2008) 'Laboratory Biorisk Management Standards', *CEN Workshop 55 – Guidance Document CWA 15793*. Accessed at: http://www.cen.eu/cen/Sectors/TechnicalCommitteesWorkshops/Workshops/Pages/CWA15793-guide.aspx.

—— (2009) 'About Us'. Accessed at: https://www.cen.eu/cen/AboutUs/Pages/default.aspx.

European Council (2014a) 'G7 Leaders Statement', 3 March, Brussels, EUCO 53/14. Accessed at: http://www.consilium.europa.eu/uedocs/cms_data/docs/pressdata/en/ec/141241.pdf.

—— (2014b) 'G7 The Hague Declaration', 24 March, The Hague, EUCO 73/14. Accessed at: http://www.consilium.europa.eu/uedocs/cms_data/docs/pressdata/en/ec/141855.pdf.

European External Action Service (1991) *Joint Declaration on Relations between the European Community and Its Member States and Japan*, The Hague. Accessed at: http://eeas.europa.eu/japan/docs/joint_pol_decl_en.pdf.

European Food Safety Authority (2004) *Assessment of the Current Image of the European Food Safety Authority* (Interviews with interested parties and stakeholders). Accessed at: http://www.efsa.europa.eu/en/mb040622/docs/ mb040622-ax2a.pdf.

—— (2014) 'Homepage'. Accessed at: http://www.efsa.europa.eu/.

European Parliament (2012) *Resolution to Wind Up the Debate on the Statement by the Commission Pursuant to Rule 110(2) of the Rules of Procedure on EU Trade Negotiations with Japan*, 2012/2651(RSP), 6 June.

—— (2014) *Resolution Containing the European Parliament's Recommendation to the Council, the Commission and the European External Action Service on the Negotiation of the EU-Japan Strategic Partnership Agreement*, 2014/2021(INI), 26 March.

European Parliament and Council of the European Union (2002) *Laying Down the General Principles and Requirements of Food Law, Establishing the European Food Safety Authority and Laying Down Procedures in Matters of Food Safety*, Regulation Number 178/2002.

European Parliament, Council of the European Union, and European Commission (2006) 'The European Consensus on Development (a Joint Statement)', *Official Journal of the European Union*, 2006/ C 46/01 (24 February).

Eurostat (2011) *Food: From Farm to Fork Statistics, 2011 Edition*. Accessed at: http://epp.eurostat.ec.europa.eu/cache/ITY_OFFPUB/KS-32–11–743/EN/ KS-32–11–743-EN.PDF.

—— (2014) *Renewable Energy Statistics*. Accessed at: http://epp.eurostat. ec.europa.eu/statistics_explained/index.php/Renewable_energy_statistics.

Falkner, R. (2007) 'The Political Economy of 'Normative Power' Europe: EU Environmental Leadership in International Biotechnology Regulation', *Journal of European Public Policy*, 14(4), 507–26.

Falletti, S. (2011) 'Economic Partnership: 'Scoping Exercise' Off to Slow Start', *Europolitics*, 28 September. Accessed at: http://www.europolitics.info/ economic-partnership-scoping-exercise-off-to-slow-start-art313968–40.html.

Fawcett, L. and Hurrell, A. (eds) (1995) *Regionalism in World Politics: Regional Organization and International Order*, New York: Oxford University Press.

Federal Environment Agency (Umweltbundesamt), Centre on Sustainable Consumption and Production and the Wuppertal Institute for Climate, Environment and Energy (2008) 'Resource Efficiency: Japan and Europe at the Forefront'. Accessed at: http://wupperinst.org/uploads/tx_wupperinst/ RessEfficiency_Japan.pdf.

Federal Environment Ministry (2014) 'Joint Concept Paper' from the Federal Economics Ministry (BMWi) and the Federal Environment Ministry (BMU). Accessed at: http://www.bmu.de/fileadmin/bmu-import/files/pdfs/allgemein/ application/pdf/konzept_toprunner_en.pdf.

Federal Institute for Risk Assessment (2014) 'Homepage'. Accessed at: http:// www.bfr.bund.de/en/home.html.

Federal Ministry of Food, Agriculture and Consumer Protection (2014) 'Homepage'. Accessed at: http://www.bmelv.de/EN/Homepage/homepage_node.html.

Feldman, R. (2011) 'Japan's Fiscal Woes', in B. Eichengreen, J. von Hagen, C. Wyplosz, J. Liebman and R. Feldman, *Public Debt: Nuts, Bolts and Worries*, Geneva: International Center for Monetary and Banking Studies, and the Centre for Economic Policy Research, 65–88.

Food and Agriculture Organisation (1951) *International Plant Protection Convention*. Accessed at: http://www.opbw.org/int_inst/env_docs/1951IPPC-TEXT.pdf.

Food Safety Commission of Japan (2003) *The Food Safety Basic Law* (Tentative English Translation). Accessed at: https://www.fsc.go.jp/sonota/fsb_law160330.pdf.

—— (2006) *Role of the Food Safety Commission*. Accessed at: http://www.fsc.go.jp/english/aboutus/roleofthefoodsaftycommission_e1.html.

Food Standards Agency (2008) *Annual Report of Incidents 2008*, London: Food Standards Agency Publications. Accessed at: http://www.food.gov.uk/sites/default/files/multimedia/pdfs/incidents08.pdf.

—— (2014) 'Homepage'. Accessed at: http://www.food.gov.uk.

Forge, J. (2010) 'A Note on the Definition of Dual Use', *Science and Engineering Ethics*, 16, 111–18.

Fouse, D. (2007) 'Japan's New "Values-Oriented Diplomacy"', *ISN*, Zurich: Center for Security Studies (CSS)-ETH Zurich, 29 March.

Frattolillo, O. (2013) *Diplomacy in Japan–EU Relations: From the Cold War to the Post-Bipolar Era*, London: Routledge.

Fraser, C.M. and Dando, M.R (2001) 'Genomics and Future Biological Weapons: The Need for Preventive Action by the Biomedical Community', *Nature Genetics*, 29, 253–6.

Fujita, M. (2007) 'The Development of Regional Integration in East Asia: From the Viewpoint of Spatial Economics', *Review of Urban & Regional Development Studies*, 19(1), 2–20.

Fukuda, K. (2003) 'Institutional Reform and European Governance: Political Reflections on the Treaty of Nice', in K. Fukuda and H. Akiba (eds) *European Governance after Nice*, London: RoutledgeCurzon, 41–66.

—— (2009) 'Accountability and NPM Reforms in the European Union', in S. Kuyama and M.R. Fowler (eds) *Envisioning Reform: Enhancing UN Accountability in the 21st Century*, Tokyo: United Nations University Press, 229–52.

Fukushima, A. (2014) 'Japan's "Proactive Contribution to Peace": A Mere Political Label?' Tokyo Foundation, 19 June. Accessed at: http://www.tokyofoundation.org/en/articles/2014/japans-proactive-contribution-to-peace.

Funabashi, Y. (1993) 'The Asianization of Asia', *Foreign Affairs*, 72(5), 75–85.

—— (ed.) (1994) *Japan's International Agenda*, New York: New York University Press.

Furuta, H. (2005) 'Economic Cooperation as Diplomatic Strategy: The Objectives of Japanese ODA', *Gaiko Forum*, 4(4), 43–51.

Gamble, A. and Lane, D. (eds) (2009) *The European Union and World Politics*, Basingstoke: Palgrave Macmillan.

Garby, C. and Bullock, M.B. (eds) (1994) *Japan: A New Kind of Superpower?*, Baltimore, MD: Johns Hopkins University Press.

Garcia, M. (2010) 'Fears and Strategies: The European Union, China and Their Free Trade Agreements in East Asia', *Journal of Contemporary European Research*, 6(4), 496–513.

Gasteyger, C. (1996) *An Ambiguous Power*, Gütersloh: Bertelsmann.

German Energy Agency (2013) 'European Top Runner Strategy Effective: Minimum Standards and EU Label Increase Energy Efficiency in Products', 25 January. Accessed at: http://www.dena.de/en/news/news/european-top-runner-strategy-effective-minimum-standards-and-eu-label-increase-energy-efficiency-in-products.html.

Gill, S. (2008) *Power and Resistance in the New World Order* (Second Edition), Basingstoke: Palgrave Macmillan.

Global Health Security Initiative (2014) 'Introducing the Global Health Security Initiative'. Accessed at: http://www.ghsi.ca/english/index.asp.

Government of Japan (2006) *Science and Technology Basic Plan*. Accessed at: http://www8.cao.go.jp/cstp/english/basic/3rd-Basic-Plan-rev.pdf.

Grabbe, H. (2006) *The EU's Transformative Power: Europeanization through Conditionality in Central and Eastern Europe*, Basingstoke: Palgrave Macmillan.

Grevi, G. with Khandekar, G. (eds) (2011) *Mapping EU Strategic Partnerships*, Madrid: FRIDE .

Haass, R.N. (2008) 'The Age of Nonpolarity: What Will Follow US Dominance?', *Foreign Affairs*, 87(3) (May/June 2008), 44–56.

Habermas, J. (2006) *The Divided West*, Cambridge: Polity Press.

Hamanaka, H. (ed.) (2006) *Kyoto giteisho wo meguru kokusai kosho: COP 3 iko no kosho kei* [International Negotiations over the Kyoto Protocol: The Details of Negotiations after COP 3], Tokyo: Keio University Press.

Hardy, M. and Niepold, R. (2013) 'Exploring Common Interest: Cooperation in Science and Technology', in J. Keck, D. Vanoverbeke and F. Waldenberger (eds) *EU-Japan Relations, 1970–2010: From Confrontation to Global Partnership*, London: Routledge, 267–81.

Harling, R. (2002) 'Strengthening International Collaboration to Improve Global Health Security', *Eurosurveillance*, 6(12), 21 March.

Harlow, C. (2002) *Accountability in the European Union*, Oxford: Oxford University Press.

Harnisch, S. and Maull, H. (2001a) *Germany as a Civilian Power? The Foreign Policy of the Berlin Republic*, Manchester: Manchester University Press.

—— (2001b) 'Introduction', in S. Harnisch and H. Maull (eds) *Germany as a Civilian Power? The Foreign Policy of the Berlin Republic*, Manchester: Manchester University Press, 1–9.

Harrison, K. and Sundstrom, L. (eds) (2010) *Global Commons, Domestic Decisions: The Comparative Politics of Climate Change*, Boston, MA: MIT Press.

Hatch, W. and Yamamura, K. (1996) *Asia in Japan's Embrace: Building a Regional Production Alliance*, Cambridge: Cambridge University Press.

Hayami, A. (1986) 'Population Changes', in M.B. Jansen and G. Rozman (eds) *Japan in Transition: From Tokugawa to Meiji*, Princeton, NJ: Princeton University Press, 280–317.

Héritier, A. and Rhodes, M. (eds) (2011) *New Modes of Governance in Europe: Governing in the Shadow of Hierarchy*, Basingstoke: Palgrave Macmillan.

Heron, T. (2007) 'European Trade Diplomacy and the Politics of Global Development: Reflections on the EU-China "Bra Wars" Dispute', *Government and Opposition*, 42(2), 190–214.

Hettne, B. and Söderbaum, F. (2005) 'Civilian Power or Soft Imperialism? The EU as Global Actor and the Role of Interregionalism', *European Foreign Affairs Review*, 10(4), 535–52.

Hill, C. (ed.) (1996) *The Actors in Europe's Foreign Policy*, London: Routledge.

—— (1998) 'Closing the Capabilities-Expectations Gap?', in J. Peterson and H. Sjursen (eds) *A Common Foreign Policy for Europe?*, London: Routledge, 18–38.

Hill, C. and Smith, M. (eds) (2005) *International Relations and the European Union* (First Edition), Oxford: Oxford University Press.

Hoffmann, S. (1995) *The European Sisyphus: Essays on Europe 1964–1994*, Boulder, CO: Westview Press.

Holland, D. and Pope, H. (2004) *European Union Food Law and Policy*, The Hague: Kluwer.

Hook, G.D., Gilson, J., Hughes, C.W. and Dobson, H. (2012) *Japan's International Relations: Politics, Economics and Security* (Third Edition), London and New York: Routledge.

Hook, G.D. and Son, K-Y. (2013) 'Transposition in Japanese State Identities: Overseas Troop Dispatches and the Emergence of a Humanitarian Power?', *Australian Journal of International Affairs*, 67(1), 35–54.

Hook, S.W. and Zhang, G. (1998) 'Japan's Aid Policy since the Cold War: Rhetoric and Reality', *Asian Survey*, 38(11), 1051–66.

Howe, B.M. and Jang, S. (2013) 'Human Security and Development: Divergent Approaches to Burma/Myanmar', *Pacific Focus*, 28(1), 120–43.

Howorth, J. (2013) 'The Lisbon Treaty, CSDP, and the EU as a Security Actor', in M. Telò and F. Ponjaert (eds) *The EU's Foreign Policy: What Kind of Power and Diplomatic Action?*, Farnham: Ashgate, 65–77.

Hughes, C.W. (2004) *Japan's Re-emergence as a 'Normal' Military Power*, Adelphi Paper 368–9, London: The International Institute for Strategic Studies.

Huliaras, A. (2007) 'Japan and Southeastern Europe', *Journal of Southern Europe and the Balkans*, 9(1), 15–27.

Hurrell, A. (2007a) 'One World? Many Worlds? The Place of Regions in the Study of International Society', *International Affairs*, 83(1), 127–46.

—— (2007b) *On Global Order: Power, Values, and the Constitution of International Society*, Oxford: Oxford University Press.

Ikenberry, J. (2008) 'The Rise of China and the Future of the West: Can the Liberal System Survive?', *Foreign Affairs*, 87(1) (January/February 2008), 23–37.

Inada, J. (2012) 'Japan Should Take Steps for Strategic Use of ODA', *AJISS-Commentary*, 160, 2 October. Accessed at: https://www2.jiia.or.jp/en_commentary/201210/02–1.html.

Infectious Agents Surveillance Report (IASR) (2007) 'Amendment of the Infectious Diseases Control Law, Japan, as of 2007', *Infectious Agents Surveillance Report*, 28(7), 185–8. Accessed at: http://idsc.nih.go.jp/iasr/28/329/tpc329.html.

—— (2010) 'IASR and Pathogen Surveillance System in Japan' [in Japanese], *Infectious Agents Surveillance Report*, 31(1), 69–72. Accessed at: http://idsc.nih.go.jp/iasr/31/361/tpc361-j.html.

Inoguchi, T. and Bacon, P. (2006) 'Japan's Emerging Role as a "Global Ordinary Power"', *International Relations of the Asia-Pacific*, 6(1), 1–21.

International Centre for Trade and Sustainable Development (2013) 'EU, Japan Report Progress at Third Negotiating Round', *BRIDGES*, 17(36), Geneva: ICTS.

International Energy Agency (IEA) (2010) 'CO2 Emissions from Fuel Combustion (Highlights)', Table 1, page 13. Accessed at: http://www.iea.org/co2highlights/CO2highlights.pdf.

International Monetary Fund (2013) 'Direction of Trade Statistics', Washington, DC: International Monetary Fund. Accessed at: https://www.imf.org/external/pubs/cat/longres.cfm?sk=19305.0.

Jacobson, M.Z. (2002) *Atmospheric Pollution: History Science and Regulation*, Cambridge: Cambridge University Press.

Jänicke, M. (2005) 'Trend-setters in Environmental Policy: The Character and Role of Pioneer Countries', *European Environment*, 15(2) (March/April),129–42.

Japan International Cooperation Agency (2012) *Inclusive and Dynamic Development, Annual Report 2012*. Accessed at: http://www.jica.go.jp/english/our_work/evaluation/reports/2012/c8h0vm00006f8m60-att/full.pdf.

Japan Society for the Promotion of Science (JSPS) (2006) 'Japan's Third Science and Technology Basic Plan', *JSPS Quarterly*, Autumn 2006. Accessed at: http://www.jsps.go.jp/english/e-quart/17/jsps17.pdf.

Japan Times (2012) 'Some in EU Cautious on Japan FTA', 2 June. Accessed at: http://www.japantimes.co.jp/text/nb20120602a7.html.

—— (2013a) 'Three Murderers Sent to the Gallows', 21 February. Accessed at: http://www.japantimes.co.jp/news/2013/02/21/national/crime-legal/japan-executes-three-inmates/.

—— (2013b) 'Japan, EU Paving Way for Free-Trade Talks in March', 4 March. Accessed at: http://www.japantimes.co.jp/news/2013/03/04/national/japan-eu-paving-way-for-free-trade-talks-in-march/.

Jarzembowski, G. (2013) 'The History and Role of EU-Japan Parliamentary Exchanges', in J. Keck, D. Vanoverbeke and F. Waldenberger (eds) *EU-Japan Relations, 1970–2010: From Confrontation to Global Partnership*, London: Routledge, 282–90.

Jörgens, H., Lenschow, A. and Liefferink, D. (2014) *Understanding Environmental Policy Convergence: The Power of Words, Rules and Money* (New Edition), Cambridge: Cambridge University Press.

Joyce, C. (2006) 'Japanese to Honour Briton Who Saved Them from Cholera', *The Telegraph*, 8 May. Accessed at: http://www.telegraph.co.uk/news/worldnews/asia/japan/1517796/Japanese-to-honour-Briton-who-saved-them-from-cholera.html.

Kakuchi, S. (2013) 'Japan's Aid Takes a Selfish Turn', *Inter Press Service*, 1 May. Accessed at: http://www.ipsnews.net/2013/05/japans-aid-programme-takes-a-selfish-turn/.

Katzenstein, P. (2005) *A World of Regions: Asia and Europe in the American Imperium*, Ithaca, NY and London: Cornell University Press.

Kawai, N. (2006) 'The Nature of Japanese Foreign Direct Investment in Central and Eastern Europe', *Journal of Current Japanese Affairs (Japan Aktuell)*, 1(5), 3–41.

Kawasaki, K. (2011) *Determining Priority among EPAs: Which Trading Partner Has the Greatest Economic Impact?*, RIETI Column, 31 May, Tokyo: Research Institute of Economy, Trade and Industry (RIETI).

Keck, J. (2013a) '1987–1990: Keeping Relations on an Even Keel', in J. Keck, D. Vanoverbeke, and F. Waldenberger (eds) *EU-Japan Relations, 1970–2010: From Confrontation to Global Partnership*, London: Routledge, 78–110.

—— (2013b) '1990–1995: Trade and Economics from Confrontation to Conversation', in J. Keck, D. Vanoverbeke, and F. Waldenberger (eds) *EU-Japan Relations, 1970–2010: From Confrontation to Global Partnership*, London: Routledge, 131–54.

Keck, J., Vanoverbeke, D. and Waldenberger, F. (eds) (2013) *EU-Japan Relations, 1970–2010: From Confrontation to Global Partnership*, London: Routledge.

Keohane, R.O. (2004) *After Hegemony: Cooperation and Discord in the World Political Economy*, Princeton, NJ: Princeton University Press.

Khanna, P. (2004) 'The Metrosexual Superpower', *Foreign Policy*, 143 (July/August), 66–8.

—— (2008) 'Inter-Imperial Relations: Rebuilding Global Governance in the New Geopolitical Order', *Internationale Politik*, Global Edition 9(3) (Fall), 28–33.

Kingdom, J.W. (1984) *Agendas, Alternatives, and Public Policies*, New York: Harper Collins.

Kingston, J. (2011) 'Information Disclosure in Japan', in C. Hill and S. Landwehr (eds) *Access to Information Laws in Asia, Germany and Australia: A Reader*, Singapore: Konrad-Adenauer-Stiftung, 61–76.

Kleimann, D. (2011) 'Taking Stock: EU Common Commercial Policy in the Lisbon Era', CEPS Working Paper, 345 (April 2011), Brussels: CEPS.

Korkietpitak, W. (2012) 'Japan's Foreign Aid Policy on Human Security: Its Driving Forces, and the Direction of Official Development Assistance (ODA) Policy and Japan International Cooperation Agency (JICA) for Human Security', *Policy Science*, 19(2), Ritsumeikan University, 177–94. Accessed at: http://www.ps.ritsumei.ac.jp/assoc/policy_science/192/192_14_warangka.pdf.

Krasner, S. (1999) *Sovereignty: Organized Hypocrisy*, Princeton, NJ: Princeton University Press.

Krause, J. (2007) 'Die International Ordnung in der Krise', *Internationale Politik*, 62(7/8) (July/Aug 2007), 8–20.

Krauthammer, C. (1990/91) 'The Unipolar Moment', *Foreign Affairs*, 70(1) (Winter 1990/91), 91–106.

—— (2003) 'The Unipolar Moment Revisited', *The National Interest*, 70, 5–17.

Kuhlau, F., Eriksson, S., Evers, K. and Höglund, A.T. (2008) 'Taking Due Care: Moral Obligations in Dual Use Research', *Bioethics*, 22(9), 477–87.

Kuhlau, F., Höglund, A.T., Evers, K. and Eriksson, S. (2011) 'A Precautionary Principle for Dual Use Research in the Life Sciences', *Bioethics*, 25(1), 1–8.

Kuriyama, T. (1997) *Nichi-bei Domei: hyoru-kara-no dakkyaku* [The Japan-US Alliance: From Drift to Revitalization], Tokyo: Nihon Keizai Shimbun.

Kyodo News International (2010) 'Record High 85.6% in Favour of Death Penalty: Survey', 7 February. Accessed at: http://disc.yourwebapps.com/discussion.cgi?disc=219621;article=42655.

—— (2014) 'Japan, EU End 4th Round of FTA Talks; Tariffs, Railways Discussed', 1 February. Accessed at: http://www.globalpost.com/dispatch/news/kyodo-news-international/140131/japan-eu-end-4th-round-fta-talks-tariffs-railways-di-1.

La Documentation Française (2012) 'Allemagne: le défis de la puissance', *Questions internationales*, 54.

Laird, S. (2002) 'Market Access Issues and the WTO: An Overview', in B. Hoekman, A. Mattoo and P. English (eds) *Development, Trade and the WTO: A Handbook*, Washington, DC: World Bank, 97–104.

Lancaster, C. (2010) 'Japan's ODA: naiatsu and gaiatsu; Domestic Sources and Transnational Influences', in D. Leheny and K. Warren (eds) *Japanese Aid and the Construction of Global Development: Inescapable Solutions*, London: Routledge, 29–53.

Leal-Arcas, R. (2010) *International Trade and Investment Law: Multilateral, Regional and Bilateral Governance*, London: Edward Elgar.

Lee, J-C (2008) 'Hygienic Governance and Military Hygiene in the Making of Imperial Japan, 1868–1912', *Historia Scientiarum: International Journal of the History of Science Society of Japan*, 18(1), 1–23.

Lee-Makiyama, H. (2012) 'Upholding Europe's Mandate on Trade', ECIPE Policy Brief, 11, Brussels: ECIPE. Accessed at: http://www.ecipe.org/media/ publication_pdfs/PB201212.pdf.

Legro, J.W. (2005) *Rethinking the World: Great Power Strategies and International Order*, Ithaca, NY: Cornell University Press.

Leheny, D. and Warren, K. (2010) 'Introduction', in D. Leheny and K. Warren (eds) *Japanese Aid and the Construction of Global Development: Inescapable Solutions*, London: Routledge, 1–26.

Leonard, M. (2005) *Why Europe Will Run the 21st Century*, London: Fourth Estate.

Lieber, R.J. (2005) *The American Era: Power and Strategy for the 21 Century*, Cambridge: Cambridge University Press.

Little, R. (2007) *The Balance of Power in International Relations: Metaphors, Myths, and Models*, Cambridge: Cambridge University Press.

Lord, C. (2004) *A Democratic Audit of the European Union*, Basingstoke: Palgrave Macmillan.

Lucarelli, S. (2011) 'Mirrors of Us: European Political Identity and the Other's Image of the EU', in F. Cerutti, S. Lucarelli and V. Schmidt (eds) *Debating Political Identity and Legitimacy in the European Union*, London: Routledge, 148–67.

Luo, Y. (2007) 'Engaging the Private Sector: EU-China Trade Disputes under the Shadow of WTO Law?', *European Law Journal*, 13(6), 800–817.

Luta, A. (2011) 'Japan after the Quake: Prospects for Climate Policy', Fridtjof Nansen Institute (FNI) Climate Policy Perspectives, 1(1).

Mahbubani, K. (2005) 'Understanding China', *Foreign Affairs*, 84(5) (September/ October), 49–60.

—— (2007) 'Der Westen als Nadelöhr', *Internationale Politik*, 62 (7/8) (July/ Aug), 54–64.

—— (2008) 'The Case Against the West: America and Europe in the Asian Century', *Foreign Affairs*, 87(3) (May/June), 111–24.

Manners, I. (2002) 'Normative Power Europe: A Contradiction in Terms?', *Journal of Common Market Studies*, 40(2), 234–58.

Maull, H.W. (1990) 'Germany and Japan: The New Civilian Powers', *Foreign Affairs*, 69(5), 91–106.

—— (2001) 'Germany's Foreign Policy Post-Kosovo Still a Civilian Power?' in S. Harnisch and H.W. Maull (eds) *Germany as a Civilian Power? The Foreign Policy of the Berlin Republic*, Manchester: Manchester University Press, 106–27.

—— (2005) 'Europe and the New Balance of Global Order', *International Affairs*, 81(4), 775–99.

—— (2006) 'Zivilmacht Deutschland', in G. Hellmann, R. Wolf and S. Schmidt (eds) *Handbuch zur deutschen Außenpolitik*, Opladen: VS Verlag, 73–84.

Mayer, H. (2008a) 'Is It Still Called "Chinese Whispers?" The EU's Rhetoric and Action as a Responsible Global Institution', *International Affairs*, 84(1) (January), 61–79.

—— (2008b) 'The Long Legacy of Dorian Gray: Why the European Union Needs to Redefine Its Perspective, Responsibility and Role in Global Affairs', *Journal Of European Integration*, 30(1) (March), 7–25.

—— (2010) 'France, Germany, UK: Responses of Traditional to Rising Powers', in D. Flemes (ed.) *Regional Leadership in the Global System: Ideas, Interests and Strategies of Regional Powers*, Farnham: Ashgate, 273–292.

—— (2013) 'The Challenge of Coherence in EU Foreign Policy', in M. Telò and F. Ponjaert (eds) *The EU's Foreign Policy: What Kind of Power and Diplomatic Action?*, Farnham: Ashgate, 105–17.

Mayer, H. and Vogt, H. (eds) (2006) *A Responsible Europe? Ethical Foundations of EU External Relations*, Basingstoke: Palgrave Macmillan.

Menasse, R. (2012) *Der Europäische Landbote*, Wien: Paul Zsolnay Verlag.

Menon, A. and Weatherill, S. (2002) 'Legitimacy, Accountability, and Delegation in the European Union', in A. Arnull and D. Wincott (eds) *Accountability and Legitimacy in the European Union*, Oxford: Oxford University Press, 113–32.

Messerlin, P. (2012) 'The TPP and EU Policy in East Asia (China Mainland Excluded)', ECIPE Working Paper, 15 May, Brussels: ECIPE.

—— (2013) 'The Domestic Political Economy of Preferential Trade Agreements', ECIPE Working Paper, September, Brussels: ECIPE.

—— (2014a) 'The EU Preferential Trade Agreements: Defining Priorities for a Debt-Ridden, Growth-Starved EU', GEM Working Paper, 30 January, Paris: IEP-Paris (GEM).

—— (2014b) 'The Japan-EU Negotiations on Railways', ECIPE Working Paper, 3, Brussels: ECIPE.

Meunier, S. and Nicolaïdis, K. (1999) 'Who Speaks for Europe? The Delegation of Trade Authority in the EU', *Journal of European Public Policy*, 37(3), 477–501.

—— (2006) 'The European Union as a Conflicted Trade Power', *Journal of European Public Policy*, 13(6), 906–25.

Mez, L. (2012) 'Germany's Merger of Energy and Climate Change Policy', *Bulletin of the Atomic Scientists*, 68(6), 22–9.

Miller, R. (2001) 'As Germany Comes to Grip with Its Own Mad-Cow Crisis, Where Was the EU?', *The German Law Journal*, 1(2). Accessed at: http://www.germanlawjournal.com/article.php?id=46.

Minami, H. (2006) 'Human Security and Japan's Foreign Policy', *Gaiko Forum*, 5(4), 43–50.

Minehata, M. and Shinomiya, N. (2010) 'Japan: Obstacles, Lessons and Future', in B. Rappert (ed.) *Education and Ethics in the Life Sciences: Strengthening the Prohibition of Biological Weapons*, Canberra: Australian National University E-Press, 93–114.

Minehata, M., Sture, J., Shinomiya, N. and Whitby, S. (2013) 'Implementing Biosecurity Education: Approaches, Resources and Programmes', *Science Engineering Ethics*, 19(4), 1473–86.

Ministry of Economy, Trade and Industry (METI) (2006) *New National Energy Strategy: Digest*. Accessed at: http://www.gas.or.jp/en/newsletter/images/05/pdf/newstrategy.pdf.

—— (2010a) Enerugi kihonkeikaku [The Basic Energy Plan]. Accessed at: http://www.meti.go.jp/committee/summary/0004657/energy.pdf.

—— (2010b) 'The Strategic Energy Plan of Japan: Meeting Global Challenges and Securing Energy Futures' (Revised in June 2010). Accessed at: http://www.meti.go.jp/english/press/data/20100618_08.html.

Ministry of Economy, Trade and Industry and Ministry of Foreign Affairs (METI/MOFA) (2014) *Joint Press Release – Fourth Round of Negotiations on the Japan EU Economic Partnership Agreement (EPA)*, 31 January, Tokyo: METI/MOFA. Accessed at: http://www.meti.go.jp/english/press/2014/0131_03.html.

Ministry of Foreign Affairs (MOFA) (1957) *Diplomatic Bluebook 1957* [Waga-Gaiko-no-Kinkyou]. Accessed at: http://www.mofa.go.jp/mofaj/gaiko/bluebook/1957/s32–1-2.htm#a.

—— (2002) *Japan's FTA Strategy*, Tokyo: Economic Affairs Bureau, October.

—— (2010) 19th Japan-EU Summit, Tokyo, 28 April 2010, *Joint Press Statement*. Accessed at: http://www.mofa.go.jp/region/europe/eu/summit/joint1004.html.

—— (2012) *Japan's Official Development Assistance White Paper 2011: Japan's International Cooperation*. Accessed at: http://www.mofa.go.jp/policy/oda/white/2011/.

—— (2014) 'Japan-EU Summit Meeting (Overview)', The Hague, 25 March. Accessed at: http://www.mofa.go.jp/erp/ep/page18e_000064.html.

Ministry of Health, Labour and Welfare (MHLW) (2012) 'New Standard Limits for Radionuclides in Foods'. Accessed at: http://www.mhlw.go.jp/english/topics/2011eq/dl/new_standard.pdf.

Möhler, R. and van Rij, J. (2013) '1983–1987: Export Moderation as a Panacea or Can Japan Change?', in J. Keck, D. Vanoverbeke and F. Waldenberger (eds) *EU-Japan Relations, 1970–2010: From Confrontation to Global Partnership*, London: Routledge, 58–77.

Molle, W. (2005) *The Economics of European Integration: Theory, Practice, Policy* (Fifth Edition), Farnham: Ashgate.

—— (2011) *European Economic Governance: The Quest for Consistency and Effectiveness*, London: Routledge.

Mulgan, R. (2003) *Holding Power to Account: Accountability in Modern Democracies*, Basingstoke: Palgrave Macmillan.

Munakata, N. (2004) 'Nihon no FTA senryaku' [Japan's FTA Strategy], in M. Tadokoro (ed.) *Nihon no higashi ajia kousou* [Japan's Vision for East Asia], Tokyo: Keio University Press.

Mykal, O. (2011) *The EU-Japan Security Dialogue: Invisible but Comprehensive*, Amsterdam: IIAS, Amsterdam University Press.

Nagase, R. (2005) 'Basic Information on Japan's ODA for the Last 50 Years', in *Fifty Years of Japan ODA: A Critical Review for ODA Reform*, Manila: IBON Books, 7–31.

Nakamura, H. (2013) 'The Efficiency of European External Action and the Institutional Evolution of EU-Japan Political Relations', in M. Telò and F. Ponjaert (eds) *The EU's Foreign Policy: What Kind of Power and Diplomatic Action?*, Farnham: Ashgate, 189–208.

Narlikar, A. and Tussie, D. (2004) 'The G20 at the Cancun Ministerial: Developing Countries and Their Evolving Coalitions in the WTO', *World Economy*, 27(7), 947–66.

National Center for Global Health and Medicine (2014) 'Homepage'. Accessed at: http://www.ncgm.go.jp/.

National Diet of Japan (2013) 'Resolution on Japan's Participation in the Trans-Pacific Partnership (TPP) Negotiations (17-06-2013)', *The House Standing Committee on Agriculture, Forestry and Fisheries*. Accessed at: http://www.sangiin.go.jp/eng/report/standing-committee/20130617-TPP.pdf.

National Institute of Biomedical Innovation (2014) 'Homepage'. Accessed at: http://www.nibio.go.jp/english/index.html.

National Institute of Infectious Diseases (2014) 'Homepage'. Accessed at: http://www.nih.go.jp/.

National Research Council (2004) *Biotechnology Research in an Age of Terrorism*, Washington, DC: The National Academies Press.

Nihon Keizai Shimbun (2014) 'Circulation'. Accessed at: http://adweb.nikkei.co.jp/english/media_data/the_nikkei/nikkei/circ_read.html.

Nordqvist, J. (2007) 'The Top Runner Policy Concept: Pass It Down?', *ECEE Summer Study: Saving Energy – Just Do It!*, 1209–14. Accessed at: http://lup.lub.lu.se/luur/download?func=downloadFile&recordOId=620199&fileOId=620584.

Nye, J.S. (2005) *Soft Power: The Means to Success in World Politics*, New York: Public Affairs.

OECD (1999) 'Development Cooperation Review: Japan', *OECD Development Cooperation Reviews*, 1(34).

—— (2004) *OECD Development Assistance Peer Reviews: Japan 2003*. Accessed at: http://www.oecd.org/dac/peer-reviews/japan2003dacpeerreview.htm.

—— (2011) *OECD Development Assistance Peer Reviews: Japan 2010*. Accessed at: http://www.oecd.org/dac/peer-reviews/japan2010dacpeerreview-mainfindingsandrecommendations.htm.

—— (2012) *Development Cooperation Report 2012: Lessons in Linking Sustainability and Development*. Accessed at: http://dx.doi.org/10.1787/dcr-2012-en.

—— (2013a) *Aid to Poor Countries Slips Further as Governments Tighten Budgets*. Accessed at: http://www.oecd.org/dac/aidtopoorcountriesslipsfurtherasgovernmentstightenbudgets.htm.

—— (2013b) *Development Aid at a Glance: 2013 Edition*. Accessed at: http://www.oecd-ilibrary.org/development/aid-for-trade-at-a-glance-2013_aid_glance-2013-en.

Ohta, H. (1995) 'Japan's Politics and Diplomacy of Climate Change', PhD Dissertation, New York: Columbia University.

—— (2000) 'Japanese Environmental Foreign Policy', in T. Inoguchi and P. Jain (eds) *Japanese Foreign Policy Today*, New York: Palgrave, 96–121.

—— (2005a) 'Japanese Environmental Foreign Policy and the Prospect for Japan-EU Cooperation: The Case of Global Climate Change', in T. Ueta and E. Remacle (eds) *Japan and Enlarged Europe: Partners in Global Governance*, Brussels: PIE-Pieter Lang, 99–126.

—— (2005b) 'Japan and Global Climate Change: The Intersection of Domestic Politics and Diplomacy', in P.G. Harris (ed.) *Confronting Environmental Change in East and Southeast Asia: Eco-politics, Foreign Policy, and Sustainable Development*, London: Earthscan and the UNU Press, 57–71.

—— (2009) 'Japanese Foreign Policy on Climate Change: Diplomacy and Domestic Politics', in P.G. Harris (ed.) *Climate Change and Foreign Policy: Case Studies from East to West*, London: Routledge, 36–52.

—— (2010) 'Japanese Climate Change Policy: Moving Beyond the Kyoto Process', in H.G. Brauch et al. (eds) *Coping with Global Environmental Change, Disasters and Security: Threats, Challenges, Vulnerabilities and Risks*, Berlin: Springer, 1381–92.

Okuzumi, K., Arakawa, N. and Kumasaka, K. (2007) 'The Impact of the Amendment to the Infectious Diseases Control Law on the Management of Clinical Laboratories', *Rinsho Byori*, 55(7), 671–7.

Orbie, J. (2006) 'Civilian Power Europe: Review of the Original and Current Debates', *Cooperation and Conflict*, 41(1), 123–8.

Oyane, S. (2004) 'An East Asia FTA: Japan's Policy Change and Regional Initiatives', *Kokusai Mondai*, 528 (March), 52–66.

Ozawa, I. (1994) *Blueprint for a New Japan: The Rethinking of a Nation*, Tokyo: Kodansha International.

Pigman, G. (2011) *Contemporary Diplomacy*, London: Polity.

Piris, J. (2010) *The Lisbon Treaty: A Legal and Political Analysis*, Cambridge: Cambridge University Press.

Ponjaert, F. (2008) 'Institutionalisation in East Asia after the 1997 Crisis', in T. Ueta and E. Remacle (eds) *Japan and Enlarged Europe: Partners in Global Governance*, Brussels: PIE-Pieter Lang, 185–202.

—— (2009) 'The Japan-EU Partnership within the Wider Euro-East Asian Cross-Regional Arrangement', in J.L. de Sales Marques, R. Seidelmann and A. Vasilache (eds) *Asia and Europe: Dynamics of Inter- and Intra-Regional Dialogues*, Baden-Baden: Nomos, 177–97.

—— (2013) 'Inter-Regionalism as a Coherent and Intelligible Instrument in the EU's Foreign Policy Toolbox: A Comparative Assessment', in M. Telò and

F. Ponjaert (eds) *The EU's Foreign Policy: What Kind of Power and Diplomatic Action?*, Farnham: Ashgate, 135–58.

Ponjaert, F. and Béclard, J. (2010) 'Public Research Projects in Europe and East Asia: Cooperation or Competition? A Comparative Analysis of the ITER and Galileo Experiences', *East Asia*, 27(1), 99–125.

Portela, C. (2010) *European Sanctions and Foreign Policy: When and Why Do They Work?*, Abingdon: Routledge.

Prime Minister's Commission on Japan's Goals in the 21st Century (2000) *The Frontier Within: Individual Empowerment and Better Governance in the New Millennium*, Tokyo: Government of Japan.

Putnam, R. (1988) 'Diplomacy and Domestic Politics: The Logic of Two-Level Games', *International Organization*, 42(3), 427–60.

Pyanai, A. (2014) 'Environmental Provisions in Japanese Regional Trade Agreements with Developing Countries', IDE Discussion Paper, 467 (March), Tokyo: Institute of Developing Countries.

Ravenhill, J. (2010) 'The New East Asian Regionalism: A Political Domino Effect', *Review of International Political Economy*, 17(2), 153–56.

Rayroux, A. (2014) 'Understanding the "Constructive Ambiguity" of European Defense Policy: A Discursive Institutionalist Perspective', in C. Carta and J-F. Morin (eds) *EU Foreign Policy through the Lens of Discourse Analysis: Making Sense of Diversity*, Farnham: Ashgate, 227–45.

Reid, T.R. (2004) *The United States of Europe: The New Superpower and the End of American Supremacy*, New York: Penguin Press.

Reiterer, M. (2013) 'The EU-Japan Relationship in Dynamic Asia', in J. Keck, D. Vanoverbeke and F. Waldenberger (eds) *EU-Japan Relations, 1970–2010: From Confrontation to Global Partnership*, London: Routledge, 293–328.

Remacle, E. (2008) 'Approaches to Human Security: Japan, Canada and Europe in Comparative Perspective', *The Journal of Social Science*, 66, 5–34.

Remacle, E. and Ueta, T. (2001) 'Japan–EU Cooperation: Ten Years after the Hague Declaration', *Studia Diplomatica*, 54(1–2).

Richardson, J. (2009) 'Weighing Foresight with Due Diligence and the Precautionary Principle', *Foresight*, 11(1), 9–20.

Rifkin, J. (2005) *The European Dream: How Europe's Vision of the Future is Quietly Eclipsing the American Dream*, Cambridge: Polity.

Roberts, A. (2008) 'International Relations after the Cold War', *International Affairs*, 84(2) (March), 335–50.

Robles, A.C. (2004) *The Political Economy of Interregional Relations: ASEAN and the EU*, Burlington, VT: Ashgate.

Rodrigues, M.J. (2011) 'Global Economic Governance and the EU's External Action', *Studia Diplomatica*, 64(4), 85–101.

Rodrigues, M.J. and Xiarchogiannopoulou, E. (eds) (2014) *The Eurozone Crisis and the Transformation of EU Governance: Internal and External Implications*, Farnham: Ashgate.

Rosecrance, R. (1987) *Rise of the Trading State: Commerce and Conquest in the Modern World*, London: Basic Books.

Rothacher, A. (2013) '2000–2010: Shaping a Common Future in the Decade of Japan-Europe Cooperation – Rhetoric and Policies', in J. Keck, D. Vanoverbeke and F. Waldenberger (eds) *EU-Japan Relations, 1970–2010: From Confrontation to Global Partnership*, London: Routledge, 170–83.

Rubin, J. (2008) 'Building a New Atlantic Alliance: Restoring America's Partnership with Europe', *Foreign Affairs*, 97(4) (July/August 2008), 99–110.

Rudloff, B. and Simons, J. (2006) 'European Governance of Food Safety', in H.C.H. Hoffmann and A.H. Trük (eds) *EU Administrative Governance*, Cheltenham: Edward Elgar, 146–84.

Sabel, C. and Zeitlin, J (eds) (2010) *Experimentalist Governance in the EU: Towards a New Architecture*, Oxford: Oxford University Press.

Sapir, A. et al. (2004) *An Agenda for a Growing Europe: The Sapir Report*, Oxford: Oxford University Press.

Sato, M. (2013) 'Public Attitudes to the Death Penalty in Japan', in M. Tagusari, D.T. Johnson, M. Sato, S. Lehrfreund and P. Jabbar, *The Death Penalty in Japan*, London: The Death Penalty Project, 31–53.

Scharpf, F. (1999) *Governing in Europe: Effective and Democratic?*, Oxford: Oxford University Press.

Schmidt, P. (2002) *Capital Punishment in Japan*, Leiden, Brill.

Schmidt V. (2008) 'Discursive Institutionalism: The Explanatory Power of Ideas and Discourse', *Annual Review of Political Science*, 11(1), 303–26.

—— (2010a) 'Taking Ideas and Discourse Seriously: Explaining Change through Discursive Institutionalism as the Fourth New Institutionalism', *European Political Science Review*, 2(1), 1–25.

—— (2010b) 'Democracy and Legitimacy in the European Union Revisited: Input, Output and Throughput', KFG Working Paper Series, 2, Berlin: Freie Universität Berlin.

Schmitz, H. and Messner, D. (eds) (2008) 'Poor and Powerful – the Rise of China and India and the Implications for Europe', DIW Discussion Paper, 13. Accessed at: http://www.die-gdi.de/uploads/media/DP_13.2008.pdf.

Schreurs, M.A. (2002) *Environmental Politics in Japan, Germany, and the United States*, Cambridge: Cambridge University Press.

—— (2005) 'Environmental Policy-making in the Advanced Industrialized Countries: Japan, the European Union and the United States of America Compared', in H. Imura and M.A. Schreurs (eds) *Environmental Policy in Japan*, Cheltenham and Northampton, MA: Edward Elgar, 315–41.

—— (2012) 'Global Environmental Problems, US Unilateralism and Japanese, Canadian and European Responses', *Rikkyo Hogaku*, 86, 250–73.

—— (2013a) 'Orchestrating a Low-Carbon Energy Revolution without Nuclear: Germany's Response to the Fukushima Nuclear Crisis', *Theoretical Inquiries in Law*, 14(1), 83–104.

—— (2013b) 'The International Reaction to the Fukushima Nuclear Accident and Implications for Japan', in F. Yoshida and M.A. Schreurs (eds) *Fukushima: A Political Economic Analysis of a Nuclear Disaster*, Sapporo: Hokkaido University Press, 1–20.

Schreurs, M.A. and Tiberghien, Y. (2010) 'Multi-Level Reinforcement: Explaining European Union Leadership in Climate Change Mitigation', in K. Harrison and L. Sundstrom (eds) *Global Commons, Domestic Decisions: The Comparative Politics of Climate Change*, Boston, MA: MIT Press, 23–66.

Science Council of Japan (SCJ) (2013) 'Statement: Code of Conduct for Scientists – Revised Version'. Accessed at: http://www.scj.go.jp/en/report/Code%20of%20Conduct%20for%20Scientists-Revised%20version.pdf.

Selgelid, M.J. (2009a) 'Dual-Use Research Codes of Conduct: Lessons from the Life Sciences', *NanoEthics*, 3(3), 175–83.

—— (2009b) 'Governance of Dual-Use Research: An Ethical Dilemma', *Bulletin of the World Health Organization*, 87(9), 720–23.

Serra, R. (2005) 'L'Evolution stratégique du Japon: un enjeu pour l'Union', Occasional Paper, 59, Paris: Institut d'Etudes de Sécurité.

Shinoda, T. (2004) *Kantei Gaiko: Seiji riidaashippu no yukue* [The Prime Minister's Office: the Future of Political Leadership], Tokyo: Asahi Shinbunsha.

Shu, M. (2008) 'Domestic Struggles over International Imbalance: The Political Economy of Anti-Dumping Governance in the EU', *Fudan Journal of the Humanities and Social Sciences*, 1(2), 72–94.

—— (2009) 'The Co-Existence of Supranationalism and Intergovernmentalism: The Common Commercial Policy of the EU' [in Japanese], in T. Tanaka et al. (eds) *Governance and Policy-Making in the EU*, Tokyo: Keio University Press.

Slater, D. (2004) *Geopolitics and the Post-Colonial: Rethinking North-South Relations*, Oxford: Blackwell.

Smith, K. (2013) 'The European Union and the Politics of Legitimization at the United Nations', *European Foreign Affairs Review*, 18(1), 63–80.

Söderberg, M. (2012) 'Introduction: Where Is the EU–Japan Relationship Heading?', *Japan Forum*, 24(3), 249–63.

Soeya, Y., Tadokoro, M. and Welch, D.A. (2011) *Japan as a 'Normal Country'? A Nation in Search of Its Place in the World*, Toronto: University of Toronto Press.

Sommer, T. (2012) *Diese NATO hat ausgedient: Das Bundnis muss europaischer werden*, Hamburg: Korber Stiftung.

—— (2014) 'Europa darf nicht glänzen', *Die Zeit online*, 2 September.

Stavridis, S. (2001) 'Why the "Militarising" of the European Union Is Strengthening the Concept of "Civilian Power" Europe', EUI Working Papers, RSC 2001/17.

Stewart, J.D. (1984) 'The Role of Information in Public Accountability', in A. Hopwood and C. Tomkins (eds) *Issues in Public Sector Accounting*, London: Philip Allan, 13–34.

Stocchetti, M. (2013) 'Inside the European Consensus on Development and Trade: Analyzing the EU's Normative Power and Policy Coherence for Development in Global Governance', PhD Thesis, University of Helsinki.

Stockwin, J.A.A. (ed.) (2008) *Governing Japan: Divided Politics in a Resurgent Economy* (Fourth Edition), Oxford: Blackwell.

Sutherland, M. and Britton, D. (1995) *National Parks of Japan*, Tokyo: Kodansha International.

Sweeny, S. (2005) *Europe, the State and Globalisation*, Harlow: Longman.

Szymanski, M. and Smith, M. (2005) 'Coherence and Conditionality in European Foreign Policy: Negotiating the EU-Mexico Global Agreement', *Journal of Common Market Studies*, 43(1), 171–92.

Tachiki, D. (2005) 'Between Foreign Direct Investment and Regionalism: The Role of Japanese Production Networks', in T.J. Pempel (ed.) *Remapping East Asia: The Construction of a Region*, Ithaca, NY: Cornell University Press, 149–69.

Takahashi, T. (2009) 'Laws and Regulations on Food Safety and Food Quality in Japan'. Accessed at: http://www.ab.auone-net.jp/~ttt/sub1.html.

Tardy, T. (2005) 'EU-UN Cooperation in Peace-Keeping: A Promising Relationship in a Constrained Environment', Chaillot Papers, 78, Paris: EU Institute for Security Studies.

Taylor, I. (2007) 'The Periphery Strikes Back? The G20 at the WTO', in D. Lee and R. Wilkinson (eds) *The WTO after Hong Kong: Progress in, and Prospects for, the Doha Development Agenda*, New York: Routledge, 155–68.

Tegnell, A., Van Loock, F., Hendriks, J., Baka, A. and Vittozzi, L. (2002) 'BICHAT: An EU Initiative to Improve Preparedness and Response to Bioterrorism', *Eurosurveillance*, 6(28), 11 July.

Telò, M. (2007) *Europe: A Civilian Power? European Union, Global Governance, World Order*, London: Palgrave Macmillan.

—— (ed.) (2009) *The European Union and Global Governance*, New York: Routledge.

—— (ed.) (2012) *State, Globalization and Multilateralism: The Challenges of Institutionalizing Regionalism*, The Hague: Springer.

—— (2013) 'Italy's Interaction with the European Project, from the First to the Second Republic: Continuity and Change', *Comparative European Politics*, 11(3) 296–316.

Telò, M. and Ponjaert, F. (eds) (2013), *The EU's Foreign Policy: What Kind of Power and Diplomatic Action?*, Farnham: Ashgate.

Telò, M. and Seidelmann, R. (1996) 'Where Is New Germany Going?' Special Issue of *Europa/Europe*, Rome.

Tietje, C. (1997) 'The Concept of Coherence in the Treaty on European Union and the Common Foreign and Security Policy', *European Foreign Affairs Review*, 2(2), 211–33.

Tew, R. (2013) 'ODA Loans: Investment to End Poverty – Discussion Paper', Development Initiatives, Accessed at: http://www.devinit.org/wp-content/uploads/ODA_loans_discussion_paper.pdf.

The Interacademy Panel on International Issues (2005) 'Statement on Biosecurity'. Accessed at: http://www.interacademies.net/File.aspx?id=5401.

Tiberghien, Y. (2007) *Entrepreneurial States: Reforming Corporate Governance in France, Japan, and Korea*, Ithaca, NY: Cornell University Press.

—— (ed.) (2013) *Leadership in Global Institution Building: Minerva's Rule*, New York: Palgrave.

Tiberghien, Y. and Schreurs, M.A. (2010) 'High Noon in Japan: Embedded Symbolism and Post-2001 Kyoto Protocol Politics', in K. Harrison and L. Sundstrom (eds) *Global Commons, Domestic Decisions: The Comparative Politics of Climate Change*, Boston, MA: MIT Press, 139–68.

Togo, K. (2010) *Japan's Foreign Policy 1945–2009: The Quest for a Proactive Policy*, Leiden: Koninklijke Brill NV.

Trommer, S. (2013) *Transformations in Trade Politics: Participatory Trade Politics in West Africa*, London: Routledge.

Tsuruoka, M. (2008) 'Expectations Deficit in EU–Japan Relations: Why the Relationship Cannot Flourish', *Current Politics and Economics of Asia*, 17(1), 107–26.

Tyshenko, M.G. and Krewski, D.T. (2010) 'Bovine Spongiform Encephalopathy and Variant Creutzfeldt-Jakob Disease Risk Management in Italy', *International Journal of Risk Assessment and Management*, 14(4), 273–83.

Uchiyama, Y. (2010) *Koizumi and Japanese Politics: Reform Strategies and Leadership Style*, London: Routledge.

Ueta, T. and Remacle, E. (eds) (2001) *Japan–EU Cooperation: Ten Years after the Hague Declaration, Studia Diplomatica: The Brussels Journal of International Relations*, 54(1–2).

—— (eds) (2005) *Japan and Enlarged Europe: Partners in Global Governance*, *International Insights*, No. 4, Brussels: P.I.E.-Peter Lang.

—— (eds) (2008) *Tokyo-Brussels Partnership: Security, Development and Knowledge-based Society*, Brussels: PIE-Peter Lang.

Ueta, T., Remacle, E. and Ponjaert, F. (eds) (2007) *Japan–European Union: A Strategic Partnership in the Making, Studia Diplomatica: The Brussels Journal of International Relations*, 60(4).

Uhlenhant, C., Burger, R., and Schaade, L. (2013) 'Protecting Society: Biological Security and Dual-Use Dilemma in the Life Sciences – Status Quo and Options for the Future', *EMBO Reports*, 14(1), 25–30.

United Nations Committee Against Torture (2011) *Consideration of Reports Submitted by States Parties under Article 19 of the Convention: Japan, Second Periodic Report*, New York: United Nations.

UNDP (1994) *Human Development Report 1994*, New York: Oxford University Press.

United Nations Human Rights Committee (2008) *Concluding Observations – Japan*. New York: United Nations.

United States Department of State (2002) *US Climate Action Report 2002*, Washington, DC: US Department of State.

Van Schendelen, M.P.C.M. (ed.) (1998) *EU Committees as Influential Policymakers*, Farnham: Ashgate.

Vanoverbeke, D. (2013) 'The Dynamics in the EU-Japan Relationship', in J. Keck, D. Vanoverbeke and F. Waldenberger (eds) *EU-Japan Relations, 1970–2010: From Confrontation to Global Partnership*, London: Routledge, 329–37.

Vanoverbeke, D. and Ponjaert, F. (2007) 'Japan in East Asia: The Dynamics of Regional Cooperation from a European Perspective', *Japan-European Union: A Strategic Partnership in the Making*, Studia Diplomatica, 61(1) (Special Issue), 5–19.

Vernet, D. (2007) 'Multipolare Verwirrungen', *Internationale Politik*, 62(4) (April), 25–30.

Vogel, D. (1995) *Trading Up: Consumer and Environmental Regulation in a Global Economy*, Cambridge, MA: Harvard University Press.

Vogt, H. (2006) 'Coping with Historical Responsibility: Trends and Images of the EU's Development Policy', in H. Mayer and H. Vogt (eds) *A Responsible Europe? Ethical Foundations of EU External Affairs*, Basingstoke and New York: Palgrave Macmillan, 159–80.

Vos, E. (2000) 'EU Food Safety Regulation in the Aftermath of the BSE Crisis', *Journal of Consumer Policy*, 23(1), 227–55.

Vossen, P., Kreysa, J. and Goll, M. (2003) *Overview of the BSE Risk Assessments of the European Commission's Scientific Steering Committee (SSC) and its TSE/BSE ad hoc Group*. Accessed at: http://ec.europa.eu/food/fs/sc/ssc/out364_en.pdf.

Walker, J.L. (1974) 'Performance Gaps, Policy Research, and Political Entrepreneurs', *Policy Studies Journal*, 1(3), 112–16.

—— (1981) 'The Diffusion of Knowledge, Policy Communities and Agenda Setting', in E. Tropman, M.J. Dluhy and R.M. Lind (eds) *New Strategic Perspectives on Social Policy*, New York: Pergamon Press, 75–96.

Walt, S.M. (2005) 'Taming American Power', *Foreign Affairs*, 84(5) (Sept/Oct), 105–20.

Wang, J. (2005) 'China's Search for Stability with America', *Foreign Affairs*, 84(5) (Sept/Oct), 39–48.

Watanabe, T. (2005) 'History of Japan's ODA in Brief', in *Fifty Years of Japan ODA: A Critical Review for ODA Reform*, Manila: IBON Books, 3–6.

Weidner, H. (1996) *Basiselemente einer erfolgreichen Umweltpolitik: Eine Analyse und Evaluation der Instrumente der japanischen Umweltpolitik*, Berlin: Sigmar Rainer Bohn Verlag.

Wey, K-G. (1982) *Umweltpolitik in Deutschland: Kurze Geschichte des Umweltschutzes in Deutschland seit 1900*, Opladen: Westdeutscher Verlag.

Woolcock, S. (2010) 'EU Trade and Investment Policymaking after the Lisbon Treaty', *Intereconomics*, 45(1), 22–5.

—— (2013) 'The Pillars of the International Trading System', in M. Telò (ed.) *Globalisation, Multilateralism, Europe: Towards a Better Global Governance?* Farnham: Ashgate, 203–14.

World Organisation for Animal Health (2014) 'Homepage'. Accessed at: http://www.oie.int/.

World Trade Organization (1995) *WTO Agreement on the Application of Sanitary and Phytosanitary Measures (SPS Agreement)*. Accessed at: http://www.wto.org/english/tratop_e/sps_e/spsagr_e.htm.

—— (2012) *Trade Policy Reviews*. Accessed at: http://www.wto.org/english/tratop_e/tpr_e/tpr_e.htm.

World Wildlife Fund for Nature (2014) 'About the WWF'. Accessed at: http://www.wwf.or.jp/aboutwwf/.

Yale University (2012) *Environmental Performance Index: Global Metrics for the Environment*, 2012 rankings. Accessed at: epi.yale.edu.

Yamamoto, A. (2012) *Friends of Europe Background Briefing: Japan as a Global Development Partner*. Accessed at: http://www.eias.org/sites/default/files/JICA_PolicyBackground_20121016.pdf.

Yamashita, K. (2011) *Incomprehensible Objection to the Trans-Pacific Partnership (TPP)*, RIETI Column, Tokyo: Research Institute of Economy, Trade and Industry (RIETI) 24 October. Accessed at: http://www.rieti.go.jp/en/papers/contribution/yamashita/83.html.

Yamin, F. and Depledge, J. (2004) *The International Climate Change Regime: A Guide to Rules, Institutions and Procedures*, Cambridge: Cambridge University Press.

Yanai, A. (2014) 'Environmental Provisions in Japanese Regional Trade Agreements with Developing Countries', IDE Discussion Paper, 467, Tokyo: IDE-JETRO.

Yomiuri Shimbun (2009) 'Japan Tops 11-Nation Anxiety Index', 28 November. Accessed at: http://www.istockanalyst.com/article/viewiStockNews/articleid/3670487.

—— (2013) 'Message to Our Readers', 1 April. Accessed at: http://the-japan-news.com/blog/article/643.

Yoshimatsu, H. (2007) 'Japan's Quest for Free Trade Agreements: Constraints from Bureaucratic and Interest Group Politics', in M. Pangetsu and L. Song (eds) *Japan's Future in East Asia and the Pacific*, Canberra: ANU E-Press and Asia Pacific Press, 80–103.

—— (2012) 'Political Leadership Preferences and Trade Policy: Comparing FTA Politics in Japan and South Korea', *Asian Politics and Policy*, 4(2), 193–212.

Yoshimatsu, H. and Ziltener, P. (2010) 'Japan's FTA Strategy towards Highly Developed Countries: Comparing Australia's and Switzerland's Experience 2000–09', *Asian Survey*, 50(6), 1058–81.

Zakaria, F. (2008) 'The Future of American Power: How America Can Survive the Rise of the Rest'. *Foreign Affairs*, 87(3) (May/June), 18–43.

Zheng, B. (2005) 'China's "Peaceful Rise" to Great-Power Status', *Foreign Affairs*, 84(5) (Sept/Oct), 18–24.

Zielonka, J. (2006) *Europe as Empire: The Nature of the Enlarged EU*, Oxford: Oxford University Press.

Žižek, S. (2014) 'How Capital Captured Politics: WikiLeaks Has Shown Us that Western Democracies Are Now Ruled by Market Forces that Debase the Very Notion of Freedom', *The Guardian*, 13 July. Accessed at: http://

www.theguardian.com/commentisfree/2014/jul/13/capital-politics-wikileaks-democracy-market-freedom.

Zürn, M. (2007) 'Institutionaliserte Ungleichheit', *Internationale Politik*, 62(7/8) (July/Aug), 21–31.

Index

Page numbers in *italics* refer to figures and tables.